THE INTERNATIONAL CORPORATION

THE INTERNATIONAL CORPORATION

A SYMPOSIUM EDITED BY
CHARLES P. KINDLEBERGER

THE M.I.T. PRESS
CAMBRIDGE, MASSACHUSETTS, AND LONDON, ENGLAND

Copyright © 1970 by
The Massachusetts Institute of Technology

Second Printing, August 1971
Third Printing, October 1972

ISBN 0 262 11032 6 (hardcover)
ISBN 0 262 61014 0 (paperback)

Library of Congress catalog card number: 76-103898

CONTENTS

CONTENTS

LIST OF CONTRIBUTORS

M. A. Adelman
Massachusetts Institute of Technology

Robert Z. Aliber
Graduate School of Business
University of Chicago

Donald T. Brash
International Finance Corporation

Francis J. Deastlov
Columbia University

Carlos F. Díaz Alejandro
Yale University

John H. Dunning
University of Reading

Stephen Hymer
Yale University

Harry G. Johnson
University of Chicago and
London School of Economics and
Political Science

Julien-Pierre Koszul
Senior Vice President for Europe
First National City Bank

Robert Rowthorn
Cambridge University

Seymour J. Rubin
Surrey, Karasik, Gould & Greene

Eli Shapiro
Sylvan C. Coleman Professor of
Financial Management
Graduate School of Business
Harvard University

J. Wilner Sundelson
Foreign Operations Consultant
Ann Arbor, Michigan

Raymond Vernon
Graduate School of Business
Administration
Harvard University

Kenneth N. Waltz
Brandeis University

H. David Willey
Federal Reserve Bank of New York

M. Y. Yoshino
Graduate School of Business
Administration
University of California at Los Angeles

THE INTERNATIONAL CORPORATION

INTRODUCTION

This volume is the product of a seminar on the international corporation given in the Sloan School of Management at the Massachusetts Institute of Technology in the spring of 1969. The purpose of the seminar was to assemble, week by week, outstanding scholars and practitioners to hold forth on various aspects of the subject in an orderly fashion, but with no attempt to eliminate overlap or contradictions, as a stimulus to research and learning.

The papers were not given in the order in which they are presented here. Scheduling difficulties, compounded by successive heavy snowfalls on Mondays, played hob with the order. Man as well as nature made Monday awkward, with two holidays, Washington's Birthday (February 22) and Patriot's Day (April 19), each shifted to the previous Monday by the will of the Great and General Court of the Commonwealth of Massachusetts. To cover the subject, the seminar was metamorphosed into a Conference on the International Corporation on the weekend of May 9 and 10, with three country and three industry papers given on Friday afternoon and Saturday morning before a faithful seminar audience. It was well rewarded for its academic overtime since external economies among the papers and the speakers — which will be obvious to the reader — proved stimulating.

With a distinguished group of participants, no attempt was made to impose on the group a single mode of analysis or even a common glossary. Nor was it thought worthwhile to force the papers into the Procrustean bed of an identical style. A number of presentations are informal talks committed to paper. Others are scholarly research, not always following the same practice with respect to footnotes and references. It is particularly evident that there is no uniformity as to what the phenomenon under examination should be called: whether United States business, as seen by Koszul and Sundelson; direct investment; the multinational or international enterprise, firm, or corporation. For some purposes, distinctions among these terms make a difference; for the present volume they do not.

The University of Chicago fires the opening guns, and Harvard has the last word. In Aliber's leadoff paper, attention should be paid to the initial article in the title. It is "A" Theory of Direct Investment, not "The" Theory, "a theory" alternative to the standard model based on monopoly advantages, worked out by Hymer in his thesis in 1960, to which there is much reference later. Aliber propounds a new, interesting, and challenging view that direct investment is significantly affected by exchange risk. Entrepreneurs in the country whose currency is regarded as the strongest have an advantage over local enterprise in foreign countries, and can afford to pay more than such enterprise for real assets in a host country, or for equity control of local companies. This is because ordinary investors regard, say, a factory in Belgium owned by Belgians as a Belgian-franc asset, whereas if a U.S. firm buys it, it is a dollar asset. The theory encounters difficulties in explaining cross investments in the same industry — by, say, Britain in the United States and by the United States in Britain in petroleum products — but hypothesizes that these are made at different times, when one currency or another was on top. In many formulations, exchange risk has nothing to do with long-term foreign investment, since it cancels out of both numerator and denominator in the ratio of profit to assets. Aliber's paper is provocative. It may even be right.

Next under Theory, Johnson has no difficulty in accepting the Hymer thesis that direct investment is the result of monopolistic competition and in fact ascribes most of its advantages to monopoly advantages in technology. As he has indicated on other occasions, knowledge, with its high overhead and close to zero marginal costs, presents a classic dilemma. Efficiency in use demands that it be free, but incentives for the production of knowledge require the

2

award of monopolies to give a high average return. Direct investment in this formulation results when firms can squeeze the maximum rent out of ownership and control because of imperfections in the market for knowledge. Johnson proceeds to show the impact of direct investment on output and income distribution, both inter- and intranationally. The bulk of the remaining analysis is devoted to the proposition that the arguments against the international corporation are noneconomic or rest on second-best considerations. Like most economists, Johnson is not certain that second best is good enough.

Stephen Hymer of Yale University was on leave in 1968–1969, using a Council on Foreign Relations Fellowship to study and do research in London, the British West Indies, and Chile. His seminar in Cambridge, Massachusetts, minimized transport costs in traditional economic fashion by hauling him back and forth from Jamaica. His paper, however, was initially prepared at Cambridge, East Anglia, in collaboration with Robert Rowthorn, a lecturer in the Department of Economics at Cambridge University, largely in the first part of the year. The first part of the paper is devoted to a refutation of the Servan-Schreiber thesis that larger size implies faster growth. The authors show that, while American subsidiaries in Europe grew faster than European firms, the latter's rate of growth outstripped that of the American companies as a whole.

The second portion of the Hymer-Rowthorn paper presents the interesting suggestion that, as they grow in size through plowing back of profits and mergers, European firms will expand abroad. In the long run, American and European firms will come to have the same relative market share in all markets. When this position is reached, the growth of national firms will no longer depend on the growth of national economies; with all firms proportionately in all markets, all will grow at the same rate, regardless of differences in national growth rates. A third section of the paper contrasts the Socialist principle of uniting all industries in one country with the oligopolist-capitalist "ideal" of uniting a single industry in all countries. This raises the question of the regulation of industry by nation-states. The authors are skeptical of the conventional view that the rise of the international corporation poses a question of the survival of the nation-state, asking rhetorically whether France or General Motors is more likely to survive the next 100 years and implying that their money is on France. An interesting question, but one hard to answer with assurance. A separate paper on the impact of the international corporation on the nation-state had been promised to the seminar by Stanley Hoffmann of the Department of Government at Harvard; unfortunately his appointment to the Committee of Fifteen appointed to deal with the aftermath of the sit-in of University Hall at Harvard made him cancel the commitment.

Part II deals with certain functional issues in the field. H. David Willey, on leave from the Federal Reserve Bank of New York to the Office of Direct Investment, Department of Commerce, spoke, and he writes, in his personal capacity. It would have been surprising if he had delivered a polemic against the controls, and he does not; moreover, he finds that the controls were effective. Some part of the credit for slowing down U.S. investment, however, has been due to increased competition in Europe and reduced profits. Exception is taken to Fritz Machlup's view that, since the gap between financial transfers and real transfers in the balance of payments of the United States remained fairly constant, selective controls have not been effective. Willey's paper refers at several points to the pioneering and controversial estimates of Gary Hufbauer and Michael Adler, prepared for the government, suggesting that direct investment is highly negative for the balance of payments. By implication, he supports their conclusions. An explicit analysis of the Hufbauer-Adler paper, which has received much unfavorable and in many cases misleading criticism, is not part of his assignment as he undertook it.

Coming down from the Harvard Business School to the Sloan School of Management to give a seminar on "Financing the International Corporation," Eli Shapiro was returning to his old institution. In his paper for the volume, written in conjunction with a student, Francis J. Deastlov, now of Columbia University, Shapiro focuses on the supply of finance for the international corporation, leaving considerations of demand to one side. The authors explore the diversification afforded to savers by investment in the inter-

4

national corporation, especially through the medium of the Euro-bond market, initially straight dollar debt issues, then convertible dollar debentures, and increasingly of late DM bonds. They pay perhaps inadequate attention to the tax considerations that encourage investors to hold Euro-bonds, although the question whether private and public welfare considerations converge or diverge is discussed in other connections, and especially on balance of payments grounds. The conclusion is reached that finance of the international corporation through the international capital market provides a distinct benefit to investors, albeit one not available to investors in the United States without payment of the Interest Equalization Tax, which links the discussion to that of Willey in Chapter 4.

The Dunning paper is functional, insofar as it is directed to technological transfer, and at the same time plugs a gap in the regional coverage of the book — Europe. Professor Dunning, who was on leave from the University of Reading in England at the University of Western Ontario, notes that direct investment by the United States in Europe is directed to the fastest-growing industries, and to the fastest-growing countries. Using Denison's measurements of the contribution of various factors to economic growth in Europe, and especially of technology, he draws the inference that direct investment contributed to growth rather than that growth led to direct investment. Dunning concedes that Europe suffers from a technological and managment gap but sees no reason why the gap should be closed by producing technology, rather than by buying technology under license, buying technologically advanced goods, or receiving direct investment in technologically advanced lines. He finds the Servan-Schreiber case that research and development are superior to the other three means of achieving consumption of high-technology goods not proved. United States direct investment has been effective in bringing modern technology to Europe in recent years. It does not follow, however, that it is desirable to continue unswervingly along this path in the future.

Part III on Law and Politics represents a gesture on the part of the economist-editor rather than a full treatment of an important subject. The possibility that the international corporation will undermine the functioning of the nation-state is taken seriously by Hymer and Rowthorn. It will be investigated in penetrating fashion, it is hoped, in a full-fledged study sponsored by the American Academy of Arts and Sciences, and ultimately published in *Daedalus*. The seminar, it was felt, should have a glimpse of these hypotheses. Just as the rise of the national corporation reduced the sovereign independence of the 50 states in this country, forcing them to harmonize policies in such areas as taxation, for fear of desertion by runaway firms, and national corporations gave rise to national unions and national government in Galbraith's view of countervailing power, so the need to harmonize policies respecting the international corporation among nation-states may weaken the independence of separate countries and lead to the development of international governmental institutions.

As it turned out, the thesis got slim support from Rubin and Waltz. The practicing lawyer was prepared to accept the principle that the international corporation posed problems of conflict of jurisdiction, but regarded the conflicts as all resolvable in practice. It is true, for example, that the Mandatory Controls Program invades the sovereignty of, say, France by requiring corporations organized under French law to remit profits to the United States (because they are subsidiaries of U.S. corporations), when these matters are normally questions for French jurisdiction, as in foreign-exchange control. Remember, however, that Michel Debré, then French Finance Minister, protested mildly, but in fact went along with the January 1, 1968, regulations of the United States. The U.S. balance of payments deficit, which gave the French a certain amount of *Schadenfreude,* outweighed empirically the legal issue. And similarly with Trading with the Enemy, Antitrust, and the like. Never mind the fundamental principles; what do you want done? If it is ostensibly a good thing to want, international agreement is likely to be forthcoming. It is ironic that the economist should worry more about jurisdictional questions than the lawyer. Such is the fact.

Stanley Hoffmann's last-minute enforced withdrawal from the seminar left a gap that was gallantly and admirably filled by Kenneth N. Waltz, who teaches international relations at Brandeis and is a fellow of the Center for International Affairs at Harvard. Waltz's interest, however, was less directed to the theoretical clash between the international corporation and the nation-state than to the notion that rapidly rising trade and investment have increased the measure of economic interdependence among nations, thereby advancing the cause of peace and constraining the independence of sovereign countries large and small. He is skeptical both of the facts and of the conclusions usually derived from them. Waltz started his scholarly career as an economist and has little difficulty in showing that the alleged interdependence of the United States and the rest of the world today differs in kind and degree from that of Britain at the end of the last century — and this despite jet aircraft, transoceanic television, and the like. Even if the facts were as alleged, however, he is deeply skeptical of the conclusions amateurishly drawn by economists as to the impact of rising trade and investment for mutual interdependence among nations. The United States and the Soviet Union as continental powers are much less dependent on the world for income and imports than was a highly specialized island power 75 years ago. The growth of economic interdependence through the international corporation is thus attacked as a myth.

Part IV presents studies of oil by Professor Morris A. Adelman, of automobiles by Dr. J. Wilner Sundelson, and of American banking in Europe by M. Julien-Pierre Koszul. Adelman is an academician, engaged in producing an enormous and detailed study of the world petroleum industry for Resources for the Future, Inc. Koszul is a practicing banker. Sundelson started out as an academic economist, with a Ph.D. from Columbia in the 1930s, but worked for years for Ford International before going into business as a consultant on the problems of investment in Europe. They thus bring to bear on the problem a variety of specialties, experience, and knowledge.

Adelman focuses attention on the difficulties of the international oil companies, squeezed between governments of both producing and consuming countries, which want to maintain high prices for one reason and another, and the reality of a world surplus of crude petroleum, recently increased by the discoveries on the North Slope

7

in Alaska. The interest of the producing countries in high prices is evident: royalties and income taxes. That of the consuming countries is protectionist, either of domestic oil production, as in the United States, or of coal mining, as in Europe. One must, however, not weep for the companies. The living is not as easy as it used to be, but they survive and even flourish, needed by both producing and consuming countries. What they possess in monopoly is not energy but logistical efficiency in moving fuel from well to furnace.

Sundelson's account of the world operations of the U.S. automobile big three is chatty, but full of pith. The preliminary sections on markets outside Europe provide a vivid illustration of one of the wastes from direct investment which the empirical papers in the symposium underline, the replication through defensive investment in a small market, of the numbers of oligopolistic competitors in a large one. The waste is that all must be of inefficient size to accommodate the number of firms. The phenomenon has been studied a long time in Canada, but now appears as an issue in Australia and Latin America, discussed by, in addition to Sundelson, Brash and Díaz Alejandro, and implied by Hymer and Rowthorn. Sundelson observes that the situation can be resolved, on occasion by competition, as in Brazil, where Ford seems to be emerging on an efficient scale that dominates the market, or by designation by government of a chosen instrument, as in Argentina with Fiat. The *quid pro quo* for concentrating government contracts on a single producer is its guarantee to cut prices. In this way it is hoped to break the deadlock of a substantial number of small-size, inefficient, high-cost companies, each losing money but resolved not to let a competitor steal a march on it.

The big struggle in automobiles, however, is in Europe, where 30 or 40 companies as of 1945 are slowly dwindling to a handful, as has already happened in the United States. Sundelson forecasts the emergence of one British, one German, one Italian company, plus how many American? The chances of a French company surviving, or Chrysler, are called into question. General Motors, he asserted in the seminar, has the resources to hang on, and seems to want to, but is not making the same return as in the market where it dominates. Ford looks like a winner. But how many titans can survive in Europe?

Koszul, the senior vice-president for Europe of the First National City Bank of New York, located in Paris, has a superb vantage point from which to observe the explosion of American banking in Europe from 16 branches in 1939 to 326 branches, representative offices, and participations as of last count. American bankers went abroad as camp followers of American industry; they remained after 1960 to participate in the growing Euro-dollar and Euro-dollar bond markets. In the years since the credit squeeze of of 1966, moreover, some banks have opened offices in Europe not to lend dollars but to borrow them for use back in the United States. Koszul emphasizes that much overseas investment by American banks was defensive in the sense that when their United States customers went to Europe, the banks were under compulsion to follow, lest they lose business to another American bank which had performed for the customer in Europe. In the course of pursuing their own customers, they inevitably collide with European banks with a less competitive tradition. At the same time, the American banks have not gone so far as actively to seek domestic accounts, as investment funds have done. In this respect European experience is different from that in other parts of the world, where not a few countries, and notably Canada and Australia, are unwilling to sanction the entry of new foreign banks. This reaction is rationalized on the ground that banking is what Lenin called "a commanding height" of the economy, a place where foreign bankers can gather confidential credit information on local enterprise, and perhaps pass it on to their U.S. customers who are in competition with local business. Since there is no evidence of such conduct, the fear is best regarded as Populist, and at worst as paranoid.

Europe having been covered in some detail in the functional and industry studies, the country papers concentrate on a well-studied dominion, Australia; on Latin America, which serves as a proxy for less-developed countries in general (to the extent not treated in oil); and on the one country that has resisted the international corporation thus far with impressive success, Japan.

CHARLES P. KINDLEBERGER

Though born in New Zealand, Donald T. Brash, an economist with the International Finance Corporation of the World Bank, on loan to the Commission on International Development, headed by Lester Pearson, did graduate work in economics at Australian National University and wrote a distinguished thesis on "American Investment in Australian Industry." His seminar paper on "Australia as Host to the International Corporation" in part brings this study up to date. The original investigation gave American direct investment higher marks than the writer anticipated would be due. In this paper, he chides the Australian government for its new policies toward direct investment, but himself begins to show concern that the process can be overdone. In his seminar presentation, Brash made no reference to the declining rate of profit on foreign investment in Australia, discussed in a widely noted paper by B. J. Johns, and running parallel to declining profit rates in other industry and parts of the world, noted for automobiles and banking, and by Willey and Waltz. I suspected this of being a universal phenomenon. Since the Australian data are superior to those of other countries, I thought it would be useful to have the latest figures analyzed. As it turned out, however, profits on foreign direct investment in Australia have started back up from their mid-1960s lows. This leaves up in the air the hypothesis that U.S. firms have overdone foreign direct investment in a follow-the-leader keeping-up-with-the-Joneses way. But if firms follow the leader, so do countries in their concern over too much foreign investment. In these questions, bureaucrats infect one another across national lines like student rebels.

Carlos F. Díaz Alejandro was teaching at the University of Minnesota, on part-time detached service with Mr. Pearson's Grand Assize on Foreign Aid (the Commission on International Development, on which Brash served). He is now professor of Latin American economics at Yale. Born in Cuba, he wrote his thesis and a book for the Yale Center on Economic Growth on Argentina, and has studied Colombia and Chile for the Nine Wise Men of the Alliance for Progress, and the M.I.T. Center of International Studies, respectively. He brings to the troubled question of U.S. investment in Latin America wide experience for a young man, a

10

knowledge of history, and a well-honed kit of economic tools. But the heart of the matter is political. A long history of cavalier treatment of Latin American individuals, traditions, governments, and business by American businessmen corrupts attempts to keep the discussion on an economic level, and even then such legislation as the Hickenlooper amendment leads Latin Americans to believe that the United States turns economic disputes into political shows of strength. Díaz Alejandro explores such solutions as joint ventures, Mexicanization, a code for host countries — covering a number of countries so that investors cannot play off one against another — but he does not predict the outcome in the steady state. Presumably the steady state is several convolutions away.

Professor M. Y. Yoshino of U.C.L.A. has written on Japan's managerial system. He is evidently well qualified to explore the interaction between foreign and Japanese management over the sought-after penetration of the rapidly expanding Japanese market by foreign firms. Unlike Australia, Canada, and Latin America, where laissez faire is giving way to restriction, generally on a case-by-case basis, in Japan restriction is moving at a measured pace toward laissez faire. Foreign firms are desperately unhappy at their exclusion from a briskly growing market, for reasons explored by Hymer and Rowthorn. These firms focus on the prospect of new Japanese combinations rising to financial strength behind barriers before setting out to penetrate foreign markets with investment as well as exports. They want to be able to maintain surveillance over Japanese business in action and perhaps discipline it with competition in the local market from time to time. Japanese industry and especially the Japanese government are, however, bemused by the heavy debt-equity ratios of existing firms and by the weak state of many small enterprises, using primitive techniques, and highly vulnerable, as wages rise, to foreign competition. When these situations are cleared up, business and government will proceed more directly to liberalization. Meanwhile they have started, in an effort to still foreign complaints, but liberally only for such safe industries as motorcycles, shipbuilding, cotton textiles, sake brewing, barber shops, beauty parlors, parking lots, amusement parks, toys, and wigs. Japan will come out from behind its shutters. It wants some technology that it cannot obtain by license. And Japanese firms themselves want to expand into international production, which probably requires reciprocity.

Professor Raymond Vernon of the Harvard Business School sums up the symposium without having seen more than one or two papers. His summation is one of a series of papers, plus books, which flows from a major research undertaking on the multi-national (as he calls it) corporation. It constitutes an admirable conclusion to the wide-ranging forays of the other participants in the seminar, treating the theory of direct investment (to which his product-cycle model has made such an important contribution), attitudes of home and host countries, and ending with a strong recommendation for harmonization of policies toward the multi-national corporation to enable them to respond to economic signals related to scarcity rather than differences in the artificial environment. Internationalized policies are needed to deal wtih international institutions. Vernon is not naive enough to expect that the road to international solutions will be an easy one, especially for the less-developed countries, but the facts and his analysis point in no other direction.

Unfortunately a seminar paper by Professor Melville H. Watkins of the University of Toronto on "Canada and U.S. Firms," could not be produced in written form for inclusion in this book. The volume is weaker for its absence.

Much of the contribution of the book, in my judgment, consists in putting precisely and between a single set of covers the common intellectual coinage of the field of the international corporation as seen by economists and, to a lesser extent, professors of management, practitioners, political scientists, and the like. The assembly of empirical material is up to date and useful. But there are a few surprises: a theory of direct investment emphasizing exchange risk; analysis and empirical demonstration of the waste of oligopolistically replicating market shares of the large market in the small, with numerous firms of uneconomic size — a familiar point in Canada, but here widely recognized; the unwillingness of the lawyer and the political scientist to be moved by the threat to the nation-state and its sovereignty, as economists have been; the prospect, as an ultimate result of evolution of a limited number of firms in each industry having identical shares in all national markets, without regard to their national origin, so that all firms grow at the same pace (assuming innovations are small and randomly distributed), without regard to the differential growth of national markets. Time is needed to test the durability of these notions.

One original view of direct investment not in these pages, which I have learned of since the end of the term, concentrates on economies of scale in capital markets in developed countries, without regard to exchange risk, and sees this as the major advantage in a factor market, rather than advantages in goods and markets. (Since the research is not finished, I am unable to refer to the source of the idea.) If this is true, infant-industry protection for the capital market in less-developed countries requires restriction on inward direct investment, as a second-best policy, although subsidies to savers and investors of domestic origin might be a better solution.

To one who has not read these essays, I may stand accused of nepotism. Sundelson was a fellow student at Columbia's Department of Economics in the 1930s. Adelman is a colleague at M.I.T. and Shapiro used to be. My associations with Rubin and Vernon go back to the Department of State, where one was a supervisor and the other a colleague. Díaz Alejandro and Hymer were students of mine at M.I.T., and Willey took a moonlighting course I gave at the Fletcher School of Law and Diplomacy at Tufts University before he transferred to Columbia. I plead not guilty. I got the best men there were, as will be clear when the papers are read, and if it turned out that so many of them had gone along the same path with me in the past, it merely suggests a historic sense of direction.

Thanks are due not only the participants who make these pages lively, but to the students and listeners in 15.959, Special Studies in Management. Their questions penetrated to the unresolved issues, and contributed in no small measure to the overall result.

September 1969   CHARLES P. KINDLEBERGER
Department of Economics and
Sloan School of Management
Massachusetts Institute of Technology

Part I

THE THEORY OF THE
INTERNATIONAL CORPORATION

CHAPTER ONE

A THEORY OF DIRECT FOREIGN INVESTMENT

Robert Z. Aliber

Introduction

One of the remarkable phenomena of the last ten years has been the rapid growth in international investment. Surges of international investment before World War II and in the 1920s have consisted largely of portfolio investment; funds moved from low-interest-rate areas to higher-interest-rate areas. Since World War II, the major component of the capital flow has been direct investment as firms domiciled in one country have established foreign branches and purchased foreign firms. Direct foreign investment has been viewed as a special form of international portfolio investment; the "borrower" and "lender" are parts of the same corporate family. The investment flows reflected differences in rates of return in capital importing and capital exporting countries. But this interpretation seems strained. What is lacking is a theory to explain the direct investment phenomenon.

A theory of direct investment must answer several questions. The firms engaged in direct foreign investment operate at a disadvantage relative to their host-country competitors — they incur additional costs associated with management of an enterprise at some distance, and they incur political risks. Thus the source-country firms need an advantage to overcome these costs. The primary question that a theory of foreign investment must answer is the source of these advantages. Another question is why such a

17

substantial part of direct foreign investment since World War II was by U.S. firms. Direct foreign investment totals about $90 billion — U.S. direct investment abroad is about $60 billion, while direct foreign investment in the United States is about $10 billion.[1] A third question is why the pattern of direct investment differs substantially by industry — why there is much direct foreign investment in aluminum and little in steel, why the drug industry is extensively international while the machine tool industry is not. Moreover, a theory should explain foreign investments through takeovers — the purchase of established companies abroad. Finally a theory should explain direct investment cross-hauling — why foreign firms invest in the United States at the same time that U.S. firms invest abroad.

The popular explanations for the dominance of the U.S. firms in direct foreign investment include the superiority of U.S. management techniques and the larger U.S. government-financed research and development. Some of these advantages are internal to firms; to some extent comparable advantages might be purchased by foreign firms. Other advantages are external to the firm and inherent to the U.S. economic environment. These advantages, comparable to advantages that other countries might have in the form of lower wage costs, should be neutralized by the exchange rate. These popular explanations for direct investment are inconclusive. A satisfactory explanation must account for advantages that U.S. firms have which cannot be acquired on comparable terms by their foreign competitors and which are not neutralized by the exchange rate.

A recent explanation emphasizes that firms engaged in direct investment have monopolistic elements; the perfect competition model is not relevant.[2] The advantage to the source-country firms

[1] S. E. Rolfe, *The International Corporation* (background report for the XII Congress of the International Chamber of Commerce, Istanbul May 31–June 7, 1969) (n.p.: International Chamber of Commerce, 1969), Tables 1–10.

[2] S. H. Hymer, "The International Operations of National Firms: A Study of Direct Investment," M.I.T. doctoral dissertation, Cambridge, Mass. (1960).

which enables them to compete against foreign firms on their own turf may be proprietary information — patents, know-how, and managerial skills. These advantages must not be available to host-country firms on the same prices and terms as to the source-country firms. Yet the source-country firms might sell these advantages to host-country firms and avoid the unique costs associated with direct foreign investment. Some explanations for direct investment emphasize that the advantages cannot be purchased in a perfect market; these imperfections in these markets might explain why the source-country firm, rather than sell its advantages, engages in direct foreign investment.[3] The imperfections in these markets may reflect costs associated with transactions, information, marketing, and bargaining.

> Direct investment belongs more to the theory of industrial organization than to that of international capital movements. The direct investor operates at a disadvantage in a foreign market, using foreign factors of production, and at a long distance from his decision-center. To overcome these disadvantages, he must have a substantial advantage of some kind. (In a limited number of cases, direct investment takes the form of policing of each other's markets by oligopolistic competitors, or defensive investment by erstwhile monopolists who are just about to be pushed out of a market.) The advantage may lie in technology, management entry into the industry, and so on. If the direct investor can take over a competitor, perhaps the only competitor in a national market, he can establish a monopoly which may prove costly for the economy.[4]

Another explanation derived from the theory of industrial organization centers on the advantages of vertical integration; an international dimension is given to the economies of scale. Certain economic processes have flow characteristics. Efficiencies may be realized by coordinating activities that occur in several different

[3] S. Hymer, "The Multinational Corporation: An Analysis of Some of the Motives for International Business Integration" (unpublished).

[4] C. P. Kindleberger, "Restrictions on Direct Investments in Host Countries," a discussion paper for the University of Chicago Workshop on International Business (March 5, 1969, unpublished), p. 9.

19

countries within the firm. Thus an international oil company co-ordinates the production, transport, refining, and the distribution of petroleum at lower costs than individual firms at each stage might be able to by using the market.[5] The economies of vertical integration involve reduction in transactions costs, the costs of search, and the costs of holding inventories.

Theories of direct foreign investment derived from the theory of industrial organization have limited explanatory power — while they may explain the advantage of source-country firms, they cannot predict the country pattern of foreign investment or its industrial pattern. Nor can they explain adequately foreign investment through takeovers. These theories are not integrated with alternative ways — exports and licensing — that the source-country firms might exploit the market in the host country. Finally, these explanations derived from industrial organization lack elements of "foreignness" in the sense that the explanatory variables do not include any of the factors that distinguish national economies, including participation in different customs areas, currency areas, and tax jurisdictions. These explanations are not theories of direct foreign investment but rather theories of the growth of firms applied to an international economy on much the same terms as to a national economy.

This paper argues that the key factor in explaining the pattern of direct foreign investment involves capital market relationships, exchange risk, and the market's preferences for holding assets denominated in selected currencies. These factors can explain why direct foreign investment by Dutch firms is large, while that by Belgian firms is small, and why U.S. firms buy established foreign firms. And these relationships have explanatory power for the pattern of direct foreign investment by industry. Finally, these factors have a unique international element and are based on the existence of different currency areas.

---

[5] This argument relies heavily on Coase's theory of the firm. See R. H. Coase, "The Nature of the Firm," *Economica,* New Ser., Vol. IV (1937), pp. 386–405; reprinted in *Readings in Price Theory* (Homewood, Ill: R. D. Irwin, 1952), pp. 331–351.

Direct Foreign Investment — A Currency-Area or Customs-Area Phenomenon

Direct foreign investment involves the acquisition of plant and equipment for production in a customs area or a currency area other than that area in which a firm is domiciled.[6] The "foreignness" of the investment reflects the movement across the boundaries between customs areas and between currency areas. In the absence of such boundaries, the distinction between foreign investment and domestic investment disappears.[7] Now the boundaries of customs unions and of currency areas tend to be congruent with national boundaries.[8] The significance of multiple customs areas is that the difference in the prices of a product in different customs areas may reflect more than the cost of its transportation from the market in one customs area to the market in another. Thus tariffs influence the choice of whether a market should be satisfied from production in one customs area or another. The significance of multiple currency areas is that the interest rates on securities of the same risk class issued by borrowers domiciled in different areas might differ because of exchange risk — the risk that exchange parities might be changed. The central question is whether direct foreign investment is better explained as a customs-area phenomenon or a currency-area phenomenon.

The argument proceeds on the assumption that the source-country firm has a monopolistic advantage; this advantage is called a "patent," although the term represents all possible monopolistic advantages.[9] The firm must decide how best to exploit its patent

[6] The term "currency areas" is used more restrictively than the terms "sterling area" and "dollar area" are generally used. Conceivably foreign investment might be undertaken within the same customs and currency area — as Belgian investment in the Netherlands.

[7] The world is also divided into tax areas and political areas, and the "foreignness" of direct foreign investment might be construed as a movement across these boundaries.

[8] The European Community is now one customs area and several currency areas.

[9] H. G. Johnson notes that the "transference of knowledge . . . is the crux of the direct investment process." The advantage of the source-country firm

21

to satisfy the domestic market and various foreign markets. The patent is a capital asset. The income stream of this asset is to be measured by decline in the costs of production from reduction in the amounts of various factors required to produce a given output. The value of the patent is the capitalized value of the difference between production costs before and after the patent is used.

The market in patents is extensive. Transactions in patents reflect that firms that have an advantage in producing patents may not have an advantage in exploiting them. The producers of patents seek to maximize their value, so that attention is given to the choice between exploiting the patent within the firm and selling or licensing the patent.[10] Many producers of patents are also users, because internal marketing costs are less than external marketing costs, because of the need for secrecy, the desire for immediate feedback to the patent development process from the exploitation process, etc. A firm that licenses a patent must police its use and prevent infringements, and the firm may find the information feedback is less comprehensive than when the patent is exploited internally.

One decision faced by a firm with a patent is whether to satisfy the foreign market by exploiting the patent domestically and exporting or whether to exploit the patent abroad. A second decision is whether to exploit the patent within the firm or to sell or license the patent.

The demarcation of the world into customs areas and currency areas affects both where a patent is exploited to satisfy each market and whether the patent is exploited by a source-country firm or a

---

is knowledge, and this knowledge is embodied in the patent. See his essay, "The Efficiency and Welfare Implications of the International Corporation," pp. 35–36 in this volume.

[10] There are numerous possible ways the patent might be licensed — the source-country firm might provide minimal technical information, or it might provide an extensive range of management services to facilitate maximum possible profits from the patent. Payment for the use of the patent may vary from a fixed fee to a variable fee to a share of the profits. The results in this section apply to almost all forms of licensing arrangement, except those where the host-country firms receive payment for the license solely in proportion to the profits of the licensee. Such arrangements are more nearly forms of direct investment, except that the downside risk of the source-country firm is limited.

host-country firm. The existence of several customs areas means that firms may forgo economies of scale available from concentrating production; to avoid the tariffs, they may produce with smaller-than-optimal plants in each of several customs areas. The existence of several currency areas may have differential impacts on the cost of capital to firms domiciled in different countries.

Assume first that currency areas are unified — devaluations and exchange controls are impossible — while customs areas remain separate. Then direct foreign investment would become a problem in the economics of location; tariffs could be construed as a type of transport cost. Within this unified currency area each firm would have to decide where to produce. This decision is based on access to markets, availability of materials, and prices of factors. The higher the tariffs, the more likely production will be dispersed among customs areas and that demand in each area will be satisfied from domestic production.

A unified currency area suggests that every firm's financial statement would be denominated in the same currency. But if separate currencies remain, the distinction among currencies would have no more significance than that which results because some U.S. firms own the liabilities of Chicago banks while others own the liabilities of New York banks.[11] Differences in the cost of capital to firms domiciled in each country would no longer reflect differences attributable to the denomination of their bonds and equities in different currencies.

In a world of separate customs areas and a unified currency area, tariffs affect where a patent will be exploited to meet demand in each customs area. Tariffs absorb part of the decline in the c.i.f. price of imports due to an adoption of cost-reducing patent abroad. The tariff creates an incentive to use the patent within each customs area; the amount of the incentive will vary with both the value of the patent in the source country and the height of the tariff.

The typical textbook description of the pattern for foreign in-

[11] Even within the U.S. dollar currency area, certain states and countries "devalue" through a variety of investment incentives. But this form of subsidy differs from a devaluation among currency areas in its impact on capital values.

volvement is that the firm initially exports to satisfy the foreign market. Then as this market grows in size and the firm develops experience about the market, the firm licenses its patents for exploitation abroad.[12] As the foreign market enlarges further, the firm may invest abroad.[13] In this sequence the tariff cannot explain the firm's decision to invest abroad; rather the tariff explains whether the patent will be exploited in the host country or the source country. The incentive to exploit the patent within the host country increases as that market grows. However, because of the cost of doing business abroad, the firm may sell the patent rather than engage in direct investment.

During the licensing stage, the market for patents operates. Possible imperfections in this market are dominated by the combination of the costs of doing business abroad and the diseconomies of small scale. As the host-country market expands, the costs of doing business abroad per unit of sales decline. But these costs always remain. At some point in the growth of the host-country market, the source-country firm may choose to exploit the patent internally rather than sell the patent. At that point, the inference is that the host-country firm is no longer willing to pay the scarcity rent demanded by the source-country firm. At this point, the capitalized value of the patent to the source-country firm exceeds its capitalized value to the host-country firm. If both the host-country firm and the source-country firm derive the same income from exploiting a patent in the host country (before the source-country firm deducts the costs of doing business abroad), the differences in capitalized values must reflect differences in capitalization ratios.[14]

---

[12] This pattern reflects the usual international business textbook sequence. "In some cases the firm may move directly from exporting to a foreign investment; the intermediate state of patent licensing may be skipped. In some cases of takeovers, the firm may move directly to the investment stage without either the export or the licensing state." See R. Vernon, *The Manager in the International Economy* (Englewood Cliffs, N.J.: Prentice-Hall, 1968), p. 202.

[13] This pattern also reflects the approach taken by the firm to develop information about the opportunities in foreign markets.

[14] An explanation of differences in valuation of the patent in terms of income streams may suggest that source-country firm succeeds in capturing some rents that host-country firms cannot capture; it is able "to get more

Figure 1 shows that the decision of a firm on how best to exploit a patent for a foreign market depends on the size of the market and the height of the tariff.[15] The function C shows the unit cost to a source-country firm of doing business in the host country; these

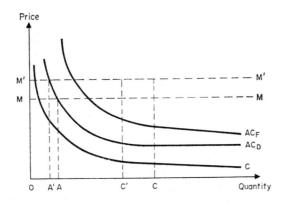

Figure 1. Unit Costs of Production in a Host Country.

costs, which are variable rather than fixed, decline. The function AC_D is the average cost function of a firm producing in the host country regardless of whether it is a host-country or source-country firm. The function AC_F is the average cost function of the source-country firm operating in the host country and is the sum of the C function and the AC_D function. The function MM shows the host-country price of imports after tariff. If the host-country market for the product is smaller than OA, then the source-country firm will supply the market from domestic production. If the market is larger than OA, the cost of supplying the market from imports exceeds

---

from the assets." The source-country firms may be able to buy certain factors at a lower price than host-country firms, or they may own managerial talents not available to the host-country firms. This suggests either that the market for managerial talent or some other advantage held by source-country firm is imperfect or that there are economies of scale in using or buying managerial talent which are available to the source-country firm but not to the host-country firm. Ultimately, the difference in income stream must be attributed to an imperfection in the market for an input or to a scale factor.

[15] The graph shows these functions for any unit of time. The major variable is the size of the market.

25

that from local production; this difference may reflect transportation costs (including the tariff) or that the host-country has a comparative advantage. As the market expands beyond OA, the firm will find that licensing may yield a higher return than domestic production.

If the host country raises the tariff, the landed costs of imports rises, as shown by the shift in the import function from MM to $M'M'$. The tariff depresses the return on use of the patent in the source country for export relative to its use in the host country; the crossover between licensing and exports shifts to OA'. If cost functions tend to fall because a new patent becomes available, the host-country cost functions may fall by more than the import function, especially if the tariff has a specific component. Then the crossover between exporting and host-country production occurs at a smaller output.

Figure 2 shows the capitalized values of the patent to the source-country firm as the patent is used in three different ways. First, Y_M shows the profit on export sales, and K_M is the capitalized value of this income to the source-country firm. Second, Y_D shows the income stream to the host-country firm; K_D is the capitalized value of

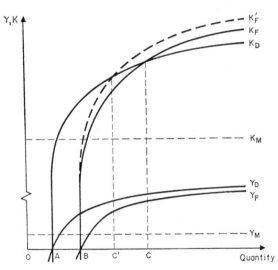

Figure 2. Capitalized Values of a Patent.

26

this income stream to the host-country firm. Third, Y_F is the income stream to the source-country firm from host-country production; K_F is the capitalized value of this stream. The capitalization ratios for Y_M and Y_F are assumed identical and exceed that for Y_D. At OC, the capitalized value of K_D and K_F are equal. At an output larger than OC, the difference in capitalization ratios dominates the difference in income streams in terms of capitalized values. Thus if the market is smaller than OA, the source-country firm will export; if its size is between OA and OC, it will license; and if its size is larger than OC, the firm will invest.

Assume now that customs areas are unified while currency areas remain separate. Separate currency areas mean that interest rates on similar assets denominated in different currencies may differ, because exchange rates might be changed. And the change in the interest rate relationship affects the relationship between capitalization ratios. Because customs areas are unified, production would tend to be concentrated to achieve economies of scale; the concentration might occur in the source country or the host country. Even if the volume of production in the host country remains unchanged, the patent will be increasingly exploited through direct investment because of the change in capitalization ratios. Thus an increase in K_F shifts the crossover between K_F and K_D from OC to OC'; direct foreign investment becomes attractive at a smaller volume of output. Thus the decision whether the source-country firm or the host-country firm exploits the patent abroad depends on the costs of doing business abroad and national differences in capitalization ratios and not on the height of the tariff.

The income stream of source-country firms may be capitalized at a higher rate than those of host-country firms for several different reasons.[16] The income streams in the source country may be grow-

---

[16] The market places a value on each firm; this value reflects its current earnings and their anticipated growth, the source of these earnings, the stability of these earnings, and the yield on competing assets. As each firm expands, it compares the rate at which the market capitalizes its earnings with the price it must pay for an income stream. A firm will buy a patent if the ratio of its price to its contribution to the future income stream is lower than the capitalization rate attached to the firm's income streams by its stockholders. Similarly, a firm sells a patent if the price offered exceeds the

ing more rapidly, either because its economy is growing more rapidly or because the share of profits in national income is increasing; the higher capitalization rate will reflect expectations of the more rapid growth of earnings.[17] The difference in capitalization rates may reflect that the assets are denominated in different currencies and that the capitalization rate of assets with certain income streams in the two countries differs.[18] The higher the capitalization rate on certain income streams, the higher the rate on uncertain income streams in the same currencies. What remains to be explained is why separate currency areas lead to differences in capitalization rates.

Capitalization Rates and the Currency Premium

The thesis of this paper is that the pattern of direct foreign investment reflects that source-country firms capitalize the same stream of expected earnings at a higher rate than host-country firms.[19] This difference in capitalization rates results because the market attached different capitalization rates to income streams denominated in different currencies. Source-country firms are likely to be those in countries where the capitalization rates are high; host-country firms are those in countries where capitalization rates are low. The dif-

---

increment of its capitalized value to that expected from internal exploitation of the patent.

[17] Alternatively, while each country may grow at the same rate, it may differ in the mix of industries which grow rapidly and those which grow more slowly.

[18] Kindleberger argues that the difference in capitalized values reflects differences in the income stream rather than in the capitalization ratio. Thus "$C = I/R$, where C is the value of a capital asset, I the stream of income it produces, and R the rate of return on investment. I is higher for the foreigner than for the local entrepreneur because of some advantage in goods markets such as a differentiated production or assured outlets or marketing skills. . . ." C. P. Kindleberger, *American Business Abroad* (New Haven: Yale University Press, 1969), pp. 24–25.

[19] The term "market" applies to the world-wide family of investors who can hold assets denominated in domestic currency or a foreign currency, depending on their prices and the investors' estimates of exchange risk. Investors may have a bias toward holding assets denominated in the currency in which most of their consumption expenditure is denominated — a bias that reflects transactions costs.

ferences in capitalization rates select which country will be the host country and which the source country. The difference in capitalization rates is evident in the difference in yields on debt issues, which generate certain income streams. Yields on uncertain income streams exceed those on certain income streams; this difference reflects a risk premium. If this risk premium is standardized among countries, then the differences in capitalization rates on equities should reflect the differences in rates on debt.

Two factors may explain why the market applies different capitalization rates to assets denominated in different currencies. The first is that the market demands a premium for bearing uncertainty about exchange risk. As a consequence, the difference between interest rates on fixed price assets denominated in different currencies may exceed the expected change in their exchange rates[20]; this difference can be called a currency premium.[21] For example, part of the difference in yield between U.S. securities and sterling securities reflects the fact that the markets believe sterling may depreciate; part may reflect a premium for bearing uncertainty about the future dollar price of sterling. The difference in the yields on equities denominated in sterling and in the dollar reflects both the expectations about the depreciation of sterling in terms of the dollar and a premium for bearing uncertainty about this change. The higher the currency premium, the greater the excess of sterling interest rates over dollar interest rates. The existence of a currency premium is well established. Because of the currency premium, host-country firms may issue debt denominated in the currency of the source country in the belief that the saving in interest rate from borrowing abroad more than compensates for taking on the exchange risk.[22] Thus Canadian firms borrow in U.S. dollars to obtain

[20] The implication is that, if the difference in yields reflected only the expected depreciation, then the capitalized value of assets denominated in the two currencies would be the same.

[21] See R. Moses, "Anticipations of Exchange Rate Changes," Ph.D. dissertation, University of Chicago (1969, unpublished).

[22] For a discussion of exchange risk and the prices of similar securities denominated in different currencies, see R. Z. Aliber, "Exchange Risk, Yield Curves, and the Pattern of Capital Flows," *Journal of Finance*, Vol. 24 (May 1969), pp. 361–370.

funds to spend in Canada. In contrast, U.S. firms rarely borrow abroad to obtain funds to finance expenditures in the United States.[23]

A currency premium is necessary to explain the pattern of foreign investment, but it is not sufficient. The second element in the hypothesis is that the market applies a higher capitalization rate to the same income stream generated in the host country when received by a source-country firm than by a host-country firm. If the market applied the host-country capitalization rate to the income stream received by the source-country firm, there would be no incentive for foreign investment. The difference in capitalization rates applied to the same income stream reflects the fact that the market does not attach a currency premium to the foreign income of the source-country firm.[24, 25] The market is subject to a bias, in that host-country equities are subject to the currency premium while source-country equities are not. Because of this bias, financial intermediaries in the source country may issue liabilities and use the proceeds to acquire the securities in the host country. The larger the currency premium, the greater the disadvantage for host-country firms.

The currency premium affects the terms on which source-country and host-country firms borrow, as well as the rates at which their income streams are capitalized.[26] The significance of this disadvan-

[23] While host-country firms can denominate their liabilities in the source-country currency, they cannot determine their equities in the source-country currency.

[24] Presumably, when a Canadian firm borrows U.S. dollars to reduce its interest costs, the market does not compensate by reducing the capitalization rate to reflect the increase in exchange risk. Or the impact on capitalized value of the reduction in interest cost is greater than the impact of the reduction in capitalization ratios. The presumption is that the uncertainty premium applied to foreign currency transactions of firms is smaller than that applied to marketable securities.

[25] The market may apply a higher capitalization rate to a source-country firm with income from foreign sources as well as domestic sources, because of the belief that the combined income stream will be more stable than either of its components.

[26] Kindleberger recognizes that the source-country firms may be able to obtain capital more cheaply than host-country firms. But this affects the income to be capitalized and not the capitalization rates. See Ref. 18, p. 23.

30

tage to host-country firms depends on both the share of the capital in value added and the size of the currency premium. In some industries the capital may account for as much as 25% of value added, while in other industries it may account for no more than 5 or 10%. Where the capital component is important, a currency premium of one or two percentage points has a substantial impact in enhancing the income stream of the source-country firm relative to the host-country firms.

The Patterns of Direct Foreign Investment

The geographic pattern of direct foreign investment reflects the dispersion in capitalization rates for equities denominated in different currencies. The United States is now the largest net source of foreign investment because capitalization rates for U.S. firms are higher than those of foreign firms. Higher capitalization rates attached to U.S. equities reflect a preference by the markets for having assets denominated in dollars; the currency premium on dollar-denominated assets exceeds that on assets denominated in other currencies. The surge in U.S. direct foreign investment which occurred in the 1920s coincided with the fall in the currency premium on dollar assets relative to that of sterling assets. Prior to World War I, the currency premium on sterling assets was higher than that on dollar assets, and Great Britain was the largest source country for direct foreign investment.

The Netherlands and Switzerland are large source countries for foreign investment; each has had a currency that has high currency premium. The net users of direct foreign investment, in contrast, are those countries that have currencies subject to a low currency premium. Canada is a large net user of foreign investment; the U.S. dollar has traditionally been at a currency premium relative to the Canadian dollar.

The differences in the pattern of direct foreign investment reflect the size of the host-country market, the value of patents, the height of tariffs, the costs of doing business abroad in a particular industry, and the dispersion in capitalization rates, both by country and by industry within countries. Other things being equal, for any given difference in the capitalization rates of countries, foreign investment will tend to be greater in those industries in which the spread in capitalization rates is greatest. The higher the tariffs, the greater the incentive to exploit the patent in the host country; the greater the dispersion in capitalization ratios, the larger the incentive for foreign investment relative to licensing in a host-country market of any given size.[27] In some industries, differences in the size of the market among possible host countries will dominate differences in capitalization rates; thus foreign investment may be higher in developed countries than in the developing countries, where markets are smaller. Where the cost of economic distance is high and the value of the patents is low, direct investment will tend to be low.

One consequence of this view is that foreign investment will tend to be larger in the more capital-intensive industries, since the disadvantage of the host-country firms is larger, the larger the contribution of capital to production. Similarly, foreign investment should tend to be high in research-intensive industries, since research is a form of capital investment. Foreign investment may be small in some capital-intensive industries like steel production either because the cost of doing business abroad is higher or because the value of patents is low.

Foreign direct investment through takeovers can be explained by the difference in capitalization ratios. The takeover involves the purchase of a patent, distribution system, or managerial talents by source-country firms; the source-country firm incurs added cost of doing business abroad. In some cases, the explanation for takeovers may be in terms of certain complementarities not necessarily available to other host-country firms.[28]

The test of a theory of foreign investment is its ability to explain investment crossflows — why foreign firms invest in the United States in those industries in which U.S. firms invest abroad. One answer is historical — British, Dutch, and a few other European

[27] In this context the volume of foreign investment is measured in terms of the share of the host-country market supplied by host-country production by source-country firms.
[28] In the process of takeovers, source-country firms seek out host-country firms in the same industry. This practice — domestically as well as internationally — suggests economies of scale.

32

firms invested in the United States when the U.S. capitalization rate was lower than their own. They have retained and nourished these investments even as the national differences in the relationship in capitalization rates reversed. Thus in recent years, the number of foreign firms which have invested in the U.S. market for the first time is much below the number of U.S. firms which have gone abroad. Moreover, the historical explanation is inadequate to explain U.S. direct foreign investment in Great Britain before World War I.

Much cross-hauling is explained by a very few firms — Shell, Unilever, Philips, Bayer, etc.; even then, the question is why these firms invest abroad rather than export.[29] What must be explained is why these foreign firms have not sold their patents to U.S. firms. The answer lies in terms of the price at which they can sell their patents, and the market's valuation of their income stream generated in a country whose currency is subject to a lower currency premium. If the price offered for a patent is very low, then the firm may invest in that country rather than license, even though its profit rate will be lower than the profit rates of host-country competitors. Given the national differences in capitalization rates, the foreign firm might invest the receipts outside the United States and increase its total earnings. Each foreign firm compares the income stream from investment in a variety of countries and the capitalization ratio the market attaches to each income stream. Some foreign firms might find it attractive to have direct investments in the United States, for the presence of dollar income stream may increase the market valuations of their equities by more than would larger income streams from sources outside the United States. The difference in the capitalization rates applied by the market to the income is consistent with a currency premium, as long as the market recognizes that the foreign firm receives an income stream generated in a currency in which the market attaches a high currency premium.[30]

[29] The industrial organization hypothesis speaks in terms of cross-patrolling.
[30] This explanation suggests a possible asymmetry between the market's valuation of nondollar income of U.S. firms and of the dollar income of U.S. firms. In the former case, U.S. firms may exploit their patents abroad because the market attaches a higher capitalization ratio to the foreign earnings of a U.S. firm than to the identical earnings of a non-U.S. firm.

Conclusion

This paper has examined whether foreign direct investment is better explained as a custom-area phenomenon or a currency-area phenomenon. The central hypothesis is that the key factor in the explanation of the pattern of direct foreign investment is that the world is divided into different currency areas and that there is a bias in the market's estimate of exchange risk. The bias in the evaluation of exchange risk determines whether a country is likely to be a source country or a host country for foreign investment.

Moreover, the bias attached to securities denominated in a foreign currency differs from that attached to the income in that currency of a source-country firm. If the world were a unified currency area, exchange risk and a currency premium would not exist; then the analysis of direct foreign investment would be in terms of the economics of location. In this world, tariffs would be a type of transportation cost; the higher the tariffs, the greater the tendency that demand in each customs area would be satisfied from production within that area. Tariffs explain whether a patent is utilized at home or abroad and not whether a host-country firm or a source-country firm utilizes the patent.

National differences in capitalization rates are the major factors that explain the country pattern of direct foreign investment; otherwise the pattern would tend to be random. The difference in pattern by industry reflects differences in the size of the host-country market and the cost of doing business abroad. Similarly takeovers can be explained by these differences in capitalization rates.

The market may also attach a lower capitalization ratio to the U.S. earnings of a foreign firm than to the identical earnings of a U.S. firm; however, the capitalization ratio may be significantly higher than on its non-U.S. alternatives.

CHAPTER TWO

THE EFFICIENCY AND WELFARE IMPLICATIONS OF THE INTERNATIONAL CORPORATION

Harry G. Johnson

Monopolistic Competition in Knowledge

Direct foreign investment by the large international corporation, and especially by the large American international corporation, has become an increasing source of political concern in countries where such investment has been significant since the Second World War and particularly in the past decade or so; and there has been much discussion, and some practice, of the application of restrictions to such investment. Much of the concern about direct foreign investment has merely expressed xenophobic or nationalistic sentiments of a type that cannot readily be reasoned with; but there are obviously theoretical possibilities that the consequences of such investments may be adverse, either by comparison with the situation as it would be in their absence, or, less stringently and more plausibly, by comparison with alternative methods of handling the transference of knowledge, which is the crux of the direct investment process. These possibilities of adverse effects have usually been discussed — as exemplified by C. P. Kindleberger's contribution to a recent seminar in Chicago[1] — in

---

[1] C. P. Kindleberger, "Restrictions on Direct Investments in Host Countries," a discussion paper for the University of Chicago Workshop in International Business (March 5, 1969, unpublished).

terms of the standard arguments for tariff protection, together, more recently, with considerations drawn from the analysis of market organization and competition, due particularly to the work of Stephen Hymer.[2] This paper will be concerned with essentially the same possibilities as other authors have noted, but it seeks to place the issues in a broader and more fundamental perspective by relating them to the welfare economics of technological and managerial knowledge as a factor of production.[3]

As has long been known from the economic analysis of the patent system, the production and utilization of knowledge in a private enterprise system poses an insuperable dilemma from the point of view of welfare maximization. The dilemma arises from the fact that the creation or development of new productive knowledge requires an investment of resources which must be recompensed if there is to be an incentive for private investment in knowledge creation, but that once new knowledge has been created it has the character of a public good, in the sense that use of such knowledge by one person does not preclude use of it by another, so that optimality requires that it be made available to all potential users without charge. Ideally, therefore, the production of useful new knowledge should be financed collectively through the government, and the results made available to potential users free of charge. This is the practice with respect to some sectors of the

---

[2] S. H. Hymer, "The International Operations of National Firms: A Study of Direct Investment," M.I.T. doctoral dissertation, Cambridge, Mass. (1960). "Direct Foreign Investment and National Interest," in *Nationalism in Canada*, P. Russell, ed. (Toronto: McGraw-Hill, 1966). "Anti-Trust and American Direct Investment Abroad," published in *International Aspects of Anti-Trust*, Hearings before the Subcommittee on Antitrust and Monopoly of the Committee on the Judiciary, United States Senate, 89th Congress, Second Session (Washington, D.C.: U.S. Government Printing Office, 1967). "The Impact of the Multinational Firm," published in French in *La Politique industrielle de l'Europe integrée*, M. Byé, ed. (Paris: Presses Universitaires de France, 1968), pp. 167–185.

[3] For an earlier and in some respects more detailed treatment, see H. G. Johnson, Wicksell Lectures for 1968, *Comparative Cost and Commercial Policy Theory for a Developing World Economy* (Stockholm: Almqvist & Wiksell, 1968), reprinted as a Supplement to the *Pakistan Development Review* (1969).

economy, most notably agriculture; but for the most part a private enterprise system relies on private enterprise for the production of commercially useful knowledge. Private production of commercially useful knowledge is encouraged by granting or allowing its producer a temporary monopoly in the use of it. Formerly, an explicit grant of a temporally limited monopoly through the patent system served this purpose; in contemporary conditions, public tolerance and legal protection of commercial secrecy has become more important than the patent system. The practice of rewarding the production of commercially useful knowledge by the right to charge a monopoly price for the product for a period limited either legally or by the natural erosion of commercial secrecy necessarily tends to generate economic inefficiency in at least four major ways.

First, as long as the temporary monopoly enables price to be set above marginal cost of production, the implicit tax on the use of the knowledge restricts such use below the socially optimal level.

Second, the reward to the private producer of new knowledge is less than the social gain from its existence, both the actual gain enjoyed from it in the presence of monopolistic restriction on use, and the potential gain that could be derived if the knowledge were made available free of charge.

These two points are illustrated in Figure 1. In the figure, DD' is the demand curve for a new product, this demand curve being assumed to be latent in the utility functions of consumers but not expressed in the market because until it is introduced the new product has an infinite price; to avoid certain obvious complications, either DD' must be defined as a compensated demand curve, or the effect of introducing the new product must be assumed to be too small to affect the marginal utility of income. Once the new product has been invented, socially optimal policy would require it to be sold at its cost of production (shown by SS', constant cost being assumed for simplicity). From the equilibrium output Q_s that would result, society would derive a consumers' surplus DSP, composed of triangles A and C and the rectangle B. Monopoly would result in the price OP_m, with a monopoly profit of rectangle B and a total social gain of triangle A plus rectangle B.

The first point implies that existing knowledge will be used to a

HARRY G. JOHNSON

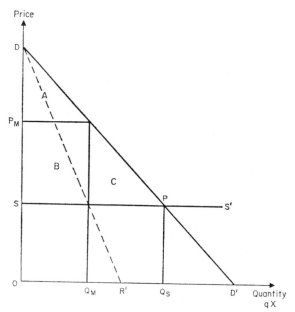

Figure 1. Optimal and Monopoly Pricing of a New Product.

suboptimal extent. The second implies that the private return from the creation of new knowledge will be less than the social return — a further reason for this is the temporal limitation of the monopoly privilege — and that there will therefore be a tendency toward underinvestment in the creation of new knowledge, from the standpoint of social optimality.

Third, since the reward available to the private investor in knowledge creation will depend on the size of the market available to him, and since this will be influenced by a variety of other factors than willingness and capacity to undertake research and development expenditure, which influence firm size and market organization, there will be inefficiencies in the allocation of resources among investments in the production of new knowledge, since private profitability and social profitability are unlikely to be closely correlated. This point has a bearing on the subject of direct foreign investment, because one of its implications is that both large firms and firms existing in large and rich home markets — American firms *par excellence* — will have a comparative advantage in the

38

production of new commercial knowledge and in the application of it in other markets.

Fourth, because success in the production of new knowledge is rewarded by monopoly profits, there is likely to be a waste of resources in investments designed to replicate successful discoveries and capture a share of the profits resulting from them. This point also has a bearing on the subject of direct foreign investment, because it gives domestic businessmen competing with foreign firms incentives to try to get their government either to invest public resources in helping them to develop the knowledge necessary to enable them to compete, or to impose restrictions on foreign investment either to give themselves protection or to force the foreign firms to let them in for a share of the profits generated by the foreign firms' superior knowledge.

Exploiting Technological Monopolies in Foreign Investment

The foregoing points are perfectly general observations about the welfare effects of entrusting the production of commercially useful knowledge to private enterprise and competition, insofar as no reference is made to differences of nationality between producers and consumers. But they do help to put in perspective some of the common reactions in host countries to direct foreign investment in them, if we identify such investment — which involves overcoming the cost disadvantages of operating production and distribution facilities in an unfamiliar environment — as being motivated by the opportunity to profit by the application of superior commercial knowledge.

In the first place, while it is generally recognized that the transplantation of superior technical and managerial knowledge is most probably beneficial to a country receiving foreign direct investment, complaint is frequently made about the high profits derived by the foreign companies from their investments. Usually this complaint is a simple case of wanting to have one's cake and eat it too, that is, specifically, of wanting to have the benefits of knowledge developed by others without contributing anything to defraying the costs they have incurred in developing it. High measured rates of profit on capital, often taken as an indication of "exploitation," may in fact

39

not be so, since the "excess" profits may represent a return on past investments in creating capital in the form of knowledge, which does not appear on the firm's books as an addition to material capital. Of course, if the foreign firm has been given heavy protection in the domestic market to induce it to establish operations there, its profits may reflect an element of monopoly profit, but that will be a consequence of the excess protection awarded it, and presumably remediable.

There is, however, more to the issue than that. On the one hand, resentment of the high profits earned by advanced foreign enterprises may be credited with a vague understanding of the theoretical point that, for welfare optimality, existing knowledge should be made available as a free good, to maximize the social benefit from it, rather than monopolized and charged for. This argument leaves unanswered the question of how the production of additional knowledge is to be motivated, and so is inconsistent and incomplete as a basis for policy. It can be argued, however, that for most of the countries in the world, and especially the less-developed countries, the contribution that the opportunity to earn a profit in their markets makes to the encouragement of investment in the creation of new commercial knowledge is negligible, so that any profit they allow to be earned from the command of advanced technology is for them a short-run loss with no compensating long-run gain from the encouragement of technical progress. To make the point somewhat differently, playing the rules of allowing monopoly gains to be made from economically useful knowledge involves the cost of paying for foreign knowledge that would probably be available anyhow, in the hope of a gain from the reciprocal obligation on foreign countries to pay monopoly profits on the use of knowledge commanded by your own producers; and since most developing countries are unlikely for a long time to be in the position of holding substantial direct foreign investments made by their own domestic firms, they are unlikely to obtain sufficient *quid* to justify the *quo*. In short, there might be a good case for the less-advanced countries to insist on playing by a different set of rules. Apart from that, if the need for recompensing those who make investments in the development of new knowledge is accepted, it does not necessarily follow that

40

recompense through monopoly profits on the use of the knowledge is the ideal arrangement for the host country. On the contrary, the principles of Pareto-optimality suggest a lump-sum payment by the government of the host country in return for the knowledge, and the placing of the knowledge at the free disposal of all firms, foreign as well as domestic, operating in the economy.

On the other hand, given that productive knowledge has the character of a public good, one would expect a firm possessing it to behave as far as possible like a discriminating monopolist: since any additional earnings obtained by applying the knowledge in an additional market will be a net addition to its profits from the initial investment in creating the knowledge, the firm will have an incentive to extend its operations to any market that offers a positive profit, and to fix the price it charges for the use of its knowledge so as to maximize profit in each market. This implies, incidentally, that, because poorer and less-developed countries are likely to have more elastic demand curves for knowledge-intensive products than richer and more advanced countries, the former are likely to pay less, and the latter more, than their *pro rata* share of the costs of development of the knowledge; in other words, there is a general presumption that discriminating monopoly redistributes real income from the rich to the poor. However, the fact that the firm will gain from any positive profit on the knowledge that it is able to make means that there may be an opportunity for governments to squeeze the firm's profits, to the firm's loss but to the social gain. In the second place, foreign firms have frequently been criticized for failure to develop technologies and products appropriate to the factor price relationships, income levels, and local conditions of the countries in which they operate. This complaint overlooks the two considerations of the cost of developing new technologies, and the need for an appropriate payoff. It is presumably cheaper to transplant an already known technology to a different environment to which it is not entirely appropriate, paying some extra cost in terms of inferior efficiency, than to develop a new technology more appropriate to that environment; otherwise firms would not engage in the practice, and there would be no direct foreign investment.

Third, foreign firms have frequently been criticized for employing their own nationals, rather than residents, especially in top positions. Since this is typically relatively expensive, it is presumably explained by the superior competence of the individuals in question in applying the firm's superior knowledge efficiently, rather than by discrimination on behalf of nationals.

Fourth, there is considerable resentment and dismay over the domination of the American corporation in the most technologically advanced sectors of industry. That dominance, however, is a natural reflection of comparative advantage, in two senses. First, the large rich market, high wage level, and relative abundance of capital of the United States tend to give American firms a comparative advantage in the production of new technology; in particular, the United States economy provides strong incentives for labor-saving innovations, either in production processes to economize on the use of workers' time or in new consumption goods to economize on the use of consumers' time. Second, the high wage levels in the United States relative to other countries imply that if the United States is to have a comparative advantage, either in exporting or in establishing and operating productive enterprises to compete in foreign and unfamiliar markets, it cannot be in unskilled-labor-intensive and technologically standardized industries: it must be in technically advanced and technologically dynamic industries. Other countries may well resent this, but it is questionable whether their own market sizes, income levels, and availabilities of scientifically trained personnel would permit them to invest with profit in the development of rival advanced technologies.

Fifth, there has been concern, especially in recent years, over the preference of foreign companies for raising as much capital as they can on the domestic market, thereby competing in that market with domestic companies and minimizing the direct foreign exchange gain from such investment. Apart from questions of minimization of foreign exchange risk, the explanation may well be that the comparative advantage of these companies lies in their possession of superior technology rather than in access to a cheaper source of capital than is available to their domestic competitors, and that this advantage enables them to raise capital on the same terms as their domestic competitors without impairing their competitive ability.

Welfare Effects of Direct Investment

To turn specifically to the question of the welfare effects of foreign direct investment, and whether restriction of inward investment might in some cases be desirable, it is convenient to idealize such investment as involving an increase in the country's capital stock and an improvement in its technology. The standard theory of trade and growth suggests that, as far as the capital inflow is concerned, the country's terms of trade will tend to improve if its imports are relatively capital intensive, and worsen if its exports are relatively capital intensive, the latter case carrying with it the possibility of "immiserizing growth,"[4] especially when the welfare of the resident population is at issue and remissions of interest and dividends to foreign owners of capital are excluded. More recently, Murray Kemp[5] and Ronald Jones[6] have investigated the concept of an optimal tax on international capital movements, parallel to the concept of the optimum tariff, and Jones has developed conditions for optimization of welfare with respect to both the tariff and the capital tax. It turns out that in some cases a subsidy rather than a tax on either goods flows or capital flows (but not both simultaneously) may be necessary to maximize national welfare. Similarly,

[4] J. Bhagwati, "Immiserizing Growth: A Geometrical Note," *The Review of Economic Studies,* Vol. XXV, No. 3 (June 1958), pp. 201–205, reprinted in *Readings in International Economics,* R. E. Caves and H. G. Johnson, eds. (Homewood, Ill.: R. D. Irwin, for the American Economic Association, 1968).

[5] M. C. Kemp, "Foreign Investment and the National Advantage," *Economic Record,* Vol. 38, No. 1 (March 1962), pp. 56–62. "The Benefits and Costs of Private Investment from Abroad: Comments," *Economic Record,* Vol. 38, No. 1 (March 1962), pp. 108–110. "The Gain from International Trade and Investment: A Neo-Heckscher-Ohlin Approach," *American Economic Review,* Vol. LVI, No. 4, Part 1 (September 1966), pp. 788–809.

[6] R. W. Jones, "International Capital Movements and the Theory of Tariffs and Trade," *Quarterly Journal of Economics,* Vol. L, No. 1 (February 1967), pp. 1–38.

technical progress in the export industry will tend to turn a country's terms of trade against it, and in the import industry to turn the terms of trade in its favor.[7] Undoubtedly there is an optimum tax on technological transplants, or on inward foreign investment as a mixture of capital inflow and technological transplant, waiting to be analyzed by a mathematical trade theorist. However, it does not seem worthwhile to dwell on the point, both because it is an obvious one and because it is hard to believe that actual national policies are governed sufficiently closely by consideration of possibilities of national gain of this kind. It is worth remarking, however, that just as the optimum tariff argument is the only economic argument that leads to restrictions on international trade, as the first-best policy solution, all other arguments being either noneconomic arguments or economic arguments in which tariffs figure as a second-best solution that may or may not improve welfare, depending on the empirical circumstances, so the optimal capital tax argument is the only economic argument that leads to restrictions on international capital flows as a first-best solution. (As such, it suggests restrictions on such flows by both capital-importing and capital-exporting countries, in their own national interests.) Henceforward this paper ignores both terms-of-trade and terms-of-borrowing arguments for intervention in direct international investment.

Host-Country Gains

Before we proceed to an analysis of the second-best arguments for restriction of inward private foreign investment, something must be said about the presumptive gains to the nation from such investment. Technical progress such as is brought by inward foreign investment is generally assumed to be beneficial by definition. But, assuming constant terms of trade, this is true in general only to the

---

[7] See, for example, H. G. Johnson, "Economic Expansion and International Trade," *The Manchester School of Economic and Social Studies,* Vol. 23, No. 2 (May 1955), pp. 95–112, reprinted in *International Trade and Economic Growth* (London: Allen & Unwin, 1958); also R. Findlay and H. Grubert, "Factor Intensity, Technological Progress, and the Terms of Trade," *Oxford Economic Papers,* New Ser., Vol. 11, No. 1 (February 1959), pp. 111–121.

extent that technical progress is a free good. If the return on the superior technology brought by foreign investment is entirely absorbed by the foreign companies, prices of commodities to consumers and the prices of factors of production in the economy remaining unchanged, there is no direct benefit to the economy. The only benefit it gets, though it may be a quantitatively important one, is the right under double taxation agreements to tax the earnings of the foreign capital invested in it, earnings which will include both the earnings of the capital as such and the earnings of the "technological capital" represented by the superiority of the foreign firm's technology and its consequent ability to earn profits higher than those earned by domestic firms. Apart from this tax benefit — which will be ignored in what follows, despite its possible significance — the residents of the country gain only to the extent that the benefit of the superior technology is passed on either in lower prices to consumers and the prices of factors of production in the economy both. This point provides a rationale for the insistence of the Watkins Committee[8] on the desirability of maximizing the benefits and minimizing the costs of foreign investment in Canada. This is really a meaningless statement, since what is to be maximized is net benefit, and this is not usually achieved by separate maximization of gross benefit and minimization of cost. Presumably, it means minimizing the rents that foreign firms derive from their possession of superior knowledge. This in turn implies attempting to obtain for Canadian capitalists and Canadian labor a share of the monopoly profits derived by foreign enterprises from their superior knowledge, and attempting to force the benefits of this knowledge to be transferred to the Canadian consumer in the form of lower prices.

Redistributive Effects

It is an interesting theoretical point that, if, as may seem plausible in spite of much recent work on the Leontief paradox,[9] direct

---

[8] M. Watkins *et al., Foreign Ownership and the Structure of Canadian Industry,* Report of the Task Force on the Structure of Canadian Industry (Ottawa: The Queen's Printer, 1968).

[9] Compare W. Gruber, P. Mehta, and R. Vernon, "The R and D Factor in International Trade and International Investment of United States Indus-

foreign investment tends to flow into the more capital-intensive sectors of the economy, and if the failure or prevention of the extraction of the whole of the monopoly rent on superior knowledge is reflected in changes in the general levels of factor prices, rather than in premium prices for the factors employed by the foreign companies, the effect of the inflow of foreign capital will be to raise the rate of return on capital and reduce the wages of labor. This point is illustrated in Figure 2, where XX and YY are the isoquants for the two sectors of the economy as they are before the foreign

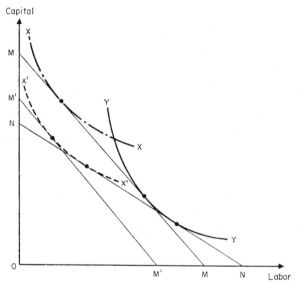

Figure 2. Redistribution of Factor Income from Direct Investment.

investment, and $X'X'$ is the isoquant for the situation after the introduction of the foreign technology. If the foreign companies absorb the whole benefit of their superior efficiency in profits on the technology, factor prices remain unchanged and they derive a profit on their technological superiority as a proportion of cost at the rate MM'/OM'. If they pass it on to the consumers completely, in the form of a price reduction proportional to their technical superiority,

tries," *Journal of Political Economy,* Vol. LXXV, No. 1 (February 1967), pp. 20–37. These authors find that the technologically advanced sectors of American industry are not exceptionally intensive in material capital.

the price of X falls by MM' in terms of capital and factor prices are unchanged; if they keep commodity prices unchanged and let the benefits be absorbed by the community through altered factor prices, the new factor-price ratio is the slope of NN, which implies a relative and absolute increase in the price of the services of capital and an absolute and relative decline in the price of the services of labor. This point may explain the otherwise rather implausible fact that in Britain the employers are favorably inclined toward American investment in the country, while the trade unions are generally hostile towards it.[10] One would expect labor to favor direct foreign investment as bringing in more capital to compete for the services of labor and so to raise real wages, and the owners of capital contrarily to be opposed to inward foreign investment; but if the effect of inward investment by foreign firms is to increase the demand for capital and reduce the demand for labor, these class reactions are understandable. (Of course, views on the desirability of capitalism may play a more important part than assessments of probable class gain or loss from particular phenomena.)

Justifications for Restrictions

It would appear from the foregoing analysis that, first-best effects of foreign investment on the terms of trade and the terms of borrowing, and second-best effects on the distribution of national income between owners of labor and owners of capital, apart, inward foreign direct investment cannot harm a country and may confer substantial benefits upon it. What then are the arguments against freedom of foreign direct investment, and in favor of restriction on it? As already mentioned, such arguments must be either non-economic arguments, that is, arguments directed at the maximization of something other than the privately consumable flow of goods and services, or arguments that produce the policy of restriction on inward private foreign investments as a second-best (possibly third-best) policy with an uncertain effect on the achievement of the desired economic aim.

[10] J. H. Dunning, *The Role of American Investment in the British Economy,* PEP Broadsheet 507 (February 1969).

The classical example of a noneconomic argument for protection is the national defense argument: the argument for protecting those industries that supply military equipment, foodstuffs, and materials vital in times of war. In principle, the economist cannot debate the necessity of national defense — though in recent years economists have in fact been arguing the necessity of relating defense policy to the kinds of wars that have a nonzero probability of occurring — but he can legitimately raise the question of whether protection of domestic output (as contrasted say with stockpiling) is the cheapest form of investment in future defense capability. As applied to the question of restrictions on domestic investment and production by foreign firms, however, the national defense argument would seem to have very little in it. By establishing branch enterprises in a country, the foreign firm gives a hostage to fortune which can be only too readily imprisoned in the event of war or the prospect of war. The only risks a country runs in allowing foreign enterprises in defense industries are:

1. The risk of espionage: this is so obvious as to be probably unimportant in practice.

2. The risk that top personnel in the enterprise will refuse to operate it in time of war if their country of origin is on the opposite side: this is unlikely to be a major problem both because few people are prepared to endure prolonged idleness in prison for the sake of principle, and because it is unlikely that the foreign enterprise will be so closely controlled by nationals of an enemy state that substitutes for uncooperative foreigners cannot be found among residents employed either by the foreign firm or by other domestic competitors in the same industry.

3. The risk that, because the foreign firm will be relying in part on research and development conducted in the parent country, the country will be cut off from the results of on-going research, even though it is not cut off from the existing knowledge embodied in the foreign firm's current production techniques: this point cuts both ways, since the presence of the foreign firm will, up to the point of a serious prospect of war, make more information on production technology available to the country than it otherwise would have.

48

These risks are likely to be of negligible importance by comparison with the costs of developing a modern weapons system on a national economic base, for the vast majority of countries, especially since the countries capable of and politically obliged to develop such systems are likely to provide the results of their investment in them at a subsidized price to friendly countries.

Nationalism as a Public Good

In the contemporary world, the national defense argument is more likely to appear in the more general form of a "national independence" argument: that is, the argument that it is valuable to have at least certain kinds of production controlled by resident nationals rather than by foreigners. Albert Breton,[11] and following him myself,[12] have developed a theory for this situation, in which nationalism figures as a collective consumption good that can be invested in by sacrifice of private consumption in order to increase the collective consumption of nationalism. This theory explains many of the phenomena of nationalist economic policies. In the context of direct foreign investment, it explains the desire, reflected in a variety of policies, to have technologically advanced industries controlled by national rather than foreign enterprises, as a facet of the desire to demonstrate national competence in an internationally competitive game. (Backward countries take inordinate pride in success in Olympic sports, and invest resources in achieving it; advanced countries take inordinate pride in success in the international basic research and technological progress races, and are prepared to invest resources on a large scale in achieving it.) Again, in this context, the economist cannot in principle dispute the public tastes, though he can question whether the policies adopted are well

---

[11] A. Breton, "The Economics of Nationalism," *Journal of Political Economy,* Vol. LXXII, No. 4 (August 1964), pp. 376–386.

[12] H. G. Johnson, "A Theoretical Model of Economic Nationalism in New and Developing States," *The Political Science Quarterly,* Vol. LXXX, No. 2 (June 1965), pp. 169–185; also "An Economic Theory of Protectionism, Tariff Bargaining, and the Formation of Customs Unions," *Journal of Political Economy,* Vol. LXXII, No. 3 (June 1965), pp. 256–283.

designed to secure their ostensible objectives, and stress the need for examination of alternative methods of securing those objectives.

In the course of a correspondence distinguished by its terse ambiguity, C. P. Kindleberger has attempted to induce me to treat nationalism as a producers' good rather than a consumers' good. I find it difficult to understand the distinction he seeks to draw. From one point of view, the distinction is merely semantic: nationalist policies directed at the production of more of the collective consumption good of nationalism clearly generate a producers' good, the capacity to supply the collective consumption good of nationalism. From another point of view, the implication is that investment in nationalism — i.e., national rather than foreign control of productive enterprises — somehow increases future income from both collective consumption of nationalism and private consumption of goods and services. For this to be the case, it must be assumed that there are externalities from national ownership and control of productive enterprises, as compared with foreign ownership and control, which raise the productivity of other national enterprises above what it would otherwise be. The only possibility of this that I can see is that somehow superior productive knowledge possessed by nationals is communicated more readily and rapidly to other nationals than is superior productive knowledge possessed by foreign enterprises. This proposition in turn assumes that, for sociological reasons, businessmen are more ready to confide their commercial secrets to fellow nationals than to foreigners — a not entirely credible proposition. In any case, treating nationalism nonsemantically as a producer's good involves reintroducing second-best economic arguments for protection.

Second-Best Arguments

I now turn to the second-best economic arguments for protection of domestic firms against the intrusion of foreign direct investment. One of these, just mentioned, is that national rather than foreign ownership of certain industries conveys externalities that are valuable enough to be worth subsidizing at public expense. This argument, which entails permanent subsidization of the industries in question, is to be distinguished from the standard infant-industry

50

argument, which calls for temporary subsidization of a given industry during the period it takes to get the industry established.[13]

The infant-industry argument for protection, as is well known, requires that there be an opportunity for investment in the acquisition of productive knowledge that is socially profitable but privately unprofitable. For this purpose, it is not sufficient that the protected industry will eventually become competitive with foreign suppliers; it must eventually either be able to charge prices low enough to the domestic consumer, or to pay prices high enough to the owners of domestic factors of production (including profits on domestic capital invested), to yield a socially adequate rate of return on the investment involved in the initial protection. Nor is it sufficient that an initial loss must be incurred as an investment in obtaining the ultimate gains. If private entrepreneurs could capture the gains in the form of profits greater than those prevalent elsewhere in the economy, they would be led to undertake the investment required if it were socially profitable, and to avoid it if it were socially unprofitable — at least on the assumption that the cost of capital to them is the social alternative opportunity cost of capital. What is required is that the social benefits of investment in the acquisition of productive knowledge exceed the private benefits. In this connection, it is necessary to observe that the argument commonly used — that the infant industry trains labor, which is then available for other firms at a wage lower than the true cost of production of the trained labor, the training being paid for by the infant industry but not recompensed by the use of the trained labor — is fallacious. In a well-organized market system, training that is freely transferable to other employers will not be paid for by the initial employer who provides the training, but will instead be paid for by labor itself through an appropriate apprenticeship system which pays the employee under training a wage lower than his current marginal product to the extent of the training costs incurred by the employer.

---

[13] For this distinction, and a full analysis of second-best arguments for protection, see H. G. Johnson, "Optimal Trade Intervention in the Presence of Domestic Distortions," pp. 3–34 in Baldwin *et al., Trade, Growth and the Balance of Payments; Essays in Honor of Gottfried Haberler* (Chicago: Rand McNally, 1965).

The infant-industry argument for insisting on confining participation in an industry to domestic firms must therefore rest on the assumption that there are social benefits from investment in the creation of new knowledge which are not capturable by the firm undertaking investment in the creation of such knowledge, *and* which are greater in the case of a domestically owned firm than in the case of a foreign-owned firm. This is a doubtful proposition from at least two points of view. First, insofar as the external effects of the development of advanced technology are a "demonstration" or "public goods" effect — that is, insofar as superior knowledge developed by a firm can be understood and applied by other firms without their having to incur the costs of developing the knowledge for themselves — it should make no difference whether the firm providing the external effects is domestically or foreign owned. Second, since the foreign firm is likely to be using knowledge that has already been developed, and is immediately applicable for a rental price that is likely to be lower than a fair rate of return on the cost of developing it for the reasons explored earlier in this paper, insistence on development of a substitute for this knowledge by domestic firms is likely to be a poor social investment, first because it will delay the development of the knowledge yielding the externalities, and second because the national enterprise will have to obtain an adequate rate of return on the investment in knowledge creation, whereas by relying on foreign enterprises the country may only have to pay a rate of return on knowledge creation which is substantially below the country's alternative opportunity cost of capital.

It is for this reason that the restriction of inward foreign direct investment in order to subsidize the acquisition of technological knowledge by domestic firms is a second-best argument. Insofar as the difference between foreign-controlled and domestically controlled enterprise is relevant to the determination of the extent of non-privately-capturable benefits from the availability and application of superior knowledge, optimal policy consists in securing that the knowledge is available to and applied by domestic rather than foreign firms, at the least possible acquisition cost. This would normally require arranging for the requisite knowledge to be acquired by domestic firms from foreign sources, through licensing or partnership arrangements or, optimally, through outright purchase by the state, rather than excluding foreign firms from the domestic market as a means of giving domestic firms an incentive to invest in replicating the knowledge of foreign firms — an incentive to which they may not find it profitable anyway to respond, given the protection provided them.

Another and very obviously second-best argument for excluding foreign firms is that the products they provide are "socially undesirable" — either "luxury goods" for the despised rich or "recreation goods" for the resented idle of all classes. First-best policy here would involve either changing the overall income distribution by taxes and transfers, if it is the prevailing income distribution that it is sought to alter, or putting consumption taxes on the goods in question, if it is the consumption of these particular goods that is regarded as socially undesirable. A second-best policy of doubtful efficacy would be to prohibit all production of the disfavored goods, whether by domestic or foreign firms. Prohibition of investment and production by foreign firms only will, unless only foreign firms have the know-how to produce the product and they are unwilling to make it available to domestic firms at any price (which would be irrational on their part, in view of the preceding analysis of the economics of knowledge as a monopolized public good), have the paradoxical result of encouraging domestic firms to invest one way or another in acquiring the know-how to produce goods considered socially undesirable or noncontributory to economic growth, and diverting scarce domestic capital and entrepreneurial talent from industries considered to be socially desirable or to be socially productive.

The Balance of Payments

Another type of second-best argument for restricting foreign direct investment in a country concerns the balance of payments. Any such argument must be either a second-best argument — because the balance of payments is determined by macroeconomic relationships and should be controlled by macroeconomic policy instruments (specifically the exchange rate and monetary and fiscal policy) rather than by microeconomic policies (which in any case are of very doubtful efficacy) — or it must be a subtle and unacknowledged version of the terms-of-trade argument for capital taxes. One version of this argument — that the balance-of-payments cost of the earnings on a foreign direct investment will be "too high" to justify the investment — reflects partly the resentment previously mentioned against paying the price of acquiring foreign productive knowledge, and partly the possibility that overvaluation of the currency coupled with import controls and domestic inflation has made the money profits earnable by foreign investors artificially high (by comparison with (1) what they would be if the exchange rate were an equilibrium rate and there were no import restrictions; (2) the real alternative opportunity cost of capital to the country).

Another version of the balance-of-payments argument for restricting foreign direct investment is that the country will be unable, when the investment has occurred, to generate the foreign exchange earnings required to service the investment, through increasing exports or reducing exports. This argument assumes either an unwillingness to devalue the currency and restrict aggregate demand sufficiently to balance the balance of payments, or that balancing the balance of payments requires a worsening of the terms of trade, whose adverse effect on domestic real income more than wipes out any gains from the foreign investment captured by the country through lower product prices, higher factor prices, or receipts from the taxation of foreign capital and foreign knowledge. In the latter case, what is at issue is the optimal capital tax argument, which is a first-best argument excluded from the 'analysis of this paper.[14]

Monopoly

A final second-best argument for restriction of foreign direct investment, popularized by Stephen Hymer, is motivated by the

---

[14] Reference 1, pp. 8–9, concedes this case for restriction of foreign direct investment without, apparently, realizing that it involves the analog of the optimum tariff argument that earlier in his paper he dismisses as "unrealistic in policy terms."

possibility that the presence of foreign enterprises may increase monopoly and thus affect the social welfare adversely. This is a second-best argument, because the intrusion of foreign enterprises may either increase or decrease competition in the domestic economy, and if more competition is desired it can be achieved more reliably by domestic antitrust policy, or still more reliably, by reducing the tariff protection enjoyed by industries where the presence of monopoly can be verified. Moreover, the question of whether foreign ownership of part of industry leads to social loss through increased monopoly requires more careful analysis than it has usually received. Social loss would seem to require either an increase in prices to consumers above what they would otherwise be, or additional wastes of resources on the nonprice aspects of monopolistic competition. Higher profits derived from the superior efficiency of foreign firms are not evidence of such loss, but rather the contrary from a cosmopolitan point of view, reflecting the saving of resource costs through greater efficiency; and from the national point of view, there is a gain to the extent that prices to consumers are lowered, prices of domestic factors of production are raised, or the nation shares in the increased profits of the foreign firms through taxation.

It has been suggested that, to maximize the chances of preserving and increasing competition when inward foreign direct investment occurs, takeovers of existing domestic firms should be discouraged, and the construction of new domestic production facilities encouraged instead. This rule of thumb seems poorly grounded in economic analysis, since for the foreign firm the choice between the two alternatives of takeover and new construction is a matter of relative cost of entry into domestic production, and reflects nothing of the purpose for which that firm wishes to establish itself as a producer in the market (that is, whether its purpose is to compete, or to organize more effective monopoly arrangements). It should be remarked also that if takeovers are forbidden, foreign entry via new construction will probably mean capital losses for domestic firms if the foreigner intends to compete vigorously, whereas entry by takeover, since it requires payment of a price for the domestic firm higher in the owners' eyes than the capitalized value of their prospective future profits under existing management, gives those owners the capitalized value of a slice of the profits the foreign firm expects to make through the application of its superior technology. The same consideration probably applies to the case where the foreigner enters to organize a more effective monopoly.

In conclusion, it is evident that with sufficient analysis one can construct cases in which there is a second-best argument for restriction of inward foreign direct investment. The fundamental problem is that, as with all second-best arguments, determination of the conditions under which a second-best policy actually leads to an improvement of social welfare requires detailed theoretical and empirical investigation by a first-best economist. Unfortunately, policy is generally formulated by fourth-best economists and administered by third-best economists; it is therefore very unlikely that a second-best welfare optimum will result from policies based on second-best arguments.

CHAPTER THREE

MULTINATIONAL CORPORATIONS AND INTERNATIONAL OLIGOPOLY: THE NON-AMERICAN CHALLENGE*

Stephen Hymer and Robert Rowthorn

The large-scale migration of United States capital to foreign countries in recent years and the coming to prominence of the multinational corporation have stimulated a world-wide discussion about the nature and significance of this latest stage in the evolution of business organization. The purpose of this essay is to examine the problem of direct foreign business investment in its European context, using a simple oligopoly model combined with data on the 500 largest industrial corporations in the world (approximately 300 U.S. and 200 non-U.S.). Our aim is to analyze what might be termed the dialectics of the multinational corporation, the thrusts and counterthrusts of U.S. and non-U.S. corporations as they compete for shares in the world market using direct foreign investment as one of their chief instruments. Our hope is to clarify

* The research for this paper was in part financed by a grant from the Council on Foreign Relations in the case of Stephen Hymer and by the Faculty of Economics of Cambridge University in the case of Robert Rowthorn. Preliminary versions of this paper were presented at seminars at the University of Toronto, Cambridge, M.I.T., and the Instituto de Estudios Internacionales of the University of Chile, where much helpful criticism was obtained. (Geoffery Whittington also made a number of helpful comments on a preliminary version.) The authors would also like to thank Miss P. Cunningham, Miss J. McKenzie, Miss R. Henderson, and Miss H. Lackner for their help in preparing the statistical material of this essay. Finally, they would like to thank Miss J. A. Barnes and Mrs. M. N. Simmonds, who typed the manuscript.

the debate on the "American challenge," a debate that we think is in many ways a manifestation on the political level of the oligopolistic rivalry of large corporations on the business level. We also wish to draw out some of the implications of the current European policy to merge and rationalize in order to meet the "specter of the American Multinational Corporations."[1]

Servan-Schreiber's[2] analysis of the American challenge provides a useful starting point. His analysis rests on three basic propositions. First, modern technology requires large corporations. The large corporation, because of its ability to concentrate capital and administer it effectively, is an essential requisite of growth and modernity. The parallels on this point, between Servan-Schreiber's analysis and that of Galbraith in *The New Industrial State*,[3] are of course obvious. Second, a country (continent) without its own multinational corporations will become a colony. If Europe does not create corporate capitals to match the American giants it will

---

[1] The Editor, "The Multinational Corporation: the Splendors and Miseries of Bigness," *Interplay* (November 1968), p. 15. This source provides as good a definition of the multinational corporation as any — "an organization which, while remaining in private hands, transcends national boundaries and national regulation."

[2] J.-J. Servan-Schreiber, *Le Défi Américain* (Paris: Editions de Noel, 1967). Servan-Schreiber is chosen because he is the most articulate propagator of a certain view. The literature on the subject is too extensive to be quoted here, but at the very least we must mention C. Layton, *Trans-Atlantic Investments* (Boulogne-sur-Seine: The Atlantic Institute, 1966); M. Byé, ed., *La Politique industrielle de l'europe intergrée et l'apport des capitaux extérieurs* (Paris: Presses Universitaires de France, 1968); C. P. Kindleberger, "European Integration and the International Corporation," *Columbia Journal of World Business,* Vol. I, No. 1 (Winter 1966), pp. 65–73; G. Y. Bertin, *L'Investissement des firmes etrangères en France* (Paris: Presses Universitaires de France, 1963); S. H. Robock, "The American Challenge — an Inside Story," *The Hermes Exchange,* Vol. 1, No. 2 (October 1968), pp. 9–12; B. Balassa, "American Direct Investments in the Common Market," *Banca Nazionale del Lavoro Quarterly Review,* No. 67 (June 1966), pp. 121–146; E. Mandel, "International Capitalism and Supra Nationality," in *The Socialist Register 1967,* R. Milliband and J. Saville, eds. (London: The Merlin Press, 1967); G. Adam, "Standing up to the American Challenge," *The New Hungarian Quarterly,* Vol. IX, No. 3 (Autumn 1968), pp. 57–139.

[3] J. K. Galbraith, *The New Industrial State* (Boston: Houghton Mifflin Company, 1967).

be reduced to playing a secondary, colonial role, not just in the economic sphere, but in the political, social, and cultural spheres as well. Third, the appropriate remedy lies in positive rather than negative measures. Negative measures to restrict the inflow of U.S. corporation investment, as the Japanese have done, would in Servan-Schreiber's view avoid the American challenge rather than meet it. Instead he argues that positive measures are needed on a European-wide basis to create giant European corporations using advanced methods of business organization and working in close collaboration with universities and government to create an economic structure suited to modern technology.

This brief summary of Servan-Schreiber's analysis does not pretend to do justice to his views. Rather we have singled out certain key features, widely accepted in Europe and in the United States, which we feel require further investigation. The view that Europe's challenge is to emulate the United States model of industrial organization raises certain important questions for analysis, and the task of this essay will be to formulate some tentative answers to them:

1. What has been the relative performance of U.S. corporations and non-U.S. corporations in recent years and how much of an advantage has size been?

2. What is likely to be the impact of the European merger movement on the strength and performance of European corporations and on the pattern of trade and investment?

3. With regard to Servan-Schreiber's political analysis, how is the creation of European giant corporations likely to effect the "independence" of Europe?

An International Comparison of the Size and Performance of U.S. and Non-U.S. Industrial Corporations

Size[4] A major focus of the debate on the American challenge has been the large size of U.S. corporations. Table 1 shows the

[4] The data are taken from *Fortune* magazine's annual listing of the 500 largest industrial corporations in the United States and the 200 largest industrial corporations outside the United States (100 in 1957). The data are subject to numerous deficiencies but are the only ones available, since government statistics typically use the industry rather than the corporation

Table 1. The Size Distribution of Large Industrial Corporations.

Size Class of Sales (millions of dollars)	Cumulative Number of Firms							Cumulative Sales (billions of dollars)						
	1957		1962		1967			1957		1962		1967		
	U.S.	Non-U.S.	U.S.	Non-U.S.	U.S.	Non-U.S.	U.S. as % of Total*	U.S.	Non-U.S.	U.S.	Non-U.S.	U.S.	Non-U.S.	U.S. as % of Total*
(1)	(2)	(3)	(4)	(5)	(6)	(7)	(8)	(9)	(10)	(11)	(12)	(13)	(14)	(15)
19,999 to 26,005	—	—	—	—	1	—	100	—	—	—	—	20.0	—	100
15,345 to 19,999	—	—	—	—	1	—	100	—	—	—	—	20.0	—	100
11,724 to 15,345	—	—	1	—	2	—	100	—	—	14.6	—	33.3	—	100
9,033 to 11,724	1	—	2	—	3	—	100	10.9	—	24.2	—	43.8	—	100
6,931 to 9,033	2	1	3	1	4	1	80	18.8	7.4	32.3	—	51.5	8.4	86
5,318 to 6,931	3	1	3	1	7	2	78	24.6	7.4	32.3	6.0	68.9	13.9	88
4,080 to 5,318	5	1	4	2	9	2	82	33.3	7.4	37.0	10.1	78.2	13.9	85
3,131 to 4,080	6	2	7	2	12	2	86	36.9	10.8	47.7	10.1	89.2	13.9	86
2,402 to 3,131	11	2	11	3	28	5	85	50.2	10.8	58.2	12.6	133.4	22.0	86
1,843 to 2,402	16	4	20	4	37	10	79	60.5	14.9	76.6	14.6	153.0	32.8	82
1,414 to 1,843	22	5	29	8	50	18	74	69.9	16.5	91.9	21.2	173.5	45.7	79
1,085 to 1,414	33	7	41	11	73	34	68	83.1	18.9	106.3	25.0	202.3	65.6	76
0,823.5 to 1,085	45	8	56	23	101	61	62	94.0	19.8	121.0	36.1	229.5	90.9	72
0,639.8 to 0,823.5	57	18	77	36	137	87	61	102.9	26.9	136.2	45.9	256.2	109.7	70
0,490.1 to 0,639.8	81	27	108	61	175	112	61	116.5	31.8	153.4	59.5	277.5	123.4	69
0,376.0 to 0,490.1	105	51	138	88	225	142	61	126.5	42.0	166.2	70.9	298.9	136.3	69
0,289.5 to 0,376.0	143	67	180	118	278	185	60	139.2	47.3	179.9	80.9	316.4	150.7	68
0,221.4 to 0,289.5	196	88	235	155				152.8	52.7	193.9	90.2			
0,169.9 to 0,221.4			284	183						203.3	95.5			

* 1967.

Table 2. The Relative Size of U.S. and Non-U.S. Corporations Firms.

Firms Ranked†	1967 Sales (billions of dollars) U.S.	Non-U.S.	Relative Size Ratio in 1967* Sales	Assets	Employees
1–10	82.2	32.8	2.5	1.9	1.2
11–20	30.7	15.7	2.0	2.0	1.2
21–30	25.3	12.7	2.0	1.4	1.5
31–40	20.1	10.7	1.9	1.7	0.7
41–50	15.2	9.5	1.6	1.4	1.0
51–60	13.5	8.7	1.5	1.7	0.5
61–70	12.0	8.0	1.5	1.7	0.9
71–80	10.6	7.1	1.5	1.1	0.9
81–90	9.9	6.5	1.5	1.2	1.2
91–100	9.1	5.6	1.6	1.2	0.9
101–110	8.1	5.2	1.6	1.3	0.7
111–120	7.7	4.7	1.6	0.9	0.9
121–130	7.1	4.4	1.6	1.5	1.0
131–140	6.5	4.0	1.6	1.1	0.8
141–150	6.0	3.7	1.6	1.4	0.9
151–160	5.5	3.5	1.6	0.9	1.3
161–170	5.2	3.3	1.6	1.1	1.0
171–180	4.9	3.1	1.6	1.4	0.9
181–190	4.6	2.9	1.6	1.1	1.2
191–200	4.4	2.8	1.6	0.7	0.5
1–50	173.5	81.3	2.1	1.7	1.1
1–100	228.6	117.2	1.9	1.6	1.0
1–200	288.8	154.8	1.8	1.5	1.0

* The relative size ratio is the ratio of total sales, assets, or employees of U.S. corporations to non-U.S. corporations within a given ranking.
† 1–10 means the 10 largest firms (by sales size), etc.

distribution of the 500 largest corporations by size of sales in 1967 and illustrates the "giantism" of the U.S. corporations. The United States accounts for about half of the industrial production of Organization for Economic Cooperation and Development countries but U.S. firms have a much larger share of the sales of corporations in larger-size categories.

The phenomenon of giantism can also be seen in Table 2, which

as the unit of analysis. *Fortune* ranks firms by sales rather than assets or employees and we have accordingly used sales for most of the tests in this paper. To the extent that *Fortune* correctly reflects business thinking on the "best" measure of size, sales may well be the appropriate index for analyzing oligopoly strategy.

61

shows that the sales of the top ten U.S. corporations are about 2½ times as large as the sales of top ten non-U.S. corporations, but that the relative size ratio declines for smaller corporations and stabilizes at about 1.6 from the 40th largest corporations to the 200th. When size is measured by assets rather than sales, giantism, though still present, is less marked. The relative size ratio is slightly under 2 for the 20 largest firms and about 1.5 thereafter. (The differences in the sales asset ratio may reflect differences in accounting practice.) When size is measured in terms of number of employees, U.S. firms have only a slight size advantage.

Table 3 compares the size of U.S. corporations to the size of leading non-U.S. corporations on a country-by-country basis. These binary comparisons exaggerate the giantism of U.S. corporations, and are of interest because countries and regions frequently com-

Table 3.   Relative Size Ratio by Country (1967 Sales)*

Rank of Firm	U.K.	Sweden	Switzerland	Germany	France	Italy	Benelux	Canada	Japan
1	2.7	29.7	11.1	8.6	13.2	9.7	8.3	22.3	11.6
2	2.4	20.1	15.9	6.7	9.9	6.9	13.8	15.7	8.0
3	3.5	19.7	16.2	6.3	9.4	8.1	13.8	14.7	7.6
4	2.9	17.5	14.5	4.7	2.3	6.4	10.6	10.9	6.0
5	2.5	22.6	11.7	4.2	6.5	6.9	10.6	12.0	4.9
6	4.4		12.7	3.9	6.2	8.4	12.4	11.3	4.6
7	4.1		15.0	4.2	6.0	9.8	12.0	11.3	4.3
8	4.5		18.4	4.2	5.7	16.7	13.9	12.9	4.4
9	3.9			3.7	4.8		12.3	11.3	4.1
10	3.8			4.0	4.7		13.4	12.0	4.3
11	3.8			3.8	4.7			12.1	4.3
12	3.4			3.4	4.2				4.4
13	3.4			3.3	4.7				4.5
14	3.6			3.8	5.4				4.6
15	3.6			3.7	5.9				4.5
16	3.6			3.7	6.6				4.7
17	3.8			5.0	7.7				5.7
18	4.0			5.2	8.4				6.2
19	4.0			6.6	8.7				6.3
20	4.1			7.1	8.8				6.2
21	4.1			7.0	9.8				6.1
22	4.0			7.0	9.4				5.9
23	4.6			7.4	9.4				5.9
24	5.2			7.8					6.1
25	4.6			8.6					6.2

* See notes to Table 2.

pare their corporations directly with those of the United States and naturally feel overwhelmed. United States corporations, of course, are interested in the strength of their rivals collectively and not separately.

Table 4 shows that the relative size of U.S. and non-U.S. corporations differs substantially from industry to industry, and serves

Table 4.   Relative Size Ratio by Industry (1967 Sales).*

	1	2	3	4	5	6	7	8
Firms Ranked	Auto	Electrical Machinery	Oil	Chemicals	Food	Iron and Steel	Non-ferrous Metal	Machinery and Eng
1	8.6	3.2	1.6	0.5	1.6	2.4	1.2	1.5
2	5.5	2.7	1.9	0.9	2.5	1.8	1.1	1.5
3	4.1	2.1	3.8	1.2	2.6	1.0	0.9	1.5
4	0.6	2.3	3.2	0.9	2.1	0.9	1.1	1.5
5	0.6	2.3	3.4	1.1	2.2	0.9	1.6	1.4
6	0.6	2.4	3.8	1.1	1.8	1.0	1.0	1.3
7	0.6	2.3	3.8	1.2	1.6	0.9	1.1	1.2
8	0.8	2.2	3.3	1.1	1.8	0.8	1.4	0.9
9	0.8	1.9	3.9	1.2	1.9	0.4	1.3	0.9
10	0.6	1.8	4.2	1.3	1.8	0.4	1.1	0.9
11	0.5	1.6	4.3	1.4	1.8	0.5		1.1
12	0.5	1.6	4.1	1.4	2.2	0.6		1.3
13	0.5	1.6	4.2	1.3	2.1			1.5
14	0.6	1.9		1.3	2.1			1.5
15	0.7	1.9		1.2	2.3			1.5
16	0.7	1.8		1.2	2.1			1.6
17	0.8	1.5		1.4	2.2			1.6
18		1.5		1.3	1.9			
19		1.5		1.2	2.0			
20		1.5		1.2	2.1			
21		1.5		1.1				
22		1.5		1.1				
23		1.5		1.2				
24		1.5		1.2				
25		1.4		1.2				
26		1.5		1.2				
27		1.5		1.2				
28		1.5		1.3				
29		1.5		1.3				
30		1.4		1.3				
31				1.3				
32				1.3				
33				1.2				
34				1.2				
35				1.1				
36				1.1				

* See notes to Table 2.

as a warning against overgeneralization. In the chemical industry, U.S. and non-U.S. corporations are just about evenly balanced; the large U.S. corporations are smaller than their non-U.S. counterparts while medium-sized U.S. firms are a bit larger.[5] In the automobile industry, U.S. corporations have an overwhelming size advantage over the leading non-U.S. corporations because production is much more concentrated in the United States than in Europe (taken as a whole). In addition, large-scale foreign investments by the U.S. giants have enabled them to capture a significant proportion of the European market, and this accounts in part for the small size of their non-U.S. competitors. Other industries show variations on these two patterns.

United States corporations are thus formidable competitors. Their ability to mobilize very large amounts of capital for specific purposes gives them a great financial advantage, especially in modern industries. However, this advantage is somewhat overstated in the size comparisons, since many non-U.S. corporations, though operationally separate from each other, are linked through banks and financial institutions and form a corporate group not unlike the large U.S. corporations. United States corporations also appear to have a qualitative advantage in their administrative structures which gives them a certain flexibility and mobility that non-U.S. corporations do not have. In order to meet the challenge of their peculiar market, U.S. corporations had to develop an administrative structure capable of managing units spread out over an entire continent in an environment of rapidly and continuously changing markets. Their answer — the national corporation (circa 1900), the multidivisional corporation (circa 1920), and now the multinational corporation[6] — involved enlargement of the corporate "brain," and the development of business administration as a spe-

---

[5] We have counted Unilever as a chemical firm rather than a food firm. If Unilever is excluded from chemicals, the relative size-ratio shifts in favor of the U.S. firms in this industry.

[6] See A. D. Chandler, Jr., *Strategy and Structure* (Cambridge, Mass.: The M.I.T. Press, 1962; paperback edition, New York: Doubleday & Company, 1966) for an analysis of the development of the United States structure of business organization in response to the challenge of the continental market and the rapidly changing composition of output.

cialized profession with its own elaborate division of labor and its own system of education.

The U.S. corporation thus represents a very highly developed form of capital (where capital is defined in the businessmen's sense of a concentration of wealth combined with the ability to use it for productive activities) and it is no wonder that European business enterprises wish to emulate it in size and organization. But as we shall see, it is not sufficient to point to the large size of the U.S. corporation, the apparently smooth functioning of its mechanism, and its ability to defend itself in international competition to establish its superiority as a mechanism for organizing economic activity to meet today's problems.

Performance Size comparisons by themselves are of little importance. What interests us is performance. The available evidence on the growth of industrial corporations in the ten years following the formation of the Common Market (1957 to 1967) shows that U.S. corporations have not been outstripping their rivals in recent

Table 5. Changes in the Relative Size of U.S. and Non-U.S. Firms 1957 to 1962, 1962 to 1967.

Firms Ranked	Sales			Assets			Employees		
	1957	*1962*	*1967*	*1957*	*1962*	*1967*	*1957*	*1962*	*1967*
1–10	2.2	2.3	2.5	2.2	1.9	1.7	1.3	1.0	1.2
11–20	2.9	2.1	1.9	3.7	1.9	2.0	1.4	0.9	1.2
21–30	2.4	2.1	2.0	2.3	1.7	1.4	1.3	0.8	1.5
31–40	2.4	1.8	1.9	1.6	1.5	1.7	1.0	0.8	0.7
41–50	2.0	1.9	1.6	2.0	1.5	1.4	1.3	0.8	1.0
51–60	1.9	1.7	1.5	2.5	1.8	1.7	1.3	0.8	0.5
61–70	1.9	1.6	1.5	2.1	1.3	1.7	0.7	0.7	0.9
71–80	2.0	1.5	1.5	2.0	1.4	1.1	0.6	0.7	0.9
81–90	1.9	1.5	1.5	2.5	1.1	1.2	0.8	0.8	1.2
91–100	2.0	1.6	1.6	1.6	1.7	1.2	1.2	0.9	0.9
101–110		1.5	1.6		1.3	1.3		1.0	0.7
111–120		1.5	1.6		1.4	0.9		0.6	0.9
121–130		1.6	1.6		1.0	1.5		0.7	1.0
131–140		1.5	1.6		0.9	1.1		1.0	0.8
141–150		1.5	1.6		0.9	1.4		0.5	0.9
151–160		1.5	1.6		1.0	0.9		0.8	1.3
161–170		1.6	1.6		1.1	1.1		0.6	1.0
171–180		1.7	1.6		1.2	1.4		0.6	0.9
181–190		1.7	1.6		1.5	1.1		1.1	1.2
191–200		1.7	1.6		1.0	0.7		0.8	2.5

(Relative Size Ratio)*

* See notes for Table 2.

years. Rather, they fell behind from 1957 to 1962 and only managed to keep pace between 1962 and 1967. Table 5 shows a shift in the relative size ratio (except in the largest size category) against U.S. corporations between 1957 and 1962, and an approximate stabilization thereafter. Table 6 indicates that this pattern holds for nearly all industries. There is thus a sense in which the U.S. corporations have been challenged rather than challenging.

Table 6.   Changes in the Relative Size of U.S. and Non-U.S. Firms by Industry Relative Size Ratio of Three Largest Corporations in Each Industry.*

	1957	1962	1967
Auto	11.6	6.2	6.4
Electrical Mach.	4.2	2.5	2.7
Oil	1.3	1.9	1.9
Chemical	0.8	0.8	0.8
Food	2.5	2.1	2.1
Iron and Steel	4.7	2.3	1.8
Nonferrous	1.8	1.5	1.3
Mach. and Eng.	1.7	1.6	1.5
Rubber	3.3	2.2	2.2
Paper	n.a.	2.3	1.9
Textiles	n.a.	2.4	2.1
Aircraft	n.a.	3.4	4.1
Stone	n.a.	1.2	1.6

* Ratio of total sales of the three largest U.S. to total sales of the three largest non-U.S. firms.

To what extent was size an advantage in international competition during this period? To help answer this question a regression analysis was performed relating the data on growth of a corporation to its size, nationality, and industry. The size of a corporation S was measured in terms of its sales at the beginning of the period. The growth rate g was measured by the average annual percentage change in sales over the period.[7] Country and industry were indicated by a set of dummy variables C_i and I_j, where $C_i = 1$ for a

[7] Certain adjustments were made to deal with inaccuracies in the *Fortune* data and mergers. The adjusted data yielded better results than the crude data and only equations for adjusted data have been reported. The differences, however, were small.

66

firm from country i and 0 otherwise, and $I_j = 1$ for a firm from the jth industry and 0 otherwise.

For econometric reasons it was necessary to exclude the dummies of an arbitrary country (the United States) and an arbitrary industry (Miscellaneous). The basic estimating equations were then of the following form, where a_1 is coefficient of the country dummy variable for the United States and b_1 is the coefficient of the industry dummy variable for the Miscellaneous industry.[8]

$$g = \text{const} + \sum_{2}^{m} (a_i - a_1) C_i + \sum_{2}^{n} (b_j - b_1) I_j + eS + fS^2 + u.$$

The sample for 1957 to 1962 and for 1957 to 1967 consisted of the 100 largest U.S. and the 100 largest non-U.S. corporations. The sample of the second period, 1962 to 1967, consisted of the 500 largest corporations, approximately 300 U.S. and 200 non-U.S. (A number of firms dropped off the *Fortune* list during the period, and so the actual number of firms which could be used was 188 for 1957 to 1962, 438 for 1962 to 1967, and 178 for 1957

[8] Suppose we had instead estimated

$$g = \text{const} + \sum_{i=1}^{m} a_i C_i + \sum_{j=1}^{n} b_j I_j + eS + fS^2 + u. \tag{1}$$

Since every firm belongs to exactly one country, $\sum_{1}^{m} C_i = 1$. Similarly since every firm belongs to exactly one industry $\sum_{1}^{n} I_i = I$. The set of variables $(C_1 \ldots C_m)$ and $(I_1 \ldots I_n)$ are thus linearly dependent. To get around this problem we chose an arbitrary country (country 1) and note

$$a_i c_i = (a_i - a_1) c_i + a_1 c_i, \tag{2}$$

$$\sum_{i}^{m} a_i c_i = \sum_{2}^{m} (a_i - a_1) C_i + a_1 C_i \tag{3}$$

$$= \sum_{2}^{m} (a_i - a) C_i + a_i, \tag{4}$$

since $\sum C_i = 1$. Similarly, letting industry 1 be an arbitrary industry,

$$\sum_{2}^{n} b_i I_i = \sum_{2}^{n} (b_i - b_2) I_i + b_2. \tag{5}$$

Substituting Equations 4 and 5 into 1 gives us the equation in the text which can be estimated, since the vectors $(C_2 \ldots C_m)$ and $(I_2 \ldots I_n)$ will normally be linearly independent.

Table 7. Regressions Results.

Description	Germany –U.S.	France –U.S.	Benelux –U.S.	Italy –U.S.	U.K. –U.S.	Other EFTA –U.S.	Japan –U.S.	Canada –U.S.	Other –U.S.	S	S²	R²
1957 to 1962												
Excluding S												
Parameter estimate	7.1**	2.8	–4.5*	10.2**	–2.4**	4.7*	10.6**	–5.1**	4.3			0.314
t value	4.15	1.36	–1.73	2.82	–1.99	1.81	2.89	–2.18	0.96			
Including S												
Parameter estimate	5.8**	0.9	–2.8	8.6**	–3.2**	3.2	8.9**	–6.1**	2.9	–3.1067**	0.2923**	0.357
t value	3.42	0.45	–1.10	2.43	–2.65	1.22	2.47	–2.64	0.66	–3.27	2.75	
S in logs												
Parameter estimate	5.5**	–0.9	1.5	7.2**	–4.4**	1.0	7.2**	–6.7**	–0.2	–20.8217*	0.9880**	0.372
t value	3.25	–0.43	0.57	2.02	–3.41	0.36	1.96	–2.93	–0.05	–1.94	1.72	
1962 to 1967												
Excluding S												
Parameter estimate	–3.9**	–1.5	–1.2	–0.6	–0.8	0.2	6.9**	–0.0	1.4			0.206
t value	–3.22	–1.13	–0.61	–0.29	–0.94	0.13	6.26	–0.02	0.57			
Including S												
Parameter estimate	–3.6**	–1.9	–1.5	–0.8	–0.8	0.0	6.4**	–0.3	0.8	–1.8516**	0.1160	0.231
t value	–3.04	–1.38	–0.77	–0.36	–0.87	0.00	5.88	–0.19	0.32	–3.40	2.37	
S in logs												
Parameter estimate	–2.8**	–1.6	–1.3	0.0	–0.8	0.2	6.4**	–0.2	0.7	–11.5656**	0.5579*	0.254
t value	–2.34	–1.18	–0.65	0.01	–0.89	0.09	5.90	–0.13	0.30	–2.24	1.91	
1957 to 1967												
Excluding S												
Parameter estimate	2.6**	2.7**	3.4**	5.8**	–1.7**	2.4	11.3**	–0.4	4.5*			0.381
t value	2.44	2.12	2.01	2.74	–2.29	1.58	5.20	–0.27	1.72			
Including S												
Parameter estimate	1.9*	1.7	2.4	4.9**	–2.1**	1.5	10.3**	–0.9	3.8	–1.6455**	0.1409**	0.417
t value	1.76	1.28	1.43	2.35	–2.89	1.00	4.82	–0.59	1.46	–2.92	2.23	
S in logs												
Parameter estimate	1.6	0.5	1.7	4.0*	–2.9**	0.1	9.1**	–1.3	1.7	–12.8019**	0.6062**	0.439
t value	1.58	0.38	1.03	1.92	–3.72	0.07	4.22	–0.84	0.62	–1.97	1.74	

Note: *t* values are the coefficients divided by their standard errors. Two asterisks means significant at the 5% level with a two-tailed *t* test. One asterisk means significant at the 10% level with a two-tailed *t* test. *S* is measured in billions when regressions include *S*, and in hundreds of thousands when they include log *S*.

to 1967). The main results are presented in Table 7. For simplicity, the constant term and the coefficients for industry dummies have been excluded, since they are not relevant to the hypothesis under test. Three regressions are presented for each period; first excluding the size variable altogether, second including it, and third using a logarithmic form. Regressions were also run separately for major industries, but the results are too long and involved to be presented here. For the moment we merely note that the main conclusions of Table 7 were broadly corroborated by the industry studies. We might also mention that the results were unaffected by additional tests involving changes in the sample, in the function fitted, and in the methods of estimation.

The first important feature to emerge from the investigation is the significant relationship beween size and growth. The coefficients are negative for S and log S, and positive for S^2 and $(\log S)^2$. This indicates a U-shaped relationship in which size first has a negative effect and then a positive effect. The exact strength of the upward twist is not well established and differs substantially according to whether we use the parabolic equation, $f(s) = \text{const} + eS + fS^2$, or its log equivalent $f(S) = \text{const} + e \log S + f \log S^2$. In the former case, for example, the turning point occurs when a firm's sales reach $8 billion (according to the 1962 to 1967 equations); in log form, the turning point occurs at sales of $3.2 billion in this period. However, in 1962 there were only three corporations whose sales exceeded $8 billion (all from the United States) and nine corporations whose sales exceeded $3.2 billion (seven from the United States). In the earlier period, 1957 to 1962, the turning points are $5.4 billion for the parabolic form and $3.8 billion for the logarithmic form and the number of firms whose sales exceeded these figures were four (three from the United States) and seven (five from the United States), respectively. The upward twist therefore applies only to a handful of giants. For the rest of the sample the relationship between size and growth is clearly negative.

An examination of the residuals suggests that even this upward twist may be an illusion caused by the types of curve we have fitted. Indeed, for the period 1962 to 1967 the industry regressions show

69

a negative relationship between size and growth rate over the whole range.

The second important conclusion of the regression analysis is that nationality has frequently been a significant variable in explaining the growth rates of firms. This is because many firms are national rather than multinational, and their fortunes depend very much upon the countries to which they are attached. Recalling that the coefficients measuring the country effects in Table 7 refer to the difference between the growth rate of companies based in a particular country and that of the United States, we note first that these coefficients are mainly positive from 1957 to 1962 and mainly negative from 1962 to 1967. This indicates a country effect or common factor for U.S. firms that was disadvantageous in the first period and advantageous in the second.

Surprisingly, when the regressions for 1962 to 1967 were run for a reduced sample of the 178 large continuing firms (i.e., those firms that were among the 100 largest U.S. or 100 largest non-U.S. firms in 1957 and were still on the *Fortune* list in 1967), the country coefficients were uniformly higher in nearly every case. This indicates that non-U.S. corporations held their own better in the middle and large range than they did in the smaller range. To put this another way, *small* U.S. corporations had some advantageous factor in common so that they performed better as a group than predicted by our equations relating size to growth.

As for other countries, in the first period it was disadvantageous to be a British or Canadian firm, relative to the United States, but this disadvantage was removed in the second period when the country effect came to closely approximate that of the United States. Germany and Italy showed the opposite pattern to the United States; a relatively strong positive country effect in the first period which disappears in the second (in the case of Germany it becomes strongly negative). Finally, the Japanese country effect, as expected, was strongly advantageous in both periods.

Before we apply these empirical findings to the second and third questions raised in the Introduction, we should perhaps stress their tentative nature. A number of empirical studies on the effect of size and growth have been conducted for samples drawn from within a country and these in general have concluded that there is little correlation between size and growth.[9] Since the problem of sorting out the effects of size, industry, and nationality is difficult and complex, our experiments far from exhaust the possible interrelationships that can be tested. However, it is clear that the data do not support the view that size has been an advantageous, much less a crucial, factor in growth during the first decade following the establishment of the common market.

Dialectics of the Multinational Corporation (1957 to 1967)

If the U.S. corporations did not grow faster than their European and Japanese rivals, where did the notion of the American challenge come from? We suggest it was due, in part at least, to myopia. Europeans felt threatened because they saw U.S. corporations gaining an increased share of the European market. They paid little attention to the fact that, in the world market taken as a whole, U.S. corporations were themselves being threatened by the rapid growth of the Common Market and the Japanese economy, and required a rapid expansion of foreign investment to maintain their

[9] See, for example, H. A. Simon and C. P. Bonini, "The Size Distribution of Business Firms," *American Economic Review,* Vol. XLIII, No. 4 (September 1958), pp. 607–617; P. E. Hart and S. J. Prais, "The Analysis of Business Concentration," *Journal of the Royal Statistical Society,* Part 2 (1956), pp. 150–181; S. Hymer and P. Pashigian, "Firm Size and Rate of Growth," *The Journal of Political Economy,* Vol. LXX (December 1962), pp. 556–569; E. Mansfield, "Entry, Gibrat's Law, Innovation, and the Growth of Firms," *American Economic Review,* Vol. LII, No. 5 (December 1962), pp. 1023–1051; A. Singh and G. Whittington, in collaboration with H. T. Burley, *Growth, Profitability and Valuation* (Cambridge: Cambridge University Press, 1968). These studies, as well as a number of others, have for the most part found that above a certain minimum size, large firms do not perform better (or worse) than small firms when judged by costs, profits, or propensity to grow. This evidence on the existence or nonexistence of economies of scale is, however, far from conclusive for an important theoretical reason. Small firms are often complementary to large firms, acting as suppliers to the large firms or filling the gaps left by large firms. The two sets are in ecological equilibrium, as bees are to apple orchards or as any parasite is to its host. International size comparisons, though subject to their own special difficulties, get around this problem, in part, since the smaller firms outside the United States are not in ecological equilibrium with the larger firms but in competition.

relative standing. To understand the divergent views on who is being challenged, and who is challenging, it is useful to distinguish between Gp, the growth rate of the U.S. parent firm (including its subsidiaries), Gs, the growth rate of its subsidiaries, and Ge, the growth rate of non-U.S. firms. The stylized facts of the period were something like the following[10]:

$$Gs > Ge \geqslant Gp.$$

European firms compared Gs to Ge and felt they were being challenged. United States multinational corporations compared Ge to Gp and also felt a challenge. The fact that both parties could feel challenged stemmed from the difference in the horizons of national and multinational corporations. Multinational corporations see the world as their oyster, and judge their performance on a world-wide basis. They look to their global market position. National or regional firms keep their eyes close to the ground and concentrate on their share of particular submarkets. Thus the same phenomenon appears different according to the eyesight of the beholder. To the short-sighted European firm, whose markets are mainly European, U.S. investment seems to be an aggressive move to dominate Europe. To the long-sighted American firm, on the other hand, this investment appears to be a desperate attempt to defend its existing world share and keep up with the dynamic Europeans.

A more interesting interpretation of the ten years between 1957 and 1967 would recognize that a firm can be challenging and challenged at the same time, just as a military strategy can be both offensive and defensive. The rapid growth of the Common Market and Japan in the 1950s challenged the dominance of the U.S.

---

[10] It is well known that U.S. subsidiaries in Europe have, on average, been growing faster than their European rivals. Between 1950 and 1965, for example, the value of U.S. direct investment in Western Europe rose from $1,720 million to $13,894 million. Few European firms, even the heavy overseas investors, could have matched this growth rate of 14.9% a year sustained for 15 years. Assuming that these figures are a reasonable guide to the relative sales performance we can conclude that $G_s > G_e$ is a fair stylization of the facts. Our regressions and tables show that, on average, $G_e \geqslant G_p$. Indeed, for the period 1957 to 1967, as a whole, the inequality is strict.

giants, who responded with an aggressive policy of foreign invest-ment. Their great strength, their past experience with continental and multinational markets, plus the open-door policy of European governments made this counter strategy successful.

This invasion of Europe threatened the position of European firms which have now begun their countermeasures. The threats, of course, have not been felt evenly. The United Kingdom, for ex-ample, seems to have felt less challenged than other countries even though U.S. penetration of the United Kingdom is far higher than for the continent. This is because linkages are well established, and because many leading British firms are themselves multinational and think in terms of world markets. Japan also did not feel as threatened as other countries, but for different reasons. By virtually prohibiting foreign investment, the Japanese government reserved its rapidly growing market for its own firms and frustrated the attempts by U.S. corporations to redress the imbalance caused by the Japanese challenge. This has created considerable tension and may soon have to be modified since Japanese corporations encoun-ter increased resistance to their penetration via exports.

What about the next round? It is a foregone conclusion that Europe will follow (is following) the policies advocated by Servan-Schreiber. The European merger movement is well under way and nearly all European governments are actively taking positive mea-sures to strengthen their large corporations. Negative measures are out of favor, in part because they are unworkable in the context of the Common Market, where an American firm denied entry to one country can always locate in another and penetrate the forbid-den market through exports. Unanimous agreement is therefore required but is not possible due to divergent interests and outlook. In any case, by now the die is cast, since all of the top U.S. corpo-rations have staked their claim in the European economy.

Where will the positive measures lead? There is no reason to believe that newly enlarged European corporations will increase their rate of growth merely because of their increased size. On the contrary, the data of the past decade indicate that, if anything, most mergers will slow down the rate of growth.

With the exception of the very largest firms, for which there does not seem to be any well-established relationship between size and growth rate, most firms are located on the downward-sloping part of the curve, where the larger their size the slower their growth. These equations for 1957 to 1967 may well not apply to the future: but taking into account the numerous other studies on the relationship between size and growth cited above, we can predict with some confidence that an analysis in 1977 or 1987 of the growth rates of firms will at least not show any positive relationship between size and growth.

The European merger movement is, however, likely to result in a crucial *qualitative* change in the nature of European business. By increasing the average size of European firms it will make them less regional in outlook and more multinational, with the result that they, like American firms, will invest heavily overseas. Among the most important reasons for this change are:

1. Mergers and rationalizations will lead to corporate reorganization and the creation of new administrative structures more akin to those of the American corporation and better suited to multinational expansion. Or, to put the matter differently, as European firms increase in size and complexity their administrative "brain" will increase more than proportionately and their attention will focus not so much on national or European markets but on the world as a whole, including the U.S. market itself. In a sense, the vision of a firm depends on the height of its head office building.

2. Greater financial strength will enable European firms to invest more overseas. Investment in a foreign country often involves a more direct challenge to established firms than does exporting. Firms that were previously prepared to tolerate some competition in the form of exports may not be willing to tolerate competitive direct investment. To protect themselves against what they consider to be a policy of aggressive expansion, they may attempt to drive the intruder out of the market before he gets too strong. The outcome of this struggle is likely to depend upon the relative financial strengths of the established firms and the firm attempting to increase its market share by investing, which in turn depend upon their relative sizes.

The financial resources associated with size confer other advantages on the big firm. It can buy its way into markets by taking over local firms. It can afford to take risks. For a firm the size of the American giants, with a capital of billions of dollars, the purchase of an overseas plant costing say $20 million may be a relatively minor affair. For a firm with a capital of millions of dollars this plant would be a major undertaking to be contemplated only if it was fairly sure to succeed. Thus the smaller firm must be cautious where the bigger firm can afford to experiment.

3. By consolidating the overseas sales of European firms, mergers will make them better able to establish subsidiaries of an efficient size. In any particular market a big firm is likely to have actual or potential sales larger than those of a small firm, either because it is already selling more in the form of exports or because it can afford to finance a costly promotion and distribution program for its products. Equally it can afford to establish a large and efficient subsidiary which can produce the output necessary to satisfy this larger market. From the point of view of both supply and demand the big firm is therefore better able to produce on an efficient scale.

As a hypothetical example, consider the case of four European firms, each with actual or potential sales of $20 million in the United States. At this level it may be hopelessly inefficient to produce locally, and therefore they export from their domestic plants. Suppose they now merge. Then the resulting firm will have actual or potential sales worth $80 million — a significant share of the American market — which may be high enough to justify setting up a local subsidiary.

A brief examination of the relevant statistics[11] supports the view that size is a major determinant of overseas investment. In 1957, out of 1,542 firms with investments overseas, 15, each having foreign assets worth over $100 million, accounted for 35% of total American manufacturing investments abroad. Together with 64 others having investments worth over $25 million each, they accounted for 69% of the total, leaving 1,463 firms to share the

[11] More evidence will be provided when G. Bertin (Université de Rennes) completes his econometric investigation of the relationship between size and foreign investment.

Table 8.   Exports and Local Production (millions of dollars).

	X	P	$X+P$	P/X	X	P (est)	$X+P$	P/X
Out of U.S.		1957				1966		
Europe	6,940	10,762	17,702	1.55	14,440	36,000	50,440	2.50
Into U.S.		1959				1966		
U.K., Netherlands, and Switzerland	2,320	4,657	6,977	2.01	3,740	7,400	11,140	1.97
Other Europe.	4,580	559	5,139	0.12	8,050	1,271	9,321	0.16
of which:								
France	690	92	782	0.13	1,050	123	1,173	0.12
Germany	1,380	47	1,427	0.03	2,700	138	2,838	0.05

Sources: *Survey of Current Business* (Washington, D.C.: U.S. Department of Commerce), various issues. *Statistical Abstract of the United States* (Washington, D.C.: U.S. Government Printing Office), various issues. *U.S. Business Investments in Foreign Countries* (1960), and *Foreign Business Investment in the United States* (undated), U.S. Department of Commerce publications.

Definitions: X = exports (c.i.f.).

P = manufacturing and petroleum sales of local subsidiaries.

Methods. The rate of growth of sales up to 1966 is assumed to be the same as that of net assets in the appropriate industry (manufacturing, petroleum). A cross check with the sales of U.S. manufacturing subsidiaries for 1965 suggested that the original estimate of $39,600 million was too high by about 3,000 to 4,000 million. The estimate was therefore adjusted to the $36,000 million given in the table. For the United Kingdom, Netherlands, and Switzerland net assets by industry were not available for 1966. It was therefore assumed that sales grew at the same annual rate as net assets between 1959 and 1967. For France and Germany no breakdown of assets was available for 1966 and the growth rate assumed was that of net assets in all industries. This probably underestimates the growth of manufacturing and petroleum sales, but the error is not likely to be important.

Finally 50% was added to the f.o.b. figures for exports and imports given by the Department of Commerce to allow for insurance, freight, and other charges.

remaining 31%.[12] In the British case, the big investor is equally dominant. Some 46 firms, most of them large, accounted for 71% of manufacturing assets overseas in 1962 and 3 firms owned virtually all petroleum assets overseas.[13] Among them they accounted for around 83% of all British investments in petroleum and manufacturing combined.

The role of investment in the expansion of American and European firms in each other's markets is well illustrated in Table 8,

[12] *U.S. Business Investments in Foreign Countries* (Washington, D.C.; U.S. Department of Commerce, 1960).

[13] W. B. Reddaway, *Effects of U.K. Direct Investment Overseas* (Cambridge: Cambridge University Press, 1967).

which shows the local production of foreign-owned subsidiaries in manufacturing and petroleum (P) and the exports (X) of various countries. Although some of the figures are rather rough estimates, the broad picture they reveal is accurate. Three European countries — the United Kingdom, the Netherlands, and Switzerland — account for about nine-tenths of the sales of all European subsidiaries in American manufacturing and petroleum. These sales are roughly twice as much as the total exports to the United States of these three countries combined. By contrast, other European countries rely mainly on exports to serve the American market, and of these the most striking is Germany, whose firms exported 20 times as much in 1966 as they produced in the United States.

As a result of investment, firms of the first group have been able to maintain a clear lead in the American market over other European firms. Despite an impressive growth of exports to the United States, which doubled in nine years, German sales by 1966 were still only a quarter of those of the first group. Moreover, the absolute gap increased dramatically as this group's sales increased by over $4 billion as compared to 1.4 billion for Germany and 0.4 billion for France.

It is clear that if French or German firms wish to establish themselves extensively or even securely in the American market they will have to invest heavily, something they have not yet done.[14] Why have they not done so? After all, the American market is important to them, as their export performance shows. More to the point, they have been investing heavily in other countries, as Table 9 shows. During the years 1961 to 1964 German firms invested an average of $220 million a year abroad and French firms an average of $100 million, compared to which their investment in the United

---

[14] At present there is a great asymmetry between commodity flows and capital flows. Europe's exports of manufactures to the United States are about equal to its imports from the United States, but direct investment by European corporations in the United States is much smaller than United States direct investment in Europe. The theory of the product cycle (from innovation to exports to foreign investment) seems to apply more closely to the experience of U.S. corporations than to the experience of non-U.S. corporations, where the sequence often runs from innovation to exports to loss of market, as the European firm's advantage is eroded by competition.

Table 9.   Direct Investment Flows of Industrial Countries (millions of dollars).

	Average 1957 to 1960			Average 1961 to 1964		
	Out-flows	In-flows	Net	Out-flows	In-flows	Net
United States	−2,830	330	−2,500	−3,210	310	−2,900
United Kingdom	− 510	310	− 200	− 670	480	− 190
subtotal	−3,340	640	−2,700	−3,880	790	−3,090
Belgium	n.a.	n.a.	n.a.	n.a.	n.a.	n.a.
France	− 10	30	+ 20	− 100	280	+ 180
Germany	− 120	60	− 60	− 220	200	− 20
Italy	− 60	220	+ 160	− 170	350	+ 180
Netherlands	− 170	50	− 120	− 120	60	− 60
subtotal	− 360	360	0	− 610	890	+ 280
Other EFTA countries	n.a.	20	n.a.	− 60	110	+ 50
Canada	− 60	550	+ 490	− 100	360	+ 260
Japan	− 50	20	− 30	− 90	80	− 10
Total Industrial	−3,810	1,590	−2,220	−4,740	2,230	−2,510

Source: M. Diamond, IMF *Staff Papers* (March 1967).

States looks trivial — an average of $5.5 million a year for the Germans and $9 million for the French.

Part, if not the whole, of the answer lies in the small size of French and German firms, particularly in those areas where European investment in the United States has been heavy. Using the sectoral distribution of investments in 1959 as a guide, we find that the bulk of them lie in areas where firms of the United Kingdom, the Netherlands, and Switzerland have a clear lead over other European firms and are of a size comparable to the American giants.[15] Unilever (Anglo-Dutch), Nestlé (Swiss), and British-American Tobacco (British) are many times larger than other European firms in their sectors of food and household products, and are about the same size or even larger than their American rivals. In petroleum Royal Dutch–Shell (Anglo-Dutch) and BP (British), which has recently begun a massive expansion into the United States, are several times larger than other European firms. In pharmaceuticals, a comparatively small-scale industry, Switzerland has the only four specialist companies on the *Fortune* list of non-

[15] Reference 12.

78

American firms. In rubber and paper, British firms are the biggest in Europe and rival the Americans, and in electrical goods the Netherlands has the largest non-American firm. Of course, there are exceptions. Switzerland, for example, is mentioned by the U.S. Department of Commerce as having investments in the electrical industry, yet the largest Swiss firm is only fifth in Europe. But on the whole the correlation holds up fairly well. In industries where the three countries are not European leaders — iron and steel, machinery, automobiles — their firms are fairly small in comparison to American firms and they tend not to invest in the United States. Even the apparent exception of chemicals, where British ICI is the largest in Europe (excluding Unilever) and relies on exporting, reinforces our argument, for ICI is planning to expand rapidly in the United States from its comparatively small base in artificial fibers.

As it stands, all this leaves the question of causality open, for it would be possible to argue that these firms are giants *because* they invest in the United States rather than the other way around, and that if European firms merge to become giants there is no reason to assume that they will follow the same path and also invest in the United States. If the European giants produced a third, a half, or more of their output in the United States, this argument would be plausible, but they do not. Over the last decade, for example, Unilever has never produced more than a sixth of its output in the American continent as a whole, both north and south. Even British-American Tobacco, perhaps the most dependent on its American investments, has only a third of its assets there. We can conclude, therefore, that as a rule the causality runs from giant size to investment in the United States at least as strongly as it does from investment to giant size. In cases such as ICI or BP, which are just beginning to invest seriously, the causality is clearly far stronger in the size-to-investment direction. This is not to deny that overseas investment does not or will not play a crucial part in the growth of large firms, particularly in the case of small countries such as Switzerland or the Netherlands. On the contrary, the most common path for European firms may well be domestic growth on the basis of home sales and exports up to the point where they are well enough established in foreign markets and financially strong enough to consider foreign investment. At first they begin by investing outside America in markets that are easier to enter. Eventually, when they have gained the experience, created the organizational structure, and, perhaps most important of all, gained the extra financial strength necessary, they invest in the United States.

Clearly, most European firms are still at the first or second stage. Either they have not invested abroad at all, or are investing outside of America. Mergers, by adding to their financial strength and consolidating their foreign sales, will enable these firms to accelerate the first and second stages or even to skip the intermediate stage so that they go straight from home production to investment in the United States. Rather than labor this point any longer, we shall assume that the European merger movement will result in both heavy overseas investment outside the United States, and in the slightly longer run in the United States itself.

How will U.S. corporations react to the challenge of outward investment by European firms? United States corporations have also been undergoing a large merger movement which may have maintained or increased their relative size. Since U.S. corporations are large and powerful there is no reason for them to accept a lower rate of growth. Moreover, precisely because they are the dominant firms, they must worry about losses in relative position and be prepared to adopt defensive measures when threatened. Although they might be willing to accept a loss of a few points in their market shares to a large number of medium and small rivals, they are not likely to regard even a small loss to a rival European giant with equanimity. Thus the merger movement makes it even more likely that they will do everything in their power to maintain the same rate of growth as non-U.S. firms: since their resources and skills are very great they are likely on the average to be fairly successful in this effort. European firms will have the advantage at first of great government support, but if the world balance is threatened, the United States government can be counted on to come to the rescue of its corporations.

The American response is likely to assign an even greater role than in the past to increased foreign investment. For one thing, it is very costly for a dominant firm to resist incursions into its own market by serious rivals (since the loss caused by a 1% reduction in price is greater for the established firm than for the new entrant). Equally, European attempts to gain a foothold in the U.S. market are also likely to be successful, for it will be easier for the U.S. corporations to counterattack abroad, and to meet inward foreign investment with outward foreign investment. Indeed, U.S. corporations might even welcome an exchange of markets since it would create a better world-wide environment for multinationalism. Another factor is that the growth of the U.S. economy may slow down, if the new Republican administration adopts a deflationary monetary and fiscal policy over the next few years. To maintain their world position U.S. corporations would have to expand even more rapidly abroad in order to compensate for their slowly growing home base. A slowdown in the growth of the U.S. market would present less of a problem to non-U.S. firms because they start from a smaller base. Investment in the United States would likely continue, and combined with deflationary policies would improve the U.S. balance of payments and facilitate the outward migration of U.S. capital. Finally, added pressure to invest abroad comes from the fact that U.S. corporations will not be able to stand idly by and allow Europeans to capture important markets in the less-developed countries or in the communist countries.

We can therefore expect a period of intensified multinationalization (almost amounting to capital flight) over the coming decade as both U.S. corporations and non-U.S. corporations try to establish world-wide market positions and protect themselves from the challenges of each other.[16] The cross penetration implied by the

---

[16] Cross investment is a long-standing feature of direct foreign investment. In many industries where U.S. corporations have substantial direct investment in foreign countries, one of the leading firms in the United States is a foreign firm, e.g., oil, soft drinks, paper, soaps, and detergents, farm machinery, business machinery, tires and tubes, sewing machines, concentrated milk, biscuits, chemicals.

81

simple oligopoly model we have just described has as its *logical* end a stable equilibrium where all of the dominant oligopolists have a similar world-wide distributions of sales. This logical end is not likely to be achieved in practice but the following equations are a useful device for illuminating current tendencies.

$$S_1 = a_{11}\ Y_1 + a_{12}\ Y_2,$$
$$S_2 = a_{21}\ Y_1 + a_{22}\ Y_2,$$

where S_1 equals the aggregate sales of the "dominant" U.S. corporations; S_2 equals the aggregate sales of the "dominant" non-U.S. corporations; Y_1, the size of the U.S. market; Y_2 the size of the non-U.S. market; and the a_{ij}'s represent the share of a firm from country i in the market of country j (obtained either through exports or local sales). The stylized fact of the present world structure of industry is that a_{21} (the European share in the U.S. market) is very low. Hence if Y_2 grows faster than Y_1, non-U.S. corporations will grow faster than U.S. corporations, unless Americans increase a_{12}. As we suggested above, this perhaps describes the period 1957 to 1967 in a rough sort of way. The increase in a_{12} and the slowing down in the rate of growth of Y_2 has threatened European firms and led them to take steps which increased a_{21}. This in turn we suggest will lead American firms to further increase a_{12}. As this dialectical process unfolds, the world distribution of sales of American and European firms will tend to approximate each other more closely. As a_{11}/a_{12} approaches a_{21}/a_{22}, relative size S_1/S_2 becomes less and less affected by differences in the rate of growth of Y_1 and Y_2. In other words, corporations of both centers will come to experience similar rates of growth regardless of whether Europe is growing faster than America or America is growing faster than Europe. But this solution to the American challenge on the level of oligopolistic competition will not remove conflicts at the political level. A breaking of the link between corporations and countries will create conflicts between the private and public interest and between one nation and another that are difficult to resolve. In the next section we turn to these more intractable and more important problems.

82

International Capital and National Interest

The concept of the American challenge as a diagnosis and prescription of Europe's current predicaments is in large part a myth resting on an exaggeration of the prowess of the large U.S. corporation and a myopic view of the dynamics of international competition. It is in fact one of the guises for a new form of protectionism and as such is an attempt to identify the national interest with the interest of certain dominant firms. The instruments of this neoprotectionism differ from those of the old. Instead of tariffs to preserve the domestic market for national firms, businessmen are asking for positive help to penetrate foreign markets. The theme, however, is the same: the growth of a certain sector of private business is elevated to a national goal and the economic problems of the entire country are viewed from a particularly restrictive vantage point.

Our analysis suggests that the main result of the strategy of "positive measures" to help large firms will be to change European business qualitatively towards multinationalism, rather than to raise the relative growth rates of European firms.

The increased multinationalism that follows increased size, by the weakening link between country performance and company performance, will help to equalize growth rates of firms of different nationality and make it easier for U.S. corporations to maintain their position.

If the goal were to develop a strong *national* business sector, it would probably be better to follow the Japanese example of fostering the growth of the internal market, restricting inward investment, and penetrating foreign markets through exports rather than investment (though this policy too has its limitations). The present strategy will strengthen a few very large corporations but divorce their interest from that of the national economy, and may well have a negative effect on international trade, since corporations concentrate on foreign investment rather than exports. For example, the data from the Reddaway report (Table 10) covering the 15 countries that receive most British direct foreign investment show that the big investors produce locally 20 times as much as they export.

STEPHEN HYMER AND ROBERT ROWTHORN

Table 10.   U.K. Exports and Local Production (£ millions) in 15
Countries.

	1956	1963	% change
1. U.K. exports (f.o.b.)	1,450.3	2,000.5	+38%
2. Exports of firms in Reddaway sample	114.2	106.2	− 7%
3. Local production of firms Reddaway sample	1,321.4	2,137.8	+62%
4. Total U.K. exports to 15 countries less those of firms in Reddaway sample (f.o.b.)	1,336.1	1,894.3	+42%

Notes and Sources: W. B. Reddaway, *Effects of U.K. Direct Investment Overseas an Interim Report* (Cambridge: Cambridge University Press, 1967), Table VI 4.

Local production has been estimated by subtracting 150% of the value of exports (f.o.b.) of firms in the Reddaway sample from the total sales of these firms in the 15 countries. The extra 50% is to allow for the fact that sales are valued at selling price whereas exports are valued f.o.b.

Furthermore, their exports to these markets have fallen by 7% whereas their local production has risen by 62%. In the same period, the exports of other British firms that did not have local foreign investments have risen by 42%. It seems inconceivable that the big investors, if not allowed to invest overseas, could not manage to raise their exports well above the £106.2 million that they presently export. More work is needed for other countries, but this example should serve as an illustration of the difference between policies to maintain a corporation's shares of the world market and policies to maintain a country's share.[17]

What will be the overall effect on economic performance and

[17] Note that local production abroad by U.S. corporations is growing much faster than exports. See also C. A. Van den Beld and D. Van der Werf, "A Note on International Competitiveness" (Berlin, 1965), published as "Nota Sulla Competitivita' Internazionale," in *Economia Internazionale,* Vol. XIX (1966), pp. 325–337; Table 6, p. 14, shows that Germany has done far better than either the United Kingdom or the United States *even when price has been allowed for.* Similarly H. B. Junz and R. R. Rhomberg, "Prices and Export Performance of Industrial Countries, 1953–63," IMF *Staff Papers,* (July 1965) show that Germany and Japan did better relative to the United Kingdom and the United States than prices would explain. In each of the above two studies the bad performance of the United Kingdom and the United States *could* be explained by the fact that their firms have tended to expand by investing rather than exporting.

political independence of a world of multinational corporations, some from one side of the Atlantic, some from the other (and perhaps a few from the less-developed world)? We can here provide only the briefest summary of various approaches.

The United States antitrust tradition, as exemplified by Kaysen and Turner,[18] for example, would tend to view the current wave of national and international mergers and takeovers suspiciously, just as this tradition viewed with alarm the merger movement in the United States at the end of the 19th century. At that time the growth of the national corporation led to great concern in the agrarian and small business sectors about "the fate of small producers driven out of business or deprived of the opportunity to enter it, by 'all-powerful aggregates of capital,' " and about "the power of monopolists to hurt the public by raising prices, deteriorating product, and restricting production"; while on the political side, "concentration of resources in the hands of a few was viewed as a social and political catastrophe," a belief, as Kaysen and Turner point out, "rationalised in terms of certain Jeffersonian Symbols of wide political appeal and great persistence in American Life: business units are politically irresponsible and therefore large business units are dangerous." The antitrust tradition would argue for competition rather than size to obtain efficiency and innovations and would resolve doubts "in favour of reducing market power rather than maintaining it." These political forces, however, had little influence in the United States. As Mason points out in his preface to Kaysen and Turner, "the struggle against size was largely lost in the merger movement of 1897–1901."[19] Similarly the battle against size on the international plane is being lost in the current international merger movement, and international antitrust is not likely to challenge the resulting size structures in any serious way. Indeed, it is supporting them.

International trade economists have in general been less concerned about the dangers of high concentration and oligopoly, and

[18] C. Kaysen and D. F. Turner, *Antitrust Policy* (Cambridge, Mass.: Harvard University Press, 1959). The quotations are from pp. 19 and 17, respectively.
[19] E. S. Mason, preface to Ref. 18, p. xi.

have welcomed the free flow of capital as a device for integrating the world economy. They have stressed the advantages of scale and argued that the multinational corporation, because of its organizing ability, will be a powerful force in allocating capital efficiently, and spreading technology from advanced to less-advanced countries. They welcome an industrial structure where large firms span the entire world producing each component in the country where costs are lowest and making technical advances and product innovations quickly and evenly available throughout the world. Their suggested model is perhaps the United States economy, where major firms are spread over most of the country and take advantage of differences in relative supplies of labor, capital, or natural resources. On the international plane, the prototype is perhaps United States–Canadian integration, which, symbolically speaking, has proceeded on north-south lines, i.e., pairing of Canadian enterprises with their counterparts to the south, rather than on east-west lines, i.e., coordination within Canada of the various parts of its economy.

Socialist economics also stresses the advantages of scale in keeping with Marx's analysis of the increasingly social nature of production (including the increasingly social nature of management). However, it does not always agree with the international trade approach on the way in which capital should be concentrated and centralized. Whereas the trade approach argues for coordinating one industry across many countries, socialist economics points to the advantages of coordinating many industries within one country. It thus argues for combining oligopolies to form monopolies (because it views the choices offered by oligopolistic product-differentiation as usually meaningless and sometimes harmful); for combining industries to harmonize complementary and competing sectors, and of course for central planning to provide overall coordination of all enterprises. Most important, it stresses the need for political control of economic decision makers. This implies that the boundaries of an enterprise should be contained by the boundaries of the political unit, since enterprises that extend over several units can escape political regulation by any one unit (on this argument the conglomerate enterprises should perhaps be organized on regional rather than national levels in order to be more sensitive to local requirements).

Since the multinational corporate system is the prevailing one, we might spend some time discussing it in more detail and especially its relations to nation-states. George Ball has put the case for the withering away of the nation-state most succinctly: "the structure of the multinational corporation is a modern concept designed to meet the requirements of a modern age; the nation state is a very old fashioned idea and badly adapted to serve the needs of our present complex world."[20] The idea behind this point of view, as expounded by Sidney Rolfe,[21] for example, is that the phenomenal progress in communications and transportation has created an interdependence of human activity that renders national boundaries obsolete. "The conflict of our era is between ethnocentric nationalism and geocentric technology." All countries, the United States included, must therefore realize that the multinational corporation is modern because it is the first of the major institutions to grasp the significant fact that "history is not of the essence here, evolution is," and "what the world faces is *le défi international* rather than *le défi Américain.*"

This argument contains a strong element of technological determinism, and in our view greatly oversimplifies and perhaps badly mistakes the trends of the modern world. Although it is quite true that modern world technology makes it possible to coordinate production and marketing on a global basis, it is also true that modern communications make centralized planning within one country possible. Moreover, the high productivity of the new technology allows countries greater scope for national independence, since it becomes far less urgent to concentrate on economizing scarce resources. Most important, improved communications make it easier for small regions and units to obtain the most advanced knowledge quickly and cheaply without formal institutional lines of communication. This provides increased scope for independence and reinforces

---

[20] G. W. Ball, "The Promise of the Multinational Corporation," *Fortune*, Vol. 75, No. 6 (June 1, 1967), p. 80.
[21] S. Rolfe, "Up Dating Adam Smith," *Interplay*, Vol. 2, (November 1968), pp. 15–19.

polycentralism rather than centralism. It is not at all clear that hierarchical authoritarian corporate structures are well suited to this environment. In an age when it is possible for every nation or city to be almost instantaneously in communication with every other nation or city, the technological distinction between hinterland and center disappears, though it can still be maintained by political or economic institutions. In short, the options available under the new technology are much wider than those suggested by the proponents of the multinational corporation and it is unjustified to foreclose debate at this time.[22]

Whatever the force of technology, it is clear that the growth of multinational corporations, by itself, tends to weaken nation states. Multinational corporations render ineffective many traditional policy instruments, the capacity to tax, to restrict credit, to plan investment, etc., because of their international flexibility. In addition, multinational corporations act as a vehicle for the intrusion of the policies of one country into another with the ultimate effect of lessening the power of both.[23] These tendencies have long been recognized in dependent developing countries, but it is now also evident that even the United States, as a *nation-state,* is losing some of its "independence" as it attempts to cope with the tangled web woven by its international business.[24]

The battle, however, is far from over. Nation-states are powerful

---

[22] For an important discussion of technology and nationalism in the tradition of Harold Innis, Karl Polanyi, and Marshall McLuhan, see A. Rotstein, "The 20th Century in Prospect: Nationalism in a Technological Society," and M. Watkins, "Technology and Nationalism," in *Nationalism in Canada,* D. Russell, ed. (Scarborough, Ont.: McGraw-Hill, 1966).

[23] For a discussion of the limitations on a nation-state brought about by multinational corporations, see M. Watkins *et al., Foreign Ownership and the Structure of Canadian Industry,* Report of the Task Force on the Structure of Canadian Industry (Ottawa: The Queen's Printer, 1968). See also K. Levitt, "Canada: Economic Dependence and Political Disintegration," *New World,* Vol. IV, No. 2 (1968), pp. 57–139. An incisive treatment designed for less-developed countries but perhaps soon to be of some relevance for developed countries is found in R. Demonts and F. Perroux, "Large Firms, Small Nations," *Présence Africaine,* Vol. 10, No. 38 (1961), pp. 3–19.

[24] Some interesting aspects of the problem are explored in L. Model, "The Politics of Private Foreign Investment," *Foreign Affairs,* Vol. 45 (June 1967), pp. 639–651.

and are not likely to die easily. Merely to ask which institution one expects to be around 100 years from now, France or General Motors, shows the nature of the problem. Moreover, the implication of Ball's point of view is that the United States must also wither away as a nation-state.[25] How exactly this is to occur is, to say the least, not clear. The growing feedback operations of U.S. corporation on the United States have already created considerable difficulty and can be expected to lead to increased attempts by the American state to control its corporations. Other countries will also try to control the eroding forces of multinational business. Even the government of Canada, which for unique reasons has been less resistant to giving up "independence" for foreign investment than other countries, has stopped short of full integration, and has, for example, used tariffs to interfere with corporate rationalization.

Nation-states and nationalism have in many ways been powerful supports of capitalism, for they have created the group solidarity that enabled the system to survive. In a private-enterprise system, some win and some lose, and a national government with the power to redistribute income and wealth is needed to convince losers to allow the game of competition to go on.[26] The manner of giving subsidies to the losers (e.g., price supports to farmers) has often been inefficient and has been subject to much criticism by economists; but this is not the same as saying the corporations can do without a strong nation-state to deal with the problems of the business cycle, social insecurity, unemployment, unbalanced regional growth, labor unrest, attacks on property and order, etc. If, for example, all countries lost their power of fiscal and monetary policy, as some observers believe Canada has, how would aggregate demand be stabilized? Or does multinationalism do away with Keynesian problems?

Hence the multinational corporations require multinational states. It is utopian to think that this will come about quickly

---

[25] The arguments put forward by Ball and the large corporations for an international system of incorporation are, of course, as much an attempt by firms to escape from U.S. regulation as anything else.

[26] Cf. C. P. Kindleberger, *International Economics* (Homewood, Ill.: R. D. Irwin, 3rd ed., 1963, p. 627).

enough to permit the full flowering of international business. It may be possible to stagger toward some level of cooperation at a higher plane on monetary and fiscal policy, tariff policy, and antitrust policy, but the degree of success will be limited. A most important obstacle to supranationality stems from the fact that many of the most important government policy instruments require patriotism to be effective. From the moral suasion exercised by governments on banks, to the voluntary guidelines established for capital flows, wages, and prices, to the demand for honesty in the payment of taxes, the government depends upon voluntary compliance by the majority of its citizens in order to operate effectively. Group loyalty of this kind does not exist at an international level. There does not yet seem to be any effective replacement for the nationalism that has in the past helped to dissolve class conflict and maintain social cohesion (witness how effectively patriotic sentiments have been used by Western governments to blunt the edge of social discontent during periods of economic hardship such as the years of postwar reconstruction).

In a regime of multinational corporations and weak nation-states, differences will become accentuated and will lead to international alliances and federations parallel to the multinational corporation.[27] And even if a strong world federal government could be established, many problems can only be solved at the national and local level. If nation-state governments are too greatly weakened, the model for the future may be the urban crisis, where strong national corporations confront weak city governments. In short, there is a conflict at a fundamental level between national planning by political units and international planning by corporations that will assume major proportions as direct investment grows.

In conclusion, we may return to the question raised in *The American Challenge* about the danger of Europe becoming a colony. Servan-Schreiber is perhaps correct that in the world of multinational corporations it is better to have some of your own than to

[27] E. Mandel, "International Capitalism and Supra Nationality," in *The Socialist Register 1967*, R. Milliband and J. Saville, eds. (London: The Merlin Press, 1967), and "Where is America Going?," *New Left Review*, No. 54 (March/April 1969), pp. 14, 15.

have none at all. This does not, however, mean that European multinational corporations will enable Europeans to control their future. Instead, difficulties arising from the internationalization of wealth may well inhibit Europe's ability to cope with its internal problems and, in this regard, the problems faced by the United Kingdom in reconciling international finance and the national interest should serve as a warning (as should the current problems of the United States). The problem of colonialism is not really a European problem since European business, despite Servan-Schreiber's analysis, is strong, not weak. Colonialism is the problem of the less-developed countries, where both state enterprise and private capital are very weak and are in no way a match for the powerful business organization of the advanced world. In the coming competition between European and U.S. corporations, the markets of the third world will be an important battleground, because the stakes will be not only the limited markets of Africa, Latin America, and Asia, but oligopoly equilibrium in the developed world itself. The lesson of Europe's past colonialism is that the harm it did to foreigners was not matched by benefit to itself (i.e., by a benefit to the country as a whole rather than to a particular group). Indeed, the nation was often called upon to sacrifice in order to maintain imperial connections benefiting only a few. Partly because of this, there is a tradition among some English economists of challenging the advantages of foreign investment (Keynes).[28] In following that tradition rather than the more prevalent one, which assumes international movements of capital to be guided by an invisible hand to improve human welfare, we are in no way suggesting policies to stop multinationalization, since we believe it to be a foregone conclusion. Our aim is to point out some likely consequences and contradictions of the laws of international industrial reorganization, as we see them. The propensity of multinational corporations to settle everywhere and establish connections everywhere is giving a new cosmopolitan nature to the economy and policies to deal with it will have to begin from that base.

[28] J. M. Keynes, "Foreign Investment and National Advantage," *The Nation and the Athenaem,* Vol. XXXV, No. 19 (August 1924), pp. 584–586.

Part II

FINANCE AND TECHNOLOGY

CHAPTER FOUR

DIRECT INVESTMENT CONTROLS
AND THE BALANCE OF PAYMENTS

H. David Willey

Introduction

Controls over foreign direct investment by United States companies as a measure to improve the United States balance of payments have been viewed as anachronistic. To subject what has now become essentially international business to national regulation seems out of step with post World War II efforts to achieve freer world trade and payments in an atmosphere of international cooperation. If, as has reportedly been suggested by Milton Friedman,[1] the two-tier gold system put the world effectively on a dollar standard and simultaneously ruled out the possibility of a major international monetary crisis, concern over the United States balance of payments is itself out of date. While there is an element of truth in these contentions, U.S. companies still bear a national "stamp," and the appetites of foreign central banks and other foreigners for U.S. dollars probably are not unlimited. To the extent that the world is on a dollar standard, our policies and those of other countries must

[1] Reuters dispatch from Geneva, "Friedman Applauds Two-Tier System," *American Banker,* Vol. CXXXIV, No. 82 (April 28, 1969), p. 3. A similar argument had been presented three years earlier by E. Despres, C. P. Kindleberger, and W. S. Salant, "The Dollar and World Liquidity—A Minority View," *The Economist,* Vol. CCXVIII, No. 6389 (February 5, 1966), pp. 526–529. The earlier argument did not imply that foreign willingness to hold dollars was without limit and suggested that an annual growth in Europe's dollar holdings on the order of $1½ to $2 billion a year was appropriate.

take care to adjust the supply of dollars to residents of other countries to fit their needs.

Few would argue that direct investment controls, or the other selective balance of payments measures adopted or reinforced by the United States Government in the 1960s, are the ideal way to deal with our role as money supplier to the world. Most economists would prefer general economic adjustments, of prices, incomes, or exchange rates, in all countries to selective controls imposed by one country. The United States adopted selective controls because general adjustment was neither automatic nor acceptable to authorities in many countries.

These selective controls were loosely interrelated and covered most capital outflows. Government outflows were tied to purchases of U.S. goods and services, purchases by U.S. residents of foreign securities were taxed, and loans to foreigners by U.S. banks and the financing from U.S. funds of direct investments abroad by U.S. companies were limited. The persistence of international monetary malaise is evidence that these selective controls did not eliminate the need for general adjustment. They may, however, have been instrumental in diminishing the amplitude of the monetary disturbances that did occur.

The purpose of this paper is to examine the relation between one of these selective controls, that over direct investment, and the balance of payments. The paper is divided into three parts: the nature of the controls, the effect of the controls on the balance of payments in 1968, and the side effects of the controls influencing future payments balances. In writing this paper I have benefited from the comments of Professor Kindleberger and his seminar. The paper, however, is my responsibility and does not necessarily reflect the view of the Office of Foreign Direct Investments, the Department of Commerce, the United States Government, or the Federal Reserve Bank of New York.

How the Controls Worked in 1968

The voluntary balance of payments program introduced in 1965 and administered by the Department of Commerce attempted to restrain both the holding by U.S. companies of liquid balances abroad and direct investment in developed countries. "Direct investment" for this purpose consisted of earnings retained abroad by foreign affiliates and net capital transfers of U.S. funds made by direct investors to foreign affiliates.[2]

The voluntary program and other selective restraint measures notwithstanding, the United States balance of payments deficit rose sharply and there was a substantial gold loss following the sterling devaluation of November 1967. On January 1, 1968, President Johnson announced a new balance of payments program, which included transformation of the voluntary program into a mandatory program. A complex set of regulations was drafted, of which only the major outline can be presented here.[3] The new program

---

[2] Direct investment as so defined is thus not "direct investments" as shown on line 33 of Tables 1 and 2 published in the quarterly balance of payments articles appearing in the *Survey of Current Business* (Washington, D.C.: U.S. Department of Commerce). Line 33 does not include retained earnings and includes capital transfers made with the proceeds of foreign borrowing. Retained earnings do not appear as such in Tables 1 and 2, but line 11, "Income on U.S. direct investment abroad," shows repatriated earnings. The foreign borrowing used by the direct investor or his U.S. (and certain foreign) financing subsidiaries to make capital transfers would appear in line 52, "U.S. securities other than Treasury issues," or in lines 54 and 55, "Other liabilities reported by U.S. private residents other than banks." Such borrowings held abroad prior to "use" should appear in lines 39 and 40, as "Claims reported by U.S. residents other than banks." "Use" may take place through the direct transfer of proceeds to a foreign affiliate or the allocation of these proceeds on the books of the direct investor, as an offset to direct investment, accompanied by their repatriation. It should be noted that data reported to the Office of Foreign Direct Investments do not in every instance match data appearing in the *Survey* tables. While data to be reported are conceptually comparable, there are differences in coverage and apparently in the information submitted. The Office of Foreign Direct Investments is working with the Office of Business Economics to resolve these discrepancies.

[3] The regulations are published from time to time in the *Federal Register* (Washington, D.C.: U.S. Government Printing Office). Updated compilations are available from time to time from the Office of Foreign Direct Investments. Partly out of date, but still of interest, is the official explanatory comment published last fall (*Federal Register,* Vol. 33, No. 198 (October 10, 1968), Part II; No. 209, (October 25, 1968), Part III). An indication of the complexity involved was offered by Representative Byrnes (Republican, Wisconsin), ". . . anybody who reads those regulations closely will end up eating bananas, or climbing walls" (*Administration's Balance-of-Payments Proposals,* Hearings before the Committee on Ways and Means, House of

also covered both liquid foreign balances and direct investment, essentially as defined under the voluntary program, but extended to the less-developed countries as well. Canada was made exempt, however, in March 1968 after official assurance that Canada would not be used as a "passthrough" to avoid U.S. balance of payments programs.

The direct investment restraints were not only made mandatory, but were also considerably more stringent than those of the voluntary program. The voluntary program aimed at restraining the growth of direct investment, but the mandatory program was intended to reduce direct investment by $1 billion from the 1967 level. This was to be done by setting individual company investment quotas for each of three geographic areas based on the experience of each company in the 1965–1966 period. Quotas were most stringent for schedule C, generally continental Western European countries, and least stringent for schedule A, generally less-developed countries. Schedular quotas were applied to total direct investment, except in schedule C, where they applied only to retained earnings.[4] As an alternative to these schedular quotas, companies could use a minimum allowable, which at the end of 1968 was set at $200,000. In addition, companies with special problems under the regulations could apply for specific relief. Such relief was given, for example, to companies with investment commitments made prior to the program, with repatriation problems, or with a need to grant additional intercompany export credit.

President Nixon and Secretary Stans eased the direct investment rules somewhat for 1969 by raising the minimum allowable to $1 million, reducing the number of companies required to file detailed quarterly reports, allowing limited transfer of investment quotas "upstream," that is, in the direction of schedule A to schedule C, and introducing an alternative quota calculation based on 1968 earnings. The latter measure was especially valuable for in-

---

Representatives, Ninetieth Congress, Second Session, February 5 and 6, 1968, Part 1, p. 265).

[4] The schedule C restriction was modified in late 1968 to allow capital transfers from foreign affiliates to direct investors as an offset to retained earnings.

vestors with sizable earnings, but low direct investment in the 1964 to 1966 period. (Some companies had low investment in that period because of cooperation with the voluntary program.) These relatively modest changes were made in the expectation of a serious 1969 balance of payments problem, with the calculated risk of further worsening the situation, in order to reverse the previous tendency toward increasingly severe selective balance of payments measures.

Direct investment fell from $3.7 billion in 1967 to an estimated $1.5 billion in 1968, a decline of $2.2 billion. (See Table 1.) The fall was greatest in schedule C and least in schedule A. The fall in the total resulted from a large increase in the use of foreign borrowing and a substantial decline in capital transfers, offset in part by a rise in reinvested earnings.

Table 1. Direct Investment Transactions, Excluding Canada, 1965 to 1969 (billions of dollars).

Selected Transactions	Data for 3,300 OFDI Reporters				Projections From 469 Major Companies
	1965	1966	1967	1968	1969
Total, all schedules, excluding Canada					
Reinvested earnings	1.02	1.08	0.92	1.21	1.67
Capital transfers, *including* use of foreign borrowings	3.10	3.44	3.35	2.47	3.42
Direct investment, *including* use of foreign borrowings	4.12	4.52	4.27	3.68	5.09
Use by direct investor of long-term foreign borrowings	(0.11)	(0.65)	(0.56)	(2.22)	(2.30)
Direct investment, *excluding* use of foreign borrowings	4.01	3.87	3.71	1.46	2.79

Source: United States Department of Commerce press release, FDI 69-5 (May 6, 1969).

The control program probably had a very significant influence on capital transfers and the use of foreign borrowing. It probably had little effect on reinvested earnings. Reinvested earnings rose in line with total earnings, for the repatriation ratio was about the same in 1968 as in prior years. The influence of the program may be seen, however, in a small decline in this ratio for schedules A and B and a small rise for schedule C.

The program influenced capital transfers in a number of ways. Introduction of the program and confusion over its meaning may have delayed some investment projects. Evidence of this is the relatively small transfers in the first quarter of 1968 and estimates of plant and equipment expenditures by foreign affiliates, which suggest postponement of some projects from 1968 to 1969.[5] The general reaction of the business community that it was possible to live with the controls in 1968 implies, however, that few capital projects were actually dropped or seriously curtailed. The reduction indicated in capital transfers was probably thus more financial than real.

Transfers were also reduced by the reduction of intercompany credits granted by the direct investor to foreign affiliates. In some cases intercompany credit terms were shortened through the adoption of new procedures for acceleration of intercompany payments. Professional advice on this subject was apparently in considerable demand.[6] In other cases, foreign affiliates borrowed abroad in order to repay earlier credits from the parent or to grant credits to the parent. Such borrowing reportedly took place on a fairly large scale in late 1968 and served to reduce fourth-quarter transfers to a very low figure. It is possible that some of this borrowing was quite short term and was repaid in early 1969.

Use of foreign financing by the direct investor rose sharply in 1968. Prior to 1966 very little direct investment had been financed by direct investor borrowing abroad, although foreign affiliates had long used foreign borrowing as a major source of funds. (Borrowing by direct investors is discussed further below.)

[5] The first-quarter "direct investment" figure in the *Survey* was the lowest seasonally adjusted quarterly figure since 1963. Estimates for 1968 and 1969 of plant and equipment expenditures by foreign affiliates of U.S. corporations were reduced for 1968 and increased for 1969, suggesting a postponement of some projects. *Survey of Current Business*, Vol. 49, No. 3 (Washington, D.C.: U.S. Department of Commerce March 1969), p. 13.

[6] One United States banking firm placed a full page advertisement in daily newspapers offering such a service. See *The Wall Street Journal* (February 19, 1969), p. 11.

The major influence of the program was thus financial, primarily an increase in the amount of long- and short-term foreign borrowing by direct investors and their foreign affiliates used as a substitute for increased transfers from the U.S. or increased reinvestment of foreign earnings. The distribution of the use of foreign borrowing was very uneven among individual companies and depended largely on the size of direct investment in the base years. In the aggregate, however, far more foreign borrowing was used than would have been necessary in strict observance of program rules. For some companies this was a safety factor to ensure compliance in the face of unforeseen end-of-year transactions. Furthermore, the program permitted a carryforward of unused 1968 quotas to 1969.

A number of considerations other than the program itself, however, tended to reinforce the reduction of direct investment. These included interest rates, foreign depreciation, and a general slowdown in the rate of foreign expansion.

Foreign and domestic interest rates came close together in 1968, and many companies found it no more expensive to borrow abroad than at home, although those with high domestic liquidity may have felt no need to borrow at all. The sharp rise in domestic rates late in the year led to fears of a domestic credit shortage early in 1969, and some companies borrowed abroad as much for domestic as for direct investment purposes. The uncovered borrowing rates on some foreign currencies were, in fact, substantially lower than U.S. rates. There was thus considerable incentive to borrow foreign currencies as a hedge against foreign currency claims coming due or as speculation against possible foreign currency regulations.

Furthermore, the cash flow from depreciation available to foreign affiliates rose substantially in 1968, reducing the need for retained earnings and capital transfers as a financing source for overseas operations.

The tendency toward deceleration in the expansion of U.S. plant and equipment expenditures abroad, which was evident before introduction of the mandatory control program, was probably also a factor. Plant and equipment expenditures by the foreign affiliates of U.S. companies outside of Canada were rising at an annual rate of more than 20% in 1964 and 1965, but declined to 12% in 1966 and 1967. While the geographic and industrial sector location of this decline has been different from year to year, the deceleration in European Economic Community manufacturing is striking; the annual rise in plant and equipment expenditures dropped from 47% in 1965 to 8% in 1967, and current estimates suggest an actual decline in 1968.

The deceleration in plant and equipment expenditures may exaggerate the slowdown in expansion of U.S. business abroad, for new acquisitions by U.S. investors of existing foreign firms are not included. New acquisitions have varied in amount over the last few years, but have tended to be higher in the most recent years.[7] Nonetheless, the number of new establishments begun abroad by U.S. companies, whether by acquisition or by new construction, has declined in each year since 1963; the number of existing establishments expanded has been markedly less since 1965.[8] The value of disinvestments, however, seems to have declined since 1964, although the 1967 total was relatively large. These various bits of evidence suggest that the foreign expansion of U.S. business has definitely slowed down, with some evidence of this starting in the mid-1960s, despite the high plant and equipment increases at that time.

The reasons for this slowdown were undoubtedly complex. One factor is probably the decline in profitability of manufacturing investments in the EEC from a ratio of earnings to book value of 11% in 1964 to 9% in 1967.[9] Overseas business is not necessarily a quick path to riches. Foreign competition has become more intense. Official obstacles to U.S. foreign business have been thrown

[7] E. Nelson and F. Cutler, "The International Investment Position of the United States in 1967," *Survey of Current Business,* Vol. 48, No. 10 (Washington, D.C.: U.S. Department of Commerce, October 1968), Table 8, p. 28, and similar annual tables in prior years.

[8] Booz, Allen, & Hamilton, *New Foreign Business Activities of U.S. Firms,* January 1961–December 1967, No. 14 (1968). These data were updated to December 1968 in "What U.S. Companies are Doing Abroad: A Statistical Summary," *Business Abroad* (May 1969), pp. 13, 16, 17.

[9] Reference 7. In some cases profits margins in Europe had apparently dipped below those in the United States. Compagnie Lambert pour l'Industrie et la Finance, "La Disparité des Taux de Profit des Entreprises en Europe et aux Etats Unis," *Annexe au Rapport de l'Exercice 1967,* Brussels, 1968.

up by some European countries that are sensitive about the proportion of new U.S. investment in key sectors of their economies.[10] Problems with local customs, labor, etc. have also been important; widespread publicity has been given to the problems faced by Raytheon, Rheem, Union Carbide, Celanese, and Marathon in Italy, by General Electric in France, and by Chrysler in Spain.[11]

These recent investment tendencies plus the financial flexibility enjoyed by many companies in relations with their schedule C affiliates probably do more than the schedular restrictions to explain the relative decline in schedule C direct investments. Similarly, the rise in schedule A capital transfers including the use of foreign borrowing is probably explained more by a growing interest in Latin American and other less-developed country investments than by relative liberality of schedule A quotas.[12] While the schedular approach was probably not effective in aiming *direct investment* away from the surplus countries of schedule C to the less-developed coun-

---

[10] A recent example is the difficulty U.S. data processing firms have had in becoming established in France. See N. Vichney, "Une Firme Américaine d'Informatique Renonce à sa Participation dans le Groupe Sema-Metra," *Le Monde* (April 20, 21, 1969).

[11] G. Melloan, "U.S. Firms and 'Il Problema,'" *The Wall Street Journal* (March 11, 1969), p. 36; C. Tugendhat, "Why U.S. Companies Abandon their European Headquarters," *Financial Times* (April 15, 1969), p. 19; F. N. Parks, "Survival of the European Headquarters," *Harvard Business Review*, Vol. 47 (March-April 1969), p. 79–84; and H. Horstmeyer, "Spain Looks for Reaction by Chrysler," *Journal of Commerce* (June 4, 1969), p. 13.

[12] To investigate the hypothesis that the ratio of actual direct investment in schedule A to that in all schedules for 1968 was raised by relatively large schedule A quotas a least-squares linear regression test was made for a cross section of 945 companies, giving the following result:

$$\frac{a_{68}^I}{t_{68}^I} = -0.015 + \underset{(0.0019)}{0.001} \; \frac{a_{67}^I}{t_{67}^I} + \underset{(0.2041)}{0.838} \; \frac{a_{68}^Q}{t_{68}^Q},$$

$r^2 = 0.018$. I is the sum of retained earnings and capital transfers, including use of foreign borrowed funds, Q is the investment quota, a is schedule A, t is total of schedules (and Canada in the case of I). Standard errors are shown in parenthesis below the regression coefficients. While the regression coefficient of the quota ratio is significant, this may simply mean that the 1965–1966 pattern of investment was related to the 1968 pattern and not that the quota ratio influenced 1968 investment. In any case, the specified relation explains little of the 1968 direct investment ratio.

tries, it did reinforce the *overall* restrictiveness of the program and the *financing* of direct investment was diverted more to surplus countries. Companies with a quota in schedule A for which they had no plans were not free to use this quota in schedules B or C and were forced to finance their schedule B or C investments above the quotas for those schedules with foreign borrowing. Most of this borrowing came from surplus countries.

Whatever the cause of the fall in direct investment, companies in the aggregate did not make full use of their quotas in 1968 and carried forward to 1969 nearly $2 billion in unused allowables. In this sense the program was self-liberalizing; the quotas carried forward were far larger than the modest liberalization introduced by the new Administration. This carryforward plus new quotas gave the possibility of nearly $5 billion in generally allowed investment this year. According to projections made in a February survey, companies do not, in the aggregate, plan to make use of this total, either because schedule limitations prevent them, or because they have investment plans smaller than available quotas. The results of the February survey, shown in Table 1, indicate that companies should invest less than the $3.35 billion target ceiling, which has been set for 1969, even when nonreporters to the survey are included. This conclusion does not take into account any outflows that might be induced by marked changes in domestic/foreign interest rate differentials or by hedging or speculation against possible exchange rate changes; such outflows have reportedly been important in the second quarter. Actual direct investment for 1969 will probably be much higher than the very low total recorded for 1968.

This rise shows that the major impact of the mandatory program came in the year of its inception, but does not mean that the program will lack effect in 1969. The use of foreign borrowing would probably be much smaller without the program than with it. The continued high use of foreign borrowing in 1969 required fewer new long-term borrowings by direct investors than in 1968. An estimated $1 billion in new borrowing will be required to finance the "use" figure set forth in Table 1, because direct investors borrowed in 1968, in advance of their needs for 1969.

In conclusion for this section, the nature of the direct investment program has been to restrict capital outflows somewhat, and to raise greatly the use of foreign borrowing. The reduction in capital transfers results mainly from economizing on parent company credit and on extra foreign borrowing by foreign affiliates. The economizing may have been partially offset by a rise in transactions velocity and the affiliates' borrowing may be quickly reversible. The principal balance of payments effect of the program would thus appear to be a shift in the structure of United States liabilities to foreigners. What would probably have been short-term liabilities of the banking system, or of the U.S. Government, or perhaps a gold loss, became instead long-term liabilities of U.S. companies. The significance of this shift for the U.S. balance of payments as well as possible offsets to this change in our other international accounts is the subject of the next section.

Effect of the Controls on the Balance of Payments in 1968

Interrelations among the various balance of payments account entries are complex, and the changes reviewed in the preceding section undoubtedly influenced other entries. No attempt has been made here to quantify these interrelations in a precise manner, but orders of magnitude are suggested. Even if the various interrelationships could be specified correctly and measured accurately, the meaning for the U.S. balance of payments position would remain open to interpretation. There are a number of possible capital and current account offsets to the changes in direct investment outlined in the previous section.

United States companies made net new long-term borrowings in

Table 2.   1968 Increase in Net "Long-Term" Foreign Debt of U.S. Companies (in billions of dollars).

New public issues		2.2
Straight debt	0.6	
Convertible debentures	1.6	
Short-term renewable		0.3
Other		1.3
Total		3.8

Note: Issues by subsidiaries incorporated in the Netherlands Antilles included.
Source: OFDI and general financial press.

1968 approaching $4 billion. (See Table 2.) An obvious possibility is that foreigners purchased the obligations of U.S. companies with funds derived from the sale of other long-term U.S. assets or with funds that would have been used to purchase other long-term U.S. assets. The evidence on this subject is mixed, but any such substitution was not clearly shown by the data.

There was some small runoff of foreign holdings of U.S. bonds, other than those newly issued by U.S. companies, but net foreign purchases of U.S. equities totaled almost $2 billion in 1968.[13] The boom in U.S. equity sales to foreigners began before 1968 and benefited from 1968 monetary and political uncertainties in Europe. The growing market for U.S. equities abroad extended to convertible debentures, and made possible large sales of these issues by U.S. companies.[14] While it is probable that the new convertible debentures diverted some foreign purchases from U.S. equities, they served to stimulate foreign interest in the securities of a broader range of U.S. companies and thus induced some additional U.S. equity sales.[15] There seems to be no good way to sort out these opposing influences. Other types of long-term borrowing by U.S. companies were stimulated by the policy of some European countries to place their surpluses in the Euro-dollar market or to encourage the foreign placement of long-term bonds through low domestic interest rates. A sizable proportion of the newly issued straight debt was denominated in German marks, for example, and carried an interest rate well below that for similar domestic borrowing in dollars.

It is important to note the role of the Interest Equalization Tax in this new borrowing by U.S. companies. The original purpose of this tax was to divert new foreign portfolio issues from the New York market. This separation of the domestic and foreign capital market was used by the direct investment programs (both volun-

---

[13] W. Lederer and E. M. Parrish, "The U.S. Balance of Payments—Fourth Quarter and Year 1968," *Survey of Current Business*, Vol. 49, No. 3 (Washington D.C.: U.S. Department of Commerce, March 1969), Table D3, p. 31.

[14] Morgan Guaranty Trust Company, Economist's Department, *World Financial Markets* (December 27, 1968), p. 4.

[15] N. M. Rothschild & Sons, *The Eurobond Market* (February 1969), p. 5.

tary and mandatory) for a different purpose, to prevent the sale of new U.S. company debt securities to U.S. residents. These securities were offered initially "for sale to foreigners," and the IET acts as a barrier to subsequent resale by foreigners to U.S. residents. Purchases by U.S. residents of these securities would appear to have been very limited.

The IET is, however, no barrier to conversion of debentures by foreigners into the underlying equity and the sale of this equity to U.S. residents. The market did favor conversion in 1968 of a few issues, and a small amount (possibly $30 million) of debentures was converted. Although the IET is no barrier to conversion, the conversion premium, the generally lower yield on the equity than on the debentures, and the absence of U.S. withholding taxes on debenture interest but not on equity dividends do act as barriers.

While the IET tended to separate domestic and foreign capital markets, the increasing resort by U.S. companies to foreign capital markets tended to bring the two markets closer together. There was some danger that the borrowing by U.S. companies abroad would so raise foreign rates that new U.S. funds would be attracted. This did not seem to have happened on any important scale in 1968. The program limited liquid foreign balances as well as direct investment, and this may have limited total company outflows. (Companies were permitted, however, to keep their foreign borrowing proceeds until needed for direct investment; a high proportion of the "unused" 1968 borrowing ($3.8 billion new borrowing, less $2.2 billion use) was retained overseas.) The story may well be different in 1969. United States corporations need to borrow much less than in 1968 to finance their direct investments, but demand by U.S. banks through their overseas branches has been intense and a number of foreign monetary authorities have ceased to favor supplying funds to the Euro-dollar market. The resulting high Euro-dollar rates and speculation over revaluation of the German mark have reportedly led to sizable outflows of U.S. funds.

It might also be argued that the controls placed pressure on some foreign currencies, thereby forcing official U.S. outflows in the form of swap drawings. Although foreign countries made substantial use of swap facilities in 1968 and at least one instance of pressure could be traced to the program, the program can hardly be blamed for speculative waves in the spring and fall.[16] In fact, the program probably had a net stabilizing effect (see the following).

Another possible capital offset to the program is the passing of funds through Canada, which was exempted from the program. Such "passthroughs" were generally covered by Canada's restraint guidelines and do not seem to have been substantial, despite press reports to the contrary.[17]

There may also have been some "end-runs" around the U.S. direct investment control program. Credits habitually granted by U.S. direct investors to foreign affiliates, which are covered by the program, may have been replaced by third party credits from United States suppliers, which are not. United States companies have also placed additional funds in "nonliquid" and "nondirect investment" assets abroad; such placements are not covered by the program. A number of companies also adjusted their accounting to reduce recorded direct investment by taking losses in 1968 or by moving from an accrual accounting basis (whereby the control program is more likely to encourage repatriation of earnings as earned) to a completed project accounting basis (whereby the program affects repatriation of earnings at the end of a contract). These and other possibilities were apparently not utilized to a large extent by direct investors, most of which adhered to the spirit as well as to the letter of the regulations. Very crude indications of this cooperation may be seen in the smaller outflow on errors and omissions in 1968 than in 1967, and in the drop in claims reported by U.S. residents other than banks.

We may thus conclude, on the basis of the still necessarily vague and imperfect information cited above, that the capital account offsets to the program were far from overwhelming, and much

[16] C. A. Coombs, "Treasury and Federal Reserve Foreign Exchange Operations," *Federal Reserve Bulletin,* Vol. 54, No. 9 (September 1968), pp. 721–742; Vol. 55, No. 3 (March 1969), pp. 210–227. The instance noted was pressure on the Belgian franc in September and October from sales of francs by U.S. corporations.

[17] R. D. Prinsky, "Hot Money is Taking Circular Trip in Quest for a Higher Return," *The Wall Street Journal* (March 5, 1969), p. 17.

smaller than most observers would have believed when the program was introduced.

It is to possible current account offsets, however, that much of the criticism of the control program has been directed. The major possible offsets are income from direct investments and merchandise trade. As noted above, income from direct investments was apparently not significantly affected by the control program; the same would seem to be true for receipts from royalties and fees. The concern over current account offsets has centered in the trade accounts. A trade offset might be expected on theoretical grounds; U.S. exports to the foreign affiliates of United States companies are a sizable proportion of the total, and our trade surplus actually fell from $3.5 billion in 1967 to almost zero in 1968.

The theoretical argument has been recently restated with new statistical support by Machlup. Financial transfers have been matched by real transfers; net financial transfers in an average year have allegedly been accompanied by almost equally offsetting real transfers, except for a persistent transfer gap, over the period 1950 to 1968.[18] Machlup's conclusion is that selective balance of payments controls over financial transactions are useless, because any reduction in financial transfers will be accompanied by a comparable and offsetting change in the trade balance. Although there is some relation between financial and real transfers, Machlup's conclusion is too pat. The statistical measure of the relation is open to question, and much of the inverse relation between financial and real transfers may be the result of underlying economic conditions and not the causal effect of financial transfers on real transfers.

There has been some documentation of the financial and real transfer relation involved in U.S. exports to the foreign affiliates of U.S. companies. Such exports, excluding those charged on the parents' books, those sold on commission, and those purchased directly by affiliates from unrelated U.S. suppliers, totaled about

[18] F. Machlup, *The Transfer Gap of the United States,* International Finance Section, Department of Economics, Princeton University Reprints in International Finance No. 11 (Princeton, New Jersey: Princeton University Press, October 1968). Originally published in *Banca Nazionale del Lavoro Quarterly Review,* No. 86 (September 1968).

one-fourth of all United States nonmilitary merchandise exports in 1964.[19] While the importance of such exports to the total is apparent, the effect of the direct investment program is not. The coverage of the program and the response of affected companies to the program must be taken into account.

The direct investment program does not cover Canada; excepting Canada from exports cuts the 1964 one-quarter ratio to one-fifth. Limiting the exports to those charged to the books of the direct investor cuts the ratio further, to about 15%. Changes over time, however, have probably raised this ratio. Reports to the Office of Foreign Direct Investments suggest that because exports to non-Canadian affiliates have risen faster than exports to all countries except Canada, the ratio rose to about one-quarter by 1966 and has remained at that level through 1968.

A further consideration is the relatively small number of direct investors that account for most of the exports. In a survey for 1965 that included Canadian affiliates, 21 United States companies, or 7 percent of the 291 parents surveyed, accounted for nearly 65 percent of the exports.[20] Similarly, an Office of Foreign Direct Investments survey (excluding exports to Canada) for 1968 revealed that about 40 companies accounted for about two-thirds of total exports to affiliates projected by 661 companies. It was thus possible in the administration of the control program to seek out companies with exporting problems and to give them specific relief.[21]

The direct investment program applies to credits and other transfers of all kinds between parents and affiliates including credits given for the shipment of U.S. exports to affiliates. The suggestion

[19] S. Pizer and F. Cutler, "U.S. Exports to Foreign Affiliates of U.S. Firms," *Survey of Current Business,* Vol. 45, No. 12 (Washington, D.C.: U.S. Department of Commerce, December 1965), p. 12.

[20] M. Bradshaw, "U.S. Exports to Foreign Affiliates of U.S. Firms," *Survey of Current Business* Vol. 49, No. 5 (Washington, D.C.: U.S. Department of Commerce, 1969), p. 44.

[21] C. Fiero, "Statement," Hearings before the Subcommittee on International Exchange and Payments of the Joint Economic Committee, Ninety-First Congress, First Session, January 13, 14, and 15, 1969, *A Review of Balance of Payments Policies* (Washington, D.C.: U.S. Government Printing Office, 1969), p. 146.

has often been made that the program should exclude credits given for U.S. exports on the grounds that the credit and the export are offsetting balance of payments transactions. To do this, however, might open up new avenues of escape from the controls and could cause a shift to investment in kind that would subject the United States to foreign complaints of trade discrimination and to possible foreign retaliation.

Although the program was designed to be nondiscriminatory with respect to trade, there have been critcisms that it is not so in fact. One argument is that the foreign financing induced by the program may be tied to foreign procurement, especially if foreign managements are making the purchasing decision.[22] Because the foreign financing induced by the program was very largely in the Euro-dollar and Euro-bond markets, where credits are not generally tied to particular procurement sources, this would not seem to be an important factor. The role of foreign management decisions, which is set by the structure of individual companies and not by the control program, may be something else. Hufbauer and Adler have suggested that the purchasing decisions of U.S. foreign affiliates may in time approach the buying habits of native firms and that crude evidence suggests that U.S. affiliates in Europe buy a larger proportion of their parts and components from the United States than do native firms.[23] Moreover, purchasing, as well as investment, decisions probably reflect the growing cost of U.S. production.[24]

The response of direct investors to the program has in many cases been to shorten the term of their intercompany export credits

---

[22] C. Stewart, "The Critical Need for an Accelerated Phase Out of Foreign Direct Investment Controls," Statement of Machinery and Allied Products Institute in Public Hearings on House Congressional Resolutions 85 and 86 by the Subcommittee on Foreign Economic Policy of the Committee on Foreign Affairs, House of Representatives (March 27, 1969), p. 15.

[23] G. Hufbauer and F. Adler, *Overseas Manufacturing Investment and the Balance of Payments,* Tax Policy Research Study No. 1 (Washington, D.C.: U.S. Treasury Department, 1968), pp. 26–28.

[24] M. Duerr and J. Greene, *The Outlook for Overseas Production and Trade, A Survey* (New York: National Industrial Conference Board, Inc., 1969), p. 5.

in addition to or in lieu of specific relief for export credit. In a 1968 survey by the Office of Foreign Direct Investment, for example, approximately two-thirds of reporting companies noted 1967 export credits to affiliates that averaged 180 days or less, and about 12% noted credits averaging over one year. Their projections for 1968 suggested that 72% would be giving credits to affiliates averaging 180 days or less, and 9% giving credits to affiliates averaging over one year. The actual shift by year end may even have been greater than indicated by these data. Such shortening of credits may be only a temporary phenomenon. The generally shorter credit terms reportedly granted to unaffiliated as compared with affiliated customers may show that companies have some flexibility in granting credits; about 90% of the companies reported average export credits to unaffiliated foreign customers averaging 180 days or less, and about 3% reported credits averaging over one year.

Even if taking into account the coverage of the program and response of investors to the program leads to the conclusion that the program had little important effect on aggregate U.S. exports to affiliates, the question of the effect on exports to unaffiliated foreign customers remains. The borrowing by United States direct investors might have denied funds to foreign customers that would have bought U.S. goods. There is, however, no evidence of a world credit shortage during 1968. Foreigners borrowed nearly as much in the Euro-bond market as they borrowed in the peak year of 1967. Payments surpluses in some European countries were channeled in good part back into international markets and reserve losses by some central banks put additional funds into the hands of private foreigners.

In any case, U.S. nonmilitary merchandise exports rose 10%, an increase comparable to an average of 6% from 1965 to 1967. Exports to destinations outside Canada were up 9% in 1968, as compared with an average of 4% from 1965 to 1967. The 1968 trade balance problem was more in imports than in exports, for imports rose 23%, as compared with an average of 13% in the prior three years. While there were special circumstances involved in the sharp import rise, inflationary pressure in the domestic economy was the dominant reason for the increase.

112

The direct investment program may have played an indirect role in this inflationary pressure by inducing extra spending on the part of U.S. companies that had borrowed money abroad to finance their direct investments instead of using domestic funds. Quantifying this linkage would be difficult, but any resulting import offset from the program would presumably be far from overwhelming. Domestic inflationary pressures and accompanying high interest rates would seem to be a common cause for a deterioration in the trade balance and for some offsetting financial inflows. At least a part of the relation between financial and real transfers would thus be indirect.[25]

From the still rather scanty evidence about capital and current account offsets to the program, it would seem that the program did have a substantial favorable effect on the U.S. balance of payments in 1968. To be more specific, the program influenced U.S. payments balances, for there are numerous measures of the international accounts, two of which — the liquidity basis and the official reserves transactions basis — have been adopted by the United States Government.

The effect on the liquidity balance from the direct investment program was mainly the shift, noted in the first section of this paper, from what would have been liquid U.S. liabilities to foreigners to nonliquid liabilities. A question may be raised as to whether this shift was only apparent. If the nonliquid liabilities are in fact liquid, and considered so in the view of the foreign holder, the statistical improvement in the liquidity balance measure is meaningless. There is no easy answer to this question, for liquidity is a relative, not an absolute, state. Some foreigners may have purchased Euro-dollar debentures of U.S. companies believing these assets to be more liquid than available assets denominated in local currencies, but certain aspects of these securities tend to make them a

[25] Furthermore, the statistical relation between financial and real transfers presented by Machlup (see Ref. 18) may be exaggerated. A scatter diagram of his data suggests that with the exception of 1969, the data fall into two groups, 1950 to 1955 and 1956 to 1967. The regression line connects these two groups, neither of which taken independently would offer the same support of Machlup's hypothesis.

less liquid asset than, say, a deposit in the Euro-dollar market. These attributes include exemption of interest payments from U.S. withholding taxes and a thin secondary market. The Interest Equalization Tax, which acts as a barrier against sale of the bonds to U.S. residents, is an important factor weakening the secondary market. The convertible debentures have the added feature of sharing in (hopeful) growth of the underlying equity. Long-term loans from foreign banks may be a different case. While these loans are perhaps nonliquid from the points of view of the borrower and lender, they are probably the counterpart of short-term Euro-dollar deposits at the lending bank, and the foreign depositor does not know that he has made, in effect, a nonliquid placement. Despite the subtleties involved in determining liquidity, the program has probably made U.S. liabilities less liquid than they would have been in its absence. In doing so, it has helped to shift dollar holdings from the hands of foreign monetary authorities to those of private foreigners.

It is this shift in holder which is of importance for the official reserve transactions balance. This shift was encouraged by monetary authorities in some surplus countries and probably helped reinforce the two-tier gold system.

No one statistical measure of our payments balance (and perhaps no combination of available measures) really tells us the current and prospective status of the payments position of the United States, for this position can vary with the changing attitudes taken here and abroad about the dollar and about the international monetary system. It may never be possible to measure the effect on attitudes from introduction of the direct investment control program. This effect may have been quite important, for the program showed the determination of this country to correct its payments imbalance at a time when this balance had seriously deteriorated, when uncertainty about the international monetary system was building up, and when the United States was delaying adoption of the income tax surcharge. This combination of circumstances may help explain how Under Secretary of State Katzenbach and other U.S. officials sent abroad to discuss the President's January 1 measures with foreign government leaders could report that the measures were recognized both as "courageous" and "absolutely unavoidable."[26] Without these measures it would no doubt have been much more difficult for the international monetary system to have survived intact the recurrent pressures it suffers.

Although introduction of the program probably helped build foreign confidence, it also introduced abroad new fears of extraordinary repatriation of income by U.S. companies, a sharp falloff in desired investment by U.S. firms, and a credit shortage for native firms. These fears proved to be generally unfounded. Nonetheless, the working of the direct investment controls did nothing to refute the charge that U.S. firms were buying up the world with money loaned to them by foreigners. Because most of the borrowing was in the international capital and money markets, however, it was difficult to identify sources and uses. Introduction of the U.S. program did not lead to widespread imitation and retaliation, for many countries were already far ahead of the United States in use of capital controls.

In conclusion for this section, direct investment controls seem to have had an important effect on the U.S. balance of payments position in 1968, although the offsets involved are not readily quantifiable and the significance of the changes induced cannot easily be assessed. Subject to even less certainty is an assessment of the side effects of the program on future balances of payments.

Side Effects on Future Payments Balances

There are many side effects of the program that will probably influence balances of payments. Most of these effects can be grouped under two headings, diversion of resources and repayment of foreign borrowing.

Significant national resources were devoted in 1968 to the program. The least of these, although perhaps important to some individual firms, was the cost of foreign borrowing. The United States would presumably have had to pay similar, perhaps higher, interest payments to foreigners had foreign-owned dollars been deposited with U.S. banks rather than borrowed by U.S. companies. Some

[26] *Department of State Bulletin,* Vol. 58 (January 29, 1968), pp. 135–142.

companies with extra domestic liquidity were faced with program borrowing requirements when they had no desire to incur additional debt, domestic or foreign, and some may have borrowed abroad at higher rates than they would have paid at home. The additional borrowing costs incurred did raise the price of foreign investment, but it is probable that this alone discouraged few investors, and that the effect on future balances will be small.

Of greater importance was the time spent in understanding, following, administering, and developing the direct investment program.

While the total number of individuals and the amount of money involved may be small in absolute terms, in relation to the planning by business and government in this area it was quite substantial. One company treasurer reports that about 15% of his time in 1968 was absorbed by the program.[27] This time might better have been spent in planning new profitable activities or in improving the profit margins on existing activities. While the Office of Foreign Direct Investments is not large (about 170 employees), it is conceivable that the energy expended by the staff might better have been spent on finding ways to improve the international adjustment mechanism. The same might be said for officials in many Government agencies who have devoted considerable time and effort to the program.

This is not to say that this diversion was a total loss. The advent of the program no doubt spurred the sober appraisal of overseas business prospects that was appropriate for many companies. Through the program U.S. Government officials began to understand the problems faced by companies in their foreign business and the complexity of developing and administering a control program for direct investment. It also heightened official awareness of contradictions in official policies (tax, foreign aid, balance of payments) toward direct investment, and it is fair to assume that experience

[27] D. A. Ellis, "Position of Tektronix, Inc. on Congressman John V. Tunney's House Concurrent Resolutions 85 and 86 calling for an end to the controls on Foreign Direct Investments," before the Subcommittee on Foreign Economic Policy, Committee on Foreign Affairs, House of Representatives (May 1, 1969).

116

gained from the program will influence future policy measures concerning the international business of U.S. firms. The statistical basis of future measures, furthermore, will be much improved because of the attention focused on international business data; both the quality and quantity of information have increased.

Repayment of foreign borrowing will, of course, be an outflow when it occurs, and the potential debt repayment by U.S. companies is very high. The total long-term foreign borrowing by U.S. companies and their financing affiliates outstanding at the end of 1968 was about $6 billion, and foreign affiliates owed large additional sums. A large part, and perhaps nearly all, of the borrowing by U.S. companies was induced by the voluntary and mandatory restraint programs, and is subject to repayment; foreign affiliates have traditionally borrowed large sums, and the amount of extra borrowing by foreign affiliates in 1968 is not yet known. Current interest rates would not favor massive repayments, even if program limitations were to be lifted, but repayments might be quite large in the absence of any restrictions should there be a change in current levels and differentials favor domestic borrowing. Many companies would seek to repay this debt because their cash flow does not require borrowing for financing direct investment or because their outstanding indebtedness is believed to be too high. If there is no limitation on repayment, the outstanding indebtedness of foreign affiliates need not be an especially important consideration, however, for the parent company can usually cover affiliates' debts.

Nonetheless, it is probable that much of this new foreign indebtedness will be renewed on maturity, for U.S. companies have found foreign financing sources to be increasingly useful, both as an alternative to domestic credit and as a means of making business contacts. To the extent that foreign financing complements direct investment rather than substitutes for it, future income from direct investment will be increased, provided that the return on investment is larger than the interest payment. The program may thus, by increasing the custom of complementary borrowing, be of future benefit to the balance of payments.[28]

[28] The substitution/complementarity problem is reviewed by G. Hufbauer

In a sense, a great part of the "foreign" borrowing in 1968 was quite "American." United States companies borrowed, through U.S. underwriters and the foreign branches of U.S. banks, funds that represented an outflow, in 1968 or earlier years, from the United States. As suggested above, however, this was more than simple financial intermediation, for this intermediation helped prevent a run on the 'bank" by transforming a part of its short-term liabilities into long-term liabilities, and by encouraging the retention of dollar assets by private foreigners.

This borrowing also had a profound effect on international capital markets. Although the borrowing generally shunned the less efficient foreign national capital markets, it indirectly made those markets more efficient by strengthening the foreign institutions that conduct transactions in national as well as international capital markets.[29] It also broadened the foreign market for U.S. securities. At such time as barriers separating the international and foreign national capital markets from the domestic capital market are removed, the resulting union will probably involve much larger foreign long-term lending to the U.S. market than was the case in the past.

United States business has responded very flexibly to the direct investment program. The "goose that lays the golden egg" still lives, despite reports of an impending demise.[30] Because of these side effects and difficulty in assessing the impact of the program on actual investment overseas by U.S. companies in 1968, the type of analysis such as used by Hufbauer and Adler in calculating payback periods is not readily applicable. It is thus hard to know how the 1968 control program will affect future golden eggs. The 1969 program is

and F. Adler, Ref. 23, pp. 12–14 and "Foreign Investment Controls: Objective — Removal," *Columbia Journal of World Business,* Vol. IV, No. 3 (May-June 1969), pp. 34, 35.

[29] European Economic Community, *The Development of a European Capital Market,* Report of a Group of Experts appointed by the EEC Commission (Brussels: European Economic Community, November 1966), Summary p. XXX and N. M. Rothschild & Sons, Ref. 15, p. 12.

[30] Joint Economic Committee, "International Trade and Finance," *1968 Joint Economic Report; Report of the Joint Economic Committee Congress of the United States on the January 1968 Economic Report of the President together with Statement of Committee Agreement. Minority and other Views* (Washington: U. S. Government Printing Office, 1968), p. 19.

less restrictive, and the new administration has announced its resolve to end this and all selective balance of payments controls.

This resolve implies that general economic measures, at home and abroad, will be taken to perfect and speed the international adjustment mechanism, for national balances of payments are not yet irrelevant. The general measures would presumably not include any specific attention to international direct investment, and many problems associated with conflicting domestic policies and national jurisdictions over international business activities would remain. Less attention to direct investment as a balance of payments problem might permit a clearer view and resolution of these other difficulties.

CHAPTER FIVE

THE SUPPLY OF FUNDS FOR U.S. DIRECT FOREIGN INVESTMENT

Eli Shapiro and Francis J. Deastlov

Availability and Cost of Finance Capital

In contrast with the extensive, albeit inconclusive, literature dealing with the determinants of demand for foreign direct investment, our topic has been relatively neglected. Because of the paucity of literature on this topic it would appear desirable to spend some time at the outset in motivating the reader to a concern for our subject.

The appeal of further accumulation of knowledge about the sources of finance for foreign investment in general, and United States foreign investment in particular (as well as more insights into the independent variables that might be taken as indicative of the forces that induce the supply of finance) lies in the fact that this information is prospectively useful to both business firms and public policy makers. In fact, it is of interest to all who are concerned with the economic development process and concomitant balance of payments phenomena.

The availability and cost of finance capital raised at home or attracted from abroad have long been a concern of policy makers in both national and international agencies whose mission has been to promote world economic growth. One obvious practical use of information about the sources of funds is in the determination of the amount of public capital that must be raised in the future to supplement private flows, in order that any one of the various possible

121

target growth commitments may be met. The geographical sources of such supply, as well as the asset preferences of wealth holders to be found at each source, must be known if public development authorities are to select markets in which, and instruments with which, to raise capital at minimum cost with negligible disruption to those credit market sources of development funds. The lower the cost of this intermediation process, the larger will be the expansion of income financed by the existing volume of the world's savings; the smaller the disruption of capital markets caused by such intermediation, the more political certainty there will be that it will be allowed to continue or increase in the future.

More generally, if one believes that the interindustry structure of the U.S. economy is sufficiently stable to permit intermediate-term prediction of the pattern of demand for industrial inputs, then a part of the future pattern of demand for U.S. direct foreign investment can also be estimated some years in advance.[1] Mining, smelting, and manufacturing have historically accounted for a large fraction of this total, and many of the individual industries within these aggregates are characterized by processes that can be associated with specific areas of the world. From this it would appear to follow that a large fraction of the geographical distribution of demand for U.S. foreign direct investment can be roughly inferred from the pattern of final demand in the United States.

According to this argument, the volume of realized direct investment in each area will depend upon the supply costs of capital (other things being given) to the agent desiring to make that investment. Finally, these costs must be a function of some recognizable determinants, just as it is meaningful to speak of the determinants of the demand for foreign investment. International agencies, foreign governments, investors, and students of growth and development all have reason, therefore, to inquire into the nature of foreign investment supply.

---

[1] This argument does not hold, of course, for foreign direct investment connected with the distribution and sale of exports. Moreover, the conclusion is also partly based on an "accelerator" or capacity theory of investment demand.

Government Policy

There is the special case of the relationship between effective demand for foreign investment and the national economic plans of countries that possess these plans. If countries could predict the "ex ante" supply of finance from domestic and foreign sources, they could make better predictions about the conditions they would confront in their capital markets over the span of the planning period. Such information would assist the countries in formulating monetary and fiscal policy as well as specific regulations governing their credit markets.[2] Less-developed countries, which obviously have an interest not only in predicting private capital inflows but also in assessing the relative costs of alternate sources, should be especially eager to understand the determinants of supply of foreign investment.

In addition to those governments which practice economic planning and often impose concomitant restrictions on the operations of capital markets, many advanced countries in Europe impose severe restrictions on their credit markets. There is growing criticism of such policies on the ground that governments are removing, from the private sector, funds that have a higher rate of return at the margin there than, in fact, exists on such funds in the uses to which they are put by the governments. Analysts critical of this state of affairs should also be interested in the determinants of the supply of foreign finance. If the ultimate source of much foreign investment finance is the saver who is faced with a captive domestic capital market, then analysts should look with favor upon the welfare gain the saver obtains by improving the financial aspects of his portfolio as more real investors compete for his funds with the attractive asset packages necessary to do so. These aspects might be either a higher yield than his government will offer for the same risk, or a lower perceived risk for the same yield than his domestic industry can provide. They might also be related to a maturity

---

[2] The "real transfer" process would require separate treatment. However, the conclusions resulting from the financial analysis suggested above is a necessary input in a study of the transfer process.

schedule preferred by the saver but unavailable from domestic sources without a sacrifice in yield; there are perhaps other aspects. Rather than see their domestic sources of funds shrink in such a manner, the governments concerned might act to further restrict their markets. They may be effectively prevented from doing so or from doing so completely by pressure, diplomatic as well as economic. Thus, these governments will be forced to meet the competition at least part way in the matter of yield and other aspects of savers' preferences. The welfare gains might not be temporary and restricted to those who find the international option attractive in the light of their preferences or to those who merely discover the option before the crowd. The gains available from investing abroad might become permanent and generally available to all domestic savers or at least more of them. Of course, if the government finds it undesirable to make the contemplated investments now that it must pay the true opportunity cost of their finance, then the classical welfare gain of allowing resources to flow into their most productive uses accrues to the economy as a whole. Savers then obtain their gains in the form of increases in real income.

Grubel has shown that there exists a different welfare gain to international diversification of portfolios, which is to be distinguished from holding all one's financial wealth in one country's assets.[3] Positing a model whose chief constraints are public policies independent of one another in the two countries concerned, and savers' preferences which are a function of expected yield and perceived standard deviation, Grubel shows a welfare gain from the necessary reduction in the variance of the whole diversified portfolio, provided only that the covariance of the two countries' interest rates is not unity. Whether or not this is a partial explanation of the foreign supply for United States foreign investment that has come forth during the last decade is an empirical proposition and a difficult one to test. However, this welfare gain remains as an inducement to such supply in the future for savers possessing the preference function Grubel assumes for them.

[3] H. G. Grubel, "Internationally Diversified Portfolios," *American Economic Review*, Vol. LVIII, No. 5, Part 1 (December 1968).

124

Balance of Payments Considerations

Still another application of information regarding the sources of funds for foreign investment lies in the area of balance of payments prediction and policy. One cannot stop with the knowledge of the demand for, say, U.S. foreign investment. Such flows, financed with home borrowings or internal sources, imply one range of immediate and eventual balance of payments effects, while utilization of foreign sources of funds implies a very different set of both immediate and eventual outcomes.[4]

An investment in a foreign country has a well-known effect on the balance of payments of the country of origin and the country of destination, respectively. The act of investment generates an initial tendency to surplus in the former and to deficit in the latter. In a world of incomplete adjustment this condition persists at least in part. However, the attitude of the policy makers in the two countries toward this condition, insofar as that attitude is derived solely from their concern with the viability of existing exchange rates, will depend entirely upon the manner in which the original investment is financed. A U.S. investment in France financed by borrowing from a local source results in no accumulation of foreign-held dollars, hence no immediate potential change in the foreign reserve position of either country. If the investment is financed in dollars, or any other currency except the franc, an accumulation does occur.

In the first case, French officials may act to contract some other component of national income in order to cancel the expansionary effect of the foreign investment on income and its balance of payments implications. They may even go so far as to create a surplus in order to finance the eventual dividend withdrawals while striving to maintain the present level of reserves. In the second case they will

---

[4] Within well-known models of a static trading world these ultimate balance of payment effects on both the capital-exporting and capital-importing countries can be made identical, i.e., nil. These models can be broadly divided into two categories — those emphasizing balance of payments changes originating in changes in money stock and the price level and those in which fluctuations in income are the driving force in balance of payments adjustment. However, we live in a multicountry nonstatic world characterized by friction in the adjustment process and in which complete transfer is not automatically completed.

not be forced to do so on these grounds, since their reserves will already have been swollen by the capital inflow. Policy makers in the United States will react with equanimity to the first situation, perhaps even moving to expand domestic income. In the second case, however, they may take steps to neutralize the effect on reserves of the capital outflow by raising interest rates in an effort to attract foreign capital, thereby retarding the rate of growth of domestic economic activity. Both measures should serve to improve the U.S. balance of payments.

To generalize, the policy makers in both countries concerned primarily with their balance of payments position rather than domestic employment, growth, or other objectives, react very differently according to how a foreign investment is financed. In a world of imperfect adjustment, any accumulation of currencies in foreign hands is a potential threat to the stability of fixed exchange rates. In the context of the contribution of foreign investment flows to such potential instability, it is not the currency of the country in which the demand for foreign investment originates whose exchange rate is threatened with depreciation. Rather it is the currency of the country from whose flow of savings and stock of money the investment is financed that is threatened. Thus to identify the currencies that will be threatened in the future by activity in their capital accounts, it is necessary to determine the sources of supply for foreign investment.

This conclusion must be qualified to take account of the actual and potential existence of portfolio demands for currencies other than the home currency. The presence of such demands mitigates the foregoing argument so that a balance of payments deficit cannot automatically be considered a threat to the exchange parity of the currency in question. Thus, for example, the U.S. monetary authorities closely watch the constellation of individual country balances of payments in order to determine in advance the identity of those who will be accumulating dollars, the most important trading and reserve currency. Some countries have sizable demands, private and/or public to hold dollars and/or strong commercial ties to the U.S. Such countries' accumulations do not represent functional claims on U.S. reserves, but other countries in balance of payments surplus do represent threats to the U.S. reserve position. By predict-ing the future pattern and amounts of such accumulations, U.S. authorities can take appropriate current policy actions, if necessary to limit our own deficits, the ultimate source of this threat. Of course, there is little that the authorities can do about the transfer of existing claims from one country to another through balance of payment balances between them.

Hedgers, speculators, and arbitragers are also vitally interested in the evolving constellation of international payments balances be-cause these will affect exchange rate movements, forward discounts, and interest rates, all of which are crucial variables that must be esti-mated in advance for these operations. Finally, portfolio and direct investors have an interest in this constellation since it is an impor-tant factor in assessing the exchange risk to which they are always subject and against which they cannot adequately hedge, given the currently available maturity schedule of forward contracts.

Factor Price Equalization

While much of the preceding discussion is heavily cast toward policy, there are at least two distinctly theoretical applications of knowledge of foreign investment supply. The first is within the body of international trade theory.

Under the premises of the Heckscher-Ohlin theorem, an unin-hibited flow of goods across international boundaries is shown to be a perfect substitute for the flow of factors in bringing about an international equalization of factor prices, at least in the two good–two factor–two country model. However, if relative country endow-ments differ sufficiently it is possible that equalization of rewards will not occur without factor migration. This theoretical possibility, in combination with the empirical fact of labor migration, has given rise to much testing of the motivation behind this observed interna-tional mobility of labor, particularly among European countries where goods have been allowed to flow relatively freely, and where one would expect transportation costs to play less of a role than the one that they inevitably must play in other trading relationships.

It is interesting to speculate about the increasing volume of in-ternational capital movements including those for direct investment that have been a feature of the world economy since the return of currency convertibility and before the institution of U.S. controls as well as the restoration of tighter control over capital movements in other countries. Assuming that intra-European labor migration is economically motivated and, even, for the sake of argument, positing that it has been the movement of this factor which has been the important element in adjusting country endowment ratios with the resulting tendency toward factor price equalization, one cannot automatically extend these findings to the whole trading world. In particular, intercontinental labor migration for purely economic motives would not seem to be such an important phenomenon during the recent past as the large international flows of capital would seem to be.[5] The existence of the Euro-bond market then suggests itself as a vehicle by which capital flows are an important, perhaps dominant, factor price equilibrating mechanism, especially for, but not restricted to, a condition of intercontinental endowment disparities. In summary, though it is far beyond our topical limits to design, much less execute, a test of the following, we can at least suggest that flows through the Euro-bond market may be a principal mechanism by which country endowment ratios change, bringing about the subsequent tendency toward equality in factor rewards for similar employment in both countries. The policy implication of this is, of course, that the same world-welfare argument against restriction of free labor migration applies also to controls on capital outflows and on access to local credit markets for foreigners making a local investment.

---

[5] The Heckscher-Ohlin model, in its modern form, needs only generalized factors. Calling these "land" (or "capital") and "labor" is a heuristic device, not a logical necessity. Thus, our substitution of finance capital for the real capital used in many expositions is not a logical contradiction of the basic model. Of course, depending upon circumstances, real capital imports may follow immediately. Again these remarks make no attempt to minimize the difficulties of a strict analysis of our suggestion. However, there is no immediate reason that we can see which would make these difficulties any worse than some of those encountered in a strict test of the theory based on observation of labor migration, e.g., the well-known difficulties involving human capital.

Private and Public Efficiencies

This last point raises the question of the financing strategy for foreign subsidiaries of U.S. firms. During the early part of this decade subsidiaries minimized finance costs by borrowing in the United States. Because of the efficiency of U.S. public policies in keeping prices stable and interest rates low relative to, say, European experience, this financing strategy led to use of low-cost sources of funds. This combination of private and public efficiencies contributed to worrisome balance of payments flows on capital account and eventually prompted increasingly severe government measures to stem these flows. The combination of official controls and public policy inefficiencies in the United States according to the same criteria by which American policy was previously quite successful, made efficient managements resort to international sources of finance for new and existing subsidiaries. Since the direct capital controls have always been regarded as temporary in any case, the current financing behavior of foreign investors and the existence of high U.S. interest rates raises the question of whether the controls are now no longer necessary. This argument is answerable on the grounds that when the current determined official effort to remove inflationary forces brings success, long-term interest rates in the United States will again fall to levels where direct investors will once more use domestic financial sources, implying the concomitant balance of payments difficulties that were experienced earlier.

Such an argument raises an interesting, more general question. Does efficient private resource allocation conflict with efficient public policy in the international sector? Other things the same, e.g., lack of equal European investor interest in placing their own capital in American assets and continued "efficiency" of American credit and capital markets relative to their European counterparts, it would seem that short-term private profit maximization may conflict with efficient public policy. As it is difficult to resolve the conflict by arguing for either inflation and/or high domestic-interest rates, perhaps short-run managerial goals of minimizing finance costs have within them the seeds of destruction of the long-run profitability of the subsidiary, including its possible expansion. In particular, in view of the precedent set by the direct controls, implying society's preference for discriminating against U.S. asset holders rather than current consumers when someone's interest must be sacrificed, perhaps managers should plan to continue employing international sources for all or a portion of their foreign investment, even after the removal of controls. The differential costs of so doing can be rationalized as insurance against diminution in the value of shareholders equity, either by market discounting of such shares because of the risk of capital controls and its possible effects on earnings, or by the market's expectation that future establishment of such subsidiaries will be difficult, which may affect, in turn, the growth potential of the parent's earnings stream.

In the preceding section we pointed out a few conspicuous gaps in the ability of public and private policy makers to plan future actions in such diverse areas as development planning, discretionary balance of payments adjustment policy, the future of captive capital markets in industrialized countries, private international cash management, speculation, and subsidiary financing. A rather theoretical issue concerning the leading foreign trade model was also shown to depend for its resolution upon the common lack of knowledge of international credit phenomena linking the preceding, otherwise quite unrelated problems, i.e., the unavailability of an accepted logical structure relating the sources of supply of foreign investment to the demand for it. Given this relatively undeveloped field, the comments that follow are not given as the final word, but rather as some tentative conclusions about U.S. experience in financing foreign direct investment since the advent of widespread currency convertibility after World War II.

Instruments, Intermediaries, Lenders

In looking at the manner in which U.S. direct investment has been financed during the decade of the sixties, we divide our general question into three more specific ones. What debt or equity instruments were offered to attract finance? Who were the intermediate sources? Who were the ultimate lenders?

Some of the data available to the authors concerning the first of these questions are presented in Table 1. A Euro-bond is defined as

Table 1. International Bond Market: Instruments of Finance U.S. Companies (millions of dollars).

	1965	1966	Year 1967	1968	1969*
Total	368	478	610	2,235	655
By Security					
Convertible	110	167	227	1,642	414
Straight debt	258	311	383	593	241
By Currency					
U.S. $	236	398	522	1,915	547
DM	80	56	40	226	67
Others	52	24	48	94	41
By Markets					
Euro-bonds	358	454	562	2,046	551
Foreign bonds	10	24	48	189	104

* First six months.
Source: Morgan Guaranty Trust Company, *World Financial Markets* (July 17, 1969).

one underwritten by an international syndicate and sold in countries other than the currency in which the issue is denominated. A foreign bond issue is underwritten by a national syndicate and sold principally in the country of the syndicate and denominated in the currency of that country. An international bond issue is sold outside the country of the borrower, i.e., is the set of which the other two types of issue are subsets.

Before proceeding, we must be clear about our intentions regarding the use of these data and the degree of their suitability for our purposes. In the first place, research in the area of foreign investment finance currently works under a severe data-availability constraint. The reason for beginning with the international bond market rather than with the domestic U.S. capital markets is that it is easier to isolate the results of U.S. corporate financing activity. Not only is financing of direct foreign investment not restricted to the international capital market, but not all financing through the international capital market is for foreign investment. That is to say, even when finance is secured specifically through the Euro-bond market, it does not necessarily follow that funds so raised will be employed in foreign investment. We have not been able to find a direct estimate of the amount of Euro-bond financing for direct investment pur-

Table 2.   Foreign Plant and Equipment Expenditures of Investments by Major U.S. Industries (billions of dollars).

	1960	1961	1962	1963	1964	1695	1966	1967	1968*
Total excluding Canada	2.5	3.1	3.6	3.8	4.6	5.6	6.3	7.0	7.6
Less net capital outflow for direct foreign investment (excluding Canada)	1.2	1.3	1.3	1.6	2.0	2.5	2.5	2.6	n.a.
	1.3	1.8	2.3	2.2	2.6	3.1	3.8	4.4	
Less undistributed subsidiary earnings	—	—	0.3	0.2	—	1.5	—	—	
Other sources including institutional borrowing, international capital market and trade credit			2.0	2.0		1.6			

* Preliminary figure.
Source: *Survey of Current Business* (Washington, D.C.: U.S. Department of Commerce, various issues).

poses, so we have constructed a crude table (see Table 2) showing that net capital outflows from the U.S., plus undistributed earnings, cannot by themselves "explain" the total financing of the U.S. direct investment that took place. This does not mean that the entire residual was secured through the international bond market, since institutional borrowing and trade credit are still unaccounted for, but we are assuming some did. In particular, after 1965, when U.S. interest rates began to rise and capital export became more difficult because of rising home demand as well as because of controls, we assume that the Euro-bond market was increasingly resorted to for direct investment finance. In any case, there is a presumption that all Euro-bond activity by U.S. firms is not in behalf of home use. The presumption is reinforced by indirect evidence consisting of various passages from the annual *Survey of Current Business* year-end summaries by Pizer and Cutler of U.S. foreign investment activities.[6]

[6] For example, in the survey for 1965–1966 (*Survey of Current Business,* Vol. 46, No. 9 (Washington, D.C.: U.S. Department of Commerce, September 1966)), on p. 36 they say: "Capital outflows from the United States for direct investments rose sharply from $2.4 billion in 1964 to $3.4 billion in 1965, and earnings retained abroad increased $0.1 billion. These sources of funds are an important part of the financing of the plant and equipment expenditures abroad described in the preceding section . . . the share of

Obviously, U.S. direct investors are not the only competitors for funds in international capital markets. Table 3 quickly makes this apparent. Thus, the sources of finance shown in all our data are not uniquely the results of U.S. foreign investors' efforts to secure funds. Since an instrument is a contract between borrower and lender, by examining its characteristics we are actually investigating the terms of that contract, which is one possible method of determining the motivation of the two parties that brought about the transaction in the first place. As all real investors in the Euro-bond market, U.S. and non-American alike, are tapping a common source of funds, at least on the present level of aggregation, then all will be competing to satisfy a common list of wealth-holder asset preferences.

We now propose to examine U.S. companies' borrowing in the international bond market in more detail. Table 3 shows that, after a steady growth in U.S. companies' Euro-bond financing during the period 1965 to 1967, with an increasing share being dollar-denominated convertibles, in 1968 there occurred a sevenfold jump in sales of convertibles accompanied by a sixfold increase in Deutsche mark issues with a fourfold change in dollar denominations.

Table 4, which shows the international bond market as a whole, enables us to derive some further suggestive associations. The share of U.S. companies is lowest in the years when U.S. interest rates are lowest (1965, 1967), and highest when those rates are highest (1966, 1968), suggesting an international horizon in their finance planning.[7]

However, the data on currency of denomination are a more complicated matter. During the period 1965 to 1967 the dollar gains in share against all currencies, principally against a declining share of

---

capital flows and undistributed profits in financing such expenditures has been well over 50 per cent in manufacturing and close to 50 per cent in the petroleum industry." Thus if the bench mark figure for the proportion of total finance accounted for by capital outflows and retained earnings is to be 50%, a large balance is left. The source of finance for this balance must be the international capital market and foreign financial institutions.

[7] Of course, this suggestion is weakened by the existence of the mandatory controls for all of 1968. The existence of the Interest Equalization Tax makes the data on the other participants useless for comparison purposes in the matter of "horizon." Also, international institutions have many reasons other than yield for selecting sources of finance.

Table 3.   Euro-Bond and Foreign Bond Issues Outside the United States (in millions of dollars).

	1965	1966	1967	1968	Jan.–June 1969
Euro-Bonds: Total	*1,040*	*1,186*	*2,002*	*3,517*	*1,682*
By Category of Borrower					
U.S. companies	358	435	562	2,046	552
Other companies	429	514	1,017	946	776
Governments	189	118	303	500	354
International organizations	64	101	120	25	—
By Currency of Denomination					
U.S. dollar	726	921	1,790	2,547	932
German mark	202	122	161	864	694
Other*	112	143	51	106	56
By Type of Security					
Long-term straight debt	870	738	1,427	1,105	877
Medium-term straight debt	60	251	260	430	121
Certificates of deposit	—	—	55	75	—
Convertible bonds	110	197	260	1,907	684
Foreign Bonds: Total	*379*	*344*	*404*	*1,185*	*514*
By Category of Borrower					
U.S. companies	10	10	48	189	104
Other companies	148	78	80	69	96
Governments	65	56	143	311	71
International organizations	156	200	133	616	243
By Currency of Denomination					
Belgian franc	12	10	21	30	6
French franc	25	41	41	—	—
German mark	123	—	10	724	379
Italian lira	24	139	24	72	24
Dutch guilder	29	—	14	30	—
Swedish kroner	—	—	20	10	—
Swiss franc	78	80	153	238	105
British pound	65	56	102	19	—
Other	23	18	19	62	—
By Type of Security					
Long-term straight debt	368	343	378	956	394
Medium-term straight debt	1	1	26	229	120
Convertible bonds	10	—	—	—	—
International Bonds: Total	*1,419*	*1,530*	*2,406*	*4,702*	*2,196*

* European Unit-of-Account and £/DM option issues are included.
Source: Morgan Guaranty Trust Company, *World Financial Markets* (July 17, 1969).

the DM (Table 3). As the dollar amounts grow by a factor of 2.5, the volume of DM denominations falls in 1967 to 50% of its 1965 amount. Thus, despite the continuing U.S. balance of payments deficits and German surpluses, despite a devaluation of sterling and

Table 4. International Bond Issues by Country of Borrower (in millions of dollars).

	1965	1966	1967	1968*
Denmark	35	48	72	106
Finland	11	1	47	86
Iceland	—	—	—	5
Norway	120	20	95	31
Sweden	86	34	30	11
Belgium	40	40	63	—
France	42	35	157	137
Germany	28	94	69	—
Italy	79	60	65	75
Luxembourg	—	47	10	—
Netherlands	58	39	101	180
Austria	21	37	85	88
Switzerland	15	—	18	13
Spain	—	—	65	—
Portugal	—	29	34	15
Ireland	3	34	—	—
United Kingdom	48	57	94	146
Canada	—	—	—	245
Japan	35	—	—	194
Australia	50	25	100	89
New Zealand	48	59	82	34
South Africa	12	25	63	85
Argentina	—	—	25	50
Colombia	—	—	7	—
Peru	—	6	12	—
Mexico	14	20	85	141
Venezuela	—	—	—	25
Jamaica	9	8	—	7
Other Caribbean	15	—	—	7
Iran	—	—	—	20
Israel	—	—	15	—
Malaysia	—	—	21	6
U.S. Companies	386	478	610	2,235
Multinational Companies†	—	47	110	33
International Institutions	197	283	234	622
Total	*1,355*	*1,479*	*2,369*	*4,673*

* Preliminary.

† Includes such companies as Société Européenne pour la Financement de Matériel Ferroviaire — EUROFIMA, Transalpine Finance Holdings S.A., and B.E.C. Finance N.V.

Source: Morgan Guaranty Trust Company, *World Financial Markets* (July 17, 1969).

135

continued speculative pressure accompanied by widespread mention in the press of the world of the potential for such speculation spreading to the dollar, wealth holders with international horizons still demonstrated a preference for dollar-denominated long-term assets, by the "share" measure as well as the tougher test of absolute amounts, throughout the period 1965 to 1967.

In 1968 there was an abrupt change in three of the above trends in dollar-DM relations. Together, the two currencies increased their dominance over all others as measured by their combined share of the total. But, while dollar volume grew to 144% of its 1967 amount, the DM figure for 1968 was more than 500% of its 1967 value, causing the DM share to jump to one-fourth of the total, while that of the dollar fell. A possible explanation of this phenomenon is that foreign wealth holders anticipated a future scarcity of dollars during the 1965 to 1967 period and/or desired entry into the U.S. capital market. In 1968 these motives suffered a relative decline as the DM strengthened on the exchanges and revaluation was widely rumored in the press, even becoming front page news during the crisis of the French franc in November.[8]

This tentative explanation suggests, in turn, a further, more general observation related to our ultimate aim of discovering the determinants of supply for U.S. direct investment. From the preceding it would seem that the currency of denomination appears more related to the preferences of suppliers of funds rather than to the ultimate use by borrowers of funds acquired by sale of these assets. There is no necessary reason why the currency of denomination should be the same as that with which the asset is purchased. This fact makes the hypothesis less surprising and affords added confidence in the procedure of attempting to obtain supplier preferences from analysis of "ex post" data.

Table 5 shows the enormous growth in the volume of convertibles issued by all parties. It also shows that in 1968, as in 1967, the

---

[8] These preferences are also reflected in yield data as well as volume figures. The interest differential between the higher dollar denominations and the lower DM bonds widened markedly in 1968 and 1967. Issuers were then more willing to accommodate lenders in the matter of currency denomination.

136

Table 5. Euro-Bond Issues (in millions of dollars).

	1968	1967
Total Convertibles Issued	1,907	260
Convertibles Issued by U.S. Firms	1,642	227
Use of Dollars by all Borrowers	2,547	1,790
Use of Dollars by U.S. Firms	1,915	522
Straight Debt Issues by U.S. Firms	593	383
Straight Debt Issues by Non-U.S. Firms	942	1,304
Use of DM Issues by U.S. Firms	226	40
Use of DM Issues by Others	638	121

overwhelming majority was issued by U.S. firms. The data suggest that convertibles issued by U.S. firms were probably denominated entirely in dollars, though we can not establish this definitively.

Likewise, there is a perceptible movement into DM-denominated securities in the market for straight debt, at least in the segment accounted for by non-American borrowers, although other currencies were also employed there. In this case the figure for straight debt issued by non-American borrowers, $942 million, exceeds the total amount of DM's employed by these borrowers for any purpose, $638 million. Furthermore, although the level of utilization of straight debt by non-Americans actually declined in 1968 from the previous year volume of $1304 million, the level of utilization of DM rose in absolute amount from the previous year figure of $121 million. Therefore, in a smaller issue market there was a large shift into DM's, indicating the intensity of the substitution was even greater than the increased resort to dollars in the expanding segment of the market, i.e., that accounted for by U.S. borrowers.

Thus, the growth in convertibles is a result of the increased resort of U.S. companies to the Euro-bond market, where they denominated their issues in dollars. The increased use of DM's is a result of other participants' choice of DM denomination for a reduced volume of straight debt issues from 1967. Thus, to minimize costs U.S. borrowers capitalized on a "bull' stock market while other borrowers, not having this advantage, denominated issues in DM's which had become a strong bull currency in the markets for foreign exchange.

The implication that foreign wealth holders see assets of nations with bull capital markets, but weak currencies, as substitutes for assets of nations with bull currencies, but relatively bearish capital markets, has a more general and far more important corollary for their behavior and, in turn, for the impact of the latter upon balance of payments theory and policy. It is quite possible that the existence of the Euro-bond market has had the effect of enlarging, perhaps permanently, the opportunity set of foreign wealth holders such that they have simultaneously discovered the desirability and feasibility of hedging long-term assets against perceived exchange risk. The prospective yield and capital gain, instead of being looked upon as a net income, are seen as the compensating virtue for the exchange risk involved in choosing dollars instead of, say, DM's. The commercial possibilities of the asset are the hedge against the exchange risks of both the dollar and the home currency of the wealth holder.

The social implication of this private behavior is obvious; a strong capital market outlook can provide capital inflow for a country with a currency of uncertain future international value, thereby improving the outlook for the latter. Furthermore, if the foreign hedger of long-term domestic (to him) assets has made his assessment of the capital market for the same time horizon as the maturity of the foreign (to him) asset in which he has placed his confidence, then fluctuations in that market from restrictive public policy undertaken for business-cycle reasons will not necessarily mitigate the balance of payments implication we have drawn.

Conclusion

We began this discussion with an attempt to generate interest in research upon the question of the determinants of the supply of finance for direct foreign investment. We suggested that the topic was pregnant both with theoretical issues and with important policy implications. In order to provide an empirical context for our discussion, we attempted to bring into focus a new source of finance for American direct foreign investment, the Euro-bond market. Care was taken to distinguish this market from domestic capital markets open to foreign borrowers, and also from the foreign bond market. We pointed to the indications in our data that a growing number of wealth holders throughout the world, for that is the field over which underwriters in the Euro-bond market spread their fund-raising activities, were actually behaving in a manner that economic theory would sanction. That is to say, long-term asset holders have found a way, or have been provided with an opportunity, to hedge their assets against perceived exchange risk, something not attainable through present forward exchange contracting arrangements. Also, there is more than one way to do this, and wealth holders seemed to be acting as if they perceived the correct parity relationship between these two methods. Finally, this desire to hedge and the parity relation involved were sufficient to explain why wealth holders might prefer foreign to domestic assets, and which currency they will choose, without further modification of portfolio theory. Of course, these investor preferences indicate why issuers choose one market over another and one currency of denomination rather than another. We were, however, compelled to leave aside the very interesting and important question of why investors choose to purchase their foreign assets in the Euro-bond market rather than through the other two alternatives for obtaining the same currency. This last question warrants substantial investigation by itself.

CHAPTER SIX

TECHNOLOGY, UNITED STATES INVESTMENT, AND EUROPEAN ECONOMIC GROWTH

John H. Dunning

Introduction

The subject of this paper is technology and economic development, with particular reference to the contribution made by U.S. direct investment to European economic development since 1950. For the purposes of most of our argument, we shall think of economic development in terms of the growth rate of real national output per person employed (Denison 1967), and shall pay only passing attention to its composition or its distribution between factors inputs.

A. Association between U.S. Investment and Growth in European Output per Head. We first start with one or two fairly well-known observations. First, a casual inspection of Table 1 reveals a generally close association between U.S. direct investment (i.e., the increase in U.S. direct capital stake) and European development between 1950 and 1965.[1] Roughly the same picture emerges for later years and from other cross-sectional studies. In particular, U.S. manufacturing investment in Europe has been directed to those countries that have increased their manufacturing output the

[1] Switzerland is an exceptional case. Most U.S. (and other foreign) investment there is of a "window dressing" character and much of it is immediately reexported to other countries, particularly Italy (EFTA, 1969).

Table 1.   United States Direct Investment in Europe and European Economic Development, 1960 to 1965.

	Increase in U.S. Direct Capital Stake			Increase in Gross National Product per Capita		
	1950/58 1950 = 100	1958/65 1958 = 100	1950/65 1950 = 100	1950/58 1950 = 100	1958/65 1958 = 100	1950/65 1950 = 100
Europe (total)	275.2	320.6	882.3	132	131	173
EEC	303.0	351.1	1064.0	144	134	193
Belgium and Luxemburg	400.0	298.0	1192.0	117*	132	154
France	251.2	318.6	800.5	133	130	173
W. Germany	330.2	389.6	1286.3	165	135	223
Italy	532.0	369.2	1964.0	147	138	203
Netherlands	280.3	344.7	966.3	127	133	169
EFTA	258.6	299.1	773.5	120	127	152
United Kingdom	261.5	248.6	650.0	116	123	143
Denmark	148.4	434.8	645.2	116	138	160
Norway	226.1	292.3	660.9	118	135	159
Sweden	196.4	291.7	572.8	120	134	161
Switzerland	316.7	1473.6	4667.2	122†	128	156

* Estimated on basis of 1953/8 data.
† Estimated on basis of 1954/8 data.
Source: U.S. *Survey of Current Business* (Washington, D.C.: U.S. Department of Commerce, September 1966), and *U.S. Business Investments in Foreign Countries* (Washington, D.C.: U.S. Department of Commerce, 1960). OECD *Statistics of National Accounts* (Paris: OECD, 1950/61; 1956/65).

most rapidly, while Krause (1968) has shown that such investment in the EEC has also been largely concentrated in the faster growing manufacturing sectors.

Such data as these, of course, may imply no causal relationship. Both U.S. investment and economic development in individual European countries (or industries) may be the result of other factors. One might have hoped that a time-series approach — particularly with the introduction of time lags — might help settle this issue, but in this case (as Bandera and White (1968) have shown) it does not. The level and distribution of U.S. investment appear to both influence, and be influenced by, European growth. One difficulty, of course, is that investment (and particularly the net capital outflow component of it) is discontinuous, while its effects are spread over many years. When first differences, i.e., the rate of change of investment, are related to growth variables, the results are inconclusive (Bandera and White 1968). Our impression is that one can waste a lot of time trying to manipulate and refine the few macrostatistics that are available. As they are, they are broadly suggestive, but insufficiently detailed or reliable to help us test any but the very simplest of propositions.

On the other hand, it is not difficult to formulate theories of *why* U.S. direct investment has been attracted to certain countries and industries in Europe and of how this might have affected their development. There would seem little doubt that in the early 1950s American firms were prompted to begin, or expand, manufacturing and petroleum refining operations in Europe, partly by the prospects of growth (both absolute and relative to that in the United States) and the profits likely to be associated with such growth (Mikesell 1967); and that, after 1958, this was accentuated by forces making for *more* growth, e.g., the impact of the EEC. This holds good for both aggressive and defensive investment, and is most clearly seen in the shift of American interest away from the United Kingdom to the EEC at a time when the supply conditions for U.S. investment were most favorable.[2] Between 1957 and 1966,

[2] It will be noted, however, that even in the United Kingdom the increase of plant and equipment expenditure by U.S. firms has continued to outpace that of their U.K. competitors.

for example, plant and equipment expenditure by U.S. firms in the EEC rose by 8 times while in the United Kingdom it increased by only 2½ times.

In the last two or three years, the pace of new U.S. investment in Europe has slowed down a bit, partly due to the resurgence of the U.S. economy, partly to the curbs placed on outward U.S. investment, and partly to the decline in the profitability of capital in European economies, both absolutely and relatively to the United States. There is, indeed, evidence that in various directions the European economy is catching up with the U.S. economy. This, coupled with the cyclical boom in the United States, explains why, relative to domestic investment, the rate of U.S. investment in Europe is now about three-quarters of that of the early 1960s.

B. *The Growth Contribution of Inward Investment. Some Macroeconomic Considerations.* Part of the difficulty in calculating the impact of U.S. direct investment, on either overall European economic development or that of individual economies, is that, in relation to domestic capital formation it is still quite small and there are so many other determinants of growth. Table 2 shows that the proportion of gross domestic fixed capital formation in various EEC countries and the United Kingdom accounted for by the expenditure of U.S. subsidiaries on plant and equipment ranged, in 1965, from 4.0% in France to 10.0% in the United Kingdom. If one could assume that this capital (and any local expenditure generated by it) represented a net addition to resource formation in the host countries, then the value of sales of U.S. firms (less imports and remitted profits), might be said to represent their direct contribution to the growth of European output. The second part of Table 2 expresses the sales of U.S. manufacturing subsidiaries in selected European countries in relation to the gross national product of these countries in 1957 and 1965 and the increase in sales to the increase in gross national product between these years. These calculations however, ignore the technological multiplier effect of U.S. investment on the output of competitors, suppliers, customers, and so on (Quinn 1968).

If the alternative assumption of full employment in the host countries is made, then U.S. investment must replace either other

144

Table 2. Relative Significance of Plant and Equipment Expenditure and Sales of U.S. Firms in Selected European Countries, 1957/1965.

	Plant and Equipment Expenditure by U.S. Subsidiaries as % of all Gross Domestic Fixed Capital Formation*					Manufacturing Sales of U.S. Subsidiaries as % of GNP			Δ in sales/Δ in GNP, 1957 to 1965
	1957	1959	1961	1963	1965	1957	1963	1965	
Belgium	2.2	2.6	3.3	3.8	4.5	†	†	†	†
France	1.8	1.9	2.1	3.0	4.0	1.4	2.5	2.8	4.7
W. Germany	1.8	2.9	4.2	3.9	4.1	2.2	3.3	3.9	5.3
Italy	2.0	1.3	2.9	4.1	5.0	0.9	1.8	2.2	3.4
Netherlands	2.6	1.2	3.2	5.4	4.8	2.3	3.4	4.4	6.5
EEC	2.2	2.6	3.3	3.8	4.5	1.7	2.8	3.5	4.6
United Kingdom	7.8	5.7	7.4	7.9	10.0	5.9	6.9	7.5	9.7

* In machinery and equipment.
† Included in Netherlands.
Sources: United Nations. Economic Commission for Europe, *Economic Bulletin for Europe*, Vol. 19, No. 1 (November 1967), p. 67. U.S. *Survey of Current Business* (Washington, D.C.: U.S. Department of Commerce, November 1966), p. 8, and OECD *Main Economic Indicators*, various issues.

domestic expenditure or imports (unless capital imports rise by the same amount). If it replaces other investment, then its net effect on economic development is the difference between the level of output actually produced and that which would have otherwise been produced by domestic firms. If it replaces consumption, then, because the savings ratio has been raised, the long-term benefits will be equal to the investment/net output ratio.

What, too, of the effect of inward investment on the balance of payments, terms of trade and prices of goods and services? In the main, our analysis will omit consideration of these and the impact any changes in their value are likely to have on resource allocation, utilization, and growth. However, depending on the assumption one makes about government policy, e.g., whether a country operates a flexible exchange or fixed exchange rate, it is possible that the indirect impact of U.S. investment on European development could be more important than the direct impact (Powie 1969). But I fear that if we went much further along these lines we would soon stray from our brief, which is less to evaluate the overall contribution of U.S. investment to Europe's economy, and more the extent to which it has advanced growth and development, through supplying additional factor inputs and knowledge. And here macrodata are not very helpful. We have, instead, to turn to data on individual sectors of the economy and/or on the components of growth and development.

In his book *Why Growth Rates Differ,* Edward Denison sets out the main determinants of European growth between 1950 and 1964. How far has the participation of U.S. affiliates contributed to this growth? Basically there are three ways in which such a contribution might have been made. First, U.S. firms might have used (or have caused to be used) resources that would otherwise have remained unemployed. Second, they might have brought about (directly or indirectly) an improvement in resource allocation, by redirecting resources from slow-growing to fast-growing industries. Third, by the injection of new technology and more progressive managerial attitudes, they might have helped raise the efficiency of production in whatever sectors they invest, and/or speeded their rate of growth. The first two of these effects essentially arise from

146

the (money) "capital" component of U.S. investment and the efficiency with which U.S. enterprises choose their European outlets; the third arises from the "knowledge" component — though, in practice, the two effects cannot easily be separated.

One way in which some idea might be obtained of the relative significance of the second aspect of growth is by use of shift and share analysis (Thirlwall 1967; Dunning 1969a). Let us illustrate from the data in Table 3. Between 1957 and 1964, the total manufacturing sales[3] of U.S. subsidiaries in Europe rose by 160.2% compared with an increase of 45.3% for all European firms.

To calculate what part of this differential growth is due to differences in the structure, or industrial mix, of U.S. investment and what part to the faster rate of growth of U.S. affiliates within particular industries, one can first estimate what the average rate of growth would have been in U.S. affiliates had their rate of growth in each group of products been that of European firms. This works out at 51.7% (Σ column 1/Σ column 4). The difference between this and their actual rate of growth (108.5%) measures the differential sector growth component, and that between the adjusted rate of growth and the actual rate of growth of European firms (7.6%) the structural or composition shift effect. In the present example, it can be seen that almost all of the faster growth of the output of U.S. firms is explained by the former effect. What part of this, in turn, reflects differences in the efficiency of U.S. affiliates and European firms cannot be adduced without further data on the inputs of the two groups of firms.

C. The "Knowledge" Capital Ingredient of Direct Investment.

It is now, I think, generally accepted that the main distinction between portfolio and direct foreign investment is that the latter incorporates knowledge and entrepreneurship, which the former does not — and which, moreover, is unlikely to be possessed by local competitors. This may take various forms, as outlined by Kindleberger (1969), and includes not only technical expertise but attitudinal advantages as well. These — through what Quinn (1968) and others have called the "technological" multiplier —

---

[3] Of those considered in the table.

147

Table 3. Sales of U.S. Affiliates in Europe and all European Firms.

	All European firms			U.S. affiliates			
	(1)	(2)	(3) 1957/64	(4)	(5)	(6) 1957/64	(7) Col.4 ×
	1957	1964	1957 = 100	1957	1964	1957 = 100	Col. 3
Food Products	34,183	44,796	131.1	734	1,308	178.2	962
Paper and Allied Products	7,188	10,846	150.9	34	148	435.2	51
Chemicals	18,310	34,039	185.9	822	2,273	276.5	1,533
Rubber Products	2,451	3,697	150.8	262	517	197.3	395
Nonelectrical Machinery	19,420	26,807	138.0	1,009	2,735	271.1	1,392
Electrical Machinery	10,802	16,958	157.0	678	1,968	290.2	1,064
Metal Products	32,868	42,634	129.7	435	1,115	256.3	564
Transportation Equipment	20,506	31,956	155.8	1,700	4,700	276.5	2,649
Total	145,728	211,733	145.3	5,674	14,764	260.2	8,610

Source: All European firms: G. C. Hufbauer and F. M. Adler, *Overseas Manufacturing Investment and the Balance of Payments*, Tax Policy Research Study No. 1 (Washington, D.C.: U.S. Treasury Department, 1968). United States firms: *Survey of Current Business* (Washington, D.C.: U.S. Department of Commerce, November 1966), and *U.S. Business Investments in Foreign Countries* (Washington, D.C.: U.S. Department of Commerce, 1960).

affect the productivity and growth of particular sectors in the host country, as both new markets are opened up and production processes improve.[4] When a firm in a technically progressive industry in an advanced industrial country invests in a less-advanced industrial country, but one that is gradually assimilating the economic structure of the advanced country, it follows not only that the knowledge content of the investment is likely to be significant, but that it will be directed to growth sectors. This explains why many U.S. firms have been able to gain a foothold in the newer European industries — simply because they were first in the field in America. Once established, by a judicious reinvestment policy, they are able to grow rapidly.

The product-cycle thesis of Vernon (1967) and Hirsch (1967), tested by Wilkinson (1968), Wells (1969), and others, is now familiar to most economists. This suggests very strongly that certain types of international investment are inherently growth oriented, not only because they are directed to industries supplying products, the demand for which increases proportionately to the growth in GNP per head (Wells 1968), but because of the various advantages, e.g., access to knowledge and markets, size, integration, and finance, possessed by the investing companies over their host competitors. Even the most cursory glance at the structure of U.S. firms in Europe reveals that their activities are heavily concentrated in two sectors: first the science-based, or research-intensive, industries supplying both producer and consumer goods, and second, industries subject to economies of scale and producing products with a high income elasticity of demand. Between 1958 and 1964, for example, the four most research-intensive industries in the United States spent 2½ times the amount on new plant and equipment in Europe than 14 other industries (Gruber, Mehta, and Vernon 1967). Moreover, these same "knowledge" industries (e.g. computer, instruments, electronics, chemicals, etc.), by providing a kind of infrastructure of knowledge, create substantial spillover

---

[4] Edwin Mansfield (1968) cites the electronic computer as an example of an investment with an exceptionally high technological multiplier and illustrates some of the ways it has affected the production function of various firms and industries.

effects, and act as a catalyst for growth which may far outweigh the initial demand-stimulating effects.[5]

The Determinants of Economic Growth in Europe

Having briefly described the character of U.S. investment in Europe, I now want to examine the sources of economic development to see how far the ingredients of one are common to the other. Several economists, notably Beckerman (1965), Denison (1967), Lamfalussy (1963), and Maddison (1964), have tried to pinpoint the reasons for differential growth rates in Western Europe in the last two decades or so. Their explanations differ according to the emphasis they place on supply- and demand-oriented factors — and also to the techniques used. Our purpose in using these theories in this paper is simply to identify the main components of growth which one might reasonably expect to be affected by the international transfer of capital and knowledge.

We shall concentrate mostly on Denison's results because his classification of the sources of growth is more appropriate to our interests than that of the other writers. His approach is based on an accounting scheme that estimates total factor inputs by weighting the individual factor inputs by their respective prices. Similarly, growth in total factor inputs is derived by weighting the individual factor inputs by their respective shares of all inputs. An increase in aggregate output resulting from increased input is then separated from growth resulting from increased output per unit of input (i.e., total factor productivity). Changes in total factor productivity are, in turn, explained by (1) intersectoral resource shifts,[6] (2) economies of scale, and (3) a residual, advances in knowledge.

---

[5] This technological multiplier of an investment is achieved by *inter alia* — (1) increasing the productivity of the sectors in which it is employed; (2) lowering the factor costs of those who use the output of that sector and releasing their resources for other purposes; (3) stimulating responsive innovations in customers, suppliers, or competition, (4) encouraging research and development to derive the maximum benefit from the new innovations (Quinn, 1968, p. 11).

[6] The following four paragraphs lean heavily on an approach adopted by Scarfe (1969).

A summary of Denison's findings is given in Table 4, from which it is clear that increases in total factor productivity were the main component of economic growth in the period 1950 to 1962; cf. (line 3/line 1). Some of the items in this table require explanation since they have a special relation to inward technology. First, however, it should be observed that the table refers to relative growth rates in national income *per person employed*. This explains the small contribution of labor inputs and the corresponding large contribution of capital inputs to that part of growth which is explained by increased factor inputs.

According to Denison, most of the contribution of improved resource allocation (3d) to productivity growth arises from a shift of resources from agriculture to secondary industry. In this connection, it is worth observing that four-fifths of U.S. direct investment in Europe since 1950 has been concentrated in manufacturing and petroleum refining, and that its growth has been particularly marked in countries that have recorded the largest gains in intersectoral productivity. Moreover, *within* manufacturing industry, investment has been directed to above-average growth sectors. (Krause 1968). In the United Kingdom, for example, nearly 80% of U.S. investment is concentrated in industries — the output per unit of input has risen *above the average* in the last ten years (Dunning 1969a).

Next, Denison considers the contribution of knowledge to increased output per unit of input under two headings, viz., advances in knowledge (3a) and changes in the lag in the application of knowledge (3e). The first of these is simply his estimate of the same component's contribution to U.S. growth during these years; the second is his evaluation of the extent to which advances in knowledge in Europe are greater or less than this rate — the implication being that if they are greater, the technological gap is being narrowed; if they are less, e.g., as in the case of Denmark, it is being widened. Clearly one would expect this source of economic growth in Western Europe to be particularly closely associated with technology importation from the United States. It will be observed, however, that it has been very uneven in its impact among the Western European countries, contributing most to productivity in

Table 4. Sources of Growth of Total National Income per Person Employed, 1950 to 1962.*

	U.S.	Germany	U.K.	France	Italy	Netherlands	Belgium	Denmark	Norway
1. Growth Rate (2 + 3)†	2.15	5.15(2)	1.63(8)	4.80(3)	5.36(1)	3.65(4)	2.64(6)	2.56(7)	3.27(5)
2. Total Factor Input	0.79	0.72	0.45	1.13	1.07	0.86	0.62	0.62	0.86
(a) Labor	0.22	−0.12	0.10	0.37	0.54	0.09	0.36	−0.11	0.02
(b) Capital	0.60	0.93	0.37	0.76	0.57	0.78	0.28	0.77	0.85
(c) Land	−0.03	−0.09	−0.02	0.00	−0.04	−0.01	−0.02	−0.04	−0.01
3. Output per Unit of Input	1.36	4.43(1)	1.18(8)	3.67(3)	4.29(2)	2.79(4)	2.02(6)	1.94(7)	2.41(5)
(a) Advances in knowledge	0.75	0.75	0.75	0.76	0.76	0.75	0.76	0.75	0.76
(b) Economies of scale	0.36	0.69	0.27	0.51	0.62	0.54	0.40	0.42	0.45
(c) Adjustments and other	−0.04	0.26	−0.09	0.22	0.01	0.21	0.17	0.15	−0.02
(d) Improved allocation of resources	0.29	1.00(2)	0.12(8)	0.95(3)	1.42(1)	0.63(6)	0.51(7)	0.67(5)	0.92(4)
(e) Changes in the lag in the application of knowledge	0.00	0.83(2)	0.04(7)	0.74(3)	0.88(1)	0.43(4)	0.07(6)	−0.27(8)	0.18(5)
(f) "Economies of scale" assoc. with income elasticities	0.00	0.90(1)	0.09(8)	0.49(3)	0.60(2)	0.23(4)	0.11(7)	0.22(5)	0.12(6)
4. Residual Sources of Growth (3d + 3e + 3f)‡	0.29	2.73(2)	0.25(8)	2.18(3)	2.90(1)	1.29(4)	0.69(6)	0.62(7)	1.22(5)
5. Difference from U.S. in 4	—	2.44	−0.04	1.89	2.61	1.00	0.40	0.33	0.93
6. Growth of U.S. Capital/ Stake (1950 = 1.00)	1.00	7.24(2)	3.85§(7)	4.74(3)	8.79(1)	4.48(4)	4.15(6)	3.63(8)	4.42(5)

* Source: E. F. Denison, *Why Growth Rates Differ* (Washington, D.C.: The Brookings Institution, 1967), Chap. 21, Table 21-1 to 21-20, pp. 298–317, and B. Scarfe, *Capital Accumulation and Comparative Advantage: A Critical Appraisal* (Ph. D. thesis, Oxford, 1969). (Figures in parentheses are rankings, excluding the United States.)
† The following growth rates of *gross national product* per person employed over the period 1950 to 1962 are given by W. Beckerman, *The British Economy in 1975* (Cambridge: Cambridge University Press, 1965), Table 1.2, p. 15: U.S. 2.0; Germany 5.1; U.K. 2.0; France 4.2; Italy 4.7; Netherlands 3.5; Belgium 2.5; Denmark 3.2; Norway 3.4; Japan's rate of growth has outstripped all of these.
‡ This item does not appear in Denison's Tables, but is derived directly from them as indicated.
§ Excluding increased investment by Ford U.S. in Ford U.K. in 1961.

Germany, Italy, and France, and least in Denmark, the United Kingdom, and Belgium.

The contribution of economies to scale to European economic development has also been divided into two parts, the first of which (3b) is associated in a straightforward manner with the growth of markets. The second part (3f), which is no less important, requires further elucidation. Essentially, it arises from the index-number problem of international comparisons of real national income and consumption levels. The technical implications of this need not concern us here. What is important is the fact that the overall growth rates of real national income of the various European countries are higher if individual commodities are weighted by appropriate domestic prices than if they are weighted by U.S. prices. Denison argues that this phenomenon is a result of the interaction of income elasticities and increasing returns to scale. With the growth of incomes in Europe, increased consumption has been concentrated on those commodities such as automobiles and consumers' durables, which have high income elasticities of demand (Wells 1968), but which, in 1950, were sold in Europe at relatively high prices (in comparison with the United States). The increase in demand made profitable the introduction of new and more mechanized methods of production which could be readily borrowed from the United States. As Europe's output of these products rose, so their unit costs fell, and prices moved more in line with those in the United States.

It follows, then, that the significance of "economies of scale associated with income elasticities," as a growth variable depends upon three elements: (1) the existence of other growth-producing mechanisms; (2) the ability to borrow technology from abroad and, hence, to decrease the lag in the application of knowledge to economic processes; and (3) the ability to adjust the structure of production and to reallocate resources between various productive sectors (Scarfe 1969). Since the process through which this is achieved cannot easily be separated from that arising from the improved allocation of resources and changes in the lag in the application of knowledge, a case may be made for combining the three components, 3d, 3e, and 3f, into the category "Residual Sources of Growth."

If we now compare the increase in the U.S. capital intake[7] with these various sources of growth (particularly 3d, 3e, 3f, and 4), we see a pretty close correlation in each case, although the marginal contribution of U.S. investment to European growth appears to be a declining function. Moreover, with one or two notable exceptions, both reinvested profits and net capital outflows appear to be equally well associated with the growth variables. On the other hand, there is little connection between the absolute size of the increase in U.S. capital stake or its share in the capital formation and of various European countries and their rates of growth (Bandera and White 1968). For example, in the period 1957/65, U.S. investment in Britain was $3,224 million compared with $1,836 million in Germany and $720 million in Italy. As a proportion of gross fixed domestic capital formation, the plant and equipment expenditure of U.S. firms over this time was 9.7, 5.3, and 3.4%, respectively. This, of course, may simply reflect the fact that Britain invests less (as a percent of GNP) than Italy and Germany, or that her industrial structure is less geared to growth. It could also mean that the composition of U.S. investment or its productivity was somewhat less growth stimulating than that in other countries.[8] Furthermore that new investment reflects the size of existing investment and the profits earned on these. A better measure of investment might be net capital outflows or plant and equipment expenditure, though it is not difficult to think of situations in which these need not have any marked impact on productivity.

The Technological Gap and Technological Transplants — Their Economic Implications

So much by way of broad introduction, which suggests not only that the rate of U.S. capital inflows is positively associated with economic development in Europe, but that, in those areas in which such investment is likely to make the most pronounced contribution, the relationship seems particularly close. One result of this

---

[7] Either total or in manufacturing industry and petroleum.

[8] This hypothesis is supported by Chase Manhattan Bank statistics of the industrial structure of new U.S. companies setting up in Europe in recent years. See their *Report on Western Europe* (March-April 1966).

technological borrowing — which we have dealt with in another paper (Dunning 1969b) — is the convergence of the composition of European and U.S. exports. But the questions to which this paper addresses itself are, first, the extent to which host countries (either singly or collectively) maximize the net benefits of U.S. investment, and, second, whether or not the net benefits (particularly the technological benefits) associated with this investment could be obtained by other, and cheaper, means. Before discussing these questions, a word about U.S. investment and the so-called "technological gap."

The fact of the technological gap between U.S. and Europe, measured in terms of technology actually produced, is hardly debatable — although its extent is easily exaggerated. We would make simply four observations to illustrate this point. First, the latest available data show a five-to-one advantage ($264 million to $46 million annually) for the United States in receipts from technological royalties from four European countries[9] (OECD 1968). Second, the United States spends about four times as much on research and development as Western Europe combined (although Europe's population is larger) and about twice as much in proportion to gross national product (OECD 1967). Third, the United States tends to dominate world trade most in those industries that are the most research-intensive (Keesing 1967). Fourth, the contribution of U.S. subsidiaries in Europe (as a proportion of output produced) is most pronounced in the science-based industries (Behrman 1969; Servan-Schreiber 1968). (Seventy-five percent of the computers sold in Europe and an even larger proportion of integrated electronic circuits come from U.S. companies; so do one-half the pharmaceuticals bought by the U.K. national health service.)

The economic implications of the technological gap and the associated managerial gap (Diebold 1968) are, however, by no means clear. It seems to be widely regarded as a bad thing, and is frequently cited as the main cause of Europe's economic backwardness. Since technology and growth are closely linked (Williams 1967), then, so the argument runs, those countries that are most

[9] United Kingdom, Germany, France, and Italy.

155

behind in the production of technology must necessarily be the slowest growers. This is a nonsequitur. It is not the production of technical or managerial know-how (or even the production of the goods that incorporate this know-how), but the extent to which this know-how is used which is the important determinant to economic development. In theory, it is possible for one country to be entirely parasitic on another for technology; and providing the tradeoff between technology and other goods and services is worthwhile, it is right and proper this should be so. Indeed, of the eight countries with the highest output per head in the world, only the United States has a surplus on its technological balance of payments account, and only the United States, the United Kingdom and Switzerland are currently net exporters of direct capital account.

Most countries then, find it worthwhile to import most of the technology they need or to import technology-embodied products. But the comparative advantage of being a technology producer, technology borrower, or importer of technology-embodied goods varies over time between countries and sometimes in the same country, and is strongly influenced by the ease with which both factors and goods are traded. Most discussion of Europe's economic future seems to assume that Europe must assimilate the U.S. techno-economic structure to reach its standards of living. Occasionally, it is recognized that some specialization of activity within particular manufacturing is desirable, but, for the most part, the popular belief seems to be that only by adopting U.S. production methods and producing U.S.-style products can this objective be achieved. That this could be the best way of advancing Europe's growth, we do not wish to deny, but, as a first-best solution, this has by no means been proved. It is, at least, arguable that the United Kingdom could advance her growth and benefit her balance of payments more by investing £100 million in building hotels and encouraging U.S. tourism to the Bahamas, than by spending the same money trying to prop up her aircraft industry to meet U.S. competition.

In the final analysis, economic welfare and economic growth are measured by the rate of growth of consumer goods and services produced, and, in some cases, foreign technology is best transferred in finished goods traded between countries. Indeed, where there are

156

substantial barriers to factor movements this is the *only* way it can be transferred. But it may not always be the cheapest or the most practical way of transferring knowledge; where costs favor local production or where trade in goods is deliberately restricted, the international migration of technology is better accomplished by other routes. It is important, when trying to assess the effects of inward direct investment on the technology of the host country, to be clear about the assumptions one is making about the conditions of trade and exchange rates. The classical theory of trade presupposed a perfect and instantaneous transmission of knowledge (indeed it either virtually ignored it or assumed it to be a free good), and that, irrespective of its country of origin, production would immediately be shared between those countries (comparatively) best suited to the task. Nowadays, not only is technological innovation generally recognized as one of the main components of growth (Denison (1962) asserts "advances in knowledge" accounted for 40% of the total income per person employed in the United States between 1929 and 1957), its production is costly in both manpower and capital. But the "correct" distribution of the production of goods embracing new technologies, from the viewpoint of world economic welfare, may well depend upon freedom of such knowledge to move across boundaries. For, because of different resource endowments, it by no means follows that the best country (or countries) for a firm to research or innovate in will necessarily be the best country (countries) for it to produce or market in. If there are differences in comparative advantages of this kind, then international investment is a prerequisite of, or at least complementary to, international trade — a fact that multinational corporations are not slow to emphasize to governments wishing to curb their foreign activities.

Summarizing then, there are three ways a nation can benefit from the fruits of world technology.

1. By importing the products of technology, be they capital or consumer goods.

2. By importing the technological know-how and producing technology-embodied products.

3. By producing the technological know-how itself.

157

Switzerland and New Zealand obtain their technology mainly in the first way, Japan and Germany in the second, and the United States the third. As we have seen, the popular conception of technological "gap" refers essentially to the amount of technology indigenously produced. It implies that (1) a country's growth is best served by the encouragement of competitive production of products with a high technological content; (2) it is better to produce the technology itself rather than import it.

I do not wish to argue the case for or against the first proposition, but simply to reiterate the obvious point that present-day restrictions on trade of both factors and goods, by distorting the best distribution of product-embodied technology and technological borrowing throughout the world, make it difficult to estimate what this best distribution should be.

On the second point, I have seen no reasoned economic assessment of why technological borrowing is, by its nature, against the interest of host countries, and it is better for a nation to be as technologically independent (or at least technologically competitive) as possible. This is not to deny that there could be some genuine costs to the host country — both economic and noneconomic — involved in technological borrowing (which will, in part, depend on the form of the borrowing) which must be set against its benefits. These we will consider in a later part of this paper. Again, the problem is conceptually simple. Is the European economy likely to grow faster (or more efficiently) by borrowing technology (or particular kinds of technology) from the United States and using its resources in other directions, or by sacrificing the obvious gains to be derived from knowledge transplants, and allocating more resources to education and research and development to produce this knowledge itself? Part of the answer must obviously depend on the efficiency of knowledge creation in Europe and the United States. To argue that it is better for France to operate an independent computer industry implies that, once it has had a chance to build up its own technological infrastructure, the industry can serve the needs of the French economy better and/or more cheaply than by importing the technology direct from the United States. Or should Europe aim at developing a more specialized technological strategy

158

and exchange the output of its own research and development for that of a different kind originating from U.S. laboratories?

Unfortunately, this is not a matter that can be left to market forces to resolve, simply because technological advances are powerfully influenced by the policies of public authorities toward higher education on the one hand and the support of research and development activities on the other. Servan-Schreiber acknowledges this in *The American Challenge* and argues that the only way for Europe to escape U.S. domination is for it, or more particularly a supranational authority acting on its behalf, to make a massive investment in both lines of activity. I am by no means persuaded that this should be the main thrust of European policy, particularly if it adds to, rather than reduces, the brain drain across the Atlantic.

However, let me try to be more specific, and tackle the question from the viewpoint of the costs of acquiring technology from abroad. Now, technology can be transferred between nations in a variety of ways. Sometimes the technology is owned (or controlled) specifically by particular institutions — we shall call such technology proprietary technology. It is mainly transmitted by (1) direct investment of multinational corporations and (2) licensing of patents, and a variety of manufacturing or technical service agreements, and some kinds of consultancy services. Nonproprietary technology includes not only the results of new knowledge contained in the technical literature, but

1. Direct purchases of hardware or services, such as new machinery and equipment, test devices, computer software, and related consulting services.
2. Technical-service activities backing up these sales or introducing new products.
3. Demonstrations of modern management technologies at seminars, conferences, exhibitions, etc.
4. Technical assistance to suppliers and customers on special problems.
5. Observation and imitation of nonproprietary technologies (Quinn 1968).

Each of the above kinds of technological transfer has led to the development of whole industries in specific countries. For example, shipbuilders in Norway and Sweden simply observed the new construction techniques developed in the United States during World War II and at once applied them, after using surplus (U.S.) government equipment. More recently, the Japanese have been very adept at observing and imitating U.S. technologies in a variety of knowledge industries, particularly consumer electronic products.

In this paper, we shall be primarily concerned with the dissemination of proprietary technology via the medium of the multinational corporation. We illustrate our argument from the experience of the United Kingdom.

The Technological Impact of U.S. Investment in the United Kingdom

There are, in general, two views of the technological impact of U.S. investment in the United Kingdom. The first of these, which prevailed up to 1960 or thereabouts, and still holds in some quarters, is that this is entirely beneficial. By the presence of U.S. firms, so the argument goes, Britain is able to tap the flow of technological (and managerial) knowledge of the U.S. economy, valued at many times the amount she spends on indigenous research and development each year at a cost — in the form of royalties, fees, profits, and interest — considerably lower than that which she would have had to pay to produce the knowledge herself.

The costs are of two kinds. First there are the actual costs associated with U.S. investment in the United Kingdom; these deducted from the benefits give the technological net return to the host country of inward investment. Second, there is opportunity cost of this net return in terms of net returns that could have been gained by obtaining this knowledge in a different way. We deal with each of these costs in turn.

The main cost of inward investment arises wherever it weakens the host country's competitive position in the world economy. Here, America is seen as a technological competitor to the United Kingdom, with the power to retard as well as to accelerate its rate of development. If, by their activities in the United Kingdom, U.S. firms can add to their stock of technology, skilled labor, and ideas

160

— at the expense of the United Kingdom — then the technological gap may widen rather than close. For example, a very small financial investment in the United Kingdom, U.S. companies could (1) gain access to the results of U.K. research and development which they may be able to exploit more profitably than the firms originating such research and development; (2) stifle indigenous research and development, and polarize it to the United States, thus increasing the technological dependence of the United Kingdom on the United States; (3) use their presence to monitor human capital back to the United States and, in so doing, encourage the brain drain from the United Kingdom. Were these policies widely practised, then the technological costs of inward investment could well be high, *unless* these gains were properly reflected in the price paid by U.S. firms for them[10] (Dunning and Steuer 1969). Not only would her rate of development become even more dependent on that of the United States than it is now, but she would have borne the costs of producing technology without receiving any of its benefits. A separate, though related argument, is that when the "knowledge-producing" operations of multinational subsidiaries are centrally controlled, then there is always the possibility that these might be diverted from the United Kingdom to other countries (Dunning 1969a). But, equally, the United Kingdom might be the beneficiary of such shifts, and, in any case, multinational firms of U.K. parentage might find it profitable to act in a similar way.

There has been no systematic measurement of these costs (or potential costs), though it is known that they have arisen in a number of cases. On the other hand, the fact that some U.S. firms do little research in the United Kingdom has been argued as being beneficial to the host economy, since it releases scarce skilled personnel for other activities. Much depends here on the state of the (U.K.) market for research workers. If, as we are often led to believe (Peck 1968), this type of human capital is in short supply in Britain, U.S. firms might be doing the United Kingdom a service by undertaking no research. On the other hand, there is no doubt that American companies have helped create a demand for certain

[10] For example, in the takeover of a U.K. firm by a U.S. enterprise.

161

types of scientists and engineers, which otherwise might have found no suitable employment in the United Kingdom. The fact that there *is* quite a substantial brain drain to the United States (Chorafas 1968) suggests there is no room for additional sources of employment in the United Kingdom and that this latter hypothesis is as likely to be as true as the former.[11]

The evidence on the amount of research and development undertaken by U.S. firms is a little conflicting. On the one hand, a report of the Stanford Research Institute (1963) indicated that, while one-half of a sample of 200 American firms undertook research and development in Europe, most spent 4% or less of their research and development budget there. The report went on to say that many U.S. firms regarded their European operations primarily as a means of steering the results of European research and development back to the United States and of gaining entry into the European scientific community. On the other hand, U.S. manufacturing firms in Britain tend to spend more on research and development than their U.K. competitors and more often than not, it seems, when American firm take over U.K. enterprises, they increase rather than diminish the research and development activity.

I have dealt with some of the wider implications of inward foreign investment which are complementary to the technological implications in the PEP paper mentioned earlier (Dunning 1969a), and a good account of them is given in the Watkins Committee report on foreign ownership in Canadian industry (Watkins 1968). However, in Canada, the technological issue is not the central issue surrounding the costs and benefits of U.S. investment. Rather it is the extent to which such investment may impinge upon national political and cultural autonomy. The same is probably true of the attitudes of most developing countries to foreign ownership and control. But these nations can hardly hope to be technologically competitive to the United States in the way Europe can — and it

[11] This is an example of a reverse flow of technology from the United Kingdom to the United States. The difference between this and U.S. investment in the United Kingdom is that, while the latter remains the property of the exporting country and earns it a return, the migration of skilled manpower is essentially a gift from the exporting to the importing country.

162

is for this reason (and the fact that technological dependence may be the first step along the road to political and cultural dependence) that the views of Servan-Schreiber have been so widely acclaimed.

Maximizing the Net Benefits of U.S. Investment

It may be, of course, that European host countries (individually or collectively) are neither gaining the benefits from U.S. investment that they should, nor are geared effectively to coping with the economic power associated with it. That the technological costs may be too high and the technological advantages may not be exploited or disseminated as efficiently as they might, may reflect some weakness in the institutional or competitive structure of the local economies. (Here a distinction needs to be made between the position of individual European economies and an integrated European community). In its report, the Watkins Committee repeatedly emphasized the point that, in the absence of effective competition to inward investment, most of the benefits will simply accrue to the investing rather than the recipient country. Only a quick glance at the economy of Europe reveals that, at the moment, it is not organized to take full advantage of inward investment. In general, her research and development effort is too uncoordinated and her industries and her markets too fragmented to offer the competition needed to combat U.S. giant firms; and, because of obstacles in framing a rationalized merger and fiscal policy and updating company law, one cannot see an effective industrial strategy developing for some years.

From a cost viewpoint, the type of market structure most suited to the type of U.S. firms now operating in Europe is oligopolistic in character. At least, it is oligopolistic in the United States, with markets several times the size of most individual European countries. The firms are generally research and capital intensive and able to benefit from economies of scale. In most European countries, one firm could comfortably supply the total market. This means that the firm first in the field often creates its own barriers to entry, which sometimes can be overcome only by firms of comparable size. At the moment, these are few and far between in Europe, for what is sometimes overlooked is that, from a technological viewpoint, European firms are competing against the facilities of U.S. corporations and not just those of their European subsidiaries. Compared to 82 U.S. firms with a sales turnover of more than $1 billion in 1967, there were 28 European firms — and most of these are not concentrated in the science-based industries. In the motor vehicles industry, the combined assets of the three largest European producers are still smaller than that of the third largest U.S. firm. Of the largest ten mechanical engineering firms in the world, only one is European. In the pharmaceutical industry there are ten U.S. firms with assets of over $100 million; in Europe the largest specialist pharmaceutical company has assets of less than one-half this amount. The combined assets of the six largest European aircraft companies are still smaller than the Boeing company of the United States (Behrman 1969).

It is outside the scope of this paper to examine the extent to which size confers advantages. Most comparisons that economists have so far made (which, on the whole, play down the size advantage) are not really helpful for our purposes. Very rarely is like compared with like, and usually the industrial (and sometimes the size) classification chosen is far too broad. Moreover, size is correlated with profitability and not with growth. But, insofar as research and development expenditure tends to be closely correlated with size, and there do appear to be marked economies of scale in this sector (Mansfield 1968), it would seem to follow that the growth potential of large firms is likely to be greater than that of small firms. The fact that some large European firms have expanded faster than the largest U.S. firms in recent years (Dunning and Pearce, 1969) in no way invalidates this hypothesis, since much of the growth has been accomplished by merger and acquisition.

The United Kingdom has probably gone further with rationalizing its industrial structure than other European countries, the best-known mergers being the BMC/Leyland merger in the automobile industry, the Plessey, English Electric, and ICT merger in the computer industry, and the General Electric and AEI merger in the electrical industry. Most mergers in recent years have been horizontal rather than vertical by nature (Utton 1969). The larger of these rationalization schemes are often backed by the government

164

(through the Industrial Reorganisation Commission), who also uses other forms of countervailing power to help British industry combat U.S. competition.

But, one cannot help feeling that, in the end, corporate alliances by firms within a country are not likely to be sufficient to counteract the American invasion, and, in any case, sooner or later one comes up against local antitrust legislation. (In parenthesis, one might make the point that the growth of economic power of U.S. corporations in the world economy has gone hand in hand with the internationalization of their activities. The United Kingdom might do well to note this fact at a time when policy is actively directed to discouraging foreign direct investment.) When one looks at the practicability of intracountry corporate mergers, or a "European" industrial policy, one runs into all sorts of difficulties — such as those already mentioned — relating to company law, taxation, fiscal policies, patents, and standards. There has been only one merger between two European firms in recent years, that between Agfa — a subsidiary of West Germany's Bayer Corporation, producing photographic equipment — and Gevaert, a Belgian company.[12] This was a classic case of Europe's response to the challenge of American size: in this case, the Kodak company. Neither of the two leading European companies could, by itself, raise the financial resources to meet the U.S. company's advanced technology. At the time of the merger, Kodak's expenditure on research and development was roughly equivalent to Gevaert's entire turnover (Layton 1969).

In his book *European Advanced Technology,* Christopher Layton examines some of the difficulties facing Europe in her attempts to pool her resources and to rationalize its industrial structure and the measures required for Europe to effectively challenge U.S. competition. There are, of course, many other aspects of American strength besides size. Indeed, some authorities feel that the provision of risk capital to dynamic small firms in advanced technology is an equally important need, together with the further development

---

[12] We should, however, observe that an official or semiofficial level there has been a great deal of intra-European technical cooperation of which the European Nuclear Energy Research Organization (CERN) has been an outstanding example.

165

of the European capital market. Nevertheless, I think that a European research director, quoted by Layton, put the matter very succinctly when he said, "If America wishes to close the technological gap with Europe, all she needs to do is erect 51 different sets of customs barriers, tax systems, space and defence programmes, science policies and public buying arrangements; the gap will be gone in a year!" (Layton, p. 50).

To some extent, the success of European competition with U.S. investment will affect the attitudes of host countries to the technological character of such investment. For example, to encourage U.S. firms to establish research and development laboratories may bring with it beneficial effects where there is little or no competition either for the skilled manpower used by such firms or their end products. These firms would then add to the research and development input of the host country. Where, however, U.S. subsidiaries siphon off skilled personnel from other parts of the economy, the effect, depending on the relative efficiency of U.S. and U.K. firms, may be to weaken indigenous research. The same sort of argument applies to the encouragement of foreign firms to install fully integrated production facilities, to hire local nationals, to use local suppliers, and to encourage joint ventures. In some cases, this kind of resource allocation might raise efficiency and make for faster growth: in others not so, and while this may be an acceptable price to encourage the full involvement of foreign countries, it may be only a second-best policy to some other alternative, e.g., the extension of licensing agreements and the encouragement of more effective domestic competition in the first place.

An alternative course of action for Europe is to try and specialize in certain areas of research and development for which it has (or is likely to have) a comparative advantage vis-à-vis the United States. Some economists, notably J. B. Quinn of Dartmouth College, strongly favor a selective economic/technological strategy in Europe. At the moment, national growth efforts tend to be scattered, "with a little bit for everyone." Not enough resources are committed to any sector for it to achieve economic viability in world terms. Nations may well learn from firms. Many a small enterprise has exploited "holes in the armor" of their larger competitors by concentrating its research and development efforts in a particular field.

Here we would offer just three comments. First, assuming Europe were able to integrate her individual economies effectively in the way earlier suggested, and that she continued to have a comparative advantage in labor costs, then one would expect her to gain most by concentrating her attentions on relatively labor-intensive vis-à-vis capital-intensive activities. This holds good even if factor endowments are tending to converge with those of the United States, as long as Europe does not completely catch up with the United States.

Second, one must be careful not to exaggerate the importance of proprietary technology in economic development. Industries that spend more than 1.5% of their net output on research and development still only account for a fairly small proportion of total manufacturing output. And the contribution of manufacturing output to GNP has for some years been steadily declining. It is true, as we have argued, that advances in technology in one industry often act as a catalyst to growth in others but, again, these can often be obtained from abroad by other means than direct investment. It may be that Europe should be encouraged to specialize in trading goods that have a high income elasticity of demand, but whose knowledge content is of a kind which, while utilizing substantial amounts of skilled labor does not require the scale of research and development expenditure (e.g., on laboratory facilities) which can only be undertaken by large firms. Examples include unstandardized and high-income furniture, clothing, metal products, electrical fittings, etc.[13]

Third, one can foresee that there may be more specialization, not only in the end products produced by multinational companies in various countries, e.g., horizontal specialization, but also in the stages of production processes as well, e.g., vertical specialization. In this instance, in genuine geocentric companies (Perlmutter 1969) there is a minimum of nationalism in the way the company operates.

---

[13] It is perhaps interesting to note that, relative to U.S. exports, European exports of these products have grown particularly in recent years. See Dunning (1969b).

(Incidentally it is sometimes felt that many of the problems arising from the presence of U.S. firms in Europe is due to the nationality of their parent companies — and if only there could be more geographical diffusion of ownership, these would disappear. This is a fallacy. It is true that European citizens would share in the profits earned by such companies; it is not necessarily the case that if companies broadly seek the same aims, e.g., maximization of profits, the geographical structure of the activities of these companies would be very different. In other words, the nation-state/multinational company conflict would still arise.)

It is a fact that many of the larger multinational companies are tending to concentrate their output of particular products and research and development facilities in certain countries and practicing specialization of stages of production process. I mentioned this back in 1958 in *American Investment in British Manufacturing Industry,* and I believe this trend has become more pronounced over time. The theory is simply that, where it is in the best interest of a firm to distribute geographically the various stages of its production process, this will be done on the basis of factor costs and productivity, and the cost of transporting inputs and outputs between countries. Since the early stages of knowledge-producing are very labor-intensive, then assuming equal efficiency of research personnel, Europe rather than the United States may be a better place to do this: the knowledge commercialization process, through to the pilot stage of production, is more capital-intensive and may need the facilities of large centralized laboratories and testing plants, and may be better done in the United States. The costs of the actual manufacturing process will be largely dependent upon the structure of wage rates, rents, and material prices, but where these are cheaper in Europe—and 'sufficient to outweigh any differences in marketing costs which may favor a U.S. location — it may pay to specialize at least manufacturing operations in Europe and export the goods to markets previously served by the United States.

I have not put this theory to the test in any systematic way, but the growing international specialization of multinational firms and the quite substantial development of sponsored research in Europe by U.S. controlled companies certainly seems to lend support to it.

It is also consistent with the product-cycle theory of international trade.

Alternatives to Inward Investment

So far I have been discussing some of the actual (or possible) technological costs and benefits associated with inward investment. Some of the costs I have suggested are inherent in the operations of multinational companies irrespective of their nationality; some could be minimized or even eliminated by freer international trade, an appropriate research and development strategy, and institutional reform on the part of host governments.

What now of the alternatives to inward investment as a means of obtaining proprietary foreign technology? First, and most obvious, are licensing agreements, covering, e.g., grants of patents, trademarks, technical assistance, franchises, etc. It is sometimes argued that, from the licensee's viewpoint, the main merit of licensing agreements is that they do not (or may not) involve any interference by the licensor in his policy and decision-taking activities — in the same way as may happen with direct investment. This is obviously true, up to a point. For one thing, many of the activities of the licensee will be completely untouched by the agreement; for another, there is likely to be little or no impact on the managerial practices of the licensee: for a third, even the methods of production may not be affected. Indeed, in some cases, all that is being purchased is "paper" knowledge, e.g., formula, specifications, drawing designs, etc. On the other hand, the licensor may seek to impose certain controls on the buying and selling outlets of the licensee. He may limit the sale of the final product to the licensee's country and/or influence the choice of suppliers. Even the license itself may only be granted for a specified period or be subject to withdrawal at short notice (Bonin 1967).

At a macrolevel, there is a possibility that the more a country licenses knowledge from abroad, the less it tends to undertake research and development itself. This, vis-à-vis direct investment, probably increases rather than diminishes its dependence on foreign technology. That this may still be the fastest and possibly cheapest way to grow may still be true, and for a country wishing to concentrate its research resources in particular sectors, such a complete dependence for other forms of know-how — providing there is adequate "software" — supporting research and development facilities may be the best thing. It is interesting that Italy and Germany, both of which have relied on this type of technological borrowing rather more than the United Kingdom in the post-war period, have grown so much faster. Likewise with Japan; but the particularly fascinating thing about Japan is the way she has gone about acquiring *non*proprietary technology, e.g., by sending teams of scientists and technologists over to the United States to gain knowledge at firsthand. Japan has long been a first-class imitator, but in recent years she has become an important competitor to the United States in high-technology products, e.g., in the field of consumer electtronics. One observes that the industries in which Japanese exports have increased most are precisely those in which Japan has endeavored to absorb Western technology in the way I have suggested. She is now building both her own indigenous research and development and allowing inward investment on this quite firm technological infrastructure.

To the licensed firm, there are two important benefits of licensing agreements. First the access to new technology while remaining free to produce the products or engage in the methods of production it chooses, and second the savings realized in research costs, enabling it to market the product more speedily than if it had been forced to depend entirely on its own resources or on a purely national technology. This latter advantage is becoming more important as the time lag between the discovery of new product is becoming less, and the need to keep up with one's competitor is that much greater.

Direct investment, on the other hand, is likely to be favored whenever the expertise most required is of a kind that cannot be easily incorporated into a licensing agreement and where "on the spot" managerial involvement is especially valued. It is not unusual to come across two firms with technologically nothing to choose between them, but one much better managed than the other. One suspects that such differences — which are partly a reflection of managerial attitudes — are at least as important a cause of the difference in profit rates of U.S. subsidiaries and their U.K. competitors in Europe as any technological differences. One further possible advantage of knowledge transmittance via direct investment is that the parent company may charge its subsidiary less than the market price for the knowledge it transmits. Should this be passed on to the local consumer in the form of lower prices, the host economy gains as it does, indeed, if the foreign subsidiary could produce more efficiently than the licensee. And if profits are higher than they would be otherwise, the local exchequer gains from additional tax revenue.

Such empirical data as we have suggest that, as a percentage of gross or net output, U.S. subsidiaries are charged considerably lower royalties and fees than European firms under license to U.S. firms. On the other hand, any wholesale transfer or assimilation of U.S. technology by their European subsidiaries, may, because of differences in market and/or prices of factor inputs, be ill suited to local conditions. In Canada, for example, Safarian found that foreign companies were often at a disadvantage because of their "inability to buy or develop products, designs or machinery more suitable to Canadian market conditions" (Safarian 1966). Where the licensing agreements enable European companies to obtain (or maintain) a technology better suited to their needs, this would represent an important benefit. At the same time, the secondary or technological multiplier effects of licensing are likely to be less than those arising from direct investment, even if the immediate technological benefits and costs may be broadly comparable. It is difficult to give an *a priori* assessment here. Among the factors to be considered are (1) the amount and direction of existing foreign investment in the country, (2) the strength of local competition, (3) the national importance of industries in which foreign investment is concentrated, and (4) the availability of research and development personnel.

If, as has been suggested, the eventual aim of Europe is to create a viable technology of its own and to reduce the technological gap between itself and the United States by adopting a selective program of research and development, then, insofar as licensing agreements economizes in research personnel, this is all to the good. On the other hand, if European industrial strategy is geared to com-

171

peting across the board with the United States, then licensing agreements have more limitations than direct investment. Indeed, the more complex the running of a business enterprise becomes, the less the knowledge content can be embodied in licensing agreements (which essentially enable standardized "know-how" to be transmitted), and the more important are the techniques of decision making and managerial judgment (which cannot be embodied in formula, drawing, specifications, etc.).

Joint Ventures. Joint equity ventures represent a midway house between the fully owned subsidiary and licensing agreements. It is not our purpose to examine the advantages and disadvantages of these, but simply to observe that these are an alternative way of obtaining technology to those already mentioned, and at (generally) a lower cost involved than that of the fully owned subsidiary. Basically speaking, their contribution to technology is the same as in the fully owned subsidiary, although the extent of management involvement may be rather less. However, there is likely to be a better appreciation of local economic conditions and needs, and less likelihood that the foreign company will use the host company's technology to meet its own ends. Joint ventures also generally make for good relations with host governments and the more nationalistic sectors of the host country.

On the other hand, there are certain well-known problems in the operation of joint companies, e.g., the disposal of profits, organization of production, staff transfers, etc. (Bonin 1967). These often involve high costs, but again, in some cases, the net technological benefits to the host country may be higher than those offered by alternative schemes.

Other Forms of Obtaining Technology. These are the days of experimentation of different forms of the international dissemination of technology. There are many models and proposals — particularly as they relate to the growth of LDC's. These vary from technical assistance and coproduction agreements to jointly public and privately financed enterprises, and the observation and imitation of product technologies. Mass production in cars, techniques for welded ship construction, mathematical systems for production, and quality control are examples of high-impact technologies trans-

172

ferred through these latter means by Japan and Italy. Each type of technology transference has its particular costs and benefits: though certain principles can be laid down as to which is likely to be the best method or mix, under which conditions of assimilation, far more research is necessary before any definitive answer can be given from the particular standpoint of Europe.

Conclusions

We have seen in this paper that Europe has leaned heavily on the United States for technology since the war, and that conditions in Europe have generally favored the transfer of this technology in the form of direct investment and licensing agreements. Partly this simply reflects the fact that European economy has gradually moved more in the direction of the U.S. economy, and that the products the demand for which are growing most rapidly are those first produced in the United States.

The share of U.S. investment in Europe's industries is still small but strongly concentrated in the research-intensive and growth sectors. This implies a strong technological impact, the costs and benefits of which we have sought to examine and appraise. Chief among the benefits is that Europe's per capita real income has grown more rapidly than otherwise would have been the case and certainly faster than that of the United States. This is partly because (1) the technological improvements have been largely embodied in new vintages of capital goods; (2) Europe was, at the beginning of our period under review (1950), less well endowed with capital equipment than the United States; and (3) during those years Europe has increased capital per head at a faster rate than the United States. The result has been that the effects of changes in technology and changes in factor proportions have worked together to yield not only convergence in patterns of production but also a higher growth rate in Europe along with the process of adapting to the borrowed technology. Given that it is desired to attract technology by direct investment, the problem of European economies is to maximize the resulting technological multiplier and to minimize its costs. We have suggested ways in which this may be done and certain obstacles in the way of doing it.

173

BIBLIOGRAPHY

V. N. Bandera and J. T. White, "U.S. Direct Investment and Domestic Markets in Europe," *Economia Internazionale,* Vol. 21 (February 1968), pp. 117–133.

W. Beckerman and Associates, *The British Economy in 1975* (Cambridge: Cambridge University Press, 1965).

J. N. Behrman, "Some Patterns in the Rise of the Multinational Enterprise," Graduate School of Business Research Paper, No. 18, University of North Carolina (1969).

B. Bonin, "Licensing and Joint Ventures as Alternatives to Direct Investment," a study prepared for the Task Force on the Structure of Canadian Industry (October 1967, unpublished).

D. N. Chorafôs, *The Knowledge Revolution* (London: Allen & Unwin, 1968).

E. Denison, *The Sources of Economic Growth in the United States* (New York: Committee for Economic Development, 1962).

E. Denison, *Why Growth Rates Differ* (Washington, D.C.: The Brookings Institution, 1967).

J. Diebold, "Is the Gap Technological," *Foreign Affairs,* Vol. 46, No. 2 (January 1968), pp. 276–291.

J. H. Dunning, "The Role of American Investment in the British Economy," PEP Broadsheet No. 507 (February 1969a).

J. H. Dunning, "European and U.S. Trade Patterns, U.S. Foreign Investment and the Technological Gap," paper presented to Conference of International Economic Association on *The Mutual Repercussions of North American and Western European Economic Policies,* Algarve, Portugal (September 1969b) unpublished.

J. H. Dunning and R. D. Pearce, "The World's Largest Industrial Companies: A Statistical Profile," *Business Ratios,* Vol. 3, No. 3 (1969).

J. H. Dunning and M. Steuer, "The Effects of U.S. Investment on U.K. Technology," Moorgate and Wall Street (Autumn 1969c).

European Free Trade Association, *Foreign Investment* (Geneva: E.F.T.A., 1968).

W. Gruber, D. Mehta, and R. Vernon, "The R and D Factor in International Trade and International Investment of United States Industries," *Journal of Political Economy,* Vol. LXXV (February 1967), pp. 20–37.

S. Hirsch, *Location of Industry and International Competitiveness* (Oxford: Clarendon Press, 1967).

R. H. Kaufman, *Strategies for Atlantic Technological Development,* background paper for the conference organized by the Atlantic Institute, and sponsored by the Committee for Atlantic Economic Cooperation (Paris: Atlantic Institute, April 1968).

D. Keesing, "The Impact of Research and Development on United States Trade," *Journal of Political Economy,* Vol. LXXV (February 1967), pp. 38–48.

L. B. Krause, *European Economic Integration and the United States,* (Washington, D.C.: The Brookings Institution, 1968).

A. Lamfalussy, *The United Kingdom and the Six: An Essay on Economic Growth in Western Europe* (London: Macmillan, 1963).

C. Layton, *European Advanced Technology* (London: Allen & Unwin, 1969).

A. Maddison, *Economic Growth in the West: Comparative Experience in Europe and North America* (New York: Twentieth Century, 1964).

E. Mansfield, *The Economics of Technological Changes* (New York: W. W. Norton, 1968).

Organization for Economic Cooperation and Development, "Technological Gaps: Their Nature, Causes, Effects," OECD *Observer,* No. 33 (April 1968), pp. 18–28.

Organization for Economic Cooperation and Development, *The Level and Structure of European's Research and Development Effort* (Paris: OECD, 1968).

M. Peck, "Science and Technology," in *Britain's Economic Prospects,* R. Caves, ed. (Washington, D.C.: The Brookings Institution, 1968).

H. V. Perlmutter, "The Tortuous Evolution of the Multi-National Corporation," *Columbia Journal of World Business,* Vol. IV, No. 1 (January/February 1969), pp. 9–18.

175

JOHN H. DUNNING

T. L. Powie, "The Influence of International Capital Flows on the Effectiveness of Domestic Policy Instruments," in *Canadian Economic Policy and the Impact of International Capital Flows,* R. Caves and G. Reuber, eds. (Toronto: University of Toronto Press, 1969).

D. Quinn, "Scientific and Technical Strategy at the National and Major Enterprise Level," Paper for UNESCO symposium on *The Role of Science and Technology in Economic Development* (Paris, 1968).

A. Safarian, *Foreign Ownership of Canadian Industry* (Toronto: McGraw-Hill, 1966).

B. Scarfe, "Capital Accumulation and Comparative Advantage: A Critical Appraisal" (unpublished Ph.D. thesis, Oxford, 1969).

J.-J. Servan-Schreiber, *The American Challenge* (London: Hamish Hamilton, 1968).

Stanford Research Institute, Long Range Planning Report 198 (1963) (quoted in B. Williams).

A. P. Thirlwall, "A Measure of the Proper Distribution of Industry," *Oxford Economic Papers,* Vol. XX (March 1967), pp. 46–58.

R. Vernon, "International Investments and International Trade in the Product Cycle," *Quarterly Journal of Economics,* Vol. LXXX (May 1966), pp. 190–207.

M. Watkins *et al.,* "Foreign Ownership and the Structure of Canadian Industry, Report of the Task Force on the Structure of Canadian Industry (Ottawa: The Queen's Printer, 1968).

M. A. Utton, "Diversification, Mergers and Profit Stability," *Business Ratios,* Vol. 3, No. 1 (1969), pp. 24–28.

L. T. Wells, Jr., "A Product Life Cycle for International Trade," *Journal of Marketing,* Vol. 32, No. 3 (July 1968), pp. 1–6.

L. T. Wells, Jr., "Test of a Product-Cycle Model of International Trade: U.S. Exports of Consumer Durables," *Quarterly Journal of Economics,* Vol. LXXXIII (February 1969), pp. 152–162.

B. Wilkinson, *Canada's International Trade: An Analysis of Recent Trends and Patterns* (Montreal: The Private Planning Association of Canada, 1968).

B. Williams, *Technology, Investment and Growth* (London: Chapman & Hill, 1967).

Part III

LAW AND POLITICS

CHAPTER SEVEN

THE INTERNATIONAL FIRM AND THE NATIONAL JURISDICTION

Seymour J. Rubin

The Practicing Lawyer's Approach

There is a certain simplicity to the task of the lawyer who, in his natural habitat, is asked to speak on the subject of the international firm and the national jurisdiction. This simplicity arises not because the subject is an easy one but because the job of the lawyer is usually defined by the needs and desires of his client. When the client has decided to make a certain investment abroad, whether in the usual sense of direct investment, or by way of a licensing agreement, or some other more or less recognized way of doing business, the lawyer is a technician. He is employed to analyze the possibilities and the methods that may be employed, to define the risks, to devise ways of minimizing risks and of maximizing profits. So engaged, his work may be arcane and difficult, as he treads his way through the maze of laws and regulations which affect the proposed course of conduct, and it may be sufficiently important to determine whether the investment will in fact be made, whether it will be made in the way originally anticipated, or whether it can be recast so as to attain a better risk/benefit ratio than might otherwise have been attained. But he is not asked to make national policy. Essentially, his concern with matters of policy is not to evaluate them but to take them into account, to recognize that the policies of at least two national jurisdictions — that of the "home" state and that of the "host" state — may substantially affect or alter or cancel a business decision. This done, other factors being duly appraised, he may then draw up for his client the best possible (in his judgment) method for carrying out a business decision.

The lawyer writing as social or political scientist is, however, faced with a rather more complex task, its complexity deriving from the fact that he does not start with his conclusion and then concentrate on methods of attaining it. In commissioning this paper, Professor Kindleberger has admonished me that I am to give heed to "questions of national and international policy, more than (to) problems facing the corporation" — though these are "by no means excluded." Whether lawyers are by training and inclination competent in broad questions of national and international policy is for many at best an open question. Certainly there are those who suggest that, both in prescribing policy and in its practical application as diplomacy, lawyers had better leave the game to others. Sir Harold Nicholson, for example, quoting an eminent if early French expert, de Callières, states that ". . . the training of a lawyer breeds habits and dispositions of mind which are not favorable to the practice of diplomacy." And George Kennan, Walter Lippmann, and others have echoed this sentiment and extended the doubt beyond "the practice of diplomacy," suggesting that lawyers suffer, when they come to consider policy, from an occupational deformation — an excessive reliance on the written word, resulting, for one example, in what some believe to have been the pactomania of a John Foster Dulles.

But even in his traditional function, the role of the lawyer is somewhat broader than that of a technician. At least he aspires to a higher if vaguer role. Mr. Justice Frankfurter has said that he should be "a counsellor . . . a trustee to the wise conduct of his client." If he is to be such a person and discharge such an office, he must necessarily be concerned with, at a minimum, some matters of policy. And his lofty pretensions can be argued to be justified by his task. For the policy of states is relevant, insofar as transnational transactions are concerned, even to the technician. As an analyst concerned primarily with what *can* be done, the lawyer finds him-

180

self involved inevitably with the question of what *ought* to be done — at least insofar as considerations of policy affect the application of legal norms.

The International Firm

Thus self-justified, I can turn to certain of the questions of national jurisdiction which seem important.

It seems appropriate to pause at the outset for a moment to consider just what is meant by the "international firm." I do not propose to attempt here any "correct" definition, if only because the term is so broadly used as to mean a good many things, and because my definition would certainly be tedious and probably incorrect. Rather, I think it best to talk of how the term is generally used, since that usage seems to me to suffice for examination of the problems with which we are concerned.

What is generally comprehended within this term, as it is used in the discussion that today flourishes around it, is a business organization that has its roots in one country and operations of various sorts in another. It may be an American corporation with an operating subsidiary in France or in Bolivia; the subsidiary may have a substantial proportion of local ownership; the French and Bolivian subsidiaries may be held or controlled through a "base company" organized under the laws of Liechtenstein or the Cayman Islands; the parent company may itself have foreign (that is, in this case, non-American) ownership. Equally, it may be a company that has chosen to go abroad by a route other than that of direct investment: it may, for example, have a series of licensing agreements with foreign corporations in which it has little or no ownership interest.

The distinction between one or another form may have very important tax or other legal consequences, but, in the sense of the relation between internationalism or foreignness, of ownership or control, and national jurisdiction or sensibilities, it is probably not very relevant. What is important is the fact that in each situation a productive activity is taking place in the jurisdiction of one country (the host) which is to some substantial extent under the control of

181

nationals of another country (the home); and that the nationals of that country in which control resides are themselves subject to the jurisdiction of the state of their nationality.

Locus of Control

It is a truism to say that what causes concern with the "international" firm, as against the large national firm, is that the power of decision over matters of importance in and to one nation lies, or is thought to lie, in a foreign state. It is, of course, not without precedent that a national company may take decisions which its own state, or which other citizens of that state, consider to be undesirable. But when the power to say yes, no, or maybe is abroad, there is a sense of lack of control over issues of social, economic, and even political polity which tends to be profoundly disquieting. The psychological situation is not unknown in our own country: Henry Ford was fanatic in his determination to keep control of his enterprise out of the hands of the alien bankers of Wall Street. The South has never enjoyed the (former) control over its economic destinies wielded by Northern industrialists. Examples could be multiplied, particularly by economic historians.

It would seem, *a priori,* that this disquiet over foreign control would be alleviated if the decision-making authority abroad is motivated solely by considerations of good business. Unless the belief exists that the large corporation not only has common interests with its home government (what is good for GM, etc.) but that its corporate decisions are made by its government, the business decision will at least not represent an extension into the host country of the political will of the home country. The decision that is taken may reflect considerations other than those which the host would like: the profit of the home stockholders may not comport with expanded employment in the host country, for example. From the viewpoint of corporate profits and the welfare of stockholders, ore may be extracted in the host but transported elsewhere for refining. Or the management may simply feel that conditions in the host are not sufficiently stable, or prospects for profitable operation sufficiently good, to justify investment which, in the opinion of the host, is necessary to its own economic development.

The impact of these potential conflicts is somewhat lessened by the somewhat impersonal nature of the factors that enter into the private corporate decision. What is done is done to maximize private and not governmental profit. The flow of investment to foreign countries is not only a possible cause of alarm but also an effective demonstration of the willingness of the international firm to produce where there is profit in producing, and to judge that profit objectively. Chauvinism is alien to the international firm. Money, as long as it is usable, is fungible. The home-grown variety has no advantage over the foreign type. Operating or investment decisions are not likely to be based on ideological or nationalistic grounds. If the approach is unsentimental, it is at the same time reassuring.

Indeed, despite the recent wave of headlines about takeovers and the size of foreign (that is, in this context, American) ownership of production and technology, public excitement over the issue seems to be on the wane. On the other hand, literature has burgeoned as much as have acquisitions. *Le Défi Américain* may be much criticized by economists, but it has undeniably established the popularity of the subject for political scientists as well as for politicians. The Watkins Report has attracted much notice to Canadian concern over American dominance of industry in Canada. The recent report written by Professor John Dunning of the University of Reading for the Political and Economic Planning Organization states that "Britain has still not come to terms with the reality of the growing rôle of the multinational company in the world's economy and the way it can affect a nation state's sovereignty." But after the dust has settled behind the critical notations of U.S. ownership in the computer industry in Europe, after the worries about Chrysler and Simca, about Fiat and Citroën, about Euro-dollar financing of American purchases of European factories, things seem to go on much as before. And, though Professor Dunning points out that the 10% of British manufacturing output which is already American owned or controlled is likely to be 20% 10 years hence, the official British reaction is one of unflappable unconcern. The Prime Minister, Mr. Wilson, has thus said that Britain continues to welcome greater participation by "American or other overseas companies when they have anything new to bring, either in terms of technical expertise or, in some cases, management expertise." British sociologists, too, suggest that the present worries of economists and political scientists over the "attack" on national sovereignty by the international firm may already be old-fashioned; they state that 10 years ago, sociologists found public hostility toward the American business presence in Britain a favorite subject; now, no sociologist even writes about it.

Partnership of Foreign Firm and Foreign Government

If there is, however, some doubt that wide-spread public agitation exists about the role of foreign corporate managers, it seems likely that such tensions as there are would be heightened if those foreign managers were thought to be obeying the dictates of their governmental policy makers rather than those of an impersonal profit and loss statement. Tensions are ameliorated if the decisions are private, heightened if they are governmental. Yet there is some substance to the notion that the large modern corporation cannot, to some important extent, escape an association with its own government that is something like partnership.

Such an association, however one may describe it, is neither new nor surprising, and by no means implies that either government or business is the tool of the other. Early companies, chartered by special act to do business abroad, were of course closely linked to government. Aside from the fact that Isabella financed Columbus' feasibility study (which, like many later such, was valuable despite its erroneous conclusions), the early companies of exploration and trade were arms of the state — the British East India Company, the Hudson Bay Company, and so forth. With the enactment of general corporation statutes which accompanied the growth of business and vice versa, corporations of course became both more independent and perhaps more powerful. Abroad, they might well have felt that government existed not to direct but to support their activities. At home, they had no cause to contest the adage that that government governs best which governs least, and to feel a glorious freedom to act as the private interest dictated.

The last half of the nineteenth century, and the early years of the

184

twentieth, were perhaps the zenith of the independence of business and finance from governmental control or interference. Erratic forays like the trust-busting efforts of Teddy Roosevelt had little effect on the steady growth in size and power of corporate enterprise. But the Great Depression of the 1930s, and the coming to political power of the New Deal of FDR, brought about a revolution in government-business relations. Despite its early demise under the ministrations of the Supreme Court, the NRA had much to do with this. The social and economic legislation of the mid-1930s created, while preserving the rhetoric of a free enterprise system, what was in reality a mixed-enterprise system. And this process was accelerated in the 1940s, under the impetus of wartime controls, allocations, and regulations. Without much effective notice, aside from the protests of such volumes as Hayek's *The Road to Serfdom*, this process brought about a real ambiguity in concepts of private enterprise and enterprise that was, to use a formerly fashionable phrase, affected with a public interest. Thus, government began the process of regulation of such previously private matters as the manner in which a corporation could distribute its securities and raise its capital, of the manner in which it could hire and fire its employees and, on occasion, of the prices at which it could buy and sell — even whether and to whom it could sell. Much of that bundle of rights which constitutes private property was, by the end of the 1930s, substantially in the hands of government. World War II, the Korean war, new concepts of the ability and indeed the duty of government to manage the economy, accelerated the process and dimmed the distinctions between the affairs of private business and those of government.

The results may be bad or good; the fact is stubbornly present. It gives some solid reason for the current feeling that government has more than a little to do with its corporate offspring and with the manner in which its nationals administer corporate business — abroad as well as at home. The fact that government is accustomed to affect corporate wage, labor, funding, and other activities at home influences the attitude of governments — both the home and the host state — toward that same corporation when it appears overseas.

In the interplay of the sovereignty of nations and the transnational activities of business, this background of regulation and control and this attitude are important. At the least, a mood is set which makes it not unlikely that a sober and reasonably friendly host government, not impressed by the wilder charges of government-business conspiracies, will feel that the large private firm operating abroad is tinged with governmental associations. The home government may also feel that "its" firms abroad owe it some duties.

This feeling of the home government is apt to be stronger than would otherwise be the case if it is financing the foreign activities of one of its firms. If, on the one hand, the Ford Motor Company has the financial resources to buy out British interests in English Ford, there is little that the United States can do about this decision unless and until it is willing to enact general controls over such financial transactions on balance of payments grounds. If, on the other hand, the investment of an American company in a foreign jurisdiction is dependent upon its obtaining an extended risk guaranty from the Agency for International Development, and/or a local currency loan that derives from U.S. funds, it is probable that the investor will find himself immersed with his government in rather detailed discussion of his *pro forma* balance sheet and profit and loss statement, his ability to operate the project, etc. He will probably even have to justify the kind of investment he is making, and to do so on grounds that are asserted to relate to national — not private — interests. In such a situation, the conclusion is likely to be drawn by the host that the home government and its "private" investors have more than a slight mutuality of interests.

It may be that this conclusion will be taken even if there is no governmental assistance that is sought. But when the government acts as banker or guarantor, preoccupations additional to those of the private banker are suspected. And it is at least possible that the government as banker does not keep its banking role entirely separate from its preoccupation with foreign economic or political policy.

Where the financing relationship does not exist, the international firm may still find itself affected by and disposed toward govern-

186

mental desires that are known (even if sometimes not expressed). Governments have many benefits to confer or deny. The United States government is a huge consumer of corporate products. It buys research and development, it purchases enormous quantities of goods, directly and indirectly, and it deals in all sorts of matters that can make or break a corporate profit and loss statement. This fact is likely to be noted, even if it is not much mentioned when matters collateral to purchases or sales are at issue. The consequent power is sometimes openly and directly used; a seller who violates the provisions of Regulation I of the Agency for International Development may find himself blacklisted, and by a process which is not open to judicial or other review. And denial of access to AID-financed sales (or possibly AID guaranties) may have drastic effects on a business enterprise.

There is a general tendency to limit the exercise of such power to situations in which it can reasonably be asserted to be related to the governmental action from which the business hopes to benefit; the government as banker may go beyond the criteria of the private banker, but its demands generally relate to the soundness of the loan and the attainment of the objectives for which the loan is made. Nonetheless, dependence on government facilities will bring an enterprise increasingly under governmental control, actual as well as potential; and such control is a factor in the foreign relations of the firm that is thought to be subject to it.

It is implicit in what has been said in the foregoing that there is a geographic aspect of the multinational firm–national sovereignty issue. When American — and many other — firms venture into the less-developed parts of the world, they wish guarantees, specific risk, extended risk, whatever is available. But a government, before giving such a guarantee, desires in the first place some umbrella type of arrangement with the host state and, second, wishes to examine the proposed investment from a number of points of view. The impression, as has been said, is left of a government-business partnership. When President Nixon speaks of IPC in Peru as "our" company, the impression is heightened. Moreover, sensibilities are likely to be greatest in the less-developed countries. American technology may be worrisome to a sophisticated and advanced Europe,

187

but foreign ownership of the "national resources" of the southern half of the world induces, in the halls of the United Nations, annual and (it would seem to the investor) almost psychotic resolutions. In the developing countries of the world, a large part of foreign investment is in extractive industries, always a sensitive area. Another large part of industrial investment benefits from home government guarantees, with their implication of a government-business complex in which political considerations may influence if not determine business decisions. The international firm is likely, therefore, to face quite different attitudes toward national sovereignty in the less-developed than in the developed parts of the world.

Much depends on other matters. One of the most important of these is the nationality of the international firm. Firms other than American ones have come up against the nationalistic barrier. The original proposals of Fiat toward Citroën were regarded in France as something of an affront to national honor, particularly since French tradition has firmly established the Citroën as the automobile in which bank robbers escape and Ministers ride. The Belgians did not regard with pleasure the proposed merger of their large photographic firm, Gevaert, into the German company, Agfa. A converse situation arose in 1968, when the German Dresdner Bank reached an agreement with the Compagnie Française des Pétroles to contribute the bank's 35% holding in Germany's largest locally owned petroleum refining company, and the bank itself decided to make the deal subject to government approval. This the bank did in recognition of the "special situation" of Germany's oil industry, more than 75% of which was already in foreign hands, and despite the fact that the government might disapprove the deal, though it had no legal authority so to do. In point of fact, the government did exercise the veto thus conferred on it, simultaneously announcing that it would aid Germany's oil companies in consolidation and strengthening of their operations. Another non-American case is that of the acquisition of the principal Norwegian aluminum producing company by Aluminium Ltd. of Canada, which has been extensively and learnedly commented on.

But, in general, for those who write on the subject, it is the

American company that is thought of as the acquirer and business imperialist. And the size of many American companies, their traditional eagerness to expand and ingenuity in effecting expansion, seem to justify the thought. As noted, some developed countries may in fact feel otherwise, and the scholarly attitude may not reflect the views of former colonies, where the American entrepreneur may be regarded as one who opens a new window. But the "problem" is generally thought of as an American one.

Finally, what the international firm does is obviously relevant. The good citizens of Paris may resent the American cultural influence reflected in the growth of "le snack bar" or "le Drugstore" as the Academy resents Franglais, but ownership by an American food chain of the Wimpy hamburger joints does not excite quite the same xenophobic reaction as IBM domination of the computer industry. Ownership of public utilities in Latin America has turned out, as inflation boosted costs while rates remained constant or were raised against public outcry, to be as bad for stockholders as useful for propagandists. Since the days of agrarian reform in Mexico in the early 1920s, it has been evident that the ownership of large tracts of foreign real estate, however efficiently farmed, was often a cause of unpopularity and consequently an unwise use of corporate funds. Natural resources, it has been said, have nerves lying close to the surface. Thus, suggestions like those of the World Bank, that a country like Turkey should develop and export its timber resources, has been thought to suggest an "exploitation" of national resources by foreigners, and has thus been greeted with an enthusiasm similar to that which would be shown by the Sierra Club if there were a proposal to turn Yellowstone Park over to Crown Zellerbach. Where an international firm may safely go into manufacturing or distribution of nonstrategic products, the ability of foreigners to control production of items thought, rightly or wrongly, to be related to national security — electronic equipment, for example — sends chills of hostility up the spines of hosts who want the production but not the foreign control. This sentiment, as demonstrated by American legislation on coastal shipping, and reaction to foreign ownership in the United States dyestuff industry (control by I. G. Farben of General Aniline and Film Corporation,

189

in the World War II epoch) is not one to which the United States is immune.

Intergovernmental Conflict through the Firm

From what has already been said, it will be evident that no general theory of international firms and national jurisdictions is likely to emerge, at least in these pages. There are too many distinctions that must be drawn — between the relations of one international firm and another with their own home government, between the kinds of activities they carry on abroad, between the areas in which they operate, whether less-developed or developed, and certainly between the intelligence and tact with which they conduct their affairs. It is also clear that there are economic as well as political problems; no country likes to feel that a major part of its industry is controlled from the outside, and that major economic decisions may be made for the profit of a foreign group of stockholders — much less for the profit of the polity of a foreign government. Each country likes to have some say in whether some or all of the facilities of a vertically integrated industry are located within its borders, and as to whether a major share of the total profits of the enterprise are left there. Important in the "real" world or not, there are some activities that each country likes to have under the control of its own nationals. Finally, host countries may well feel that there is rather more than a chummy relationship between international firms and their home governments, and that there is rather too much intermingling of business and government decision making.

This assumed if not proven, it seems useful, in this empirical manner, to turn to certain of the situations in which it is commonly asserted that conflict has occurred between policies imposed through if not by international firms and the policies of the host governments.

A. Antitrust. The potential for conflict seems high in the field of antitrust, and indeed, those who assert that the United States has erred in trying, through the ownership or control by American firms of subsidiaries abroad, to inflict the rigors of its policies outside its national territory, use antitrust as a prime example. That there are theoretical grounds for such fears is fairly clear. The antitrust laws

190

of the United States apply not only to commerce among the several American states, but also to commerce between the states and foreign nations. It is quite conceivable that American strictures might be applied to two foreign enterprises that do no business in the United States, but which combine together to restrict American entry into a foreign market. American antitrust laws have been applied to wholly foreign defendants operating a transportation route to the United States. Conversely, where acts are done, with or without the participation of American firms, it has been held that they are not within the antitrust laws if their sole effect is on commerce in a foreign country, though the broad validity of the 1909 American Banana case so holding is today somewhat in doubt.

The authoritative Restatement of the Foreign Relations Law of the United States, in Section 18, concludes that a state has jurisdiction to prescribe a rule of law which gives legal consequences to conduct outside its territory, if the conduct causes an effect within its territory, under certain conditions. Those conditions are in general that the conduct and the activity must be parts of the activity to which the rule applies, that the effects must be substantial and be a foreseeable result of the conduct, and that the "rule is not inconsistent with the principles of justice generally recognized by states that have reasonably developed legal systems." The authority cited is the Alcoa case, in the 2d Circuit Court of Appeals in 1945. The Restatement rule seems to go rather far; the case on which it relies had rather special features. One was that one of the members of the foreign cartel was an affiliate, through common stock ownership, of the Aluminum Company of America; and the opinion of Judge Learned Hand stated that the action abroad of foreign companies must have been intended to affect the American market, and that it must be shown that the effect actually was achieved.

It is of course possible that, in such a situation, there may be conflicting mandates. In the 1951 Imperial Chemicals Industries case, ICI (British) and DuPont (American) each had monopolized certain patents, licensing only each other and in such a way that United States patented products could not be sold in Britain and vice versa. The American court ordered compulsory licensing, and ordered ICI to assign their nylon patents to DuPont, in violation of a previous assignment of an exclusive license by ICI to a British firm. The British firm then obtained, in a British court, an order that ICI fulfill the terms of its British contract. The clear conflict with the American court decree was, however, avoided, because of a saving clause in the United States decree which exempted from its scope action taken to conform to foreign law to which the company was subject.

These illustrations, and the statement of Judge Learned Hand that "any state may impose liabilities . . . for conduct outside its borders that has consequences within its borders that the state reprehends" suggest the likelihood of conflict between national jurisdictions, which is not lessened by the Supreme Court's statement in the Continental Ore case of 1962 that "a conspiracy to monopolize or restrain the domestic or foreign commerce of the United States is not outside the reach of the Sherman Act because part of the conduct complained of occurs in foreign countries." This possibility is sometimes said to be enhanced because of a general difference in philosophy between United States and antitrust laws: the United States laws generally are said to fall into the "prohibition" category — that is, they prohibit certain restrictive business practices and forbid the acquisition of dominant or monopoly power; the European laws generally are in the "abuse of power" category, with regulation designed to prevent abuses of such practices or such dominant positions.

How real are these fears of conflict?

First, it may be observed that the antitrust problems arise in relations with the developed, not the less-developed countries, though less-developed-country antitrust questions are, of course, not impossible.

Second, there is no necessary connection between ownership or control of foreign subsidiaries (the general situation of the "international firm") and antitrust. The ICI-DuPont case illustrates that.

Third, the rise of antitrust in other developed nations, notably those of Europe, suggests that the extraterritorial application of antitrust laws may not long remain exclusively an American problem. Articles 85 and 86 of the Treaty of Rome are part of the national law of each Common Market state, and may be there enforced.

Fourth, the antitrust principles found in Articles 85 and 86 have a definite similarity to American antitrust laws. The European Coal and Steel Community has had very stringent antitrust laws since 1951. Germany, France, Holland, and Belgium all have laws in the field of antitrust, the German one being the closest to that of the United States. Obviously, as the substantive law of the several nations that may be involved draw closer to each other, the possibility of conflict is diminished.

Finally, there have been several attempts to minimize conflict by consultation, agreement, or by procedural measures. The abortive draft charter of an International Trade Organization (1948) contained proposed minimal principles on antitrust, which were to be put into effect by national legislation. An unsuccessful try at comity via the international tribunal route was contained in the Report of the Ad Hoc Committee on Restrictive Practices of the UN, in 1953. But there have been some successes in the effort to reduce or eliminate conflicts. A GATT resolution of 1969 provides for a procedure for complaints and for consultation, and clauses that are now found as a standard feature of the proliferating treaties of friendship, commerce, and navigation also provide for consultation.

The OECD has a Restrictive Business Practices Committee, which meets twice annually and whose membership covers most of what is known as the free, developed world. It provides a forum for discussion of problems of mutual interest — among which may be considered possibilities of conflicting jurisdiction. The United States delegation always contains someone from the Department of State, who may be presumed by his official preoccupations to be sympathetic to foreign complaints about excessive American zeal in what foreign states may consider to be their own jurisdictions. There is a continuing liaison, on the American side, between the Departments of State and Justice. And there exists a "gentleman's agreement" between the United States and Canada, which seems to bring satisfaction to the antitrust officials on both sides of the border.

So much for the factual background. I conclude, contrary to current opinion of others more expert than I in economics and political science, that this tale moves one neither to pity nor rage. It seems to me to be extraordinarily difficult, on this record, to show that the potential for international conflict has, in fact, been realized, or that, in any case, its realization depends in any significant way upon the existence of international firms, or that such conflict is likely to increase as international or multinational firms multiply. There are, of course, conflicts between companies doing business, national or international, and the antitrust authorities of various countries. Since the United States has many such firms, since a good many of them do business abroad or have contractual arrangements with foreign firms, and since the United States has led in both the scope and the enforcement of its antitrust laws, most such conflicts have involved the United States government. But it is hard to argue that the trend has not been toward harmonization of law and policy by others moving in the direction of the United States; that where persons who are charged with violation of United States law and with adversely affecting commerce in or with the United States can be found in the jurisdiction, they should not be sued; or that where, as in the Swiss watch case, there is a real dispute over the respective sovereignties of two nations, good faith — and successful — attempts have not been made, through diplomatic channels, to reconcile the conflicting views.

Moreover, since the home government, at least in the case of the United States, applies a test based on what is done and not on ownership, there is no discrimination between the acts of subsidiaries of domestic parent and those of nonaffiliated foreign companies. Except, of course, that one has to *catch* the nonaffiliated foreigner (which these days is not so difficult to do), whereas the undisputed authority over the domestic parent makes the subsidiary immediately answerable. This is hardly a discrimination that pulls at one's heartstrings.

Only in the rather infrequent case in which an American court may prohibit action that a foreign court requires is there a real conflict: in those cases conciliation seems to have been effective; and in any case, this is part of the general problem of antitrust enforcement among nations, not necessarily related to the impact of the international firm on national sovereignty.

At least in this important field of antitrust, I am therefore inclined to feel that the international firm presents no real threat to comity between the nations.

B. *National Security and Denial Policies.* The classic example of the problem posed by the existence of the international firm, with its parent in one country and its subsidiary in another, is the imposition on the subsidiary of policies felt by the home government to be desirable but considered to be undesirable by the host government. Frequently cited in this situation are the Trading with the Enemy Act controls of the United States and the consequent attempt by the United States to impose restrictions on foreign subsidiaries which are contrary to host government policy. Thus, the subsidiary of an American company in France or in Canada is prohibited under Trading with the Enemy Act controls from conducting trade with Cuba or Communist China, even though France or Canada may consider such trade not only permissible, but in some cases, positively desirable.

(It may be mentioned parenthetically that the situation also applies to licensing arrangements made by the American company, the United States requiring as a condition of such license that the foreign subsidiary comply with American laws and American criteria. A related aspect of this same matter is the possible imposition by the home government of economic or financial policies that may contradict the corresponding policies in the host nation. Thus at the outset of the Foreign Direct Investment Controls of the United States, it was suggested that American policy would be to require the French subsidiary of an American company to repatriate dividends to the United States, while French policy would be to keep such dividends in France.)

Undeniable though the prospects for conflict are, it does not seem likely that there have been important difficulties in either of these regards, other than the psychological trauma that exists in the host country when it realizes that policies of operating entities within its jurisdiction are being determined from without.

That the United States, in these situations, will try to ensure that its own policies are not frustrated by the foreign operations of persons within its jurisdictions, is clear. It will hardly make sense for the United States, assuming that it believes an embargo on trade with Cuba is desirable, to prohibit exports from the United States directly, but to be indifferent to such exports by a Canadian subsidiary. Moreover, the home government will ordinarily try to make its policies in the monetary or fiscal field effective; and one way of so doing is to ask the American parent to comply with its policies, at home or abroad.

Nevertheless, the problem is one which is far broader than that of the national or multinational corporation. It may be that a more direct possibility of control exists when the foreign corporation is either a subsidiary or a licensee of the American corporation; but the United States has characteristically and often quite successfully attempted to impose its Trading with the Enemy concepts on foreign operating entities, even when there were no direct ownership or licensing arrangements stemming from the United States. Thus, The Mutual Defense Assistance Control Act of 1949 required the Administration to terminate Marshall Plan aid, both military and economic, if companies in Marshall Plan countries did not agree to an embargo on the shipment of what were considered to be strategic materials to what was then called the Communist bloc. Most of the foreign companies thus affected were independent entities, subject to no direction from American parents, and yet the controls were in the main successful. The right of a sovereign nation to attempt to make its policies effective was, in fact, sufficiently recognized so that even a constitutionally neutral country like Switzerland, not a recipient of Marshall Plan aid, was willing to adopt procedures to guarantee that shipments subject to the embargo were not transhipped through Swiss channels.

The possibility of a conflict, at least with allies, was greatly ameliorated by the establishment, at the initial suggestion of the United Kingdom, of an institution known as COCOM — the Consultative Committee — in which agreement was sought and very largely reached as to what, in fact, should be considered strategic. In the few cases in which agreement could not be reached, "exceptions," or withdrawals from its stated hard line, were made by the

196

United States. Thus, the United States required termination of all aid in the case of sale of oil tankers to the Soviet bloc; but a Danish decision to honor its contractual obligations with the Soviet Union and to deliver previously ordered tankers resulted only in a Presidential determination that the national interest of the United States required an exception to the law — a decision perhaps arrived at more easily because the aid in question was to build an airfield that the U.S. military felt was necessary to NATO defenses.

At various times and in varying circumstances, there has been a strongly held feeling in one country or another that foreign ownership or control of certain activities was prejudicial to the national interest. The United States has been no exception. As has already been mentioned, coastwise shipping in the United States has traditionally been excluded from foreign ownership. Similarly, foreigners have been prohibited from acquiring interests in American land, in the American telecommunications industry, etc. In the late 1940s and early 1950s, considerable agitation existed in the United States over the possibility that, through the intermediary of Swiss banks, whose actions were shrouded in secrecy under Swiss law, foreigners were acquiring substantial interests in American defense-related industry.

Security considerations have, from time to time, worried governments in whose territory foreign nationals owned substantial industrial interests. During World War II, grave apprehension was expressed in the United States over the ownership by German and, to a much lesser extent, Japanese nationals, of various segments of American industry. When companies that had been vested by the United States Alien Property Custodian at the outset of World War II were finally sold to the American public, foreign acquisition of the shares of these companies was either prohibited or limited. Worries about control from Germany over subsidiaries in Latin America stimulated the creation of something called the Replacement Program, which was designed to transfer the ownership and control from alien to friendly Latin American hands.

In the perspective given by the passage of the years, most of these worries seemed to have been exaggerated. The relevant fact was the existence of certain facilities within the jurisdiction of the host country. Where it was necessary, companies whose continued production was desired were taken over by the Alien Property Custodian, management was transferred to a government-designated Board of Directors or Trustees, and production continued, and in most cases, was substantially enhanced. Thus, General Aniline and Film, despite German ownership (assuming the validity of the assertion that the ostensible Swiss owners were merely a front for I. G. Farben), made a substantial contribution to the American war effort just as the German subsidiaries of General Motors contributed to the production of tanks and military vehicles for the Wehrmacht. Should it desire to exercise it, the authority of the host government exists over facilities that are located within its own territory. Whether that authority is exercised depends, of course, upon the degree of importance that is attributed by the host government to the desired productive or commercial activity.

All of this is not to say that no problems do exist, or that they are not of some degree of importance. For example, there has been — and continues to be — considerable irritation abroad over the rather stiff and doctrinaire interpretation of the Treasury Department of the United States of the prohibitions promulgated under the Trading with the Enemy Act. The Congress and the Securities and Exchange Commission worry the Swiss in their feeling that books and records affecting happenings in the United States are not immutably secret. It is not a complete answer to worries about conflict of national policies to say that, in most cases, these have been relatively satisfactorily adjusted. Nor is it merely the exercise of a power which is a problem; the mere existence of the power may itself give a sense of insecurity, and the fact of dominance by foreign nationals in certain industries, particularly those that are considered to be closely related to national security, may well enhance that insecurity.

Nonetheless, a close look at the realities of conflicts arising from so-called denial policies reveals that they are far from entirely those of international rather than national firms. Where the home government can control a subsidiary or a licensee through a holding company or licensor, the techniques for enforcing denial policies are, of course, easier. And it is certainly an irritant for Canada to

198

be told that the Canadian subsidiary of an American company cannot trade with Cuba, when Canadian policy is to permit such trade. But there are not many cases in which important differences of policy of this sort have not been reconciled. The sheer economic size of the United States does not always imply usable power, just as the holding of an American "spy" ship by North Korea has demonstrated that the possession of military might by the United States does not necessarily betoken a willingness to use that might. The problems that may be included in the topic of international firms and national sovereignty are, in sum, part of the much larger issues of conflicts and reconciliations of national policies.

A European Company Law

A principal current attempt to deal with the problem of the multinational firm is the proposal for a Company Law which would be common to the countries of the European Economic Community. It is suggested that such a law would, in conferring equal rights and duties in all countries of the Common Market, do away with conflicts of policy at least as among those states.

I consider the prospects for such a law to be dubious, and its effects to be considerably less than all-embracing. As to the prospects, the February 14, 1969, issue of *Business International* states that "efforts to draft supranational company law have again been sabotaged by France, which has indicated that it will not participate in further talks." Even if one assumes that this boycott will not last forever, and that the views of de Gaulle may not long survive his recent defeat and retirement, it is not entirely clear that a supranational EEC company law would be either without drawbacks or would be much of a step toward solution of problems arising out of clashes of company or governmental policy.

There appears, first, to be some question whether non-EEC nationals would be able to take advantage of the projected Common Market incorporation. If not, the new law might be a convenient vehicle for enforcement of the French desire to keep foreigners (e.g., Americans) out of the Market — a desire that has so far been frustrated, much to the benefit of the Market, by the availability of national company laws. Second, it is not clear that Common Market rather than French or Belgian incorporation would necessarily affect business or government decisions. Would the fact of Market incorporation change the ownership and control realities of a Fiat-Citroën merger? If the stockholders in a Common Market incorporated company were the Compagnie Française des Pétroles, would the Germans be more willing to have it acquire Gelsenkirchner Bergwerke AG?

A common European company law would have some advantages. It would, of course, eliminate the time and bother necessary for a company incorporated in one nation to obtain permission to operate in another; but that is really not such a great difficulty, as witness the flourishing condition of many a Delaware corporation, not only in the 50 American states, but also across Europe. A common company law would facilitate harmonization, and help to do away with varying interpretations of identical or similar provision of current law. But the statement that without such a law "the parties in international mergers . . . would have to solve incredibly difficult problems and face staggering costs" (Colonna, European Community, September 1968) seems somewhat excessive, particularly since some companies seem already to have solved some of these very problems. The suggestion is perhaps more relevant that "there would be an important psychological advantage in the creation of a type of multinational company. If such a company enlarged its share of the market, it would not be associated with any particular national flag." Perhaps the principal value of such a new law would be its establishment of a common policy toward worker participation in management (though reconciliation of these varying provisions is a tough obstacle to the proposed law itself). In areas of company law such as this, a single policy might indeed be useful.

In any case, work seems to be proceeding, on the basis of a model statute that was prepared by a group of experts from the Six and completed in 1966. The Commission of the EEC has suggested to the Council that the Commission proceed with preparation of a draft convention based on the expert draft. What, in view of the French attitude, will come of this project is uncertain; but resolution of the entirety of the difficulties is too much to ask of this proposal.

Just what those difficulties are was considered at an interview-conference between European and American businessmen and theorists in Paris on December 16, 1968. At that meeting, Jean-Jacques Servan-Schreiber alluded to the desirability of a "European power," argued that "what is lacking to help is laws," but finally agreed that "you get into psychological problems." It may well be that it is these psychological problems that are most relevant to the difficulties centered on international firms and the national jurisdictions. There are, of course, economic and political problems, arising from the ability of a foreigner — be he the home office or the government of the parent company — to make decisions that may adversely affect the national interests of the host state. And psychological problems are no less real than others. But it may be necessary to deal with them on a somewhat different basis, with more understanding for national sensibilities, than would be the case if all were merely to sit down to try to maximize economic benefits.

The Foreign Firm as Domestic Good Citizen

From this point of view, such suggestions as those of Professor Vernon that the Calvo clause be recognized by the United States (a clear nonstarter, in my opinion) has at least the merit of suggesting a psychologically meaningful approach. There is evidence that sympathetic attention to local attitudes and local problems can have startling results. The Chrysler takeover of Simca in 1963 — despite the fact that it was a rescue of a failing company — stirred angry headlines in France. The government was openly angry. But, in June, 1968, when red flags flew over the gates of many a French company, when rioting was taking place outside the Renault plant at Flins, the Simca plant at Poissy five miles away from Renault continued to turn out autos. Labor relations have been excellent. Simca now exports more autos in Europe than Peugeot, Citroën, and Renault combined — which may be a reason why its relations with a French government that needs foreign exchange earnings particularly in the present dubious condition of the franc, have been and continue to be very good.

It is not likely, nonetheless, that being on good conduct will settle all the problems. Despite my feeling that the extent of the conflict between international firms and national sovereignties has been exaggerated, many of the issues are real, and not susceptible to solution through the Lady Bountiful treatment. A decision, private though it may be, to close down a plant, like the Remington decision to shut down operations at Lyon, has direct economic consequences, would be resented if the decision were taken by a local company, and is detested if taken abroad. The association of government and business is more than a fiction, and provides a very real cause for worries that excessive or even important control of resources from abroad may mean pressure from foreign governments. The problems arise because of conflicts that do not yield merely to politeness.

It is, I believe, useful to recognize that the problem is broader than that implied in the parent-subsidiary, or licensor-licensee relationship. At the same time, it is a series of different problems, each of which is likely to be responsive to somewhat different treatment. Ownership by American and Foreign Power of the traction companies of Latin America could be and was solved by turning them over to local governments, getting out of the unpleasant task of trying to raise rates and infuriating commuters, and investing the proceeds in local industry. Such problems as there may be in connection with American ownership of some 70% of Mexican industry is a quite different matter. No one remedy answers the needs.

At the same time, it is possible to take some general steps. Perhaps, despite my general scepticism, the proposed EEC company law is one such.

Certainly, the tendency toward denationalization of international corporate activities will help — the willingness of American firms not only to have national managers and shareholders for their foreign subsidiaries, but to create a truly international manpower and management pool, for home office as well as foreign activities. As Professor Kindleberger has put it, there is a natural tendency toward good citizenship, and this may in the long run be the most effective remedy.

On the international side, increased use of the facilities of such organizations as the OECD, the various regional commissions of the United Nations, the IBRD, etc., may help to solve some of the assorted conflicts. As pointed out, consultation has already proved its utility, both in the field of antitrust, of governmental restraint policy, and in other areas (like the application of the Foreign Direct Investment controls of the United States which, it may be noted, caused worry by their threat to reduce, not to add to, the flow of United States industrial penetration of foreign markets).

It has been suggested that more forums for consultation would be useful. It seems hard to contest a proposal for more reasoning together, but it would be well to define just what is the topic around which consultation is to take place. The forum is a function of the topic: it would probably be inappropriate to discuss the problems of American-owned international firms in relation to the less-developed countries in, for example, the OECD: it would not seem useful to discuss American-French questions under the umbrella of the UNCTAD; and so forth. A new forum, or new forums, might be created — but under governmental or private sponsorship, or the sponsorship of what international organization? And how are the topics to be chosen and the issues defined, the participants selected? These are not insuperable obstacles. But the questions, to my mind, suggest that a series of meetings on questions more narrowly defined than those of "the international firm" and with a limited and relevant participation, are more likely to yield satisfaction than would an attempt to organize a new general forum.

In the end, the answer may lie with the growing maturity, and the increasing social as well as business responsibilities, of the modern corporation. As long ago as 1932, Professor E. Merrick Dodd, of the Harvard Law School, pointed out the social function, in national terms, of the modern corporation. Some years later, Adolph Berle said: "It is justifiable to consider the American corporation not as a business device but as a social institution in the context of a revolutionary century." On the international scale, the Kindle-

SEYMOUR J. RUBIN

berger rubric of "good citizenship" has in it something of this sentiment. So approached, recognizing the problems not as merely those of corporate business relations across national boundaries, but as problems of an evolving international society, something may perhaps be done not merely to reduce frictions but to increase mutual benefits.

CHAPTER EIGHT

THE MYTH OF NATIONAL INTERDEPENDENCE*

Kenneth N. Waltz

"Peace is indivisible," a slogan of the 1930s, suggests that a small war anywhere means war everywhere unless the small war can somehow be stopped. The domino theory is an old one. Its economic equivalent is found in statements, frequently made, that America cannot exist as an island of affluence in a sea of impoverished nations. From such statements the mistaken conclusion is often drawn that a growing closeness of interdependence would improve the chances of peace.

But close interdependence means closeness of contact and raises the prospect of at least occasional conflict. The fiercest civil wars and the bloodiest international ones have been fought within arenas populated by highly similar people whose affairs had become quite closely knit together. It is hard to get a war going unless the potential participants are somehow closely linked. Interdependent states whose relations remain unregulated must experience conflict and will occasionally fall into violence. If regulation is hard to come by, as it is in the relations of states, then it would seem to follow that a lessening of interdependence is desirable.

Focusing on the international corporation, however, has led

* I am grateful to the National Science Foundation for supporting my research on this subject, to Harvard's Center for International Affairs at which the research and writing were done, and to Ellyn Hessler, who assisted me on every aspect of this paper.

many economists to believe that international interdependence is high and is rapidly becoming higher. The thought is forcefully put by the various people who claim that the national state has become an obsolete economic unit. If the interdependence of nations is high and becoming higher, we must expect international difficulties to multiply. I am inclined to be sanguine because I believe that interdependence is low and, if anything, is on the decrease. Those who come to the opposite conclusion apparently do so for two reasons. What interdependence entails is often incorrectly understood. Because this is so, economic developments are looked at aside from their proper context.

The Meaning of Interdependence

A comparison of the conditions of internal and external interdependence will make it clear that in international relations interdependence is always a marginal affair. The political elements of a state are formally differentiated according to the degrees of their authority, and their distinct functions are specified. Specification of roles and differentiation of functions characterize any state, the more fully so as the state is more highly developed. The parts of a highly developed polity are closely interdependent. Some parts depend on others for services and supplies that they cannot easily, if at all, provide for themselves. Thus Washington depends upon Kansas for its beef and its wheat, and Kansas depends on Washington for protection and regulation. In saying that in such situations interdependence is close, one need not maintain that the one part could not learn to live without the other. One need only say that the cost of breaking the interdependent relation would be high. Where the political and economic division of labor is elaborately developed, high inequality may be found; and yet a mutuality of interest among unequals may be said to prevail.[1]

[1] Cf. R. E. Park, *Human Communities: the City and Human Ecology* (Glencoe, Ill.: Free Press, 1952), p. 80: "People live together on the whole, not because they are alike, but because they are useful to one another." Cf. also J. G. March and H. A. Simon, *Organizations* (New York: John Wiley & Sons, 1958), p. 159: "The greater the *specialization by subprograms* (process specialization), the greater the *interdependence among organizational subunits*."

The domestic order is composed of heterogeneous elements; the international order is composed of homogeneous units. Each state regulates its own affairs and supplies largely out of its own resources the food, clothing, housing, transportation, and amenities consumed and used by its citizens. The international order is characterized by the coaction of like units. Since the functions of all states are highly similar, differentiation among them is principally according to their varied capabilities.

Because the units that populate the international arena are the same in type, interdependence among them is low even if those units are of approximately equal size. Interdependence is further reduced by the immense disparity in the capabilities of states. This last point can be stated as an iron law: high inequality among like units *is* low interdependence.

How interdependent are these not very interdependent states, and what difference does the answer to this question make? In the European-centered great-power politics of the three centuries that ended with World War II, five or more great powers sought to coexist peacefully and at times contended for mastery. Since World War II, only two states have perched at the pinnacle of power. It follows from the law just stated that the interdependence of states is less now than it was earlier. But this deduction will not be accepted unless the force and meaning of the law are made clear. The validity of the proposition can be established by looking at international trade and investment, not simply at a moment in time and as absolute amounts, but by viewing them in relation to the volume of internal business and in comparison with the patterns of previous periods.[2]

Trade: Changes in National Involvement

Even if the interdependence of nations is in general low, we nevertheless want to know whether it is lower or higher now than in

---

[2] I have, of course, had to leave some things out of this paper. To draw a fuller picture would require consideration of monetary and balance of payments problems, short-term capital movements, etc. The conclusions reached would, I believe, be similar to those arrived at by examining international trade and investment.

earlier times. In the late nineteenth and early twentieth centuries, the external sector loomed large. Not only was the level of external transactions high in comparison with internal production, but also the internal order was characterized by a low level of governmental activity. Even if the interdependence of nations has increased in the meantime, the progress of internal integration and the increased intervention of governments in their domestic economies means that for most states the internal sector now looms larger than it once did. But it is not even clear that the interdependence of states has increased overall.

Prior to World War I, most of the great powers of the world were also great traders; economically they were closely tied together. In the years preceding World War I, for example, Germany was Britain's second-best customer, both as a source of imports and as a market for exports. Measured in terms of their own economies, the two greatest powers in the world today trade little with each other or with the rest of the world.[3] Most of this change can be accounted for by the fact that the present great powers of the world are geographically much larger than the old ones.[4] Britain, France, Italy, and Japan, it should be noticed, also trade a smaller proportion of their national product now than they once did.[5]

[3] The situation of low economic interdependence along with high political-military interdependence suggests the limits of drawing conclusions from economic conditions alone. I have, however, confined myself to worrying about the international political implications of economic developments.

[4] Cf. K. W. Deutsch, C. I. Bliss, and A. Eckstein, "Population, Sovereignty, and the Share of Foreign Trade," *Economic Development and Cultural Change*, Vol. X (July 1962), pp. 353–366; S. Kuznets, "Economic Growth of Small Nations," in E.A.G. Robinson, ed., *Economic Consequences of the Size of Nations* (London: Macmillan, 1960), pp. 14–32; H. B. Chenery, "Patterns of Industrial Growth," *American Economic Review*, Vol. L (September 1960), pp. 624–654; C. P. Kindleberger, *Foreign Trade and the National Economy* (New Haven: Yale University Press, 1962), pp. 32–37.

[5] K. W. Deutsch and A. Eckstein, "National Industrialization and the Declining Share of the International Economic Sector, 1890–1959," *World Politics*, Vol. XIII (January 1961), p. 275. Cf. S. Kuznets, *Modern Economic Growth* (New Haven: Yale University Press, 1966), pp. 312–314. Decline is marked for all of the great powers except Germany. The comparison made, however, is between all of Germany earlier and Western Germany now. The change in the size of the state, of course, affects the level of its foreign trade.

From the recent growth of world trade, however, one might be tempted to conclude that the relative decreases in trade are only temporary and that the interdependence of nations is now tending toward the old level. In the years from 1953 to 1965, both trade in manufactured goods and trade in primary products grew more rapidly than world output in each of the two categories.[6] In the economic data for the first half of this century, however, there is a strong component of war and depression. To a considerable extent we are dealing, in the past two decades, with recovery rates; and the recovery is rooted in the economic resurgence of Western Europe and Japan. In the years from 1926 to 1930 world manufactures grew more rapidly than trade in manufactured goods — about 40% as compared to less than 15%. This was in part because of the faster economic growth of the United States, a relatively self-sufficient country, as compared to the economic growth of West European countries, which are more dependent on imports. Beginning in the 1950s, the rapid growth of Japan and of West European countries has given a corresponding boost to world trade.[7]

As well as considering the decline of trade in relation to GNP and the recent growth of world trade overall, we should ask whether changes in the composition and direction of trade have affected the extent of interdependence. In advanced industrial countries a larger proportion of the national product is now composed of products whose raw-material content is low. This is true not only because the service sector has grown but also because more value is added to raw materials as they are transformed into technologically more complicated goods. The GNP's of advanced countries have thus grown faster than their demand for primary products.[8] In 1953, trade among developed countries accounted for 37.2% of world trade; 12 years later the amount had increased to 46.5%. In 1953,

[6] M. Z. Cutajar and A. Franks, *The Less Developed Countries in World Trade: A Reference Handbook* (London: Overseas Development Institute, 1967), Table 1, p. 21.

[7] A. Maizels, *Industrial Growth and World Trade* (Cambridge: Cambridge University Press, 1963), pp. 79–81.

[8] The point is often made. See e.g., R. Nurkse, Wicksell Lectures for 1959, published as *Patterns of Trade and Development* (Stockholm: Almquist & Wiksell, 1959), p. 23.

the trade of less-developed with developed countries accounted for 19.3% of world trade; 12 years later the amount had decreased to 14%.[9] The exchange of finished goods for primary products has grown less rapidly than trade in finished goods among industrial countries. A lesser portion of trade now is done out of near necessity, and more of it is merely for profit. The present relation of less-developed to developed countries is less close than was the old imperial tie.

Shifts in the composition of trade, with primary products in decline relative to manufactured goods, change the political as well as the economic significance of trade. Before World War I, as Richard Cooper points out, large differences in comparative costs meant that "trade was socially very profitable" but "less sensitive to small changes in costs, prices, and quality."[10] I would add that trade then, as well as being socially very profitable, was politically very significant. States are mutually dependent if they rely on each other for goods and services that cannot easily be produced at home. That kind of interdependence is difficult (costly) to break. The other kind of interdependence — sensitivity of response to variations in factor prices — may be economically more interesting; it is also politically less important.

Even though trade in relation to production and the proportionate amount of raw materials imported have declined, one might nevertheless imagine a country being heavily dependent on a small quantity of imports. But is this really the case? In the decades during which congressional renewal of the Reciprocal Trade Act was recurrently at issue, it was customary for the friends of free trade to emphasize the extent of American dependence on imported minerals and ores. The Report of the Commission headed by Clarence B. Randall, for example, stated that: "we depend on foreign sources today for over 30 percent of our requirements of

[9] Data taken from Ref. 6, Table 2, p. 22.
[10] R. N. Cooper, *The Economics of Interdependence: Economic Policy in the Atlantic Community* (New York: McGraw-Hill, 1968), p. 152. On p. 68, Cooper identifies a "gradual convergence of cost structures among the industrial countries — an evolution which results in narrowing the economic basis on which foreign trade rests."

copper, lead, and zinc; over 50 percent of our requirements of tungsten, bauxite, and antimony; over 75 percent of our requirements of chrome and manganese; practically all of our nickel requirements; and all our requirements of tin, natural rubber, and jute."[11] Bad economics may make good political strategy; we should, however, notice that the economic case was distorted.

The quantity of imports is not just a function of scarcity; it is also a matter of price. Reliance on imports at a particular time does not necessarily represent dependence, as the following points make clear.

1. The nearness of a country's approach to autarky cannot be measured simply by amounts imported. It is not possession but rather reliability of access that counts. Whether Lorraine was part of France or of Germany, those countries were less sure of the availability of its iron than the United States is of bauxite and nickel from Latin America and Canada.[12]

2. Not only the location of suppliers but also their numbers are important. Wayward political movements or revolutions or wars elsewhere in the world may well shut off some of a country's supplies. The larger a country's trade, in absolute terms, the larger the number of its suppliers is likely to be. The United States, as the world's largest trader, enjoys a multiplicity of sources of supply. Here as in other matters, there is safety in numbers. Worries are further reduced by remembering that the market for primary products is one that favors the buyer. Manganese, for example, is often cited as an instance of America's dependence on imports; but those imports come from a large number of eager suppliers, Brazil and India among them.[13]

3. Suppose, however, that war engulfed much of the globe and

[11] Commission on Foreign Economic Policy, *Report to the President and to the Congress* (Washington, D.C.: U.S. Government Printing Office, 1954), p. 39.

[12] (a) Department of the Interior, Bureau of Mines, *Minerals Yearbook, 1967,* Vol. I (Washington, D.C.: U.S. Government Printing Office, 1968), p. 36; (b) W. S. Woytinsky and E. S. Woytinsky, *World Population and Production* (New York: Twentieth Century Fund, 1953), Table 335, p. 791.

[13] Reference 12a, p. 711. See also P. W. Bidwell, *Raw Materials: A Study of American Policy* (New York: Harper, 1958), p. 192.

disrupted many or most of the channels of trade. This possibility was a more active worry in the late 1940s and early 1950s than it has been in the 1960s, and the response to it was more than sufficiently effective. In the considerable efforts made to stockpile strategic materials, the problem was not to acquire and store enough of them but rather to prevent domestic producers from unloading unduly large quantities upon the American government. Glenn Snyder, for example, has pointed out that as of June 1964, "about 60 per cent of the stockpile was surplus and subject to disposal . . . more than 80 per cent of the total excess was concentrated in 12 materials — aluminum, chromite, cobalt, copper, lead, manganese, molybdenum, nickel, rubber, tin, tungsten, and zinc."[14] Often domestic interests resisted the government's efforts to dispose of the surplus for fear of reducing prices.

4. The resiliency of the economy is increased, and dependence on imports is lessened, by improved methods for the use and recovery of materials. The electroplating process in tin-plating, introduced in 1949, resulted in a steady drop in imports. In recent years, the secondary recovery of antimony has yielded a larger supply than imports of the metal itself.[15] The ability to make do in the face of adversity is one of the most impressive qualities of large and advanced economies. The synthetic production of rubber provides the most impressive example. The need was not recognized until the fall of Singapore in 1942. The United States was able to develop an entirely new large-scale industry while fighting a global war on two fronts. The worry of primary producers that synthetics will further shrink their markets is more sensible than American worries about access to raw materials.

Large and economically well-developed countries, the very ones that are crucial in world politics, can more quickly move toward an autarkic condition. I am not suggesting that we should forgo imports and rely on our own resources, but merely that we can move in that direction at relatively low cost if we have to. The low cost of disentanglement is a measure of low dependence.

[14] G. H. Snyder, *Stockpiling Strategic Materials* (San Francisco: Chandler, 1966), p. 247.
[15] Reference 12b, pp. 804, 820; cf. Ref. 12a, pp. 187, 1119.

If not dependent on particular items of import, may the economy nevertheless be sensitive to adverse economic movements that originate outside of the national arena? Here also big countries are at an immense advantage. I shall give only a few illustrations of this. If a country exports a large portion of its manufactured output, as advanced countries smaller than the United States and the Soviet Union tend to do, then changes in trade will have major effects on that country's economic growth.[16] Of more relevance to the less-developed countries is the tendency for foreign trade to be most important where incomes are lowest and for the fluctuations in the trade of those countries to be unusually large.[17] Countries of large GNP are doubly protected from such effects. The circle of their customers and suppliers is wider, thus increasing the chances that some external fluctuations will balance off others. And since their trade is relatively small, even sharply adverse foreign developments do not greatly affect the domestic economy. From 1950 to 1956, for example, the year-to-year fluctuation in national income derived from changes in the terms of trade was 2.8% for less-developed countries and 1.5% for developed countries. For the United States, it was only 0.2%.[18]

A small portion of America's trade is a big portion of the trade of many another country. In 1966, for example, 42.5% of Peru's total exports and 18.2% of India's were sent to the United States; but the exports of each of those countries amounted to only 1.2% of total United States imports. The asymmetrical relation also holds for industrial countries. Japan, the United Kingdom, and France sent 30.7, 12.3, and 6.0%, respectively, of their total exports to the United States. The respective shares of U.S. imports that these totals represent were 11.8, 6.8, and 2.5%.[19] Smaller countries are

[16] Reference 7, pp. 222–224.
[17] H. W. Singer, "U.S. Foreign Investment in Underdeveloped Areas: the Distribution of Gains between Investing and Borrowing Countries," *American Economic Review*, Vol. XL (May 1950), p. 473.
[18] M. Michaely, *Concentration in International Trade* (Amsterdam: North-Holland, 1962), Table 18, p. 113.
[19] Figures computed from data in United Nations Statistical Office, *Yearbook of International Trade Statistics, 1966* (New York: United Nations, 1968). West Germany is the only country for which the difference in proportions is small.

213

strongly constrained to make domestic economic decisions with an eye on their external accounts. The United States is much less constrained to do so, and yet our domestic economic decisions will affect other states more than theirs will affect us. The political importance of this condition arises from the asymmetry of the relation.[20] Decisions by the United States, whether or not intended to harm or to bring pressure against another state, can have grave effects.

What looks to some like a thickening web of economic interdependence obscures relations that are best described as a compound of independence and dependence, and that is quite a different thing. But this point can be developed better if we add consideration of foreign investment to the discussion of international trade.

Investment: National and Corporate Stakes

Statements about whether interdependence is higher or lower now than it used to be easily obscure the fact that recent economic changes within and among nations and the political consequences attendant upon them are changes of kind rather than merely of degree. When the great powers of the world were small in geographic compass, they naturally did a higher proportion of their business abroad. The narrow concentration of power in the present and the fact that the United States and the Soviet Union are little dependent on the rest of the world produce a very different international situation. Since at the same time the size of America's foreign business in terms of world totals is large, its impact on others is considerable.

It may be, however, that the enterprise of international corporations and the recent increase of foreign investments modify these trends and move the world back toward a closer integration. But is this really happening?

[20] The 4 percent of its 1966 GNP that the United States exported amounted to 14.7 percent of the world's total exports. The corresponding figures for the United Kingdom were 15.3 and 6.8 percent. Calculated from (a) U.S. Bureau of the Census, *Statistical Abstract of the United States: 1968;* 89th ed. (Washington, D.C.: U.S. Government Printing Office, 1968); (b) Central Statistical Office, *Annual Abstract of Statistics, No. 105, 1968* (London, Her Majesty's Stationary Office, 1968); (c) Ref. 19.

When Britain was the world's leading state economically, the portion of her wealth invested abroad far exceeded the portion that now represents America's stake in the world. In 1910, the value of total British investment abroad was 1½ times larger than her national income. In 1966, total American foreign investments, both official and private, were only 18% as large as its national income. In 1910, Britain's return on investment abroad amounted to 8% of national income; in 1966, the comparable figure for the United States was only 1%.[21]

Although, in comparison, the stock of American investment is not high, the rate of its recent growth is impressive. Britain's foreign investment had tripled in the 30 years prior to 1910. From 1958 to 1966, American investment abroad grew at an average rate of 8% yearly, which in 18 years would increase the total fourfold. One should, however, be wary of assuming that such a high rate will continue long enough to raise American investments to the point where they become a much higher percentage of GNP. One may expect continued growth although I rather doubt that it will be as rapid. Not just American technology but also skills in management and marketing enabled American subsidiaries operating in the less-advanced and less-well-organized European environment to earn a higher return on capital invested in Europe than on capital invested at home. As with the opening of mines in Latin America or the drilling of oil wells in the Middle East, businessmen properly and usefully responded to the possibility of increased profits. As we have known since Adam Smith and Ricardo, the effect of everyone's seeking to increase his profits is to drive the profit rate downward. Something of the same sort is happening here. American capital in Europe earned 18% yearly in 1959 as compared to 13% at home. In 1965 return abroad and at home stood at 13% and 15%, respectively.[22] On economic grounds, one would expect a leveling off.

[21] Computed on the basis of figures on British foreign investment: A. H. Imlah, *Economic Elements in the Pax Britannica* (Cambridge, Mass.: Harvard University Press, 1958), pp. 70–75; on British national income, Ref. 12b, p. 385; on U.S. national income and foreign investment, Ref. 20a.

[22] W. Guzzardi, Jr., "Why the Climate is Changing for U.S. Investment," *Fortune,* Vol. LXXV (September 1967), p. 117.

On political grounds, one might entertain the same expectation. Precisely because the operations of American corporations abroad have concentrated in those sectors of the economy that are thought by the host countries to be most significant for economic growth and for their military establishments, political resistance to the encroachment of American firms has occurred and will continue to do so.

But such resistance has been of limited effect. Just as political fragmentation invites imperial control, so low economic capability easily leads to dependence upon another state of higher economic capability. The higher the costs of disentanglement, the higher the degree of dependence; the lagging state will only get weaker if foreign capital and technology are excluded.

The American computer industry can get along without the assistance of French companies, but Machines Bull felt it could not survive without American capital and technology. In 1962, the French government resisted the purchase by General Electric of 20% of Bull's shares. Unable to find another French or European partner, the French government was constrained in 1964 to accept a 50-50 arrangement with General Electric. By the middle 1960s General Electric's share in the company had grown to approximately two-thirds.[23] General Electric, Control Data, and other American firms may require foreign affiliations in order to compete with IBM. There may be genuine interdependence at the level of the firm. It is a mistake, however, to identify interdependence at that level with the interdependence of states. The attempts of European firms to band together are impeded by the greater attraction of establishing connections with American firms, for they are the ones with the most advanced technology, the most plentiful capital, and the most impressive managerial abilities. When German aviation companies sought ties with firms in other countries, they did not go to Britain or France. Larger benefits were to be gained by association with American companies.

Nor is it easy for foreign firms to catch up. The size of the home market enables American firms to operate on a large scale and to

[23] R. Gilpin, *France in the Age of the Scientific State* (Princeton: Princeton University Press, 1968), p. 50; Ref. 22, p. 116.

216

generate resources that can be used abroad to compete with or even to overwhelm native industries. General Motors could have given away every Opel it produced in 1965 and still have made $1 billion in profit.[24] As long as IBM spends yearly on research and development an amount equal to the gross sales of Britain's largest computer company, the American industry is likely to retain its lead. Two-thirds of the world's and two-thirds of Europe's markets in computers have been captured by IBM.[25] The size of its operations enables the company to spend money on a governmental scale. The $5 billion that IBM committed to the development of its model 360 computer was equal to the amount that France planned to spend on her nuclear force in the years from 1965 to 1970.[26]

The disadvantages of foreign firms are paralleled by the difficulties their governments face. In 1962, America's gross expenditure on research and development amounted to $17.5 billion; Britain, France, Belgium, Holland, and Germany together spent $4.3 billion. American expenditure amounted to about 3% of GNP or about $100 per capita, and for the European states named, to about 1½ % of their GNP's or about $25 per capita.[27]

Under these conditions, national governments are constrained to permit domestic firms to make arrangements with American companies. The smaller states' opportunities to maneuver are further limited by competition among them. If, say, France follows an effective policy of exclusion, American capital and firms, and the technology these firms carry with them, will locate in neighboring countries. Even one who believes that the economies of those countries would become beholden to America cannot help but notice that they would also be enriched and be enabled to compete more effectively in European markets, including the markets of countries that had excluded American firms.

In 1967, the output of American firms operating abroad amounted to some $120 billion. This product represented, in effect,

[24] C. Layton, *Trans-Atlantic Investments* (Boulogne-sur-Seine: Atlantic Institute, 1968), p. 47.

[25] Reference 24, p. 98.

[26] T. A. Wise, "I.B.M.'s $5,000,000,000 Gamble," *Fortune*, Vol. LXXIV (September 1966), p. 118; Ref. 23, p. 65.

[27] Ref. 23, p. 27.

217

the world's third largest economy, surpassed only by the United States and the Soviet Union.[28] In 1965, residents of the United States owned 44% of the capital invested in Canadian manufacturing firms and those firms accounted for 48% of Canada's exports of manufactured goods. In the United Kingdom, American subsidiaries accounted for 7½ % of the capital, 10% of the sales, and 17% of the export of manufactured goods.[29] In France, American firms "control" only 5 to 7% of the economy, according to Robert Gilpin, but America's influence is wider than the figures suggest because the companies that Americans do control are strategic ones.[30]

Who is able to regulate these vast undertakings? Most Americans who have considered the question conclude that the American government is not able to do so with very much success. Foreigners more often incline to the opposite view. On the basis of their study, the authors of the Canadian report previously cited draw "the general picture . . . of a tight legal and administrative network capable of being turned to any objective in foreign policy or to meet any future stringency, such as a further deterioration of the American balance of payments position."[31] Rules made under the authority of the Export Control Act of 1949 control not only American exports but also those exports of other countries that contain American components and embody American technical data. Under the Trading with the Enemy Act of 1917, the Office of Foreign Assets Control regulates the exports of American subsidiaries abroad whether or not the commodities they produce incorporate American components or technology. Enforcement can be secured by holding the American parent criminally liable for its subsidiaries' activity.[32]

[28] E. Littlejohn, "The Influence of Multinational Corporations on International Affairs," paper given at the Ninth Annual Convention of the International Studies Association, March 28–30, 1968 (unpublished), p. 1.

[29] M. Watkins *et al.*, Report of the Task Force on the Structure of Canadian Industry, *Foreign Ownership and the Structure of Canadian Industry* (Ottawa: The Queen's Printer, 1968), pp. 199–200.

[30] Reference 23, p. 51.

[31] Reference 29, p. 339.

[32] Reference 29, pp. 313–314, 317–318.

By an executive order issued in January of 1968, President Johnson made previously voluntary guidelines mandatory. The American government can now control the payments of foreign subsidiaries to their American parents and can regulate companies that are incorporated abroad, that operate under foreign law, and that may in part be foreign owned. Further, by requiring the approval of the Secretary of Commerce for private investments abroad, the American government may, if it chooses, control both the amount and the direction of capital flow.[33]

Whatever the extent of American control over various operations, one may nonetheless believe that with well over $100 billion of assets abroad the vulnerability of American interests to punitive regulation by foreign governments, or even to confiscation, must be proportionate to the size of the stake. Just as the sudden severance of its trade would be a hard blow for the United States to absorb, so would the nearly complete loss of its investments abroad. Surely, if all or much of this capital were suddenly wrenched from us, the American economy itself would be seriously damaged. I would not care to deny that. We do have plenty to lose, and we can emphasize the "plenty" or we can emphasize the possibility of its loss. But if we imagine a situation in which American assets in Canada, Latin America, Europe, and the Middle and Far East are simultaneously confiscated, we are imagining a situation comparable in its impact to a global war. Indeed, short of such a catastrophe, it is hard to see why or how all or most foreign governments would suddenly set upon American capital and enterprises.

Partly, as suggested earlier, the question becomes one of who needs whom more. Confiscation would result in the loss of assets and profits of American firms, and for those few of them whose foreign operations are a major part of their business, that could be fatal. It is widely agreed, however, that physical plant and capital investment have not been as important as the managerial and organizational abilities of American firms and their capacity for technological innovation. Foreign economies would lose capabilities that could

---

[33] Cf. Reference 29, p. 336; Ref. 28, pp. 3–4; A. de Riencourt, *The American Empire* (New York: Dial Press, 1968), pp. 228–290.

not easily be reproduced. Partly, also, the diversity of American investment, both in terms of types of enterprise and of their geographic location, itself provides insurance against sudden and sharp reversals. Nations do not easily bring their policies into concert, and that is a comfort for the nation whose operations are global.

Rhetoric and Reality

The American rhetoric of interdependence has taken on some of the qualities of an ideology. The word "interdependence" subtly obscures the inequalities of national capability, pleasingly points to a reciprocal dependence, and strongly suggests that all states are playing the same game.

If interdependence is really close, each state is constrained to treat other states' acts as though they were events within its own borders. A mutuality of dependence leads each state to watch others with wariness and suspicion. Near self-sufficiency and the possession of great capabilities, however, insulate a nation from the world by muting the effects of adverse movements that originate outside of the national arena. One who looks only at the activities of American firms and at their considerable stake in foreign countries, may then in one misdirected leap reach the conclusion that the size of this stake renders America vulnerable. At the level of the firm, it may be all right to dwell upon the extent of integration. At the level of international politics, it is grossly misleading to do so. It often seems that the approach of international economists would, if applied to domestic economics, cause it all to be written in terms of the firm and not at all in terms of the market. It is necessary to look at the matrix of action rather than simply at the discrete activities that fill it. One who does so reaches a different conclusion.

Someone who has a lot to lose can afford to lose quite a bit of it. This maxim is, of course, a common proposition of oligopolistic economics. That a large and well-placed firm can afford to run at a loss for some years is taken not as a sign of weakness and vulnerability but as being a considerable advantage. Where disparities are great, whether among firms or among states, the largest of them need worry least about the bothersome activities of others. Since in such situations interdependence does not reduce to zero, we can rightly say that all of the parties are vulnerable, but we should hasten to add that some are much less so. Some states, of course, are closely interdependent economically, but neither the United States nor the Soviet Union is among them. In economic terms and from their points of view, the world is loosely coupled.

Finally, as well as the insulation that permits lassitude, the highly skewed distribution of resources gives rise to the possibility of those with the largest share exercising some control. When the point is made that multinational corporations make their decisions on a global basis, one gets the impression that nations no longer matter. But that is grossly misleading. We should not lightly conclude that decentralization of operations means that centers of control are lacking.

From about the middle of the nineteenth century, the quicker transmission of ideas resulted, in the words of R. D. McKenzie, in "centralization of control and decentralization of operation." As he put it, "the modern world is integrated through information collected and distributed from fixed centers of dominance."[34] The complaints of some Europeans strikingly echo these words. One has to ask where most of the threads come together, and the answer is not in London, or Brussels, or Paris, but rather in New York City and Washington.

Decisions are made in terms of whole corporations and not just according to the condition and interest of certain subsidiaries. The picture usually drawn is one of a world in which economic activity has become transnational, with national borders highly permeable and businessmen making their decisions without even bearing them in mind. But most of the largest international corporations are based in America; most of their research and development is done there; most of their top personnel is American. Under these conditions, it is reasonable to suppose that in making corporate decisions the American perspective will be the most prominent one. Similarly, though both American and foreign governments try to regulate the activities of these corporations, the fact that most of them

[34] R. D. McKenzie, "The Concept of Dominance and World-Organization," *American Journal of Sociology*, Vol. XXXIII (July 1927), pp. 34–35.

are American based gives a big advantage to the latter government. The advantage is made much stronger by the ability of the American government to grant or withhold a variety of favors, for example, in matters of trade, aid, loans, financial arrangements, and the supply of atomic energy for peaceful purposes. If means for bringing other countries into compliance with preferred American policies are desired, the American government does not have to look far to find them. The customary response of American commentators when the regulatory instruments available to their government are mentioned is to dwell on the ease of evasion. There is something to that response, though it underplays the fact that control — domestically as well as internationally — is often difficult to achieve.

What is really important, however, is to notice that we do not need much control. The size of American operations abroad does give the United States influence in the affairs of other nations, a situation that prevails whether or not we wish it. But the fact that, in relation to our resources, the stake is small means that the exercise of influence and control is less needed. These points can be clearly seen if both the similarity and the difference between America's present and Britain's past positions in the world are kept in mind.

Britain in its heyday had a huge stake in the world, and that stake also loomed large in relation to her own national product. From her immense and far-flung activities, she gained a considerable leverage. Because of the extent to which she depended on the rest of the world, wise and skillful use of that leverage was called for. When the great powers of the day depended on foodstuffs and raw materials imported from abroad much more heavily than the United States and the Soviet Union do now, that very dependence pressed them to make efforts to control the sources of their vital supplies.

Today, the myth of interdependence both obscures the realities of international politics and asserts a false belief about the conditions that may promote peace. The size of the two greatest powers gives them some capacity for control and at the same time insulates them to a considerable extent from the effects of other states' behavior. The inequality of nations produces a condition of equilibrium at a low level of interdependence. In the absence of a system of international regulation, loose coupling and a certain amount of control exerted by large states help to promote the desired stability.

Part IV

THREE INDUSTRY STUDIES

CHAPTER NINE

THE MULTINATIONAL CORPORATION IN WORLD PETROLEUM*

M. A. Adelman

World Oil

World oil (the industry outside North America) has pride of place in any discussion of multinational firms. Everybody knows the anatomy: a few huge companies, with a fringe of smaller but still very large units. The companies are vertically integrated, and most of their crude oil, produced in the less-developed countries, is eventually sold in the developed world as their own refined products.

The structure derives from a history starting before World War I. Low-cost sources and profitable markets beckoned in distant places. Companies knew how to make money in finding, processing, and selling oil. Their skills could not be sold or leased; they could only be used. Those who found crude oil did not care to sell to a few buyers; they built their own refineries. Those who had built sales outlets for refined products did not care to buy crude from a few sellers; they looked for crude oil. A concentrated integrated market structure thereby perpetuated itself.

Our concern now is not with anatomy but physiology: the severe disequilibrium in which the industry finds itself today, which domi-

---

* This paper is based on a forthcoming book, *The World Petroleum Market* (publication in 1970 by Resources for the Future, Washington, D.C.).

nates its relations with governments and, therefore, its multinational character.

The imbalance begins with a massive innovation, the discovery and gradual development of very low-cost oil deposits in the Middle East and later North Africa. A cheaper supply source allows the innovators large profits and induces an inflow of resources. In the course of time, profits are mostly competed away to the customer. At the margin, the rate of return for the least profitable facilities necessary, just worth investing in, will under competition approach some normal cost of capital.

In world oil, as Table 1 shows, this kind of evolution has indeed

Table 1. Persian Gulf Prices and Costs

Price:	1947 (1949 price levels)		$3.80
	1949		1.65
	1957		2.10
	1969		1.20
Tax		0.88	1.08
Cost {	Maximum Economic Finding Cost, to 1983	0.08	0.20
	Development (20% return on investment)	0.06	0.12
	Operating	0.06	0.06

Source: M. A. Adelman, *The World Petroleum Market* (Resources for the Future, to be published), Chaps. II, VI.

taken place, but still has a very long way to go. A great cost-price gap serves to draw in ever more resources and offer a constant incentive to try to sell a little more at a slightly lower price, although everybody knows and often repeats that chiseling injures everybody.

The principal groups concerned — host governments, companies, and consuming country governments — all want high oil prices, though their reasons vary. Each of them does a great deal to repress competition; otherwise, the price would be far below current levels. But among them they cannot quite stop the process, because they cannot get together to control the supply of oil. Each company or government knows it must cooperate with the others, but wants to do no more than necessary, and claim as much as it can. The resulting conflict is dangerous, especially because all parties in varying degrees build their expectations and commitments on a future

228

price higher than current: it will probably be lower. They will be disappointed and their reactions are likely to be sharp.

The long-run incremental cost of oil in the Middle East is crudely but sufficiently approximated by considering the highest costs among the Big Five (Iran, Iraq, Kuwait, Libya, Saudi Arabia), whose combined resources are more than enough to supply the whole world today, tomorrow, and as far ahead as it pays to look. The price of $1.20 f.o.b. the Persian Gulf is a rough average that includes both the minor proportion sold as crude oil and the much larger portion sold as products. Product prices, less transport and refining cost — including a sufficient return on investment to induce inflow of capital — are within 5 or 10% of this figure; even a wide error would not make much difference.

Companies and Host Governments

The great bulk of the profit is, of course, absorbed by the governments of the producing nations; the companies still earn a very high rate of return. So sensitive are all parties to public reaction that it is hard to have a sober discussion of the investment decision in crude oil. Oil companies will treat a realistic estimate as though it were an accusation of insolent profiteering, and will hasten to quote estimates of a modest return on, e.g., the overall integrated Eastern Hemisphere investment. But the notion that oil production yields something approximating an ordinary market rate of return is refuted simply by looking at the scramble for concessions all over the world. People do not run great risks in exploration and then invest heavily in politically unstable areas for the sake of 10 or 11%.

The companies' published estimates of earnings from operations abroad are not reproducible and not explained. We have no indication of where, e.g., a tanker company is incorporated and its profits or losses credited. More important, within the integrated company there is no market checkpoint or interface to set the value of transfers. Because we do not know the foreign profits of the multinational oil companies, we do not know their contribution to the balance of payments or the national product, even though we cannot doubt it is large.

229

The producing countries are now moving to get the rest of the profit. (Those mouthing that wonderful phrase "grande firme, petite nation" should, but will not, reflect on how funny it sounds.) Their tax system has come full circle. Today they levy a nearly pure excise tax, not quite pure because changes in cost still are reflected to a minor extent in changes in tax due. But in effect the tax liability is in cents per barrel.

No prudent management will commit for a price that is less than operating costs plus a minimum return on investment — plus an allowance for contingencies. Thus the per barrel tax has not only served as a floor, but has actually been effective at a distance. If there were pure competition, 100 or 1,000 hard competing individual firms in oil production, each completely independent of the rest, prices might drop another 12 cents. But this is a rather small proportion of the 85 cents the governments receive, escalating to over 90 cents in the mid-1970s. In no other industry, to my knowledge, have host governments intervened so actively and successfully into the pricing process.

The governments in June 1968 proclaimed their intent to obtain everything above the minimum profit needed to keep development work and production going. In effect they will become owners. But, as the company buffer dwindles, the producing nations will themselves greatly weaken the price supports. As long as they have no quota system for allocation of output, they cannot escape acting like competitors. The temptation to shade taxes in order to let the company shade prices, to chisel in order to get large incremental revenues, will here and there not be resistable, because there is no assurance that other governments are not yielding. Already we have seen six incidents where a government has opted for a lower tax and higher revenues. There are no contrary examples, though doubtless there will be some.

But the governments are taking other measures tending to increase competition. They invite new concessionaires; most will find no oil worth finding, but some will do very well. (The great success story is Occidental Petroleum, which obtained a Libyan concession in 1966, and is now (May 1969) producing over 600,000 barrels daily.)

Finally, all of the producing governments have set up national oil companies to explore and produce. But the pace is obviously too slow for them, and they are now demanding ready reserves, or what they call "participation" in the established low-cost concessions. Furthermore, the national companies have a nonprofit incentive to grow, profits or not. The governments are out to show the world that they can run an oil company as well as Westerners. Once the government companies gain access to ready low-cost reserves, the decline in price will accelerate.

The interests of the producing nations are too diverse to permit a firm collusive understanding to fix prices, divide markets, and limit total output. A small barren country, without land or labor or water, can do nothing better with revenues than lend them out on the European money market, after first subtracting a considerable contribution to other governments and to nationalist movements. Hence future revenues are discounted at probably no more than 6 to 8% per annum. In Iran, where a high growth rate over the past decade has accelerated to about 10% during 1964 to 1968, the real social return on investment must be well over 20%. An additional annual dollar of revenues gained over the next five years has a present value of $3; an offsetting perpetual loss of a dollar per year, starting in the sixth year, has a present value of only $2. Haste is folly for one country, prudent management for the other. By the time this paper is printed, it will be apparent that the trans-Israel pipeline is a vent for incremental Iranian production to be sold in the Mediterranean. And although both governments will in their own interest tread very carefully to avoid price cutting by themselves or their customers, there will be no mistaking the direction.

Thus we head for a series of difficult and dangerous confrontations. Governments are avowedly out to take everything over and above the minimum necessary return, and also firmly committed to actions that will have the effect of lowering prices. Even if they take the last of the supernormal returns from the companies, they must eventually lower taxes per barrel. It is hard to see them doing this peacefully and without demanding more of the companies than in fact the companies can give. When total profits begin to decrease because of lower prices, negotiation between landlord and operator, each perhaps having made commitments based on higher returns which now he is in danger of not getting, can become harsh, not to say violent. Neither side knows just how far the other can be pushed, nor perhaps even knows its own reservation price. Hence there will be a series of encounters, with the government threatening to expel the company, or the company threatening to leave before it can be expelled. Doubtless most will somehow be settled quietly. But it takes only one of them to force a showdown for both sides. If a company leaves, and proposes to draw its crude oil supplies from its other concessions, or from companies working in other concessions, what then? Will the other governments pocket the additional revenue at their fellow government's expense, or will they assert a right already claimed — to regulate aggregate production and the respective shares of the companies? They may play their last card, which is a concerted shutdown of production. Either the companies must give in or else the governments of the consuming countries, confronted by an oil famine, may intervene to force the companies to accept terms.

Companies and governments alike proclaim that taxes are nothing but a kind of cost, and that prices can and must and should be raised to cover them. I fear they believe their own propaganda, and will plan or promise things they cannot do. The multi-billion-dollar misunderstanding will disrupt output, waste resources, and worsen relations between the peoples of the producing governments and the West.

Western economists will not escape some small share of the responsibility. They have made popular a doctrine of "administered prices," of great "economic power" of large corporations, who set prices by planning and not by the market, who can and do disregard such tedious facts as supply, demand, and the degree of monopoly. Big companies do not maximize profits, but always carry a reserve price-raising power: they can always raise prices if they wish. Therefore if they plead that they cannot raise prices, this only shows their bad faith. These cliches, because they are familiar, give the illusion of being clear. They are part of the intellectual baggage of most educated people, including advisers to oil companies and

governments. Whether divertingly written or mathematically refined, they are all variations on the one theme: wishing will make it
so. Oil companies and governments will find out the truth the hard
way.

Consuming Countries

The multinational oil companies must also reckon with governments in the consuming countries, including their own home or
central-office country. Their role has been rather peculiar and
above all inadvertent, yet it has been large and is increasing. Soon
after World War II, when there were only the eight large companies, all of them were concerned to expand output rapidly and
not touch price until somebody else touched it first — whereupon
everybody might have waited quite a long time. At this point the
U.S. government, which was heavily financing the European recovery program, took steps to transform the price structure from a
highly discriminatory one (U.S. Gulf-plus) to a simple f.o.b. based
on the Persian Gulf, which incidentally was about half the level
under the old system. (This revolution in the price of crude, which
was also a rough index number for product prices, was transformed
by the artful semantics of the Federal Trade Commission into a
"multiple basing point system," and their "cartel" myth lives on.)
But during 1949 to 1957 the price not only ceased to decline but
even increased significantly — about 15 to 20% at a rough guess.
The U.S. government had withdrawn the pressure.

After 1957, it was mostly downhill. After 1969, the actions of
the companies were to a large extent determined by what the producing governments allowed them to do, and the concentrated
market structure was secondary though not negligible. But if the
producing governments, in their efforts to get all of the surplus, are
about to undermine the price structure they have supported, then we
must look to the consuming country governments as the last barriers
to price reduction. It is not a new role for them, but they are becoming the only ones who can play it.

The declining price of oil after 1957 was a considerable shock
to most of the consuming countries — less the shock of pleasure
than the shock of dismay. Public and private opinion was largely

233

incredulous, and often resentful. The one-word explanation was coal.

The difficulties of the coal industry were ascribed to the selfish or predatory ambitions of the foreigner — the multinational oil companies. In fact, the companies had two objectives to reconcile, one political, the other economic, and they lost out both ways. For *maximum profit,* they should have priced heavy fuel oil moderately below coal, but enough to tempt away most price-sensitive buyers. Even a small differential between coal and oil would have sufficed to give them all the new business and eventually the old. For *minimum political grief,* the companies should have priced heavy fuel oil a trifle above coal to win only such portions of the market as governments thought it best for them to have. The companies got the worst of both worlds. Competition forced price cuts far more than enough to get the business. Thereby they sacrificed profits and incurred political wrath.

The coal industry in Europe is now in full retreat, and within ten years the final act of euthanasia will be in preparation. But as coal passes from the scene it is being replaced by other producing interests in consuming countries. Nuclear power is now being installed on a very large scale in Great Britain. The published estimates show it to be much more expensive than fuel oil at actual current prices, let alone lower future prices. (Those estimates having been revised upward; few would expect them to remain firm.) The French nuclear technology has been so obviously high cost and inefficient as to evoke protests, and may well be suspended. Although technology in Italy, Germany, Japan, and smaller nations is better than British or French, no projected nuclear plant in Europe or Asia can produce electricity as cheaply as it can be generated from oil at actual current prices, which are higher than future prices. The expectation of stable or increasing prices in oil causes the governments to make investments that will be seen as uneconomic if oil prices fail to increase.

There are other government producing interests. A British government corporation monopolizing gas distribution has been able to set its own buying price for gas produced in the North Sea. The higher the price at which it resells the gas, the higher its profit, and the more it will have for capital spending (e.g., a gas transmission network) without recourse to the public treasury. Hence the Gas Council too wants as high a price of energy as possible. Across the channel, the Netherlands government has preferred to deal itself into a gas partnership with the producing companies and take the lion's share of the revenues, which gives it, too, an ownership interest and a reason for charging the highest possible price — to the ill-concealed annoyance of its Common Market partners.

Finally, there is the direct government involvement in oil production. Great Britain is apparently an oil seller on real and balance of payments account, and French policy is to close the "oil deficit." The French government has always had a considerable direct interest in oil production, but this has been greatly expanded over the last few years by the formation of the concern known as ERAP, which has sought and obtained concessions in over half a dozen countries. Undoubtedly there will be oil discoveries, and the higher the price of oil the better they will look. Germany has given considerable subsidies for oil exploration by domestic companies, none of them particularly fortunate thus far, but continues to press on in the attempt. Italy's well-known ENI has become a large-scale refiner and marketer, and has spent considerable amounts of money on exploration, with poor results. But they continue to search for oil on an increasing scale. Finally, the Japanese government has adopted two policies, which would seem contradictory, of subsidizing oil exploration and also of trying to get the price reduced. Possibly they are simply trying to keep two options open for final choice at a later date. If so, they are about the only government trying to keep a degree of flexibility. The others all base their policy on a high level of oil prices, though it would be an exaggeration, or at least too summary, to say they are committed to high prices.

One other type of seller interest is even more complex. In the developed and less-developed countries alike it is considered desirable to have the local refining done in whole or in part by locally owned or perhaps government-owned companies. "Independence" *could* be rationalized as the desire to confront the multinational companies with one large buyer, for whose trade they would have to compete, instead of with a cloud of small buyers easily exploited by noncompeting sellers. Probably some such realization floats somewhere in the backroom of policy making, but in practice independence has been an end rather than a means. A domestic refining industry, even when privately owned, becomes to some extent a ward of the local government. The local refinery would be better off by (a) lower crude prices *or* (b) higher product prices. The former are hard to attain if only because it is so unclear to the government how prices are made. Moreover, no matter how cheaply crude oil can be bought, the multinational companies can always have it cheaper yet, since they produce from the cheapest sources. But higher product prices can achieve the same result of safeguarding "independence," and a certain share of the domestic market can be ensured for domestic companies so that their higher cost per gallon processed is translated into profits. Hence it is much easier for a consuming country government to opt for higher product prices and in fact most of them do. Thus M. André Giraud, head of the Direction des Carburants: "[French] ex-refinery prices are higher than in other countries . . . [in order] to maintain the self-financing of the petroleum industry. Otherwise, the French petroleum companies . . . would no longer be able to combat the foreign companies and after a very short time this would be harmful to our economic security. . . ."

This again leads governments into conflict with the multinational companies. (Security will be discussed in the following.)

Furthermore, those companies have a tax advantage in paying a higher book price for crude oil and usually also for transport to their own affiliates, which lowers the tax on their refining operations and gives them an additional competitive advantage. Since crude prices are difficult to verify or even specify, there have been negotiations in some countries but formal litigation only in Australia.

Income tax in the consuming countries will probably become a more acute issue in the years ahead. In part this is because the price will continue to decline, unless the consuming country governments themselves take a hand in supporting it. Furthermore, more and more knowledge of real oil prices and transport costs is coming into public domain. I would guess — in the absence of any verifiable

236

knowledge — that in the large consuming countries where the subject has at least been raised once over the last few years — the United States, Great Britain, France, Germany, Italy, Australia, New Zealand, and Japan — the additional taxes due have been settled by negotiation one way or another up to at least a recent year, but that the parties are not committed for the years to come. The governments are not likely to retreat from their position that all taxpayers must be treated alike, and that the only acceptable price is an arm's length price or equivalent. But they are also very much aware that the companies have already paid taxes to the producing country on the basis of artificially high prices for oil. To the extent that a consuming country government presses for what it considers its due, it in effect challenges a producing country government to take even as much as it does now, let alone the larger amount it claims for the future. This is one reason why the producing companies will attempt to stay in the producing countries as concessionaires as long as possible. Were they to withdraw and buy the oil from the government now become operator as well as owner, the price they paid would be a fairly clear-cut item and the basis for a higher tax assessment on the refining affiliate.

Another aspect of taxation is indicated in a widely noted speech by the public relations director of the French national oil company ERAP: "In a market free from government intervention, competition is subject to the risk of *abusing competition,* which is as bad in the long run as no competition. *Independent companies are threatened or disappear* in the face of companies infinitely more powerful because of the excessive profit leverage which can only be resisted by companies enjoying a particularly favorable treatment in their home countries, as well as access, in the same country, to an interior market with wide profit margins." (Emphasis in original.)

The resentment over favored tax treatment and over the high prices and profits in the closed U.S. market may have no small part in determining the future of American companies, and not only in France. But this statement also expresses the world-wide popular wisdom about large diversified companies: profits in one place as "leverage" in another; "siphoned" from one market to undermine

237

rivals in another; or "mobilized" in one market to crush rivals in another; etc., etc. Metaphor covers the absence of fact or logic. Little is gained by pointing out that capital is never pushed but always drawn to where a good return beckons. The guarantee of a fat profit margin — "self-financing" — is precisely what draws the detested foreigners into the French market (and others) like bees to the jam pot.

National Security

No discussion of government policy could be complete without mention of "security," which would seem to the outside observer to be an insurance problem; the risk of interruption of fuel supplies, and a search for the cheapest method of providing against it, as against fire, shipwreck, theft, etc. Yet one looks in vain through the literature of "security" to find any such approach. There is a good semiofficial French analysis dating from 1964, which was ignored. But in December 1967, a Belgian analysis begins by bluntly dismissing the coal industry as a source of national income. Once this simple fact is accepted, the nature of the security problem is clearly seen. Not until coal or other costly substitutes are off will governments consent to look at security rationally.

"Security" is really a code word, whose meaning is not what it seems. The oral tradition, to my knowledge, has only been publicly expressed by Hans von der Groeben, an EEC Commissioner. It is feared that the big international oil company, having ruined the coal industry through a "price war," would then turn around and exploit Europeans without mercy. Herr von der Groeben deserves everyone's gratitude for bringing the issue into the open, and it is a pity that he found none to continue the debate. For it would have become quickly apparent that the so-called "price wars" were something that happened to the companies, not something they did, and that the chances of their getting together to exploit the consuming nations were remote. But as long as producing interests remain strong in these countries, the multinational corporation is resented as a potent competitor. And the *less* economic power the industry has, the less power over supply and price, the more it is forced to compete prices downward, the more the companies will be blamed and execrated for their "ruthless economic power" expressed in "price warfare."

The true meaning of "independence" or "security" cannot be stated, only suggested like the mood induced by music or poetry. The following passage must be respectfully considered by anyone interested in the multinational corporation in petroleum. Observe how "security" is first mentioned without explanation and then referred to as though it had just been explained.

> . . . The six countries of the Common Market cannot fail to attach a major interest to the security and the price of their supply . . .
>
> These states have encouraged . . . their companies toward a renewed discovery effort. But this diversification policy solves their problems only in part and in the long run. New methods must be sought, different from those which leave only to the oil companies the care and responsibility for this security.
>
> It is in this direction, whoever happen to be the protagonists who conduct the action, that relations . . . will not cease to progress between oil producing and consuming countries, and most particularly between the Arab world and Europe . . . [We are approaching], no question about it, a growing cooperation between two parties whose interests, often contradictory in appearance, are in fact tightly linked.[1]

Political influence in the developing world is sought in part for "access" to oil. The economic costs of tying in with the producing nations are presumably justified by the hope of getting political influence — indeed the hour is late for hoping to keep any profits. The aims of "independence," "security," and "influence" form a closed system from which economic costs and benefits are largely excluded. There is nothing peculiarly French about this policy. There are important differences in degree to be sure, but the only reason the French energy planners are worth more attention is their old and good national tradition of clear expression, where other nations mumble and mutter.

The net result is that the consuming governments have maintained the price at a higher level by restricting competition in the sale of crude oil and products. Obviously their interests are not

---

[1] ELF/ERAP, *Bulletin Mensuel d'Informations* (May 20, 1969).

clear-cut. As net buyers they are better off with lower prices. If their producing ventures in oil, nuclear energy, etc., turn out badly, some may give up the attempt as a bad job and try to minimize their import bill. Indeed, to some extent they can have a foot in both camps: trying to decrease the cost of oil to the national economy while transferring large amounts of the income thus gained to the government producing interest, as is being done in Britain by the Gas Council. But this kind of two-faced role is of limited effect. For what keeps the price up is the maintaining of barriers to competition. If even one of the large producing countries gave up restriction as a losing game, and directed or permitted electric power companies to buy the cheapest possible fuel, the resultant competition would send prices farther down. The odds seem fairly good that at least one large country will do so in the 1970s. This will dovetail with the effort of one or more producing countries to gain more outlet even at lower prices. There will be strenuous efforts to maintain prices, possibly by an international commodity agreement under UNCTAD auspices. There may be some interim success, which I would expect not to last. Balance of payments effects may be substantial. At present, the producing nations' taxes generate a pure transfer payment from the developed nations of about $6 billions annually. It will increase rapidly in the near future, then stabilize as production increase balances price decrease, then decline.

Conclusions

Elsewhere, the multinational companies will continue to be treated in both producing and consuming governments as the messengers bringing the bad news of more competition and lower prices. In some of the producing countries, negotiations will break down, and they will either be expelled or else such impossible demands will be made upon them that they will withdraw and obtain their oil by purchase rather than by their own production. It will be increasingly difficult to distinguish this kind of arrangement from the so-called partnership or participation of a national company with a Western concessionaire. In the consuming countries

240

their tax burdens will probably be increased, as will the amount of local competition.

All this would seem to add up to a rather gloomy prognosis, but it does not. The companies' essential stock in trade is not their heavy past investment, but their continuing and improving know-how in all phases of the oil business. Whether as concessionaires or contractors, they will be active in the great bulk of the producing countries, and probably the first expulsion will work badly enough for the government doing it to slow things down. The companies' expertise in logistics grows more not less important with the growth of larger tankers and pipelines. There is a greater premium on their skilled use in combination, for it is no saving to keep a huge tanker waiting to be unloaded, or to provide excess amounts of storage for lack of efficient refining and marketing. The multinational companies will undoubtedly be under somewhat greater handicaps because of the resentment aroused by their being large and foreign, but they are not about to leave the scene.

CHAPTER TEN

U.S. AUTOMOTIVE INVESTMENTS ABROAD

J. Wilner Sundelson

U.S. Automotive Investment Abroad

Though a late starter in the roster of early cars around the world, the Ford Model T was the first inexpensive utilitarian and durable car. It swept the markets of the world beginning in 1903. When General Motors was formed in 1908, its first inexpensive utilitarian model, the Chevrolet, joined in sales abroad but trailed the Model T in the export boom for almost 20 years. Ford and GM, as well as, later, some Chrysler assembly plants mushroomed around the world, taking advantage of lower freight charges on knocked-down vehicles, lower tariffs, and using some local components and labor.

In the late 1920s the Model T's dominance came to an end. The Chevrolet superseded it as a leader both in the United States and abroad. At the same time, European taxes, based on cubic engine capacity and weight, gave rise to a new breed of light, small-engined cars made in Europe. The long foreign honeymoon with U.S.-sourced car was nearing an end.

General Motors, in what now has come to be recognized as a brilliant strategy, bought out an auto firm in England, Vauxhall. Two years later, in 1927, it paid $26 million for the Adam Opel Company based near Frankfurt, Germany. Also, the Holden firm in Australia was acquired. All three manufacturing plants became wholly owned.

Ford's experience tells of slow and spasmodic efforts to turn the assembly plants in England, Germany, and France into manufacturers of distinctive European vehicles. Lack of support from the parent U.S. company led the managers of the European companies to borrow and sell shares, giving rise to the shareholders whose elimination was so costly later on.

Just before World War II broke out, General Motors and Ford were selling or about to sell European-made vehicles. By that time, too, Morris and Austin in England, Daimler-Benz (Mercedes) and Bayerische Motor Werke (BMW) in Germany, Renault, Citroën, and Peugeot in France, and Fiat in Italy were already in production and are still surviving.

While each warring power enlisted its automotive plants into its war effort with varying degrees of success, many plants also suffered war damage. Some, such as the Ford plant in Poissy, France, became a full-fledged manufacturing plant, under Nazi control, during the war. General Motors and Ford recognized the end of a profitable period of U.S. exports, which had reached a peak of over 200,000 cars a year in the 1930s. While profits at source and those repatriated from abroad ran into the hundreds of millions, valuable tangible assets in the form of foreign manufacturing and assembly plants had come into being. At the same time, dealer networks and product recognition had been won, the latter for the new European products as well.

Investments, other than General Motors purchase of the three companies, were small and sporadic. The real fight for the foreign market between American companies and Europe's own giants took place in the 1950s and is continuing heatedly as the decade of the 1960s nears an end.

Before turning to that interesting battle of the million-unit producers, let us look briefly at the principal markets other than the United States and Europe.

The Free World. These are (1) the "accessible-to-U.S.-automotive-investment" countries of the world, Latin America, Australia, Africa, and a lot of smaller scattered markets; (2) some "behind-the-Curtain" countries; and (3) Japan. The latter two have been closed since the postwar period to the U.S. automotive industry except for occasional exports. Unlike the Communist countries, Japan has become a major export source. Canada, now part of an integrated market with the United States, was "foreign" until 1964.

Latin America began to import U.S. cars, and, soon, because of the distance, there were good economic reasons for assembly. Ford started as early as 1917, when it invested some $240,000 to help set up the Brazilian branch. GM and also Chrysler have been active in Latin America for a long time. Assembly in Brazil lasted until the late 1950s, when a wave of nationalism hit the leading countries of Latin America.

The Brazilian government decided in 1955 that it would force manufacturers to produce up to 80 to 90% of trucks in Brazil and formulated its implementing program. The required speed for using locally produced components turned out to be slow enough to enable the investing American companies to recover the investment by profits on the continuing, if declining quantities of components they exported. Also, Brazil is a big country, and there was, for local manufacturing conditions, a truck market approaching 100,000 units which was divided into not more than five slices.

The existence of assembly facilities made it necessary to invest principally in engine and other power-train manufacturing facilities. The initial amount spent by Ford is reported at $21 million, GM at $20 million, Mercedes at $18 million, Volkswagen at $12.5 million. These amounts are the going-in investments. They are now still higher, the increases attributable not only to a greater proportion of components produced but also to the movement to more manufactured end products. The real problem initially was not getting the money but finding the right people and the know-how of producing at small volumes, which was alien to companies planning model runs in the millions of vehicles. It was not easy to gear their activities to some 18,000 trucks a year. These included a full range, not as complete as in the United States, but from one to six and eight tons.

The Europeans, Volkswagen and Mercedes, decided to enter the Brazilian car business that the Americans had neglected in the early years. Chrysler made early attempts to get into the truck business but did not succeed until later. It now has a 100%-owned car and truck manufacturing facility in Brazil.

In some markets some company occasionally takes the lead. Ford now seems to have been doing this in Brazil with the car, truck, and tractor line. More recently it has bought out some parts of Willys from Renault, which had bought out Willys' entire operations in Brazil and Argentina. This brought a new, smaller car called the Corcel into the Ford line, and Ford now can produce some 90-odd thousand units in Brazil, including tractors. This is a far cry from the 18,000 trucks they started with in 1956.

The economy of Brazil has remained troubled, and, while the inflation has slowed down, vehicle prices have grown faster than incomes. For some reason other than profits, Ford, Chrysler, and GM stay in Brazil, expand, and hope for the mañana that never seems to come.

The next Latin American compulsory production program was in Argentina. This brought forth a host of companies. Mercedes was the first; Kaiser had taken over Willys and was next in 1955. In 1959 the big push developed: Ford, GM, and Chrysler from the United States, Fiat from Italy, and several smaller firms entered the manufacturing program. Since that time, there has been reshuffling with a local company bought by Kaiser and with Chrysler buying out one of the smaller companies there, Germany's DKW. Finally, in 1967, Renault bought out Kaiser and sold part of it to Ford.

Argentina may be a good example of how nationalism and the competitive instincts of manufacturers spoil it for themselves and the country. There are 13 manufacturers now turning out some 70 models of cars and trucks on a total production equal to less than 2% of the U.S. volume. These 70 models do not count differences in the size of the engines and whether gasoline- or diesel-powered. In a study made of the Argentine industry by Baranson of the World Bank,[1] the market has been characterized as having enormous swings in volume much greater than those that the industry has met in the United States or Europe. The bad years reduced the industry to between 20 and 60% of their capacity and they go be-

[1] J. Baranson (International Bank for Reconstruction and Development), "Automotive Industries in Developing Countries," Washington, D.C., 1968, p. 40.

246

tween 70 and 80% in good years. There is too much capacity for any one to go to 100%. From the government's point of view, the foreign-exchange burden continued to grow even though the proportion of imported components was declining all the time. For example, the premanufacturing program (1932) exchange cost was $42 million. It grew to $250 million in the late 1950s, when the foreign programs were in full bloom. Import substitution and exchange savings were defeated. This inefficient production led to inflationary pressures, and the profit squeeze was on the producers. It is no wonder that there is resistance to the trade integration programs such as LAFTA. Argentina is afraid that its industry would be wiped out if vehicles came in from other countries.

Recently there has been some indication that one company in Argentina thinks that it may get out of the profit squeeze, as Ford may be doing in Brazil, by growing to a point where its production is economic. As recently as February of 1969, Fiat was reported to have won the government's approval for a $95 million expansion program involving more vehicles, tractors, and even locomotives. Fiat has also bought out a company, the Auto-Motriz Santa Fe, in which Volkswagen had a minority industry, and will get some increased facilities and market outlets for its tractor and agricultural business. This program will give Fiat leadership in Argentina. To get the government's approval for this expansion, it had to agree to lower prices by 30%. By 1973 the ratio of Argentine to Italian Fiat prices will be 1½ to 1. It is now 2 or 2½ to 1. Also, the expansion has to take place outside the Buenos Aires region. Finally, Fiat pleased the government by salvaging the faltering Santa Fe Company (which it bought) and by nullifying Volkswagen interests, which will help to keep Volkswagen out of the already saturated market.

By 1960, Mexico could not resist the pressure from its various nationalistic interests to require a local automotive industry. This had been late in coming, since the Mexicans are close to the United States and see all the new model cars. The manufacturers expected there would be consumer resistance to the frozen models and higher prices. The Mexicans believed that local production would give them opportunities to sell their cars to other Latin American countries. They took LAFTA more seriously than appears to have been warranted.

The solution to the problem of the Mexicans wanting modern-looking cars was met. First, the number of models was cut down. There are just some GM, Chrysler, and Ford cars that the Mexicans allow to be produced. Secondly, bodies, new ones each year, continue to be imported.

More recently there have been starts at manufacturing programs of one kind or another in Venezuela, Colombia, Peru, and Chile. There are nascent programs inching up toward more and more local content in each country. The situations are extremely complex because the volumes are small and because there are no free-trade programs between the countries concerned. Chile and Peru are most anxious to have their own automotive industries. In good years, the total Chilean market varies between 18 and 25,000 units, which six or more producers have to share. The resistance is great and the auto companies do just enough to stay within the limits of what they have to do to get import permits. If this trend were to continue, it would be disastrous, and would make it virtually impossible for any Latin American integration to get started.

More of the Free World. New Zealand has assembly, and there is a small beginning of some local content. Elsewhere in the world there is manufacturing in Australia and in South Africa and assembly in Egypt, in Rhodesia, and in Malaysia. There are rumblings of more assembly, and increased manufacturing is on the horizon. Among the few programs that have the potential of being profitable are those of Australia and South Africa. When Ford got started in Australia, after much hesitation, it had to invest $28 million. In 1950, GM designed an Australian car to be manufactured in its earlier acquired Holden plant and attained a strong market position. GM still is a market leader and no one in sight is catching up. Ford is number two and is hard put to keep its relative position. We know that the profitability is the greatest at GM's Holden. In fact, it has been a matter of parliamentary concern how much they make and that the activity is 100% GM owned. GM has weathered these criticisms because, in the final analysis, it produces cars that people want. Chrysler is in Australia with a 96% owned facility.

248

The South African experience is most recent. Ford was in South Africa since 1925, having at that time put in a million dollars in an assembly activity. GM followed very shortly thereafter. They now all have to meet local-content requirements, but conditions are very competitive. This is brought about by the fact that there are 12 producing companies. Outside of Ford, GM, and Chrysler, there are Volkswagen, Fiat, Mercedes, Renault, and British Leyland.[2] The Philippines has now insisted on assembly, and several companies including the big U.S. three, have formed new companies and made investments. Elsewhere the companies also let dealers assemble: GM in Pakistan and Ford in Israel, the latter the reason for an Arab boycott.

Behind the Curtain. The period prior to World War II saw the only East European automotive industry of any economic significance in Czechoslovakia. This country, independent in the interlude between the close of World War I and occupation by Hitler, was producing two lines of vehicles which met limited acceptance in Western Europe. The war, which led to a Russian puppet state, did not leave the industry intact, nor did the economic leadership that took over have the know-how or the resources to restore the factories to a competitive level. Postwar Skodas and Tatras are no longer seen in Germany, Austria, or elsewhere in Western Europe. The only other noteworthy prewar industry in the countries now behind the Iron Curtain were those German plants that ended up in the Russian satellite, East Germany. One or two of the plants started in the West again. The Auto Union regrouped in the West and is now part of the Mercedes complex.

What has happened since the war may be briefly summarized as follows: cars for consumers were virtually ignored; there were not enough cars even to go around for the bureaucrats and for those who wanted cars to include as exports in bilateral trade agreements. There was an emphasis on trucks and military carriers. Not more than several hundred thousand vehicles were produced in East Germany, in Soviet Russia, and in Czechoslovakia for hundreds of millions of people.

[2] British Motors Leyland, Ltd. is referred to here as British Leyland.

In the mid-1960s the Soviet leaders recognized three factors. First, their products were not acceptable to the West. Even in countries like Finland, where there was considerable pressure forcing the Finns to accept Russian cars and trucks, they were not appreciated, and few people acquired them voluntarily. The Finns, who had to import Russian trucks, landed them on the docks and had mechanics take out the Russian engines and insert English Ford engines. This is the only way the trucks could be sold. Dealers in Belgium, hoping the small but active Communist party members would go for Soviet vehicles, were disappointed. Even dumping did not succeed in creating markets for such vehicles. Second, there was, wherever possible, a market for Western-made vehicles, particularly from England, in the country's bilateral trade agreements. Thousands came under each agreement, and vehicles disappeared behind the Curtain whenever officials and other privileged persons could travel. There are other sources. For example, some of Berlin's used cars end up in East Berlin. Third, Russia realized that to maintain the allegiance of the masses, their standard of living would have to grow, and that in a rising standard of living, even behind the Curtain, a demand grows for a small car. This recognition of the political necessity of meeting the growing needs of consumers led Russia, swallowing its pride, to approach Fiat and to propose that Fiat design a modification of one of its popular little cars, the Fiat 124 (12-liter engine displacement) for Russia. It also proposed that it design and equip a series of plants to produce initially 600,000 such vehicles in a year. This is about half the number Fiat produces in Italy. The plants themselves were to be built by the Russians following Fiat plans and specifications. The Russians agreed to pay over a period of time. Fiat, lacking political inhibitions, quickly accepted the deal. The factory should go on stream in 1970, and Russia will then be the scene of the first major large-scale consumer-type passenger car made behind the Curtain. Rumania, independent and not to be outdone, has made a much smaller but comparable agreement with Renault. Rumania, too, will have a small automotive industry.

The American companies were anxious to get in the act. Ford of Germany tried on behalf of the Ford Motor Company. Ford's president also visited Russia. However, there is no desire to lean on America or American-owned industry for the development of the Soviet bloc industry.

In Yugoslavia, Fiat and an English manufacturer of diesel engines were invited in. Fiat agreed to license the manufacture of one of its small cars, to help design and equip a plant to manufacture and assemble the chassis and body parts, and to give technical know-how and licenses for the manufacture of engines and other components. There is a large plant turning out these Fiats, which are sold under a Yugoslav name, and a large engine plant on the outskirts of Belgrade. Fiat is paid by accepting end products, such as some cars and engines. The world's biggest diesel-engine manufacturer, Massey-Ferguson's Perkins in England, set up a diesel plant in Yugoslavia, also in the Belgrade area and under the same conditions. This plant manufactures the engines for Yugoslav-made trucks and tractors. Yugoslavia is rapidly following western patterns in marketing and in the purchasing habits of its residents. That is why other Western companies have relationships with importing bodies of the government who import and sell their products. Of all the Marxist countries, Yugoslavia has, of course, the highest car density and was the earliest to have a fully developed automotive industry created by collaboration with the West. Initially critical of this step, Russia has now gone in the same direction, and by coincidence, with the same company that started Yugoslavia on its way toward being a manufacturer of automotive vehicles.

Japan. Another part of the world in which the American companies have no participation is Japan. Japan is now the second leading producing country of the world and is in the 4 million-unit-a-year class. The U.S. companies are outside, but not for want of trying. In the 1930s, Japan decided to develop its own industry. Ford bought land and prepared to build, but was denied permission by the government. The Japanese wanted a fully home-grown industry. This industry had a rough time during the war years and failed afterward to retain a lot of the know-how that had been acquired abroad in the early postwar period. The government was less restrictive in those days than it had been. Thus, Ford was invited to form a joint venture with Toyota. This was one of several mistakes the Ford Motor Company made. It thought at the time that it was too busy with its U.S., and Canadian, and nascent European production problems. It also thought that it could come into Japan at a later date at its pleasure. Then Japan closed the doors, and since then the U.S. industry has been clamoring for entry. While the Japanese do not allow foreign investments in the automotive industry, Toyota, Nissan, Honda Toyo-kogyo, and Mitsubishi Heavy Industries have all enjoyed growth and have expanded their car sales. Three developments are taking place. First there is pressure by the U.S. government and by U.S. automotive manufacturers to allow investments. There are also veiled innuendos about asking for restrictions on Japanese imports in the United States unless Japan yields. Volkswagen is also pushing its government to impose a ban on Japanese car imports into Germany. Volkswagen is angry because Japanese imports pushed them out of Australia. Second, the Japanese government is pushing mergers and tie-ups so that its industry can be powerful enough to withstand the shock of foreign competition in the country. Nissan and Fuji Heavy Industries would become the nucleus of one of the big units. The other would be the grouping of smaller companies around Toyota. A third group would be formed around the Mitsubishi Heavy Industries and Isuzu Motors. Production by only three companies would place the Japanese industry near par with the United States and the leading European giants. Thirdly, Europeans are trying to edge in. Swedish Saab has been talking with a company, Marubeniida, which is a distributor of imported Fords. Fiat, which is the fifth-ranked importer behind the three U.S. companies and Volkswagen, has opened an office. There are also confirmed reports linking Nissan and Toyo-kogyo in a venture with Ford to manufacture automatic transmissions. Most recently it became known that joint production of more car parts and components was under study. At the same time, Borg-Warner has already applied to the Ministry (MITI) for approval of a joint venture on automatic automotive transmissions with a Toyota subsidiary, the Aishinseiki Company. Borg-Warner's investment, a $6 million joint venture, is split between the United States and the Japanese company 50–50. But Borg-Warner will receive its equity share and royalties for the technical know-how rather than for any cash investments. Chrysler is, at this moment, negotiating with Mitsubishi Heavy Industries for a joint 35–65% (Japanese) venture. Conflicting reports mention plans to sell a car from Japan in the United States, engage in joint research, or even produce a car jointly in Japan. Mitsubishi and the government still insist no agreement has been reached.

Canada. As early as 1922, the U.S. industry realized that money could be made in Canada. The early $100 Ford Canadian shares a few years later were worth over $6,500 as production expanded. Now facilities and market shares in the Canadian market are ranked about the same way they are in the United States proper. Soon Ford fell behind GM and Chrysler behind Ford. The situation was unsatisfactory for Canadians because they had a limited number of models for which they paid higher prices. However, the Canadian market boomed, and the assets employed by U.S. companies in Canada grew to some $500 million each. This prompted the Kennedy administration to try to develop a historic agreement. In 1964 the negotiations were concluded, and one automotive market was created. There is some limitation on U.S. imports into Canada unless they are matched by Canadian shipments to the United States, and there is grumbling on the part of spare parts and components manufacturers to find the big auto companies occasionally buying from Canadian sources. But the integration has proceeded, and now the United States and Canada are one market to the extent that the large U.S. companies can plan a unified United States–Canadian operation. They allocate functions to an Ontario-based assembly plant as they would to one in Ohio or in California. The program has resulted in such a degree of integration that it could hardly be dropped. The real question is: Is this a forerunner of the future? Have we, via the automotive industry, the beginning of a truly economic integration of the United States and Canada?

The Automotive Boom in Western Europe in the 1950s and 1960s

One can conveniently group the 1950s and the 1960s in Europe as the time of the boom that led to a concurrent growth of the

253

automobile industry. The European consumers began to behave the way the American consumers did in the 1920s. They bought consumer goods, including durables; they learned to use consumer credit; they gained leisure and then wanted the means of enjoying it; they moved to the suburbs. All these developments led to their becoming car buyers. The economic recovery also led to an increased demand for commercial vehicles. A European development, the large box-shaped van designed to carry goods that were bulky but were not necessarily heavy, dethroned the one-half- and the one-ton American type trucks that were designed to carry steel ingots or scrap iron. Light commercial vehicles became very popular, and the United States copied the idea later.

During the boom period of 20 years that we are considering, the countries all moved from the consumption of hundreds of thousands of vehicles a year to millions. Finally, by the end of the period, Western Europe (for our purposes comprising the two trading blocs, the Common Market, and the Outer Seven, together with Spain) was buying 6 million new vehicles a year, some 95% of them made in Europe.

How were the American companies in Europe poised to enjoy this boom? It appears now in retrospect that they had ideal and unique capabilities of riding with the boom. GM and Ford both had manufacturing facilities in Germany and England. Ford, in addition, had a manufacturing facility in France. They had a network of assembly plants from Scandinavia southward which enabled them to take advantage of lower tariffs on components. The two companies had European products designed for the European market. Both had many dealers and product reputation, and behind them stood virtually unlimited resources of money as well as the all-important resources of know-how and talent in the form of experienced men.

Besides the Americans and the big Europeans, there were also dozens of small companies. In Europe there soon began a dropping out of the inefficient manufacturing companies, both of trucks and of passenger cars. A series of mergers and takeovers occurred which reached its fruition in the last few years when giants took over big companies outside their own country and when in some

254

cases a host of little companies that had managed to survive when gobbled up.

The company that had the best opportunity of enjoying the boom was probably General Motors. It had the largest resources in its domestic market, where it had achieved an unparalleled 50% or more of the total demand. It had an experienced body of international automotive management and staff. GM had no inhibitions against employing American talents where they were needed, and had no bothersome minority shareholders. Early in the postwar period GM had provided capital and other resources for its German Opel plant, which grew as a motor passenger car manufacturer in Germany, second only to Volkswagen. Opel was the leader in the profitable middle-class vehicle segment of the market. GM showed no hesitation in doing what was needed to stay in markets outside its manufacturing centers.

The records are not clear as to how much GM put into its plants but it certainly must have expended more than a half a billion dollars in Europe alone. It expanded Opel to a capacity of 650,000 vehicles, but never succeeded in getting Opel to be a truck producer. Making trucks was left to the English company, which became one of the leading truck producers and the U.K.'s leading truck exporter. On the other hand, the English Vauxhall plant never developed a leading position as a car producer. In a sense, GM, which had the most going for it, did not do enough to capitalize on what it had to attain a leading position.

Some of the things which GM and also Ford did should be recognized. The Americans have felt, and perhaps rightly so, that there can be no profitable production of really small cars, the kind that Renault, Fiat, and some of the new defunct Germans, Gutbrod, Glas, and others, tried to develop. It is fortunate that outside of Italy the leading companies can avoid putting too much of their resources in these little- or no-profit vehicles and can concentrate, as Fiat, Simca, Renault, and British Leyland are now doing, on increasing the proportion of their over-one-liter cars. By a utilization of some existing components GM managed to enter the one-liter class, which appears to be the size limit at which European cars can be profitably made.

255

It is interesting to see just how GM overseas did grow while its export shipments from the United States gradually declined. GM entered the 1950s with as many as 137,000 vehicles shipped from the United States and 180,000 made abroad, principally in Europe. The U.S. exports had declined to 106,000 two years later and the European production had grown to almost 600,000 units, a third of them in England and two-thirds in Germany. A year later, foreign production, aided by the Australian and Brazilian production of about 150,000 units, hit the million mark. The boom can be seen in the fact that between 1963 and 1964 the overseas production grew by a quarter of a million, while the U.S. exports remained stable. The importance of the overseas markets began to be a factor in the finances of the domestic company only recently. Foreign sales of $2.9 billion were about $\frac{1}{7}$ of total sales, which has now become roughly the proportion of cars produced overseas compared to those made in the United States. One in seven GM cars are now made abroad. Also recently foreign incomes began to be interesting in the total picture. In the last year of which we have a complete record we have sales abroad reaching $3 billion, Opel and Vauxhall producing slightly under 900,000 units with Opel generally twice as big as Vauxhall, and GM telling us that they make 59 different car-body styles overseas.

In 1960 GM had assets of about $600 million abroad, but held a reserve against depreciation of currencies and listed the assets at about $450 million. In that year also GM earned abroad 14% of its total $873 million, or $148 million. The percentage of earnings abroad fell in 1962 to 7%. By 1963 it recovered to 8% and meant that some $127 million came from abroad. There seems to be a wide fluctuation in recent years in the profit proportions derived from the foreign investments, reflecting both the size of U.S. earnings and the fluctuations in foreign returns. In 1964 total foreign earnings were $226 million, the highest ever reported by any U.S. automotive company. Of the total, Opel earned $86 million and Vauxhall $27 million in that year. (In 1964 the foreign earnings still included Canadian operations.) This also represented 13% of the $1,735 billion net earnings of GM on which they had record return on sales of over 10%. Assets abroad continued to creep up, reflecting reinvestments as well as new undertakings, but the earnings percentages and the totals never reached the 1964 record. In 1967 and 1968 the percentages have been 6.6 and 7%, respectively — almost stable earnings yielding $108 million and $121 million. Some idea of the transfers other than net profit can be seen by the statement in its 1968 annual report — that since 1945, GM has contributed $12.3 billion to the U.S. balance of payments. This is also an all-time record for any single company. It shows that in addition to repatriated profits, GM sold a great many components and equipment and received other payments. (Nonautomotive products are also in the total.) In conclusion, the United States's and the world's biggest automotive company is abroad on a large scale, but not in proportion to its overwhelming position in the world's biggest market, the United States.

Ford was also well placed at the beginning of the European boom. In fact, relative to its position in the U.S. market, its sales were proportionately much better in Europe. But Ford Motor Company, too, made a major mistake in the too-slow recognition of the importance of its German source. That important source was late in expanding and late in getting designs of mass popular appeal. German Ford was also late in reaching the level of integration established by the other big producers in its country, that is, in reaching that proportion of "make" as distinguished from "buy" items which characterizes the European market in general and the German market in particular. The German company also failed, as did GM in Germany, to get into the truck market. It produces only the light transit vans. Unlike Opel, Ford Germany tried, but came out with a disastrous model that not only lost the company a great deal of money but also financially wrecked many dealers.

Ford eliminated the base it had in France. Ford had a choice in the late 1950s of spending $100 million to design new products or to tool up for their production. It was not that the $100 million was lacking; there was in the management of Ford Motor Company a considerable body of men in key positions who had come up through General Motors. They carried with them two of GM's favorite policies — 100% ownership and stay out of France. Both policies were carried out, first in the sale of the French Ford Company to Simca in return for 15.2% of Simca shares. Subsequently, a change of heart led Ford to investigate whether it might acquire more shares and rebuild in France, on the basis of the Simca Company. Fiat held those shares, although this was not publicly known at the time, and refused to sell. By 1958, the interest in maintaining a small minority share of Simca vanished. Also, the possibility of making a profit, which could bolster up the sad 1958 U.S. Ford earnings, prompted Ford to sell the shares to Chrysler at a gain of some $17 million. Fiat by then must have had its own ideas as to how it was going to grow into the French market. It sold enough shares to Chrysler to give Chrysler control of Simca. Ford was thus out of the French market and Chrysler finally got a car-manufacturing foothold in Europe.

Earlier, Ford had made one good move. It realized that the post-World War II period would not involve merely selling American products but would involve investments, marketing and design advice, engineering know-how, and people. Ford then formed an International Division. GM had already set up its overseas division in New York. The head of the new Ford division, Graeme Howard, an ex-GM overseas vice-president, followed the same pattern. Prior to becoming a vice-president of Ford, he worked as a consultant on plans for the acquisition of more ownership shares. In the case of Canada, Ford bought shares that gave it 51.85%, or control of the company. It did not have that control until that time. More important, in August of 1949, Howard developed a brilliant scheme. The English Ford company had declared dividends throughout the war, but transfer of Ford U.S. shares had been blocked. After the war, England felt an obligation to provide dollars for the transfer of those shares. It was thus delighted at the proposal that the United States instead use its sterling resources, some £4½ million, to buy the ownership of the Guernsey Holding Company, which held the majority shares of the continental Ford companies. Fortunately for Ford, the £4½ million each bought $4.03 worth of shares. Had the scheme been put through one month later in September of 1949, the U.S. company would have received only $2.80 worth of shares due to the devaluation of the pound in August. For these blocked pounds, Ford U.S. got 99% of the Egyptian company; 100% of the Italian company; 57% of the Belgian company; 60% of the Dutch, Danish, and Spanish companies; 21% of the French company; and 6% of the German company. The United States already had controlling shares of both the French and German companies — 55 and 58%, respectively. Also, by owning the Danish company, they received indirect holdings in the Swedish and the Finnish companies, and by having control of the Spanish company they received control of the Portuguese company.

The company that really moved ahead on all fronts — cars, vans, trucks, and tractors — was Ford of England. It had excellent management. It moved by reinvesting its earnings in expansion and in acquisitions, not of other automotive companies, but of component manufacturers. It bought control of the U.K. Briggs body plant through an exchange of shares. This dropped Ford's U.S. ownership in 1953 to 54%. Another result of the purchase continues to plague Ford to this date. There were some left-wing aggressive labor stewards representing several unions in the Briggs operation that Ford took over. The Briggs operation was located on the main Ford industrial park outside of London. Continued agitation and strikes have led to a plague of labor problems which have cost Ford of England profits in almost every year since 1954 and have been a major deterrent to even a greater lead in the European race. Ford of England, nevertheless, started to move ahead as fast as it could.

At the end of the 1950s, the leaders of the Ford operation in Germany were reluctant to ask for assistance, and the little they asked for, Ford U.S. was reluctant to give. In the meantime, Opel, the GM base on the continent and the government-owned plant, Volkswagen, moved ahead in a lead that Ford's revitalized management, cash, and technical assistance in Germany could not overcome.

In the 1960s, the Ford effort on the continent intensified. Germany turned the corner with new U.S. management and new capital, all of it coming from the United States. With U.S. technical assistance and investment, Ford spent some $380 million in expansion in Europe in 1964 and 1965 and reported that it was planning

259

to spend $200 million more. This is part of the total of some $900 million that Ford invested overseas in the decade, more than ⅔ of it in Europe, and which gave it the capacities it now has.

Ford showed also a great appreciation of the potentials of the Common Market. It wagered that the Common Market would last, and that it would have a major effect on the automotive industry. Ford reacted to this belief by accelerating the growth of its one facility in the Market, in Germany, and it sought to overcome the absence of trucks and tractors there. The Common Market had the same effect of rendering some assembly plants as surplus. This led the German Ford to build a facility in Belgium because of labor availability, help from the Belgian government, and better access to parts of Germany than its Cologne plants could give it. It succeeded in the tractor area by using the Antwerp assembly plant rendered useless by the Benelux, necessitating only one facility in both countries. Ford found a way of getting English-made tractors into the Common Market changing the Antwerp plant into a tractor assembly and manufacturing base for some components.

Unlike tractors, the efforts to get into the truck business on the Continent was not successful. As noted above, the truck program in Germany fell flat. Then Ford Cologne flirted with various producers, Krupp, Henschel, and others, but never made a successful purchase. It is now assembling U.K.-made trucks on the continent, but so far not successfully. Ford also set up a sales office in Brussels which, whatever its costs and shortcomings were, concentrated sales efforts in the markets of Europe, which were moving from assembly companies to selling bases.

While everyone else was growing slowly, Ford in England went ahead and spent as much as $196 million out of its own resources, primarily in a huge plant outside of Liverpool on the Mersey ($85 million) and at Basildon in the London suburbs ($28 million). The balance went for engineering centers and other facilities. Dagenham also continued buying out companies and parts producers. It bought, as did the United States, a part of the Auto-Lite Motor Products in England. It also acquired facilities and the rights to certain products for some $4 million from the Simms Motor Company Ltd. It took an expenditure of $500 million in the five years

1964 to 1969 to reach new capacities. Now Ford of England can manufacture over 750,000 units a year; it is the biggest U.S.-owned automotive operation abroad.

Facing the fact of the Common Market and the Outer Seven led to the realization by Ford that it could not apply strategies designed to meet the complex political and trading situation in Europe unless it controlled all the shares of the manufacturing companies. With such control it could do what was necessary regardless of where the profits were made. The minority-acquisition plan cost Ford some $500 million. The minority shareholders in the United Kingdom obtained $358 million. The German minority shareholders received over $100 million in the move to 99% ownership by Ford. The balance went to acquisition of some Canadian shares. European shareholders were paid about $450 million.

Ford could now begin to design cars and sell the same product, with some minor cosmetic indications of origin, in both trade blocs. It began with vans, which were successful, and more recently has a new product, the Capri, which is a major play by Ford for the middle-class market with five engine choices between 1.3 and 2.3 liters. The second step Ford took was to create Ford of Europe manned by some U.S. Ford vice-presidents and to decentralize the European operation entirely from Detroit. It centralizes product development and engineering and manufacturing control in the outskirts of London where Ford of Europe is based. This leaves all the European Ford companies with local responsibility for selling. Together with Esso, ITT, and Corn Products, Ford is one of the few big American companies setting up a European-base profit center and the only one of the big automotive three. GM remains in New York, and Chrysler, after experimenting with a tax haven operation in Geneva, now has its international operations controlled from Detroit.

The channeling of funds has been accomplished by a willingness to forego dividends and allow the funds to go into reinvestments, as well as by new cash from the United States — a billion or more dollars since the mid-fifties. More recently, since the investment controls, channeling of funds has occurred by the issuance of Eurobonds and debentures. GM, Ford, and Chrysler have sold some.

The expenditure of vast sums is the price of leadership in Europe.

Since 1965, Ford has sold more vehicles abroad, consisting of a small number still coming from the United States and the rest units made abroad. It is Europe's fourth leading producer after Volkswagen, Fiat, and British Leyland, in that order. However, Ford has been unable to have a comparable lead in earnings. Its manufacturing facilities have not been very profitable. Most of what they earn they have to reinvest. Ford hit over the $100 million mark of dividends and profits after tax in the United States in 1966 when it made almost $112 million and in 1968 when it reached its own all-time high of $125 million. One of the problems is that Ford still has minority shareholders in the selling companies, particularly in Europe. Good profits are made, and it has to give away a large part of what it earns to minority shareholders.

Annual reports show a growth of assets but a rather sad return on sales abroad. However, there has been no diminution of the interest in growing abroad and in maintaining the blue ribbon of leadership. Annual reports show that assets after reserves were $532 million in 1960, and these have inched up to where they are now at $1 billion 370 million. Ford makes about 20% of its profits from foreign sources, a much higher proportion than does GM. In some years when there are domestic strikes, as in 1967, the proportion, the foreign share of total earnings, soared to 49%. (This is reminiscent of the Great Depression year when Ford exported 42% of the cars it produced.) The leadership is made possible by production of 1,204,183 units abroad: over a million cars and the balance trucks.

Finally, Ford believes that it, too, has helped the balance of payments. It has provided some $4 billion in the postwar years to the U.S. balance. This includes the sale of U.S. products, the receipt of payments for technical assistance, as well as dividends and the return from the sale of the Simca shares.

It would have been much better for Chrysler if it had earlier recognized that a position in Europe could be won only with European-produced vehicles. Europe is now the scene of three Chrysler operations, which have something under 7% of the European market. Of the big three, Chrysler is the only one in Spain. Spain decided some years ago to have its own industry, and favored a Fiat operation in which the government had shares. It made newcomers reach the same level of local content which that older establishment, SEAT, had obtained. This made entry extremely costly and suggested no profits could be made because of a limited volume from which to recover the heavy investments.

However, a truck manufacturer had a previously issued license for car production which he could exercise at the old rates of local content. Chrysler bought into the Spanish truck plant. It had 77% of the company and is a factor, albeit a small one, in the Spanish market. Spanish costs are such that no one has seen a Spanish vehicle in recent years commercially sold outside of Spain. Next, Chrysler was able to take control of Simca, of which it now has 77% of the shares. More recently, it bought Rootes, and it has now a foothold in both European trading blocs. Simca is the fourth-ranking car company in France — one that has difficulties in exports. Rootes is a relatively minor company in England. Neither company manufactures trucks or tractors. Chrysler's big problem is how to achieve profitability out of its operations. This has more recently been accomplished in Simca where, in 1968, the first small profits appeared. In 1967, Rootes lost some $29 million; market-share declines are among Rootes problems. Most recently, Rootes showed its first modest profits on almost a half a billion dollars of sales. Profitable European operations for Chrysler are not in sight.

Compared to its relatively small European sales, Chrysler participates more intensively in almost all the other foreign markets of major importance — Brazil, Argentina, Mexico, Australia, and South Africa. In the 1968 fiscal year, it reported $1.5 billion in sales and net earnings of $17.6 million. Those came largely from outside of Europe. Chrysler has indicated it will spend $100 million a year abroad for the next four years. Chrysler cannot even maintain its present position unless it makes such investments. It is believed that such amounts are not enough to move ahead.

While GM and Ford went ahead, Europe's own automotive leaders grew at a faster rate and are now virtually unreachable in their individual leadership positions. Some, like Fiat, did this in a protected market, and as quasi-monopolists rode the boom in their own countries. Fiat achieved a major market elsewhere in Europe with the opportunities presented by the Common Market as well as with its strategic pricing policy. (The Europeans have long ago decided to sell vehicles in export cheaper than they sell them at home. There are admitted discounts. Volvo sells in Germany for 82% of the Swedish selling price. Fiats in Germany sell for some 80% of the price in Italy. English Ford products are sold at little or no profit margins to come into France. These European-sponsored price cuts, or what our Treasury might call dumping, have been very successful and have contributed to growth.)

Fiat also grew by buying up smaller producers such as Bianchi, OM, Macchi, and others. Diversification — locomotives, ships, planes, electronics, even superhighways — also helped Fiat's development. Fiat, we have learned, is an aggressive operator overseas, and besides having leadership prospects in Argentina, has major participation in the growth behind the Curtain in Russia and Yugoslavia.

In France there have been few mergers, and the companies have grown, although not to a position where they can be leaders in Europe. De Gaulle tried to bring about mergers in France to give at least one major French company a chance to compete with Europe's leaders, Fiat and Volkswagen. But there were animosities between the privately held companies, and the mergers did not come about until a defensive reaction occurred to Fiat's move into Citroën. Everyone assumes that the present close relations of Renault and Peugeot will lead to a merger. This leaves Simca alone with the Chrysler resources behind it and an ownership link with Rootes. France has missed the boat in not creating leading automotive producers.

In Germany, leadership came to the companies that made the products which the Germans as well as the car- and truck-importing world wanted. Volkswagen is an outstanding example of having designed a car that had a tremendous hold on the buyers of that particular type of vehicle — 1.3-liter four-seater air-cooled beetle-type car — which meets a great deal of the world's demand. Gradual loss of its hold in Germany and in the neighboring markets has come about largely through the upgrading of consumers' purchases.

264

They are buying bigger, more powerful cars. As the veteran automobile people say, "Lightning strikes only once"; Volkswagen has not succeeded in designing a car in the 1.6-liter class that has any degree of popularity comparable to its earlier vehicle. Volkswagen will be in trouble in Europe if it does not win enough time to design a completely new successful car to succeed the beetle.

Mercedes' success in the two-vehicle categories that are the most profitable, better-grade cars and trucks and buses, possibly contributed to its decision to remain in those areas. It fares poorly in the count of the number of units sold, but it has a great volume of money gross sales in Germany and is one of the profit leaders in Europe. More recently, Mercedes has been playing the acquisition game. Only one other German company has survived. That is BMW of Munich.

The English scene has a new leader that has lately appeared on the horizon. In 1952, two companies, the number two and three companies after Ford, merged. Austin and Morris became the British Motor Corporation. The new company was not brilliantly managed. This was reflected in its export performance, in its profitability, and in the image that its products created. The company also did not believe in investing abroad, and consequently did very poorly in exports and in foreign manufacturing centers. A much smaller company, Leyland, had a good hold on the truck market and had acquired some smaller car manufacturers. It has very able management. Leyland literally took over the much bigger BMC and formed British Leyland. This has since become, by any standard in Europe, a major producer of a complete line of cars and trucks of all categories and has put England back in the leadership running with an English-owned company. The move precluded Ford's U.K. operation from aspiring to the leadership in its home market. BML in the U.K. market has market shares almost comparable to GM's hold in the United States. New assembly plants, aggressive marketing and good products are pushing British Leyland ahead. In Europe it will spend $120 million a year for five years. The two other smaller European companies have made a good showing; one is the German BMW, the other is Volvo. Neither is a leader, but both are growing fast. Volvo competes in

Sweden against imported vehicles that have relatively low tariffs and no hindrances. In fact, the Swedish assembly plants owned by Ford and GM closed because there were no longer tariff advantages in assembling. Volvo is also a good exporter, having quickly learned the trick of price cutting in export markets.

One of the smaller remaining companies, which is very profitable, Bayerische Motor Werke, best known as BMW, bought out a financially troubled producer of small cars, Hans Glas. It dropped the Glas cars but got factory space and manpower. In an effort to keep alive, BMW will spend $130 million in the near future in order to double its capacity. This is on top of $72 million that BMW had spent in the previous three years.

Some recent developments in the acquisition field may be of interest. In 1968, General de Gaulle restated his opposition to any acquisition by Fiat or any other foreign company in France. Renault and Citroën had been talking to each other, and there was hope that Peugeot would be brought into the discussions. Over the opposition of General de Gaulle, however, Fiat announced in the fall of 1968 a joint venture with Citroën involving test tracks and factories jointly owned which would employ 6,000 people and increase the hold of Fiat and Citroën on the European vehicle market. Acquisition by Fiat, which is expected gradually to be run up into a control position, followed the failure of approaches to Citroën by Renault.

Fiat went to the Michelin family, who are big Citroën share-owners, and was able to acquire that family's shares in return for a Fiat agreement to let the French-made Michelin tires into Italy as original equipment on some Fiat cars. Fiat had earlier acquired a French truck manufacturer (UNIC), and if the expectations that Fiat will acquire complete control of Citroën are realized, it will have a major foothold in France. Analysts point out that Citroën had a bad export record, a declining market position, and losses.

A very interesting move also was that of the hookup between Mercedes and a large steel company, Rheinstahl, which had in its possession two truck companies, Henschel and Hanomag. Other companies, including Ford, had at one time tried to acquire

266

Henschel. Rheinstahl eliminates a losing truck business. (The head of Rheinstahl, a former German Ford executive, was not disturbed at building up one of Ford's major competitors.) Mercedes acquired important producers of the four to eight gross ton trucks in which the two acquired companies had previously had 70% of the German market. It also has some 30% of the EEC market, Europe's leading commercial outlet. Leading producers are now Mercedes, Fiat-OM, and the Berliet, the important French truck manufacturer which Citroën owned and which came with the Fiat package. There remains now another truck group in Germany, Klockner-Magirus-Deutz, a subsidiary of a Rhineland-based steel and engineering group complex.

It is possible that in the near future some more truck mergers affecting the Common Market and linking perhaps the Common Market with countries outside of that trade bloc will occur. Leyland had already been negotiating with Klockner but that fell through. MAN, a big factor at the heavy truck end, already works with the Saviem Company, a subsidiary of Renault in France. Büssing, a money-losing subsidiary of the state-owned Salzgitter complex in Germany has been talking with a Fiat truck subsidiary in Italy, OM. Sooner or later the job that the American companies have of getting into the truck business on the Continent will become very difficult unless they acquire the currently unbespoken Klockner-Magirus-Deutz group or the others.

Recently further moves took place. Citroën took over Maserati in Italy, adding it indirectly to Fiat. The takeover grew out of a technical and commercial agreement of two years earlier. Next, Volkswagen announced a merger with NSU. It accomplished this merger by buying NSU through its subsidiary, Autounion, so that Volkswagen now had both companies in a subsidiary. Citroën had an agreement with NSU relating to NSU's development of the Wankel patented irregular-shaped crankshaft combustion engines. Volkswagen now has a subsidiary with $350 million sales, which it achieves through the production of 255,000 units. The arrangement also allows the NSU shareholders to keep 70% of the royalties from the sale of the Wankel engines. (It is now reported that they want more.) In total, it cost Volkswagen $32 million to acquire NSU and to accomplish the increase in sales and volume and profit which the acquisition had made possible.

The big companies are not content, however, merely with take-overs. They are expanding facilities and taking over distributive outlets. An example is a recent report that Volkswagen is building a $113 million plant at Salzgitter which will add 10% to its capacity. Early last winter, we read that Mercedes bought out its French distributor, that is, it got 75% of the shares for $7 million. It acquired a company that sold 10,000 cars and 4,500 trucks. Mercedes knows, as do the American companies, that the big money in the car business is in the marketing, and not necessarily in the production. Mercedes is successful in production and is now going after the margins that are earned by the distributors.

Before turning to some concluding remarks about the outlook, let us take a brief glance at measures of performance and position in the European market. In the European Common Market in 1967 there was an interesting indication of profitability, namely returns on sales. The leader was the above-mentioned BMW, which made 11.7%; Fiat made 10.7%; Mercedes made 10.6%; Peugeot made 10.5%; and Volkswagen made 10.0%. Of the big companies in Europe, the only one who made as little as Ford does in the United States was Renault, with 4.9%. GM's latest figure comparable on its total operations around the world was around 7 and 8%, once going to 10%. The leaders with the greatest volume of money sales, Fiat, Mercedes, and Volkswagen, were among the sales leaders and very close together with the rankings of 10.7, 10.6, and 10.5% respectively. Net profit was the greatest at Fiat; next greatest at Volkswagen; and Mercedes followed. Renault had the sales volume but not the return on sales or the profitability. BMW's profit of $7.1 million is large in proportion to its sales, making BMW one of the most profitable automobile companies in Europe.

By growth and by merger, Europe is facing a concentration of industry. We in the United States have seen some 240 companies decline to four survivors with major disparities between the leader and the last. GM currently has a lion's share, 56% of the market; American Motors has another 7%, less than Volkswagen in the

United States. Europe is not sufficiently economically and politically integrated to permit the type of consolidation that has occurred in the United States, but it went quite far in the 1960s toward a smaller number of dominant companies.

What Lies Ahead

The U.S. market is so big that leadership here gives its own leaders a world position. GM probably produces in the United States alone some 40% of the world's total vehicle production. Ford probably produces some 20%. In Europe there is a growing concentration with companies that have smaller volume than the U.S. leaders, but whose margins of profit on assets and on sales is greater than in the United States. They also have the drive and the management and the resources to lead the Americans in Europe a hot pace. In the third major area of the world, Japan, there are already million-vehicle-a-year producers, like Toyota. A government-sponsored merging of the industry is creating three leaders.

In another market, Scandinavia, the leader, Volvo, is so far ahead that it will no doubt hold on to its position. Volvo has published plans recently to boost production to 275,000 units from the 170,000 it now makes. In the late 1970s it wants to go up to 400,000 units. Volvo spent $117 million for expansion in the last four years, and in the next four plans to spend $260 million. These are the magnitudes necessary for little companies to stay alive; they give yet another clue to what the leaders will have to spend to hold their positions.

In other big areas of the world, the land masses of South America, Africa, Continental Asia, and Australia, vehicles are produced, but are rarely exported.

There is no question that the boom in car volume will continue in the major market areas. We know that the projections in the United States are up to total car markets of 15 million a year. In Germany, a recent survey suggests that cars and accessories will enjoy a 74% growth over their present volume by 1975. They lead all other product categories in the German market including the fast-growing industries of leisure and housewares. There is indication in other countries as well, in spite of traffic jams, pollution,

269

and other deterrents, that the urge to own cars is still irresistible. The rate of car ownership per 1,000 residents in Europe is still where the United States was in the 1930s. Keeping up with its potential increase will take a lot of money and other resources. In the United States, GM has not announced its plans; Ford has announced that it has spent $181 million overseas in 1968, and if the same proportion of its $600 million expenditures in 1969 go overseas, the expenditure will be some $220 million. We know Chrysler has announced $100 million.

The present market share of the leaders gives a clue to their probable position in years ahead. Fiat has almost 19% of the total European car market; Ford has 11.6%; GM, 11.1%; Volkswagen and its subsidiaries, 10.6%; British Leyland, 8.5%; Renault, 8.4%; and Chrysler, 6.5%. The three big U.S. firms have over 23% of the European market; this is a comfortable lead over Fiat. This means big volumes if the market grows, and more capacity.

An expenditure of $100 million is a minimum each year for the leaders to stay where they are. Growth will be by acquisition as well as by their own expansion. All the others have some 25% of the European market. Some of these will lose their identity and some of them may be distributed among those leaders, depending on who buys from whom first.

Knowledgeable experts in Europe foresee eventual winners in Volkswagen, Fiat, British Leyland, and Ford. When Renault and Peugeot merge, the "big four" could become a "big five." This could happen if the new combination proves better than its parts. Fiat, which owns a great many small companies in Italy, is reported to be in line to take over Lancia and Ferrari, literally wiping out everybody except government-owned Alfa-Romeo. Volkswagen is vulnerable if its hold on the big U.S. import market is threatened for one reason or another. In Germany, a union of Volkswagen-Mercedes-BMW would create the number one giant, the General Motors of Europe, and an unbeatable combination with major holds in most categories of vehicle classes, especially a grasp on the light transit vehicles and trucks of all sizes. This leaves only Chrysler subsidiaries and Volvo which are not bespoken or mentioned in the imagined future lineup.

270

It will be interesting to see whether Chrysler in Europe can survive. Perhaps one of these days some offer will be more attractive to Chrysler management than the prospects of spending hundreds of millions each year for the privilege of staying where it is and not making any money.

The big advantage the two large U.S.-owned competitors in Europe have is a huge size in their own markets that no other firm can derive from its home market and exports. This is the fundamental strength of the U.S. companies according to Sampson[3] in his *New Europeans*. This is what European vehicle companies, even the giants, feel and fear the most.

Is this fight going to involve the American companies in a profitable operation? Hardly — they are not making a return on assets in Europe comparable to the one they earn in the United States. They certainly do not make it on their foreign operations outside of Europe, but they have accepted the challenge and the stockholders do not object. They are striving toward a position where perhaps eventually leadership shared by a few companies will restore some sanity to the pricing situation and allow all the companies to be reasonably profitable. This has happened in the United States, where a majority market-share owner provides a price umbrella for the others. Perhaps when this happens in Europe, the returns will be commensurate with the assets employed. The hope for such an ideal situation may be attractive to the U.S. companies. They certainly have good prospects for being there whenever that millennium is reached in Europe.

[3] Anthony Sampson, *The New Europeans* (London: Holden and Stoughton Ltd.), p. 119.

CHAPTER ELEVEN

AMERICAN BANKS IN EUROPE

Julien-Pierre Koszul

It is a privilege to be your guest and have this opportunity to break a lance for the cause which, as you might imagine, I believe to be an honorable one: American banks in Europe. The privilege is no doubt a somewhat perilous one, if only because the expansion of American banks in that part of the world since World War II has given rise to a flurry of comments, not all of them of an enthusiastic nature. Perhaps in breaking a lance it will be possible to bury some swords.

American Banking Penetration in Europe: A Recent Development

Before World War I, there were practically no branches of American banks in Europe except in London and in a very few other European cities. All in all, in 1914 American banks and American foreign banking corporations had 26 branches overseas, mainly in Europe. It may be worth recalling that this was a time when the United States was a net importer of capital, of course primarily from Europe. United States overseas trade was not large. Branching overseas had little attraction for American financial houses.

Between the two World Wars, American banks spurred their expansion in South America and in Asia on the heels of growing American trade with, and investments in, these areas. In Europe, they actually reduced the number of their branches, more than ever relying on correspondent bank relationships. American banks had 25 branches in Europe in 1922 and only 16 in 1939[1] (out of which 7 were First National City Bank's.).

World War II brought in its wake the closing of almost all the branches of American banks in Europe, save of course those in London and in one or two places on the Continent. It was not before the early 1950s that American banks regained their prewar strength in Europe. This was about the time when each year their European colleagues began to experience what they quickly began to refer to as the American bankers "springtide." Spring because business mixed well with pleasure, they supposed. Then the movement gathered momentum, so that today the position of American banks in Europe can be summed up about as follows.

Today, American banks have:

1. Nothing in the so-called Eastern countries (where a very few American banks had some branches before the last war, all of them long since taken over by the local authorities).

2. Nothing in Sweden, Norway, and Finland, nor in Portugal (which in this respect appear to be the most highly protected banking areas in the free world).

3. Very little in Austria, Denmark, and Spain.

Their implantation in Europe is largely concentrated in the United Kingdom, the Common Market countries, and Switzerland. As far as can be assessed from fragmentary information and late official statistics, this now consists of some 326 branches, representative offices, and participations, of which 69 are in the United Kingdom (see Table 1). These 326 outposts were established by 39 American banks[2] of which the 3 largest account for about 167 and American Express for 40.

---

[1] Not included are the branches held in Italy by Bank of America in 1939 or by its predecessor in 1922.

[2] American Express, Bank of America (including the 85-odd branches in Italy of its subsidiary, Banca d'America d'Italia), National Bank of Detroit, Bank of New York, Bankers Trust, Brown Brothers Harriman, Butlers Bank, Chase Manhattan Bank, Chemical Bank, City National Bank of Detroit, Continental Illinois, Crocker Citizens Bank, Detroit Bank and Trust Company, Fidelity Philadelphia Trust, First National Bank of Boston, First National Bank of Chicago, First National City Bank, First National

274

Table 1.   Distribution of American Banks in Europe.

Country	Representative Office	Branches	Participations	Total
Austria	1	3	2	6
Belgium	1	13	5	19
Denmark	1	1	—	2
France	7	21	12	40
Germany	2	23	2	27
Great Britain	2	45	22	69
Greece	—	10	1	11
Ireland	1	2	—	3
Italy	6	93	5	104
Luxembourg	—	—	1	1
Netherlands	—	10	4	14
Spain	6	1	3	10
Switzerland	2	14	4	20
Total	29	236	61	326

American Banks' Motivations

If it is recalled that European banks were very active in branch banking in the rest of the world well before 1940, one might be less surprised by the development of American banks in Europe in the last 20 years and more amazed that this evolution did not begin earlier. British, French, German, and Dutch banks had a wide network of branches abroad, some dating back to the nineteenth century.

Here are a few figures concerning French banks, which take on added significance seen in the light of the English overseas branch banking system, which at the time was substantially more developed. In 1922, 13 French banks had collectively more than 320 overseas branches and affiliates including some 125 in Algeria and 195-odd in the rest of the world. For these French banks, as for

Corporation of Los Angeles, First Pennsylvania Banking & Trust Company, First Wisconsin National Bank of Milwaukee, Franklin National Bank, Girard Trust of Philadelphia, Irving Trust, Manufacturers Hanover, Manufacturers National Bank of Detroit, Marine Midland, Mellon National Bank, Morgan Guaranty, National Shawmut Bank of Boston, National Bank of Commerce, Seattle, Philadelphia National Bank, Security First National Bank, Texas National Bank, Union Bank of California, United California Bank, Wachovia Bank and Trust Company, Wells Fargo Bank.

the English, Dutch, and German banks, the motivation was essentially to track the expansion of their countries' external trade and overseas investments. The particular intent was to serve domestic customers in their colonial and foreign ventures, to provide them with the services they required, to finance their imports and exports, and to help finance their investments.

It is striking that the same sort of motivation produced the expansion of American banks in South America, Asia, Africa, and Europe. Exactly as in the case of the English, French, German, and Dutch banks formerly, the American banks were eager to meet their customers in the places where they were expanding, to finance their exports and imports, and help them finance their overseas investments.

As George S. Moore, then President, now Chairman of First National City Bank, pointed out some time back when embracing the problem from a broader point of view and considering the evolution in its world-wide perspective:

> Historically, there has been a close correlation between the high levels of international trade and investment on the one hand, and international activities of U.S. banks on the other. During the Twenties, when trade and investment were expanding, U.S. banks expanded abroad. During the Thirties, when world depression and the drive toward autarky contracted world trade and investment, there was a corresponding contraction of the international activities of U.S. banks. The same correlation is evident today . . . .[3]

The postwar expansion of American banks in Europe has in large part been a logical consequence of the passing of American isolationism, of Marshall Plan aid, of the quick recovery of Europe's shattered economies, and of the dramatic development of United States trade with the rest of the world. In 1967, total U.S. exports and imports were, respectively, approximately nine and eight times what they were in 1937. Table 2 gives the figures for 1968 as compared to 1937. United States foreign trade experienced an even more marked increase with Switzerland and the EEC (Table 3),

---

[3] G. S. Moore, "International Growth: Challenge to U.S. Banks," *The National Banking Review,* Vol. 1 (September 1963), p. 3.

Table 2. Comparison of Total U.S. Exports and Imports in 1937 and 1968 (millions of dollars).

	1937	1968	1937/1968
Exports (excluding military aid)	3,361.0	34,087.0	× 10
Imports f.o.b.	3,176.0	33,252.0	× 10

Source: IMF *International Financial Statistics*.

Table 3. Comparison of U.S. Exports and Imports with Switzerland and the EEC (millions of dollars).

	1937*	1968†	1937/1968
U.S. Exports to Switzerland	9.6	527.4	× 55
U.S. Imports from Switzerland	26.9	436.1	× 16
U.S. Exports to EEC	479.1	5,994.1	× 12
U.S. Imports from EEC	296.4	5,848.8	× 19

* U.S. Bureau of the Census, *Statistical Abstract of the United States: 1968*, 89th ed. (Washington, D.C.: U.S. Government Printing Office, 1968).
† OECD overall trade by countries.

but the expansion was decidedly less pronounced as regards the United Kingdom (Table 4).

This evolution was enhanced by other favorable events that made European investment attractive: the gradual liberalization of foreign exchange controls and capital movements, the lowering of trade barriers, the return of the main European currencies to external convertibility, the appearance and development of the Euro-dollar market, and foremost, the formation of the Common Market with the subsequent spreading in that area of subsidiaries of American firms accompanied by a strong increase of American private investments (Table 5). Direct investments in the EEC, Switzerland,

Table 4. Comparison of U.S. Exports and Imports with the United Kingdom in 1937 and 1968 (millions of dollars).

	1937*	1968†	1937/1968
U.S. Exports to the U.K.	536.5	2,332.0	× 4
U.S. Imports from the U.K.	202.7	2,015.6	× 9.9

* U.S. Bureau of the Census, *Statistical Abstract of the United States: 1968*, 89th ed. (Washington, D.C.: U.S. Government Printing Office, 1968).
† OECD overall trade by countries.

277

Table 5.   U.S. Direct Investments (all industries, millions of dollars).

	1936	1966	1936/1966
World total	6,691	54,711	× 8
EEC	498	7,584	× 15
Switzerland	9	1,211	× 134
U.K.	474	5,657	× 12

Source: U.S. Department of Commerce.

and the United Kingdom increased more as a percentage from 1936 to 1966 than the total of U.S. direct investment overseas.

Incidentally, such an evolution is in no way limited to Europe. The total number of foreign branches and Edge Act Corporations increased from 100 in 1950 to 171 in 1963. No exact figure is available for 1968, but the total has more than tripled in the last six years. To take the example of the three largest American banks: while in Europe, Bank of America has 100 branches, First National City Bank 35, and Chase 14, they have 162, 579, and 73, respectively, around the globe, not including their branches within the United States.

This growth is not restricted to American banks. Since the end of World War II, American industrial firms have been swarming throughout the world, especially in the Common Market, an area which promised a brilliant future. I have already indicated the urgency felt among American industrial firms, who hastened to settle down there (opening subsidiaries or acquiring participations) for fear of seeing their products prevented from entering an economic area protected by the EEC external tariff.

The largest American banks could not ignore this expansion, since it interested their most important customers. Staying out of Europe would have been too great a financial risk when so many of their domestic customers were setting up subsidiaries or taking important participations in the European market. Competition is very intense among American banks. It is clear that if one American bank opens a branch in a part of the world where American firms are located, it will stand a good chance of getting the local companies' banking business. This would be too much for the other American banking competitors to sit back and watch. There would

278

be considerable risk that their important American customers might concentrate their financial operations in each foreign country with the American bank represented there.

But there is more at stake. One should not forget that most of the main institutional customers of American banks have investments throughout the world, and that in the United States these corporations maintain an account with not one, but several American banks. The main concern of an American bank is not only to keep the foreign subsidiaries of its prime domestic customers from resorting to the services of any other bank locally; it is also to prevent the Head Offices of these foreign subsidiaries from globally shifting their huge business to another more international American bank. This explains why the expansion of American banks in Europe feeds on itself as it does in other parts of the world and historically as it did with the English, French, Dutch, and German banks. The problem is not only to lose customers abroad; it is indeed not to lose them at home. In brief, the reasons for the expansion of American banks in Western Europe are basically the same as those for their expansion in the rest of the world and the same as those which prompted the overseas expansion of the English, French, Dutch, and German banks.

American Banks' Activity in the Euro-Dollar and Euro-Bond Markets

The minute one starts thinking about Euro-dollars, it is good to make sure of the meaning lent to the terms used. Let us accept the expression "Euro-dollar market" for short-term money (up to two or three years) and that of "Euro-bond" or "Euro-capital" market for medium and long-term money (although, of course, there is a good deal of overlapping). On both markets, American banks have taken a rapidly expanding position.

The appearance in the early fifties and the development of the Euro-dollar market soon provided a new stimulus to American banks' activity in Europe. It was only natural for American banks to seek participation in a market that had grown among non-American banks, particularly European banks, for dollars deposited with banks in the United States. It is not out of place here

279

to recall that one of the determining factors for the existence of the Euro-dollar market is the regulations that prevent banks in the United States from paying for money the price that market conditions warrant. As everybody knows, interests cannot be paid on demand deposits and are strictly limited on time deposits. Banks outside the States quickly discovered the discrepancy between the rates that American banks were authorized to pay by American regulations and the rates that the world market was prepared to support. Logically American banks were attracted to that market essentially for the purpose of pumping it — a not negligible business if one bears in mind that the whole American banking system is now globally indebted to the Euro-dollar market to the extent of some $8.8 billion, about 35% of that market's total resources. This motivation is behind the setting up of most branches opened by American banks in London in the last 10–12 years. These branches are not prevented by American regulations from paying for dollar deposits according to the conditions prevailing on the international market and they hand over most of these borrowed dollars to their respective Head Offices.

The Euro-dollar market is not only a very large one but also a highly competitive one, a fact which led First National City Bank to introduce into it the Certificate of Deposit instrument, which this bank had successfully launched a few years before in the United States. American financial institutions also helped in developing a secondary market for these CD's, another truly American contribution to the European scene.

Soon, American banks found another compelling reason for being present in that Euro-dollar market, since more and more the treasurers of their large customers short-circuited New York and resorted to the Euro-dollar market as a very convenient and remunerative way of temporarily investing their spare cash.

The commercial banks involved in the Euro-dollar market use their deposits in providing working capital for a wide range of local and international companies, organizations, and even governments. The amount of each loan can vary from an insignificant size to a very large one, although the average amount is several million dollars. The period ranges from overnight facilities, covers

30-, 60-, 90-day loans, and extends to several-year term facilities. All of this is familiar ground to commercial banks, who have easily adapted proven techniques to the international Euro-dollar market.

Besides this involvement in the short-term Euro-dollar market, American banks have been taking more and more interest in the *Euro-capital market*. The appearance of this market dates back to the early 1960s, at a time when the setting up of the interest equalization tax closed for all practical purposes the American market to most foreign issues, while in Britain new regulations were restricting the sterling capital market to sterling area users. Its development was given impetus by the "U.S. voluntary balance of payments program" launched in 1965. It was further stimulated in 1968 when this program became obligatory. American firms were thus led to go overseas for the financing of their expansionary plans outside the States. They pumped the Euro-capital market and more particularly so for the money that they intended to spend in Europe. Here again it was only natural that American banks accompany their customers to that market and not let them be wooed away by the local banks. Indeed, such a move was all the more logical since the very numerous subsidiaries established in Europe by American corporations were banking in most cases with the local branches of banks which were serving their parent companies in the United States.

For several years American financial houses have been increasingly active in this medium- and long-term market, either through special offices opened in Europe, fully owned new investment banks, or participation in joint ventures with banks in Europe. In the same way as they made a very helpful contribution to the development of the short-term Euro-dollar market with Certificates of Deposit, the Americans brought to the Euro-capital market a new instrument which quickly proved admirably adapted to the needs of the borrowers as well as to the taste of the lenders. Actually, the American finance houses soon discovered that straight debentures were not so easily placed in Europe even at very high rates and that it was much easier to find purchasers for convertible bonds issued in the names of first-class internationally known American corporations or with their guarantee for their subsidiaries in Europe. The convertible bond was found extremely attractive by investors since it not only provided a fair return of interest but ensured to the purchaser a stake in the prospects of world-wide, often very dynamic, and profitable corporations, the rate of interest being lower as the standing of the issuer was higher. For their part, these American corporations thought it advantageous to be spared the burden of high interest rates, at the cost of a convertibility option given to the lenders.

In the medium-term range, new international banks were created by American financial names in cooperation with European institutions. In the course of the last seven years, there have been at least thirty-five of these incorporated in Europe, domiciled primarily in London, Paris, and Luxembourg. Two-thirds of these international banks have active American shareholders and most of them have three or four nationalities represented among their shareholders — sometimes more. Two banks recently formed include eighteen different financial names representing eight countries, five from America. One of the most successful international banks has four shareholders, which consist of an English merchant bank and three American commercial banks. This type of organization permits the banks to pool their talent and financial resources, encouraging the multinationality so characteristic of the Euro-capital market today, and at the same time providing medium-term Euro-capital facilities, the principal objective.

In the long-term field, American banks are now represented in each syndicate underwriting an American corporate issue. There are about 100 underwriting houses, most of them European, out of which currently half would be called on to sell the bonds to their own national clientèle. In order to do this, they in turn must establish selling groups which include other national institutions not members of the underwriting syndicate. The result is an interesting blend, the manager often being American, but the issue's success often depending primarily on the cooperation at the international level. This introduces an element somewhat rare up to now and provides the fluidity in the European capital market which had not been readily developed before.

A few figures will highlight the extent of the American banks' involvement. A rating of the most active institutions in 1968 showed that four out of the top ten were American (two were British, two German, one French, and one Italian). Out of 165 issues underwritten by these 10, 67 were managed by American houses representing roughly 40% of the total value.

On the borrowing side, American companies took $3¾ billion, i.e., 37% of the money raised during the period 1963 through February 1969. Significantly, this percentage rose to 60% in 1968.

The market also exists because the Federal Reserve's Regulation Q fixes deposit interest rates in the United States at levels that have not proven to be competitive. As long as this regulation is not altered significantly, and I see little indicating that it will be, the Euro-dollars will continue to be available.

These are significant points that suggest that the participants will not be easily inclined to bring to an end a market that has proved to be so useful.

American Competition Not Always Welcome

Understandably enough, this sudden expansion of American banks in Europe has not always been enthusiastically welcomed by the local banks. There is no business community and no part of the world where new competitors are accustomed to receiving a warm welcome. The local banking fraternities' reaction is similar to that noted in a number of countries against the establishment of subsidiaries of American industrial firms or the purchase for their account of equity in local corporations. Competition upsets habits and makes life more difficult for the competitors. It obliges them to work harder, to make greater use of their imagination and business acumen, to reduce their prices, to accept smaller profit margins, to look for new opportunities, to be more dynamic, and to lose no occasion of increasing productivity.

American banks in Europe are sometimes accused of spoiling markets and being too eager in the quest for customers, in short, being too hot on the warpath.

This sort of reaction could be expected. Particularly in the banking business, which in Europe so efficiently protects itself against

283

foreign competition, no one likes to have to work harder, to watch expenditure more closely, to wrack his brains in order to prevent profit margins from shrinking, if not just to survive.

It may be that in some instances a local employee of an American branch becomes a little bit too dynamic in his quest for customers, but I would submit that American branches do not have a monopoly on exaggerated zeal. I have been told, indeed I have myself seen, that when American banks follow up on complaints and ask for specific facts they do not often get very far. The case usually boils down to extremely little, if not to nothing at all.

Customer Welfare

When hearing complaints such as these, we should not forget that the customers' welfare is also worth consideration. Competition is bound to bring in its wake the usual advantages for the clients (reduced cost of services, new and improved services) while it stimulates the banking community's initiative and imagination in helping pull down barriers instinctively raised by habit and tradition, behind which banks at times have too easily shielded themselves. Extensive branch banking abroad leads to faster and easier communications between the different elements of a bank, a benefit to the customer and a competitive advantage. It makes it easier for head offices to follow their customers' total bank credit exposure and deposit situation throughout the whole bank around the world. It enables them to be better informed on how each customer fares in his overseas ventures as well as at home. The time-honored system of correspondent banking does not offer these advantages to the same degree.

Now, we all well know that fierce bank competition has often been accused of being detrimental to the depositors' interests. If it became too difficult for banks to make a living, some of them might be induced to overpay on deposits and to be less strict in evaluating the credit risks they accept, the danger being that money entrusted to them by depositors could be committed to unsound operations, possibly resulting in the banks' insolvency and, ultimately, the depositors' anguish. But this argument has lost a good deal of its

284

pertinence with the proliferation of regulations and banking controls.

At the risk of being spurned by my banking colleagues both in Europe and in the United States, I will venture to avow that I have long thought that the argument about the welfare and safety of the depositors, which of course has a historical foundation and which is not without some justification, has been somewhat generously used as an excuse to justify the maintenance of habits and practices, as a pretext not to modernize banking structure as the evolution of the times would warrant, and as a handy device to ward off harsh competition.

Furthermore, one should not forget that the expansion of American banks in Europe helps, as in other parts of the world, to open a huge American market to foreign goods and to foreign investments.

European Banking, a Highly Protected Business

From all I have said, it might appear that in view of the increased American competition, prospects for European bankers in Europe are bleak indeed, but I think there are points that might bring them comfort. First, the local deposit base of foreign banks in Europe is, as a rule, narrow. As everybody knows, deposits are gathered through branches, and in Western Europe the extensive networks of branches developed by the main local banks are like tentacles to collect deposits from customers. Furthermore, in a number of European countries there are government or semigovernmental institutions like savings banks or Crédit Agricole, Crédit Populaire, or Girozentrale and the like, which are extremely well situated to attract deposits. As a consequence, branches of foreign banks always have a problem in finding the money to finance their loans. They must resort to the local monetary markets, which is a way of saying that these branches have to buy, often at a high price, the money which the main local banks through their local network of branches manage to get at a much lower cost. This is specially so since in many European countries regulations restrict payment of interest on demand deposits and strictly limit the interest that may be paid on time deposits. These branches often must have recourse to costly borrowings of currencies on the Euro-markets.

The result of all this is that their profit margins tend to be more limited than those of their indigenous competitors. This situation can prove to be a very strong handicap, so strong a handicap indeed that it helps illustrate what I said before, i.e., that if it were not to meet the needs of their international customers, American banks might be more reticent about European branch banking.

Second, it is also a fact that for all its growth in the last 20 years, American banking in Europe does not muster more than a very, very small percentage of the local banking business (with the exception of activity in Euro-currencies and Euro-capital).

In Great Britain, the local sterling deposits carried by American banks do not exceed 3% of total sterling deposits in the entire British banking community. In France, this percentage is only 1.7%, in Germany published figures do not isolate the overseas banks' portion, but it seems a fair guess to assess the American banks' share to be similar to that in Great Britain and in France.

Since it is improbable that foreign banks will ever be able to emulate the pace set by local banks in breeding branches in Europe, a sharp increase in the American banks' percentage of the local business is unlikely in the foreseeable future.

Third, and above all, banking is a highly protected business in Europe. It is guarded from foreign competition by a century-old establishment, long-standing relationship with local customers, thorough knowledge of the local markets, and a huge network of local branches. In this respect I cannot help remembering the question I was asked in the middle of a very pleasant lunch in a certain European capital. My host, the most courteous of men, suddenly flushed and said: "But do they really believe in the United States that Europe is an underdeveloped area? This country," speaking of his own, "is fully developed as far as banking goes." I hastened to assure him that in the States there would be no hesitation in agreeing with this. Actually, American banks are fully aware that prospects for them in Europe are in no way comparable to what they have been or can be in other parts of the world. They also know that banking in Europe is encircled by regulations of all

286

kinds. There are few businesses that are more closely watched by the local authorities than banking. The opening of branches or acquisition of sibsidiaries is, in most cases, subject to formal application and inquiries. Credit, monetary, and administrative regulations, as well as official controls, are in no way lacking in Europe. Furthermore, foreign exchange regulations, used in one way or — as in Switzerland and Germany — in another, transform banks into delegates of the local monetary authorities and load them down with special responsibilities and controls; not to speak of fiscal regulations, a world in themselves.

American banks are extremely attentive to regulations. Regulations in the United States are not to be tampered with. The American banks in Europe never forget that they are guests in the host countries and they have the definite will to behave like good citizens. Further, American people are law-abiding and dislike being at odds with regulations. Their branch management as well as their head offices are acutely aware of the necessity to be aboveboard abroad as at home. Moreover, it seems to them absolutely natural. Put in another way, let us say that, when in other parts of the world the local attitude toward regulations is not as strict, this loose approach is something entirely distasteful to the American instinct.

There are also in some European countries regulations that strictly limit the number or the percentage of foreign employees to local or total staff. In fact, if I may take the example of an American bank I have reason to know especially well, it often happens that the percentage of Americans in these European branches is much below the maximum percentage permitted. Ample opportunities are given to the local people, so that the average of nationals as a percentage of the total staff is often very high. In First National City Bank establishments in Europe the figure is above 95 percent in most branches, 98 percent or even higher in some cases. Nationals are in no way confined to operational jobs; in all branches many of them are given executive responsibilities.

But it is really confining the discussion to minor points to concentrate on what is perhaps sometimes too dynamic a quest for deposits, too generous interest rates paid to depositors, or not high enough interest rates asked from borrowers. It is somewhat paradoxical that in some of the countries where, as a matter of principle, American investments are welcomed for the spirit, the methods, the know-how, the drive, the increased marketing facilities they bring with them, the attitude is far less broad-minded in the field of banking. Local banks display a definitely less open attitude toward foreign competition than most other kinds of businesses do.

After all, American banks' expansion in Europe is merely a specific case of a more general phenomenon: the expansion of American businesses around the world and, more especially since World War II, into Western Europe. There is a growing realization among large American banks that they, as all big firms, must cross continental frontiers and become multinational entrepreneurs.

There is more. At a time when American corporations seem to be discovering the advisability of becoming conglomerates, and when the banking field is being entered by business firms like travel agencies or other firms still more loosely connected with banking, it seems only natural for American banks to follow a similar evolution although certainly limited to activities directly related to financing. There is also the growing feeling that the banking business is going to become less profitable if it is confined to the banking field as strictly defined.

Since American banks, like all American corporations, are not ashamed of working for their shareholders and never forget that it is their primary task to see that the shareholder's money be used at a maximum profit, the idea of a congeneric application to banking was bound to appeal to bankers and to lead them to look outside and venture into neighboring financial fields. Besides commercial and personal banking, these include launching new issues, holding equities, portfolio management, factoring, leasing, life insurance, travel agencies, selling accounting and computer services, and any other financial business that may look profitable such as insurance broking, credit cards, company mergers. As very well summed up by Richard Fry in the London *Times* of November 27, 1968, "what matters is a willingness to experiment." This is, indeed, why so many American banks are now adopting the legal status of one-bank holding companies. One cannot help being struck by such a development, which is bringing us back to the times of the London Merchant

288

Bankers, who establish their reputation in import/export, shipping, insurance, commodities, stock exchange, and money business, and by the same token brought money, business, and fame to the City.

As far as American banks' expansion in Europe is concerned, there should be no fear that the rules, which in most European countries so closely circumscribe the banking business, will be relaxed to an extent that would permit in Europe such a development in the near future (although many German banks are known to be active in ventures which often do not necessarily appear directly related to banking).

To sum up, world-wide American banks cannot afford not to be in Europe where so many of their huge customers are settling in, but they are aware that they are waging an uphill battle in terms of local competition on a country-by-country basis. They harbor no illusions, I think, as to the difficulty of the task. It may be that the prospects of traditional branch banking are now quite limited for American banks in Europe, anyway definitely more limited than in the developing countries. This is why I personally wonder whether the time is not at hand when a number of American and European banks will devote more of their business in this part of the world to associations and joint ventures. Developments in the last few years are perhaps an indication in this respect.

There is a final point I should like to make. As all American corporations that open subsidiaries or branches in Europe, American banks are deeply convinced that they bring something with them: new methods and sometimes a new spirit, which is an asset in itself, and this belief is supported by success achieved in all parts of the world. American banks are prepared to confront their methods and ideas with foreign methods and ideas, and let the better win. They believe that if they succeed in making money, it will be the best proof that their activity is of service to the community, not of course necessarily to the benefit of the competitors but to the benefit of the customer and of the community as a whole. To be of service to the community is an expression typical of American philosophy and is as rare in Europe, I am sorry to say, as it is common in the United States. If American expansion were to bring to Europe this attitude of mind, it would, in my opinion, be another great contribution to the European part of the world.

289

THREE COUNTRY STUDIES

CHAPTER TWELVE

AUSTRALIA AS HOST TO THE INTERNATIONAL CORPORATION

Donald T. Brash

The Data

To judge by the number of guests, Australia's reputation as host to the international corporation stands high indeed. Over the two decades 1947/48 to 1967/68, total foreign capital invested in Australian companies amounted to A$6,579 million.[1] Of this, A$3,134 million (or 47.6%) came from the United Kingdom, A$2,573 (39.1%) from the United States and Canada, and A$871 million (13.2%) from all other sources combined. Corporate direct investment was by far the most important part of the total (A$5,286 million, or 80.3%), despite the great increase in the relative importance of portfolio investment toward the end of the period. (See Table 1.)

Putting these figures into perspective is made difficult by the inadequacy of the statistical data published by most capital-exporting countries except the United States. For U.S. corporations, the attractions that Australia offers are clear from the fact that by the end of 1967 there were only four countries in the world (Canada, the United Kingdom, West Germany, and Venezuela) where the book value of direct investments exceeded that in Australia.[2] In per capita

---

[1] Or U.S.$7,368 million. A$1 = U.S.$1.12.

[2] Information in this and immediately succeeding sentences is derived from *Survey of Current Business* (Washington, D.C.: U.S. Department of Commerce, October 1968).

Table 1. Annual Inflow of Private Overseas Investment in Companies in Australia, by Domicile of Investor and Category of Investment (millions of Australian dollars).*

| Year ended 30 June | Domicile of Investor | | | | Category of Investment | |
	U.S. and Canada†	United Kingdom	Other	Total	Direct	Port-folio‡
1948	13	59	5	77	74	3
1949	8	70	7	85	81	4
1950	21	106	10	137	130	7
1951	40	87	10	137	134	3
1952	61	94	17	172	161	11
1953	4	42	5	51	42	9
1954	35	89	14	138	137	1
1955	79	114	17	210	198	12
1956	64	144	26	234	224	10
1957	55	123	31	209	191	18
1958	55	122	30	207	192	15
1959	94	129	25	248	208	40
1960	127	209	52	388	320	68
1961	178	223	70	472	374	98
1962	143	125	29	297	221	76
1963	185	207	70	463	380	82
1964	200	193	53	446	418	27
1965	242	259	76	576	534	43
1966	318	260	104	682	476	207
1967	281	115	96	493	317	175
1968 (provisional)	370	364	124	857	474	383

* A$1 = U.S.$1.12.

† Almost entirely from the United States, if one important U.S. investment that is channeled through an American subsidiary in Canada is included in the U.S. figure.

‡ Including institutional loans.

Source: Commonwealth Bureau of Census and Statistics, *Annual Bulletin of Overseas Investment: Australia,* issues dated 1963–1964, 1964–1965, and 1966–1967; *Overseas Investment 1967–1968* (*Preliminary*) (Canberra: Government Printer).

terms, only Canada and Venezuela surpassed Australia as a field for U.S. direct investment, as Table 2 indicates.

United States direct investment in Australia expanded by 1071% between 1950 and 1967, compared with an expansion in total American direct investment abroad of only 403% during the same period. The growth of the American corporate commitment in

Table 2.   U.S. Direct Investment in Selected Countries.

Country	Value of U.S. direct investment, year end 1967 (millions of U.S. dollars)	Per capita value of U.S. direct investment, year end 1967 (U.S. dollars)
Canada	18,069	901
Venezuela	2,553	286
Australia	2,354	204
United Kingdom	6,101	112
West Germany	3,487	58
France	1,904	39
Mexico	1,342	30
Japan	868	9

Australia, though not the fastest on record, was greater than the increase recorded for the United Kingdom (620%) and substantially greater than the 405% increase in Canada, both areas of major American investment interest in the fifties and sixties. The level of U.S. corporate investment in Australia more than doubled between 1962 and 1967 alone.

The expansion of British direct investment in Australia was less dramatic in relative terms since it began from a higher base. But it was still very rapid. Figures published by the U.K. Board of Trade in 1968 indicate that British direct investments in Australia increased by 65% between 1960 and 1965, and by the latter year were 16.6% of total U.K. direct investment abroad (in industries other than oil, banking, and insurance, which were excluded from the statistics). Indeed, the U.K. corporate stake in Australia in 1965 was substantially the largest single foreign commitment of British industry.[3]

At present international corporate guests occupy some of the most important "rooms" in the Australian economy; certainly, to push the metaphor still further, most of the main public rooms. In 1965, the then federal Minister for Works, Senator Gorton, estimated the foreign share of the Australian motor vehicle industry at 95%, of motor parts and accessories at 55%, of telecommunications at 83%, of pharmaceutical and toilet preparations at 97%, of soap and de-

[3] *Board of Trade Journal* (London: Her Majesty's Stationery Office, January 26, 1968), p. viii.

tergents at 80%, and of petroleum refining and distribution at 95%.[4] He could have quoted similar figures for chemicals (including petrochemicals), aluminum, other nonferrous metals, some branches of the ferrous metal industry, photographic supplies, electrical appliances and processed food (especially breakfast foods and soft drinks). By the mid-sixties, 26–27% of total company income after tax was payable abroad.[5]

Basis of Inflow

The reasons for the massive inflow of corporate capital are not hard to find. To begin with, Australia has justly acquired an enviable record for political stability. Like the United States, it has a federal structure of government; like the United Kingdom, a parliamentary form. For two decades, the party in power at the federal level has been a conservative one with a basic economic philosophy favoring development through private enterprise. English is the only language spoken by the overwhelming majority of the people, and the legal system is based on the British. At the international level the country has been linked in many ways to the two countries supplying most of its foreign capital. With Britain, Australia shares a common history and membership of the Commonwealth; with the United States, some of the same history and a common interest in the stability of the Pacific region. Intangible factors, perhaps, but nonetheless important for that.

Australian economic growth has also been a significant factor attracting the foreign corporate investor. In real terms, Australian GNP grew by almost 5% annually during the fifties, and by somewhat more than 5% in the sixties. By the middle of the latter decade, GNP per capita had reached U.S.$1,840, a level surpassed by few countries outside North America.[6] The country has long had a high ratio of gross investment to GNP, and by the late sixties this ratio had reached 26% — a level not substantially exceeded in any other advanced economy except Japan. Population growth, partly

---

[4] *Australian Financial Review* (February 18, 1965).

[5] This compares with a ratio of 18–20% in the early fifties.

[6] *World Bank Atlas* (Washington, D.C.: International Bank for Reconstruction and Development, 1968).

as a result of the government's vigorous immigration program, has been rapid by the standards of high-income countries (slightly over 2% annually) and by 1968 total population had reached 12 million. Unemployment has never risen above 3% of the work force in recent years, but despite this the federal Treasurer, the Right Honorable William McMahon, was able to claim in March 1969 that prices have risen by only about 2¼% annually since 1960.[7] Industrial relations have been good too, and over the decade 1957 to 1966 the country lost only 331 days per 1,000 workers to industrial strife annually, a rate which was a little higher than that in the United Kingdom but only a third of that in the United States.[8]

With this record of achievement behind it, Australia's prospects looked attractive to many international corporations even before the Australian mineral boom of the sixties. The latter dispelled any remaining doubt. At the beginning of the decade, Australia imported virtually all its oil, nickel, and phosphate requirements (to take only three examples) and there was a government ban on the export of iron ore because reserves were believed to be so limited. By the end of the decade, the country was contemplating the supply of at least two-thirds of domestic oil requirements from local sources by the end of 1970, was exporting 30 million tons of iron ore annually (with further increases in sight), and saw the likelihood of major exports of nickel and phosphate. Proven bauxite reserves were the largest in the world. And yet, despite these discoveries, Australia — a land larger than the continental United States — remains geologically relatively unexplored.

These mineral discoveries are quite enough in themselves to explain the substantial investments that international corporations have made in the Australian mining industry in recent years. And the greater strength they have undoubtedly given to the Australian balance of payments must also have encouraged foreign investment in other sectors. But neither growth prospects nor mineral discoveries was a sufficient condition for much of the foreign investment that has taken place in the manufacturing sector. The additional element needed in most cases was some form of trade barrier, be-

[7] Commonwealth Treasury Press Release, No. 21 (March 10, 1969).
[8] *Australian Financial Review* (February 12, 1968).

297

cause in the absence of that, or some Australian cost advantage, there would have been nothing to prevent most international corporations taking advantage of the growing Australian market through exports from their home base. In a survey of British corporate investment in Australia, Hogan found that 53% of the companies in his sample which were established in Australia during the fifties mentioned import controls or tariffs as a "very important" motive for establishment. Most of the other companies gave long-term market growth as the main motive.[9] Looking at American corporate investment, the present writer found that expected market growth was the prime reason for investment given by 54% of the companies studied, and one of the main reasons for investment given by no less than 89%. But as suggested above, it is hard to see how market growth in itself could be the cause of American investment in Australia and it is surely significant that more than half the companies in that survey also listed trade barriers as of importance in their investment decision.[10]

Australian Policy toward Foreign Investment

Up to this point, no explicit consideration has been given to federal government policy toward foreign investment. Until very recently, this has been unequivocally in favor of foreign investment. To return to the original metaphor, Australia has maintained an almost completely open house; the only areas which have been out of bounds are broadcasting (radio and television) and banking. (Even in banking there has been absolutely no interference with, or discrimination against, two long-established British-owned banks operating in Australia.) In April 1960, the Treasury opened its policy pamphlet on foreign investment with the statement that: "The Australian Government welcomes overseas investment in Australia, particularly where it is of a kind likely to help in the balanced development of Australia's resources and brings with it the skills

---

[9] Quoted by B. L. Johns, "Private Overseas Investment in Australia: Profitability and Motivation," *Economic Record*, Vol. 43 (June 1967), p. 259.

[10] D. T. Brash, *American Investment in Australian Industry* (Cambridge, Mass.: Harvard University Press, 1966), pp. 34–40.

and "know-how" needed for the successful fulfilment of the project in which the investment is made."[11] The revised version of the pamphlet, published in April 1968, began with virtually the same sentence. Successive Australian Prime Ministers have reiterated their desire to see a strong inflow of foreign capital. That this was the view of Menzies and Holt is fairly common knowledge, but even the present Prime Minister, John Gorton, whose doubts on the wisdom of continuing the open-house policy will be discussed below, has made this clear. Speaking in London in January 1969 he said explicitly that there should be "no doubt in the minds of anybody in this room that we need, wish, welcome, [foreign] investment capital and that there is stability of opportunity for those who have it to invest."[12]

From this basic attitude of welcome stem a number of specific policies favorable to foreign corporations. There are no legislative provisions requiring local participation in the capital or management of companies set up in Australia by overseas interests. There is no discrimination against foreign-affiliated companies in the taxation levied or the tariff protection provided. All current net income after taxation — including profits, interest, royalties, and service charges — may in practice be remitted overseas without restriction, and the government has indicated that permission to repatriate capital would be "withheld only in cases where the circumstances were exceptional."[13] Agreements between Australia on the one hand, and the United Kingdom, the United States, Canada, and New Zealand on the other, shield companies based in these countries from the rigors of double taxation on income earned on investments in Australia. Investment from other parts of the Sterling Area does not require any type of government approval at all, while approval for investment from outside the Sterling Area has been granted automatically for many years.

[11] *Overseas Investment in Australia* (Canberra: Government Printer, 1960), p. 3.

[12] From a speech at an Australia Club Dinner, London (January 17, 1969).

[13] *Overseas Investment in Australia* (Canberra: Government Printer, 1968), p. 3.

By and large, the federal government has not gone out of its way to attract specific foreign companies to Australia. But there have been a few such cases. In the survey of U.S. companies in Australia undertaken by the present writer in the early sixties, referred to above, 13 companies (out of a sample of 100) mentioned government encouragement as a significant factor in their decision to invest. Three of these, for example, mentioned encouragement from the Department of Supply, one being promised duty-free admission for all imported materials if it agreed to manufacture locally, and another a premium above the price of imported goods for its output.[14] Government initiative in the establishment of Ford Motor Company in Australia during the twenties was also important.[15]

State governments have been much more aggressive in seeking out prospective investors. Three states — New South Wales, Queensland, and Western Australia — have full ministries devoted to this task, and in Victoria and Tasmania special sections of the Premier's Department handle it. State Premiers personally devote considerable time to this matter. All the states offer special inducements to companies contemplating investment within their borders, inducements that may include cheap land and auxiliary facilities, subsidized power, waiver of harbor fees, and preferential purchasing arrangements. Grant notes that when Mobil Oil decided to build its second Australian oil refinery, the South Australian government encouraged the company to build in that state by agreeing to provide not only access roads and railroad track but also housing, water, and electricity. This was in addition to an undertaking that state preferences would be given to the products of the new refinery.[16] Such arrangements are not unique.

The reasons for this "open-house" policy on the part of Australian governments, at both federal and state level, probably lie more in the realm of history and sociology than of economics. This is not to say that economics was irrelevant to the policy — far from it. State governments doubtless behaved in what they saw as the

[14] Reference 10, p. 44.

[15] C. Forster, *Industrial Development in Australia 1920–1930* (Canberra: Australian National University Press, 1964), p. 38.

[16] Quoted in Ref. 10, p. 45.

best economic interests of their state — tempered on some occasions, no doubt, by a penchant for monument-building that affects most of us to some extent — and the federal government was advised through much of the postwar period by some very able economists in the civil service. The latter perceived very clearly where the national economic interest lay. But the almost total absence of any kind of restriction on the freedom of foreign corporations is probably also a result of two other factors. One is the fact that so much of the foreign capital inflow into Australia has come from the United Kingdom and, for historical reasons, many Australians have until recently not considered such capital as really "foreign." With the weakening of the ties that bind Australia to the "mother country," this view is probably changing fairly rapidly. A second factor is the nature of Australian nationalism. Though it is not by any means a universal trait, many Australians have sought not merely the aggrandisement of their country in the abstract but its growth in political, economic, and military power in relation to the Asian countries around it. The fear of the "Yellow Peril" is deeply imbedded in the Australian national psyche, and is reflected in many facets of the national life — immigration and foreign policy most obviously, but also in defense policy, development priorities (especially in the emphasis on "developing the north" of Australia) and foreign investment policy. For foreign investment policy the fear means an uncritical acceptance of all foreign capital that is willing to come to Australia, with an eye to the strategic advantages of having a large body of investment from powerful political allies. Only occasionally have members of the parliamentary Opposition raised the possibility that such investment might be embarrassing if it came mainly not from the United States and the United Kingdom but from potentially less "friendly" countries.

Portents of Change

There has recently been considerable publicity in the world press, however, that Australia is moving toward a more negative attitude to foreign investment. The London *Economist* for February 22, 1969, for example, devoted almost a full page to what it called "Mr. Gorton's backlash," and noted that the present Prime Minister "has lampooned" the previous open-door policy. *Fortune* magazine, in its April 1969 issue, quoted speeches by the Australian Prime Minister toward the end of 1968 and observed that these were "a shocking reminder that even in such a hospitable country as Australia, political leaders may choose to play on the fear of foreign capital simply because it is foreign."

Has there really been a change in Australia's policy toward foreign investment? There seems little doubt that there has in fact been some change in policy, though it is not, by international standards, a very dramatic change and cannot with fairness be entirely attributed to Prime Minister Gorton. Perhaps more significant for the future, Gorton's accession to power at the very beginning of 1968 brought a change in *attitude* to foreign investment at the very highest level of political responsibility. In a widely reported speech early in 1969 he commented that: "Up until very recently it has seemed to me that the posture of Australia in seeking overseas capital has been the posture of a puppy lying on its back with all legs in the air and its stomach exposed, and saying 'Please, please, please, give us capital. Tickle my tummy — on any conditions!' And this is being reexamined."[17] He has made many other similar statements since coming to power.

But while it may be legitimate to accuse the Prime Minister of imprudence in choice of words, to question the motives that prompt him to make such statements, or to disagree with their economic rationality, it should also be recognized that the views he has voiced have quite a long history of expression in Australia. Edith Penrose observed the "hornet's nest" of controversy which the Australian subsidiary of General Motors stirred up in 1954 when it released its annual report for that year.[18] Much of the resentment was against the high profits earned by the company, but this in turn was closely related to the other main cause of hostility, namely that all the ordinary shares of the company were held in the United States. Popular annoyance that so few of the large, profitable, foreign-affiliated

[17] From a speech at an Australia Club Dinner, London (January 17, 1969).

[18] E. T. Penrose, "Foreign Investment and the Growth of the Firm," *Economic Journal*, Vol. LXVI (1956), p. 220.

302

companies seem willing to allow Australian investors to participate in the equity of their ventures is widespread, and finds vocal expression in much of the press. The Australian Labor Party, in Opposition at the federal level since 1949, shares this annoyance and "control of foreign investment" has been a frequent election promise of that party. The government-appointed Committee of Economic Enquiry discussed foreign investment without histrionics, but, largely on balance of payments grounds and concern lest the proportion of the economy under foreign control should rise too quickly, recommended in 1965 that new capital inflow be kept within limits and all takeovers involving overseas interests be subject to governmental approval. The Deputy Prime Minister and leader of the Country Party,[19] the Right Honorable J. McEwen, has been critical of his own government's policy on foreign investment for at least a decade. He has been particularly unhappy about the takeover of existing Australian companies by foreign capital and the restriction of the export franchise of foreign-affiliated companies. In 1964 the Minister for Territories indicated that there must be provision for Australian participation in any proposal to develop the bauxite deposits at Gove Peninsula, and later in the same year even Prime Minister Menzies said that he "would be much happier if all [the foreign investors] who came into Australia were willing to admit Australians to some share in the equity of the business."[20] Speaking in the House of Representatives the following year, the Right Honorable Harold Holt (then federal Treasurer) observed that he wanted "to guard against the situation where the basic resources of this country have fallen into the control of overseas interests without any basis of Australian participation."[21] Gorton's sentiments do not seem such a break with the past after all.

Access to the Australian Capital Market

One of the areas in which Australian policy toward foreign investment has most clearly changed in recent years concerns access

[19] The Australian federal government has been a coalition of the Liberal and Country parties since 1949.

[20] Quoted in Ref. 10, p. 2.

[21] Commonwealth of Australia, *Parliamentary Debates,* Vol. House of Representatives 45 (1965), p. 55.

to Australian fixed-interest funds. Until the mid-sixties, foreign-owned companies in Australia were quite free to borrow at will on the local capital market. Companies financing credit transactions, such as General Motors Acceptance Corporation, Australia, tended to do so on a large scale, but for the most part other companies financed their expansion from internally generated funds or resources from abroad. The writer's own survey of American-affiliated companies in 1962 indicated that only 7% of the funds employed by the 101 companies that provided information represented long-term liabilities to Australian creditors. For the 56 wholly American companies in the sample, the comparable figure was only 4.5%. While short-term liabilities to Australian creditors represented an additional 20% of the funds employed (almost exactly the same whether the companies were jointly owned or wholly American), a very substantial part of these liabilities represented taxes payable and ordinary trade credit.[22]

Several factors were probably responsible for the government's decision to restrict freedom to borrow on the Australian market. One of the minor ones may have been the passing of the Uniform Companies Act in 1961; since this removed the advantage of secrecy from proprietary status, a number of foreign subsidiaries decided to become "public" companies (though still entirely owned abroad) and their avowed purpose in doing so was to increase their access to local loan funds. Another factor was probably the sharp rise that took place in the mid-sixties in world interest rates in relation to those in Australia. But certainly the decisive factor was the introduction of the U.S. "guidelines" policy on foreign investment in 1965. The 1968 edition of the government's policy statement on foreign investment makes this causal relationship clear:

> Following the measures taken by the United States Government to restrict the flow of capital to a number of countries, including Australia, the Government requested that the Reserve Bank be consulted before overseas companies, or Australian companies in which there is a substantial overseas shareholding, complete plans to borrow in Australia. The request was repeated following measures taken by the

[22] Reference 10, pp. 79–91.

United Kingdom Government to restrict capital outflow. The general aim is to avoid overseas interests making too great use of Australian borrowings in substitution for funds that would otherwise be provided from overseas sources.[23]

Clearly, then, the request that foreign-owned companies consult with the Reserve Bank is not a measure that in itself should be interpreted as being hostile to foreign capital: on the contrary it should be seen as a form of countervailing pressure to ensure a *continued* flow of capital from abroad, despite the measures taken in capital-exporting countries to restrict the flow. In December 1968, the federal Treasurer, the Right Honorable William McMahon, made clear that the government has never used "the Australian guidelines" to regulate the kind of activities that overseas firms engage in, nor does the policy aim to influence the type of borrowing to be made in Australia. This is left up to the companies themselves and the terms that they can negotiate with lenders. He went on to explain that approval for local borrowing is not normally given where the main purpose of the operation is to facilitate the remittance of funds abroad, but he made clear that companies long established in Australia, and those that have brought in substantial capital from abroad in the past, "are generally permitted to continue to have access to Australian borrowings, provided this does not involve excessive reliance on local funds."[24]

There are still plenty of ambiguities in government statements on this subject, and a great deal of room for Reserve Bank discretion. In the speech just referred to, Mr. McMahon mentioned that the government had provided "in the case of new [foreign-affiliated] ventures, that access to Australian fixed interest funds should be linked to the provision . . . made for equity participation by Australian investors." What this means in practice is not entirely clear, since it presumably is not the government's intention, for example, to refuse new wholly foreign ventures all access to overdraft accom-

[23] *Overseas Investment in Australia* (Canberra: Government Printer, 1968), p. 1.

[24] From a speech to the Annual Convention of the American Chamber of Commerce, Commonwealth Treasury Press Release, No. 105 (December 6, 1968).

modation at the commercial banks. To date, the policy appears to have been operated with flexibility and understanding, but a clearer definition of policy is undoubtedly needed.

Local Equity Participation

This comment applies with even more force to the government's attitude toward local equity participation. Such participation has always been viewed by the government as a desirable objective. The 1960 edition of the government's policy statement on foreign investment stated that "although no rules are laid down by the Government it is in general considered desirable that there be Australian participation in ownership and management."[25] It has already been mentioned that Australian equity participation was required in the development of the Gove bauxite deposits in 1964. In 1967 the Australian Resources Development Bank Ltd. was established by the eight major trading banks, with the encouragement and financial backing of the government, primarily to help Australian-owned companies to engage in large-scale development of natural resources without having to invite foreign equity participation simply because of a shortage of capital. In recent months, the demand for local equity has been asserted more strongly still. Thus the 1968 edition of the government's policy statement on foreign investment bluntly stated: "Whilst there are no legislative provisions requiring local participation in the capital or management of companies set up in Australia by overseas interests we want some local participation both in ownership and management."[26]

It seems that Australia may now be in the worst of all possible worlds with respect to its policy on local participation. The policy of polite persuasion that was followed at the beginning of the sixties probably led few foreign companies to share ownership with locals. On the other hand, it had the advantage of deterring nobody from investing in Australia. A policy that laid down clear and specific inducements to share ownership — or penalties for not sharing

[25] *Overseas Investment in Australia* (Canberra: Government Printer, 1960), p. 4.
[26]*Overseas Investment in Australia* (Canberra: Government Printer, 1968), p. 1.

ownership — would certainly deter some foreign companies from investing in Australia and would, to the extent that equity funds raised in Australia would otherwise have been brought from abroad, reduce the capital provided even by those who were not deterred by such a policy. But presumably it would also lead significantly more companies to seek Australian partners than now do so. The present policy of virtually demanding that Australians be given the opportunity to participate in the equity, and of implying unspecified adverse consequences if this is not offered, may both induce fewer companies to share ownership and frighten more potential investors than a more explicit formulation would.

One of the difficulties with the policy of demanding that foreign companies should "at least offer" equity participation to Australian investors is the definition of what constitutes an "offer." This becomes very clear in the following excerpt from a speech made by Prime Minister Gorton in March 1969:

> It may well be . . . that so much capital is required for the development of Australia . . . that the money markets of Australia and the savings of Australians could not meet the requirements of x percent of equity. I think it likely that they could not. That is why I use the word "offer", because what is important to me is that in such cases people are prepared to allow Australians to enter with equity such companies if Australians are prepared to take up the offer. But if they are not prepared to take it up . . . or if because of existing economic circumstances in any particular year it is thought that a float could not be filled if it were offered, then at least the offer has been made. If Australians cannot accept it, then that is no reason why the development should not go on.[27]

The whole question of offer *price* is not even discussed, a critically important question since under this approach it is clearly quite possible for a foreign-affiliated company to offer shares to Australian investors at a price that would be uninteresting in the local market situation and then claim an offer had been made. Conversely, no matter what the "economic circumstances," there is

[27] From a speech at the Australian Finance Conference Seminar on "Australia 1980" (March 10, 1969).

307

always an offer price at which Australian investors could be attracted. Unless the government makes the link between domestic equity and access to local fixed-interest funds a direct and explicit one, it seems doubtful whether all the talk about "wanting" local participation will have achieved anything very tangible, even judged by the government's own criterion, except a tarnishing of Australia's investment image.[28]

Takeovers

Government policy toward the acquisition of existing Australian companies by overseas interests has also undergone modification since Mr. Gorton became Prime Minister, again with unfortunate results for Australia's reputation as a host to the international corporation. In September 1968, following heavy stock market purchases of the shares of a large Australian life insurance company, the Prime Minister announced personally that the government intended to amend the Companies Ordinance of the Australian Capital Territory (where the company was incorporated) to prevent that company and its accumulated stock of Australian savings falling "under the control of anonymous and probably foreign interests."[29] Since even the government's 1968 official policy statement on foreign investment contained no hint of objection to the takeover of Australian companies by foreign interests, this statement came as an unpleasant surprise. Surprise was even more general when it became known that the "anonymous and probably foreign" buyer was another insurance company which, though British-controlled, had been active in Australia for many years.

Less than three months later, in December 1968, the Prime Minister and the Treasurer approached the Australian stock exchanges and asked them to modify their listing requirements to allow companies to amend their Articles of Association to ensure

[28] On September 16, 1969, some months after going to press, Prime Minister Gorton personally issued a statement clarifying the main features of Australian policy on this matter. A link between Australian equity participation and the right to borrow more than limited amounts has now been explicitly established.

[29] Press release by the Prime Minister's Department, No. 83/1968 (September 22, 1968).

"that control of the company, exercised through the voting power of the shareholders, remains in Australian hands."[30] Reluctantly, the stock exchanges acceded to this request in January 1969 — indeed they perhaps had little choice, since one of the major exchanges had long permitted the quotation of shares in a large Australian company that had "disenfranchised" its foreign shareholders. And, of course, the government was not trying to place an obstacle in the way of foreign *ownership* of shares in Australian companies, only to increase the ease with which Australian companies could prevent foreigners from exercising the voting rights that would normally attach to their shares.

The outside observer almost gets the impression that since January 1969 the government has been keen to repair some of the damage done to its international reputation by these measures. Thus, in March, the Prime Minister went out of his way to make clear that he would have no objection to a foreign company acquiring 50 "or even 60%" of the equity of an inefficient Australian company if the latter would benefit from an infusion of capital, know-how, or management skill. He emphasized that he was only objecting to a "raid" on an efficient Australian company, which already had good management and "good technical application," by foreign interests "who could afford to buy it out at high prices."[31] In April, the federal Treasurer (who is widely reported to be unhappy with the changed attitude of the government toward foreign investment) delivered a speech that followed a recapitulation of measures the government had taken to control foreign takeovers with an analysis of the economic benefits these often bring.[32]

These, then, have been the three main changes in Australian policy toward foreign investment in the last five years: tighter control on the access that foreign-affiliated companies enjoy to local fixed-interest funds, greater emphasis on securing Australian equity participation, and two measures designed to discourage the acquisi-

[30] Press release by the Prime Minister's Department, No. 96/1968 (December 5, 1968).

[31] From a speech at the Australian Finance Conference Seminar on "Australia 1980" (March 10, 1969).

[32] Commonwealth Treasury Press Release No. 36 (April 2, 1969).

309

tion of existing Australian companies by overseas interests. There has, as well, been some additional attention given to the whole question of export franchise restrictions, and the 1968 policy statement explicitly states, in the second paragraph, the hope that the potential contribution of foreign investment to export income will not be restricted by such barriers. But such other changes have been relatively minor. There remain no sectoral restrictions on foreign investment (with the exception of broadcasting and banking), no controls on the origin of capital, no legislative requirement to share ownership, no limits on the employment of expatriate personnel, and no discrimination against foreign companies in any field with the exception of the discussed limits on fixed interest borrowing. If the government can erase the memory of its recent indiscretions, there seems no fundamental reason why Australia cannot regain its former reputation as host to the international corporation.

The Australian National Interest

But *should* Australia wish to regain that reputation? Would its interests not be better served by a more vigorous pursuit of the policy changes already begun? This leads us to an analysis of the economic rationality of the existing "restrictions" on foreign investment.

The rules prohibiting any foreign direct investment in broadcasting, or any new direct investment in banking, are of long standing. The rule applying to investment in broadcasting clearly has no justification in economic terms, but, since its cost in terms of foreign investment forgone is probably very small, and its return measured in psychological well-being probably fairly high, the economist is not inclined to quarrel with the measure.

The regulation affecting new foreign investment in banking is more difficult, though perhaps not impossible, to accept. Typically it is justified on the grounds that foreigners should not be allowed to occupy "the controlling heights of the economy," should not be permitted, in other words, to make decisions affecting the allocation of large amounts of domestic savings. An additional argument is that foreign investment in banking would rarely involve the

310

transfer to Australia of additional foreign capital, and would bring few skills not already very familiar to Australians.[33] (The assumption implicit in the latter argument is that, despite their modest contribution of capital and know-how, new foreign-owned banks would earn a high rate of return, essentially using Australian savings.) The "controlling-heights" argument would carry weight if there were no exchange-control apparatus preventing foreign-owned banks from exporting capital raised in Australia; in the presence of such an apparatus, and of a watchful and efficient central bank, there is surely no presumption that a foreign-owned bank would behave very differently in the allocation of its funds than would a domestically owned bank. If there were such a presumption, it would certainly be good reason not only to limit new foreign investment in banking, but also to buy out foreign-owned companies now established throughout the financial services sector. If the objection to allowing new foreign banks to set up in Australia is essentially the high profits they would earn on a small contribution of capital and know-how, then it must follow that the competitive mechanism has broken down in some way in the banking sector as presently constituted. This is indeed probable, and may justify the exclusion of new foreign banks on "second-best" grounds.

It is much easier to justify the government's decision to limit the access that foreign-affiliated companies enjoy to local fixed-interest funds. It was taken in the context of a debate on the most appropriate monetary and fiscal policies to adopt as a consequence of the curbs on private capital outflow by the American and British governments. As I have noted elsewhere,[34] orthodox economics seemed to call for contractionary measures to offset the balance of payments problem that was anticipated. But some argued, possibly with success, that Australia could maintain its level of capital inflow by a continued expansion of economic activity coupled with restric-

---

[33] Both arguments find expression in W. Hogan, *Foreign Investment and Capital Inflows* (St. Lucia, Queensland: University of Queensland Press, 1968).

[34] In "American Investment and Australian Sovereignty," *Contemporary Australia: Studies in History, Politics, and Economics*, R. A. Preston, ed. (Durham, N.C.: Duke University Press, 1969), pp. 547-8.

tions on the right of foreign-owned companies to borrow in the Australian market. Such a policy would put foreign companies in the dilemma of losing part of their market share or of continuing to bring in capital from abroad for further investment. A superficial view of the statistics of capital inflow suggests that the policy may have worked rather well.

Even in the absence of curbs on foreign investment in the United States and Britain, however, there appears to be good reason to limit the access enjoyed by foreign-affiliated companies to local fixed-interest funds. In a perfect capital market this would not be true; nor would it be true where domestic resources had a low opportunity cost. But where vigorous domestic companies find themselves at a substantial disadvantage in the capital market vis-à-vis foreign companies simply by virtue of the worldwide reputation of the latter, some countervailing interference with the market mechanism seems not inappropriate.

There appear to be two theoretical reasons that might justify measures to discourage the takeover of Australian companies by foreign interests. The first is the infant-firm argument, clearly stated by Professor Kindleberger in his most recent book on foreign investment.[35] Like the infant-industry argument in tariff theory, it rests essentially on the assumption of declining costs. But, like the tariff argument, it depends for validity on the further assumption that the owners of the firms or industry to be protected — in the one case from imports, in the other from foreign takeover — cannot themselves foresee the declining costs.[36] For, if the declining costs were foreseen, they would already be reflected in the price of the stock. Only if the government were able to predict the declining costs better than the shareholders of the company would protection from takeover on these grounds be worth considering. Even then there is no presumption that takeover should be prevented: a foreign-financed takeover, like other forms of foreign investment, is likely to result in a net addition to the country's capital stock. If the

[35] C. P. Kindleberger, *American Business Abroad* (New Haven: Yale University Press, 1969), pp. 32–33.

[36] In the tariff case, protection may also be justified if the expected economies, even if predictable, are external to the firm.

takeover is prevented, the foreign investment may not occur. In this situation, the choice is between:

1. The discounted present value of the future earnings of the company if it stays under local ownership.

2. The discounted present value of the earnings from investment of the proceeds of the takeover *plus* the discounted present value of benefits to all other domestic factors of production as a result of the increase in capital stock.

In Australia, where the capital market is normally able to spot a growth situation as reliably as government, and where the scope for investment of domestic resources released by takeover is great, the likelihood of finding a takeover that should be prohibited on infant-firm grounds seems remote.[37]

The second reason for opposing a foreign takeover might be based on the theory of second-best. There would be a good reason to oppose a foreign takeover, for example, if it resulted in a sharp reduction in competition, and if it were not possible to build adequate machinery to deal with monopoly situations *per se*. Similarly, if the takeover put a foreign company in receipt of a substantial net subsidy as a result of inappropriate tariff policy, and if it were politically impossible to improve the tariff policy, this would be reason to consider prohibiting the acquisition. Such arguments might well carry some weight in less-developed countries, but they surely should not be used in relatively advanced countries like Australia. Indeed, they have not been to the writer's knowledge. On the contrary, Australians have frequently opposed a foreign takeover even in a situation where it would clearly lead to increased competition. The most remarkable case of this in recent years concerned the

---

[37] One should guard against drawing the conclusion from the spectacular growth that followed some foreign takeovers in Australia that these should have been prevented on infant-firm grounds. Almost invariably, the new foreign owners injected an element into the company — large amounts of capital, vast technical or managerial experience, market access or whatever — which would not have been present had the company remained in local hands. Many, possibly most, foreign acquisitions of Australian companies have involved firms that faced severe financial difficulties at the time of takeover.

prolonged struggle between the American-owned Nabisco company and the locally owned Australian Biscuit Company Pty. Ltd. for control of Swallow & Ariell Ltd. in 1964. Though the failure of the Nabisco bid meant that the privately held Australian Biscuit Company increased its estimated share of the market from 70 to 80%, public opinion during the conflict was strongly against the American firm.[38]

To many Australians it is simply the idea that foreigners are permitted to take over control of assets built up by years of Australian effort which is offensive. But that this is a totally unacceptable view (except in the infant-firm case) in a situation where the owners of the assets themselves regard the price as adequate compensation for their effort should require no arguing. Unfortunately the *type* of measure so far taken by the government to discourage foreign takeovers — the pressure placed on stock exchanges to allow listing of companies that disenfranchise foreign shareholders — is not the type of instrument that can be justified by any other economic "argument." And if the measure is based not on economics but on a political resentment against foreign control, the Prime Minister has already undermined its basis by conceding, in a speech quoted earlier, his willingness to accept the foreign purchase of as much as 60% of the equity of an Australian firm where it is "inefficient." More important, such resentment ignores the very great amount of control that Australia can already exert over the behavior of the local subsidiaries of international corporations through intelligent use of ordinary economic policy instruments such as taxes on income, sales, imports, and exports.

How rational is the government's increasing insistence that international corporations invite local investors into partnership in their Australian operations? The present writer has argued elsewhere at some length that such a policy is not rational,[39] but a brief recapitulation may be in order. To begin with, the policy almost certainly deters some — perhaps not many, but some — firms from investing in Australia. Second, a domestic equity of the

[38] Reference 10, p. 54n.
[39] Reference 10, especially pp. 76–79, 231–233, 274.

314

kind proposed rarely secures national control over important corporate decisions and in reality often becomes a means of extending foreign control over domestic resources. This would often be true even were the domestic equity in a majority (because of the local company's dependence on its parent for technology or market), and the Prime Minister has made it clear that he does not normally expect Australians to be "offered" a majority.[40] Third, there can be no presumption that Australia's balance of payments is improved by the policy, since, if the local equity is acquired at a fair market price (that is, one that reflects the discounted present value of expected future earnings), the capital outflow (or absence of capital inflow) implicit in the purchase by definition just equals the discounted present value of the averted future earnings outflow. As with the infant-firm case for preventing the foreign takeover of a local company, a government policy encouraging local equity participation on balance of payments grounds can only be based on the assumption that the capital market's expectations about the future growth of foreign-affiliated companies are unduly pessimistic. There does not seem to be much evidence for this assumption in Australia.

To offset what little control domestic investors do secure there are some specific costs of sharing ownership: the affiliate's access to parent company technology is likely to be somewhat reduced; the parent is likely to limit its access to world markets more strictly than it would that of a wholly owned subsidiary[41]; the affiliate is likely to have to make specific payment for parent company technology more often than would a wholly owned subsidiary, a fact that reduces Australian tax revenue (since many of these payments are exempt from Australian tax); the jointly owned affiliate may be obliged to pay higher prices for purchases from its parent, or may receive lower prices for sales to its parent, than would a wholly foreign subsidiary. Perhaps even more important than these factors

[40] Commonwealth of Australia, *Parliamentary Debates,* Vol. House of Representatives 60 (1969), p. 23.
[41] Evidence for this point is not absolutely conclusive, and is based partly on *a priori* reasoning. But what empirical evidence there is lends some weight to the argument. See Ref. 10, pp. 231–233, and W. P. Hogan, "British Manufacturing Subsidiaries in Australia and Export Franchises" (1965) (mimeo).

— certainly of more topical relevance at present — is the fact that it may be *more* difficult, and not less, to subject a jointly owned company to rational government economic decision making. There seems little doubt, for example, that the pressure on the federal government to end the special subsidy for domestic oil production when it comes up for review in 1971 would be very much greater if Australia's largest and most widely held industrial company did not hold a 50% stake in the most important oil field now in production. The federal Treasurer implicitly acknowledged that pressure for local equity is rather irrational when he observed in March 1969 that the "Australian character is a mixture of sentiment and sanity. There is a strong sentiment that . . . we would like increasing Australian participation in ownership and management."[42]

The increased government exhortation to foreign parent companies not to limit the export freedom of their Australian affiliates probably makes good sense by drawing the attention of those companies to the scope that does exist for exporting manufactures from Australia. In so doing it may lead foreign companies to establish larger — and so more efficient — operations in Australia than they would otherwise have done. But the prevailing view in Australia that such restrictions are a major impediment to the country's export drive is not well founded, though there seems little doubt that the abolition of controls would result in some increase in exports. The restrictions are certainly very common, but they very frequently reflect a recognition that Australia's cost structures in manufacturing tend to be high by world standards. Even where exports would increase in the absence of the restrictions, the benefit to the balance of payments would of course be less than the increase in exports. For if the company in question is operating at full capacity, and total domestic demand is given, the diversion of some output abroad may well lead to increased imports or decreased exports elsewhere in the economy. If the company is operating well below capacity, the marginal cost of producing the extra output is low, and the profit that accrues abroad accordingly fairly high. There is in any case little chance of legislating effectively against such re-

[42] Commonwealth Treasury Press Release No. 21 (March 10, 1969).

strictions: many of them are already unwritten because of their prohibition under most circumstances by U.S. antitrust law.

New Policies Desirable?

Might new policies affecting foreign investment be desirable? It has already been argued that the basis for restricting foreign investment inflow into Australia on infant-firm or second-best grounds is weak. But, even in this citadel of economic orthodoxy, I am tempted to advance (albeit tentatively) another reason for restricting the entry of international corporations. Not, it should be noted, the size of the foreign investment, the ownership of the operation, or the sector in which it operates, but rather the *number* of foreign-affiliated companies in particular industries. My reason for suggesting this stems from an awareness that the combination of almost any actual or potential barrier to trade with the oligopolistic nature of most of the industries in which foreign investment is important tends to produce a great proliferation of small-scale foreign-owned units, without any real prospect of rationalization or consolidation. Striking examples of this phenomenon in the Latin American auto industry are well known, but the same type of situation also prevails in some Australian industries, even to some extent in the motor vehicle industry. If the units were domestically owned, one could expect market forces to bring about consolidation over a period; when they are owned by large internationally competing corporations, this is highly unlikely. Faulty tariff policy is partly to blame for this situation in many cases, but even a country pursuing an exemplary tariff policy may encounter the problem. What machinery Australia should establish to meet the problem I confess I do not know: it would be preferable to integrate it with the Tariff Board, but to be effective it would be essential that the Board have power to veto plans to establish new foreign-affiliated operations.

Beyond that, one can only recommend the kind of policies that should make the second-best reason for restricting the inflow unnecessary in the Australian context; intelligent tariff policy, vigorous action against monopolies, avoidance of extravagant subsidies through state competition for industry, and careful policing by the Taxation Commissioner of the prices at which foreign-affiliated companies price their imports and exports — all these are especially important. Also important for the sake of balance of payments management is a policy that attempts to minimize the instability in the capital inflow — one of the elements in such a policy is the avoidance of provocative or implicitly threatening speeches on foreign investment by prominent politicians.

CHAPTER THIRTEEN

DIRECT FOREIGN INVESTMENT IN LATIN AMERICA

Carlos F. Díaz Alejandro*

The standard caveat about Latin American heterogeneity applies *a fortiori* to the region's experience with, and attitude toward, direct foreign investment (DFI). The range spans Socialist Cuba together with some countries with attitudes not unlike the Australian Prime Minister's eager puppy. This warning out of the way, let us plunge into broadbrush generalizations.

One could discuss this topic starting from a MacDougall-type model. An alternative approach emphasizes history. The methodological choice often reflects the student's bias: those out to show the foolishness of DFI opponents tend to start from nonhistorical competitive models; those interested in exposing DFI evils find history more congenial.

This paper will rely on a mixture of history and (somewhat loose) analysis. Pure competitive models, however, will not be used as the basic framework for the simple reason that much DFI in Latin America has occurred in areas and sectors where markets and competition are weak. They would miss most of what the argument is about.

The main thesis of this paper is that on balance there is a strong case, resting on a blend of economic and other considerations, for

* I am grateful to Donald T. Brash, Roberto González-Cofiño, Javier Pazos, and Felipe Pazos for helpful discussions. But they are not responsible for the views expressed or for any errors in this paper.

319

fairly strict control over DFI by Latin American countries. Such control should preferably be exercised at a regional (or perhaps subregional) level, by multinational Latin American institutions.

Some History and a Few Facts

Original sins and past adolescent escapades plague many foreign investors now operating in Latin America. Cool Latin American bargaining is hampered by memories of that not-so-distant past.[1] While the precise extent of "horror stories" is debatable, it is doubtful that most foreign investors would care to make a full disclosure of events and negotiations surrounding their first establishment and early operations in the region.

They key point is that much DFI involved not just commercial bargaining, including bribery, but the implicit and explicit use of the political and military muscle of foreign governments to further their nationals' business interests. Without such political underpinnings, foreign investors would have been somewhat more circumspect in their dealings with host countries.

The unpleasant history of United States intervention in the Caribbean and Central America in support of U.S. business interests is well summarized by the widely quoted 1931 remark of U.S. Marine general, Smedley D. Butler: "I helped make Mexico safe for American oil interests in 1914. I helped make Haiti and Cuba a decent place for the National City Bank boys to collect revenues in. I helped purify Nicaragua for the international banking house of Brown Brothers . . . I helped make Honduras 'right' for American fruit companies. Looking back on it, I might have given Al Capone a few hints."[2]

---

[1] As put by C. P. Kindleberger: "Alien in spirit, foreign investors in the past have often acted in the less developed countries as if they enjoyed extraterritorial rights, and this history of their considering themselves above the law corrupts equitable and more nearly balanced negotiation today." *American Business Abroad* (New Haven: Yale University Press, 1969), p. 148. Much of the emotional heat in the Peruvian-IPC dispute, now in full bloom, has been generated by conflicting views of how IPC first obtained control over its Peruvian assets.

[2] Quoted in J. Gunther, *Inside South America* (New York: Pocket Books, 1968), p. 161.

Compare also the 1945 U.S. moratorium on new investment in Germany with U.S. investment in Cuba following the 1898 U.S. intervention in the Cuban-Spanish war. Taking advantage of low prices brought about by war devastation, much real estate and other assets passed into North American hands under the U.S. military government. So much real estate was purchased in the Isle of Pines that the political status of that part of Cuba remained cloudy until 1925.[3]

Other examples of shady property rights origins, of past foreign investors' misbehavior, and of unholy combinations of economic and political power could be given. Some may argue that morbid dwelling in the "irrelevant" past says little about the present and future. Whether rational or not, however, the past conditions Latin American attitudes to DFI. The spirit of the Calvo doctrine, calling for a strict separation of commercial from political relations among countries, is kept alive by those memories. And it is inevitable that Brazilians worried about land purchases by U.S. interests in the Amazonian region will remember how Texas and other open areas of Mexico were eventually transferred to the United States.

The lessons of the past may not be wholly irrelevant. Granting that foreign investors now going to Latin America do so with attitudes different from those of 30 or 50 years ago, one may wonder whether this is due more to changed world political conditions and bargaining power than to changes in the nature of DFI.[4]

[3] According to R. H. Fitzgibbon: "In the years immediately after the War with Spain the island became largely Americanized insofar as ownership of real property was concerned, though the bulk of its population is still Cuban" (p. 95). After many delays, and under pressure from Latin American opinion, Cuban title to the Isle of Pines was recognized by treaty by the U.S. government in 1925. Fitzgibbon adds: "Hope sprang eternal in the breasts of the 10,000 American investors in the island and they, their land companies, and their banks conducted a prolonged and persistent lobby against ratification of the treaty" (p. 102). R. H. Fitzgibbon, *Cuba and the United States 1900–1935* (New York: Russell and Russell, 1964). Ironically, the Isle of Pines has been chosen by the Cuban revolutionary government for the first experiment in full communism.

[4] Until the 1965 invasion of the Dominican Republic, Latin American reminiscences of marine landings were met by impatient heckling even from sympathetic U.S. liberals, who were eager to discount history. Repentance is always possible, but an old sinner should be more careful than Caesar's wife.

321

Before 1930, DFI in Latin America went mainly toward export or export-oriented activities, as well as public utilities. Much of that investment involved natural resources commanding high economic rents (oil, copper, and some other minerals) and giving rise to enclave-type operations. Some of the forward linkages arising from mineral or agricultural foreign investments were located within Latin America (sugar mills, meat packing plants); typically foreign investors were vertically integrated, and controlled most steps from raw natural resource to marketing of the finished product. Public utility investments involved natural monopolies like telephones, electricity, and railroads. Most of these investments had, on balance, a positive economic impact on host countries, accelerating modernization even as they generated new problems. Their liberalizing influence can be compared to that of DFI in post-1959 Spain.

Either because of their position as natural monopolies, or due to extensive vertical integration, a large share of foreign investors were not subject to market pressures that could be objectively and easily ascertained by public opinion and host governments. Naturally, arguments over whether foreign investors earned more than a "normal" rate of return flourished.[5]

Until the First World War, European funds dominated DFI in Latin America, although since the turn of the century U.S. interests had been very active, especially in the Caribbean and Central America. After the First World War United States predominance in fresh investments extended into South America. In areas where British capital had been prominent, such as the River Plate region, Latin American "progressives" viewed the emergence of U.S. DFI with favor. Some began to distinguish between "bad" DFI, usually British and linked to rural exports, and "good" DFI, usually North American and involved in import-substituting manufacturing. In view of more recent trends in Latin American attitudes this distinction seems ironic.

---

[5] Much DFI in Latin America occurred in activities, such as railroads, public utilities, banking, and development of natural resources, which, throughout U.S. history — more recently during the 1930s — attracted the criticism of U.S. populists and liberals, eventually leading to their regulation.

The 1930s and the Second World War did not provide an atmosphere conducive to DFI expansion; the stock of foreign investment in traditional lines dwindled, and fresh investments in new activities were weak. Trends already visible in the 1920s (increase in U.S. participation, especially in oil and manufacturing, and relative decline of traditional investments in public utilities and agricultural exports) became more noticeable after the Second World War. The value of U.S. direct investments in the Latin American republics, which had dwindled from $3.5 billion in 1929 to $2.7 billion in 1943, rose at an average annual rate of 7.3% during 1943–1950, of 6.9% during 1950–1960, and of 4.6% during 1960–1967.[6] As is well known, no comparable data exist for non-U.S. DFI.

The most significant and persistent feature of postwar DFI trends is the growing importance of manufacturing investment, mostly for import substitution. The book value of U.S. direct investment in Latin American manufacturing increased at an average annual rate of 7.5% during 1950–1960, and at an impressive 11.9% during 1960–1967. The participation of different activities in the *increments* to the stock of U.S. investments in Latin America, measured at book value, has been as follows[7]:

	1950 to 1960 (%)	1960 to 1967 (%)
Mining and Smelting	14.5	2.3
Petroleum	42.1	6.4
Manufacturing	21.3	64.8
Public Utilities	4.5	− 7.4
Trade	12.5	19.2
Other	5.2	14.7

Mining and petroleum investments follow the geographical distribution of those natural resources. United States manufacturing

---

[6] Calculated from U.S. Department of Commerce, *Balance of Payments; Statistical Supplement* (Washington D.C.; U.S. Government Printing Office, 1963), pp. 208–209, and *Survey of Current Business* (Washington D.C.: U.S. Department of Commerce), several issues (usually August issue). Post-1950 rates were computed excluding Cuba; Cuba is also excluded from data given in the rest of the paper.

[7] All data on U.S. DFI obtained from the sources listed in footnote 6.

investments are concentrated in the "big three" (Argentina, Brazil, and Mexico) plus Venezuela. In 1967 these four countries, accounting for two-thirds of Latin American population and three-fourths of the area's GDP, were hosts to 84% of U.S. manufacturing DFI.

But the most striking fact emerging from the sectoral and geographical distribution of foreign investment is its adaptability to different circumstances. It has flowed into Brazil in spite of secular inflation, and it has gone into Mexico not long after oil nationalizations and in spite of stiff regulation. The Mexican experience with foreign investment is worthy of a detailed study, as well as of comparison with the experiences of Canada and Australia, but its main lesson seems straightforward enough: a medium-sized country with a growing domestic market can get substantial amounts of DFI under rules written by the host government, as long as those rules, tough as they may be, remain reasonably steady, and foreign investors are allowed a predictable rate of repatriation of capital and profits. A determined and stable public sector, the Mexicans have shown, can get foreign investors to accept "unacceptable" conditions while obtaining a rising flow of DFI.[8]

DFI has flowed into Latin America naturally in the search for short- and long-run private profit. The lure of rich natural resources, such as oil, copper, and banana-growing lands, needs little elaboration. Manufacturing investment has been attracted by high tariff walls and import restrictions, coupled with oligopolistic rivalries among multinational corporations. Some agricultural and manufacturing foreign investment, especially in Puerto Rico and Mexico, has taken advantage of low labor costs in host countries to produce for export to labor-poor countries.[9]

---

[8] The day may come when foreign investors prefer putting their money in Socialist Cuba rather than in some capitalistic, but unstable and stagnant, Latin American republic.

[9] According to *Business Week* (March 19, 1966), p. 104: "So promising, in fact, is the U.S. market for Mexican-grown food that U.S. food packers who originally set up shop south of the border to supply Mexico's growing middle-class market now are looking to the U.S. for increased sales." An interesting aspect of this investment is that it has been stimated by the 1965 cutoff of entry into the United States of Mexican itinerant bracero farm

The Case for Controlling DFI

The more sensible arguments for controlling DFI by Latin American countries will now be presented. It is, of course, easy to list and demolish absurd and inconsistent arguments against DFI (and there is no shortage of them), but little will be gained by such an exercise here. It is also true that motivations behind Latin American criticisms of DFI, whether the criticisms are sensible or absurd, are sometimes murky and include the fear of elite businessmen, intellectuals, and bureaucrats of losing special privileges and social status. But it would be a mistake for observers in industrialized countries to assume that nothing else lies behind Latin American uneasiness over DFI, or that the masses, eager for development, are necessarily more favorably disposed toward DFI than wealthy nationalistic elites.

In the heat of discussions over DFI, economic and other arguments tend to merge. Often what is politically disliked is damned with economic reasons. Exasperation with the irrationality of some anti-DFI economic arguments lead some to ignore possible negative political repercussions of DFI. Separation and recognition of the two types of arguments are worth a try.

The economic arguments. To some it is so obvious that development needs capital and that DFI brings capital, that it appears self-evident that more DFI means more development. But this reasoning neglects the point that the welfare effect of more capital is not independent of that capital's allocation. More badly allocated capital can lead to less, rather than more, welfare, even when the additional capital is domestic.[10] When the capital is foreign,

---

hands; a neat example of trade *cum* capital flows making up for restrictions on labor flows. According to *The Wall Street Journal* (May 25, 1967); "Unlike the farm program, under which Mexican laborers entered the U.S. until such border crossings were banned in 1965, Yankee manufacturers are bringing their work to Mexican soil — more precisely to the part of Mexico that lies close to the 2,000 mile common border with the U.S." New investments included not only food processing but also products "ranging from electronic parts to clothing and furniture." Food processing for export includes strawberries, tomato paste, pineapples, chilies, mushrooms, and peaches. Many of the foreign investors are small companies, not linked to giant multinational corporations.

[10] See H. G. Johnson, "The Possibility of Income Losses from Increased

national welfare is further reduced by the need to transfer abroad factor payments. In other words, when more capital leads to a lower GDP, measured at "world" prices; because of its distorted allocation, it will *a fortiori* lead to a lower *GNP* when that capital is foreign. And even if GDP expands, GNP may not (both measured at world prices).

Possibilities for misallocating capital abound in most Latin American economies, where markets are often thin and far from competitive, and where price signals are distorted by public policies that are far from optimal from a purely economic viewpoint. Consider the latter type of distortion first.

Tariff protection and import controls, often prohibitive, have attracted much DFI into import substituting industrialization. The excesses of Latin American protection are well known. The costs of protection could have been minimized by selecting one or few firms in each new activity. Unfortunately, the pressures of international oligopolistic warfare led to a multiplication of uneconomic plants in infant activities (although seldom of infant entrepreneurs —unless GM, Ford, etc, can be called infants when they move abroad). Most host governments have been too weak or shortsighted to resist the pressures of oligopolistic strategists who favor keeping a toe hold in every market, at least for a while. In fact, tariff setting was probably not free from pressures arising from foreign investors in new activities. And without strong public sector leadership, perhaps requiring cooperation among several governments in a common market framework, it is unlikely that a rationalization of, say, the auto industry, will take place spontaneously.

In Latin American countries suffering from chronic inflation, bank interest rates are typically kept, by public policy, below inflation rates. When borrowers and lenders are nationals, that situation leads to capital misallocation plus income redistribution within the country. But when the borrower is a foreign company,

Efficiency or Factor Accumulation in the Presence of Tariffs," *Economic Journal,* Vol. LXXVII, No. 305 (March 1967), pp. 151–54. Note that this possibility of "immiserizing growth" does not assume monopoly power in international trade.

income is redistributed from nationals to foreigners. And it is known that foreign companies are, for understandable private reasons, favored borrowers in Latin American commercial banks. Yet another distortion from which foreign companies have benefited is the facility to import capital and intermediate goods duty-free at overvalued exchange rates as an incentive to new foreign investors who, no doubt, continue to insist in public that inflation creates an "unfavorable climate" for DFI.

The main point emerging from all this is that foreign investors are particularly well suited for profitable fishing in the troubled waters of second-best Latin American economies. Domestic hiring and component requirements, and impositions on foreign companies to give technical aid to their domestic suppliers, can be viewed as efforts by the host country to get back part of that "fishing."

The counsel of perfection is to eliminate policy-induced distortions. It is not the fault of DFI if Latin American countries have inflation, overvalued exchange rates, and controlled interest rates, and DFI cannot really be blamed for all of the extraordinary levels of protection. The advice is sound, but difficult to implement, as the experience of even industrialized countries shows. Consider a mental experiment: suppose that part of U.S. agriculture, say one-fifth, were owned by foreigners (Frenchmen or Japanese, perhaps). No doubt this would make U.S. agricultural subsidies less popular, but would it lead to their abolition? In all likelihood, the subsidies would stay, and new foreign investing in this industry would be tightly controlled. Or assume part of the Texan oil industry was owned by Mexicans. Would oil import quotas be eliminated, or would Mexican investors be controlled?

Even when the price system is not distorted by government action, many markets where foreign investors operate are thin and imperfect and can affect domestic resources with low mobility. Many Latin American exports of minerals and raw materials are still handled by vertically integrated foreign companies. Reliable market prices for a given commodity at different processing stages often do not exist, complicating the task of how rents will be split between investors and host governments. Governments and foreign investors, having different discount rates, are likely to disagree also on the optimal rate of exploiting natural resources. Even countries not experiencing inflation have weak capital markets in Latin America. Uncertainty and lack of information handicap the rising national entrepreneur, and especially during "credit squeezes" — such as those in Brazil during 1964–1967 — foreign investors with easier access to credit abroad enjoy a distinct advantage.

Where capacity to transform is high and the cost of resource mobility is nil, sectoral allocation of DFI matters little, assuming no other imperfections. But Latin America has experienced during the last 20 years severe balance of payments difficulties, and resource mobility has been low. Under these circumstances, if DFI is channeled toward activities with low degree of international "tradability," it may place on the rest of the economy a significant burden as it attempts to transfer domestic resources into foreign exchange to finance profit remittances. Costs of such process may include not only internal ones associated with moving resources about, but could conceivably lead to deterioration of the host country's terms of trade. Another extreme outcome could be that foreign investors may displace domestic resources (say, those in handicrafts) which have no alternative employment opportunity. Sharp fluctuations in the net flow of DFI and of profit remittances can also result in high real costs in countries with low capacity to transform.

These arguments lead only to proposals for *some* host country control over DFI, assuming the costs of running the control machinery are not exorbitant. They obviously do *not* show that all DFI is economically harmful to Latin America. These are unsatisfactory conclusions, since they fail to provide clear guidelines for policy action and can be misused to justify foolish policies. A case-by-case approach is a way to handle bewildering second-best reality, but where governments are short of economists competent in second-best analysis and efficient civil servants, and foreign investors clamor for steady and clear guidelines, crude and arbitrary rules of thumb may be the best available approximation to ideal policy.

While most (nonextremist) Latin American opinion is suspicious of DFI in general, when concrete proposals for new DFI are discussed the attitude becomes more favorable. The weak conclusion that "laissez faire for DFI is out, but we welcome some DFI" is widely held. In spite of memories of abuses and recognition of possible harmful DFI effects, its potential economic benefits are also acknowledged,[11] at least in private. Many readily grant that nowadays most foreign investors in Latin America, especially those exploiting rich natural resources, pay better wages, cheat host treasuries less, and provide better social services to their workers than most native entrepreneurs. On wages and social services IPC in Peru was a showcase, if somewhat paternalistic. In spite of all this, suspicion of DFI persists; more than economic reasoning is involved. Indeed, the heart of the DFI matter is sociopolitical.

The noneconomic arguments. A high GNP growth rate is not the only target of Latin American development; most articulate Latin Americans also include a greater degree of political autonomy and more equitable distribution of income and wealth among families and regions among the targets.

In this context, the fear exists that U.S. DFI will result in the "Portoriquenization" of Latin America, and in its cultural annihilation. The stronger the political power of the country from which DFI originates, the greater the fear that national sovereignty may suffer in the bargain. Thus, Italian investors enjoy in Latin America greater popularity than those from the United States.[12] History and the Hickenlooper amendment remind Latin America that investors from hegemonic powers are often tempted to convert economic disputes into political ones when dealing with politically weak countries, and that foreign countries are tempted to

[11] Even (or especially?) when that DFI leads to profit and amortization remittances larger than the original capital inflow.

[12] See *The Economist para América Latina* (April 16, 1969), pp. 48–50. This publication points to additional factors explaining Italian popularity and success: many executives of Italian corporations in Latin America have become citizens of the countries where they operate and their Italian experience has prepared them for dealing with the intricacies of Latin American law and bureaucracy. There is little evidence suggesting that the business ethics of Italian investors are any different from those of other foreign investors. As an extreme consider the substantial Latin American purchases of U.S. real estate (*Business Week* (March 22, 1969)); no one supposes that this will lead to U.S. territorial losses.

use the economic power of its overseas investors to further their policy goals.[13] West European preoccupation with U.S. DFI has thrown many Latin American observers into gloom: if proud and ancient nations can be so easily "taken over," how can Latin America resist? Canadian fretting is also followed with interest.

The fear may be exaggerated, but the suspicion persists that, if left alone, U.S. investors may eventually dominate most of Latin America's capital stock.[14] Without capital movements, the balance of payments constraint ensures a country against being flooded by foreign merchandise; but, just as with free international labor movements a country could conceivably become depopulated, without controls over DFI the whole of a country's capital stock could, in principle, pass into foreign hands. From the viewpoint of economic efficiency this may or may not be the optimal solution (U.S. entrepreneurs could have absolute advantage in *all* activities!). But, as pointed out by Felipe Pazos: "A workable capitalist system is one which is made up of local capitalists, not foreign capitalists and local workers. The latter obviously has adverse social implications."[15]

---

[13] Consider, as examples of the type of remark that kindles this Latin American concern, those by a U.S. potential investor in Algeria — ("It's almost physically impossible to do business without having the [U.S.] embassy here" — *Business Week* (April 12, 1969)) and by Senator Thruston Morton outlining the procedure of the U.S. Senate Finance Committee in considering the sugar bill ("We went through the matter country by country. If we liked the country we voted yea; if we did not like the country we voted nay" — *Business Week* (October 30, 1965). The conservative *The Review of the River Plate* of Buenos Aires, noting that under Argentine law the only relevant distinction for companies is domicile, not nationality, expressed concern over the fact that U.S. authorities had been circularizing companies, which they consider to be of American nationality, but which Argentine authorities cannot regard as being subject to dictations from abroad, instructing them to follow procedures designed to relieve pressure on the U.S. balance of payments, to the detriment of Argentina's balance of payments.

[14] It is doubtful whether foreign investors now own as much as 10% of Latin America's capital stock. But the percentage is much higher in new manufacturing activities, such as automobiles and petrochemicals, and effective control over the capital stock, though difficult to measure, may be larger still.

[15] F. Pazos, "The Role of International Movements of Private Capital in

330

The implication is that first economic and then political control and cultural identity would leave the nationals of the host country, unless DFI, especially that from strong powers, is regulated. It is generally assumed that bonds sold to foreigners carry considerably less danger of unfavorable political and cultural repercussions than DFI, even if foreign bondholders show keener anxiety over some aspects of the host country's economic policy than direct investors.

The purchase of going Latin American concerns by foreign investors, therefore, has been an especially disappointing phenomenon to Latin American observers. Published hard data are difficult to find, but there is a feeling that this trend has picked up force recently. After many years of fostering infant entrepreneurs and industries at high cost to the rest of society, it is galling to see those activities go under foreign control and the infant entrepreneurs turn into rentiers.[16] Public efforts to persuade local entrepreneurs to leave traditional real estate and commercial speculations and turn to industry, and many hopes for entrepreneurial "learning-by-doing" have come to naught. In the process, however, the lesson has been learned, at least by some, that building up a strong and efficient local entrepreneurial class will not be achieved by just shutting off imports of foreign goods and DFI; more rational policies on foreign trade and finance, plus the fostering of an active domestic capital market, will be required. But much remains to be done in the refinement of positive measures to encourage local entrepreneurship and joint ventures.

Promoting Development," in *Capital Movements and Economic Development*, Proceedings of a Conference held by the International Economic Association, J. H. Adler, ed. (New York: St. Martin's Press, 1967). Elsewhere Pazos has put the same thought in this way: "One cannot have Latin American capitalism without Latin American capitalists."

[16] The disappointment is similar to that occurring when a youth whose studies have been financed at public expense leaves his country. One may wonder whether a state that has directly or indirectly subsidized an infant entrepreneur for many years does not have a right at least to a share of the price paid by the foreign investors taking over a local going concern. It is ironic to recall that import substitution was viewed years ago as a nationalistic and antioligarchical strategy, even where supported by DFI. That viewpoint has lost appeal in Latin America, perhaps excepting the disciples of the exotic Frondizi-Frigerio school. Not all foreign takeovers of existing national enterprises need extinguish local entrepreneurship; research on what happens with the sales proceeds is badly needed.

Not all segments of Latin American opinion look with mistrust to DFI. Indeed, some local entrepreneurs fear their own governments more than foreign investors, and welcome the latter as potential allies against local bureaucrats. The widespread feeling that political interest follows economic involvement cuts both ways: some local businessmen (and others) fearful of political turmoil welcome foreign, especially U.S. presence, in their countries.[17]

How much should Latin America pay for generating local entrepreneurs? The cost to Mexico, in terms of forgone DFI and growth opportunities, does not appear to be inordinately high, even though Mexican rules of thumb and regulations on DFI are somewhat mystifying and their rationality is not self-evident.[18] But the key to Mexico's success in this field, i.e., a strong and stable central government presiding over a rapidly expanding economy, is something for which no recipe exists.

[17] Referring to Cuban reluctance to accept the odious Platt-Root amendment to the Constitution of the new Cuban Republic, Fitzgibbon (Ref. 3) writes: "By the middle of April (of 1901) the hectic discussions in the Cuban convention began to assume more definite form, perhaps in consequence of the frank agitation by Cuban economic interests for acceptance of the amendment" (p. 83). Even after the proclamation of independence (in May 1902) talk about annexation of Cuba by the United States persisted: "It may be concluded that Havana business interests and foreigners in general, and Spanish and Americans in particular, were sympathetic toward annexation, while the Cuban political caste was unfavorable to the idea" (p. 108).

[18] Activities in which Mexican capital must represent a minimum of 51% of total capital range from basic chemicals to production and distribution of soft drinks and fruit extracts. Radio broadcasting, television, gas, and automative transportation on federal routes are fully reserved for Mexican citizens. See Banco Nacional de México, *Mexico as a Field for Foreign Investment* (n.d), p. 15. This pamphlet also adds: "We should emphasize that the areas of activity indicated, particularly insofar as concerns the third classification [dealing with the 51% Mexican capital minimum], are covered not by laws but simple administrative rulings." It also warns: "Mexican laws contain the so-called Calvo clause that dates all the way back to the third quarter of the nineteenth century and requires that foreigners forego the protection of their home governments in the event of controversy" (pp. 15–16). Proximity to the United States is now another Mexican asset, but it is doubtful whether this explains more than a small share of Mexican success in this field. Cuba, as one is often reminded, is only 90 miles away.

Some Recent Trends and Proposals

What to do about DFI remains a lively topic of discussion, not always wholly rational, in Latin American circles. The Inter-American Committee for the Alliance for Progress has sponsored a study on the subject, and the Inter-American Development Bank is giving much thought to DFI, with the help of Dr. Raúl Prebisch. Individual Latin American countries are developing new policies, and hopes have been expressed that joint policies may be undertaken. Academic interest is also strong, and intellectuals' writings on the subject are influential.[19]

One trend involves public utilities, such as telephones, electricity and railroads, where little fresh DFI is going in, and where several foreign investors have been bought out by host governments. Sometimes arrangements include reinvesting by foreigners of part or all of the sale proceeds into other activities within the host country. For example, Mexico's 1960 purchase of American and Foreign Power assets, worth $70 million, was accompanied by such an understanding.[20] This trend illustrates Vernon's proposition that the

---

[19] See especially O. Sunkel, "Política Nacional de Desarrollo y Dependencia Externa," *Estudios Internacionales*, Year 1, No. 1 (April 1967), pp. 43–75; C. Furtado, "La Concentración del poder Económico en los Estados Unidos y sus Proyecciones en América Latina," *Estudios Internacionales*, Year 1, Nos. 3–4 (October 1967–March 1968), pp. 323–336; and A. Pinto "Political Aspects of Economic Development in Latin America," and V. Urquidi "The Implications of Foreign Investment in Latin America," in *Obstacles to Change in Latin America*, C. Veliz, ed. (London: Oxford University Press, 1965), pp. 9–46 and pp. 91–115, respectively.

[20] See M. S. Wionczek, *El Nacionalismo Mexicano y la Inversión Extranjera* (Mexico: Siglo XXI Editores, SA 1967), pp. 138–139. The same author suggests that funds used by Mexico for the purchase of Mexican Light and Power during the same year came from long-term funds supplied by the Prudential Insurance Company of America to the Mexican government. During 1965, the Brazilian government purchased the Brazilian assets of American and Foreign Power Company (electricity) for $135 million, and those of Brazilian Traction Light and Power Company (telephones) for $96 million. In the latter transaction, there was an initial payment of $10 million; the balance of the purchase price is payable over a 20-year period and the company has agreed to invest 75% of this sum in other Brazilian enterprises. See *The Wall Street Journal* (December 23, 1965). Colombia recently ended a six-year dispute with American and Foreign Power Com-

advantages perceived by LDC's in a given foreign investment declines as the enterprise ages.

"Traditional" DFI exploiting exhaustable natural resources has also come under increasing pressures from policies such as "Mexicanization" and "Chileanization," not to mention the more radical Peruvian actions against IPC. Mexico, which in 1938 nationalized the oil industry,[21] purchased in 1967 majority control of Pan American Sulphur Company's assets, not without not-so-subtle pressure. New sulfur concessions are to be granted only to companies at least 66% Mexican-owned.[22] During 1969 Mexico moved to persuade two other U.S. mining firms, subsidiaries of Anaconda and Gulf Resources and Chemical Corporation, to sell part of their assets to Mexican investors, presumably a controlling interest.[23]

In 1966, the Chilean government and Kennecott Copper Corporation formed a new company to operate the giant El Teniente mine, with 51% participation by the state-owned Chilean Copper Corporation. Chile paid Kennecott $80 million, which Kennecott lent back to the new company. In addition, Kennecott agreed to put another $120 million ($110 million covered by a 15-year EXIM-BANK loan) to expand El Teniente's output. A management contract provides that the operation of the mine remains in Kennecott's hands. Other partnerships were created with Anaconda and Cerro Corporation, although the Chilean interest is here of only 25%. Furthermore, the Anaconda deal covered only the Exótica mine,

pany by paying $38 million for their assets (*Business Week* (April 26, 1969)). It will be recalled that the Perón regime used large foreign exchange reserves accumulated during the Second World War to purchase foreign-owned railroads and public utilities in Argentina during the late 1940s.

[21] *The Wall Street Journal* (January 26, 1967) candidly headlined a story on PEMEX, the Mexican oil monopoly, as follows: "Nationalized Oil Agency in Mexico so Successful it Worries the Industry — Firms Fear Other Lands May Follow Example of Pemex . . . ."

[22] See stories in *Business Week* (April 22, 1967) and *The Wall Street Journal* (October 5, 1966). For an interesting history of DFI in Mexican sulfur see M. S. Wionczek, Ref. 20, pp. 171–305.

[23] *Business Week* (February 1, 1969). The article is entitled "Go Mexican or else. . . ." Mexico's manipulation of the production and export quotas of Gulf Resources ". . . gave Gulf Resources an irresistible pocketbook reason to sell control to Mexicans." The Anaconda subsidiary has been hit by a new production tax.

since that company was reported to balk at giving the Chilean government any interest in Chuquicamata, the largest Chilean mine, or in its other mine, El Salvador. Cerro Corporation had not previously operated in Chile, and its partnership with the government involved a new mine, Río Blanco. All agreements included output expansion plans, with considerable external financing, together with tax concessions and Chilean assurances that tax rates would be held steady for 20 years.[24] By these actions the Chilean government hoped not only to extend its control over the production and marketing of copper, but to increase the shares of copper refined in Chile and of domestic supplies in total inputs of the industry.

Since 1958 Venezuela has announced an oil policy of "no new concessions" for foreign investors and has nudged upward their tax share by insisting in valuing oil output at posted rather than realized prices. New concessions are reserved for the state-owned oil company (CVP), which also has one-third of the Venezuelan service station market allocated to it. CVP expects to award service contracts to private companies to develop government-owned leases, but this new relationship has had trouble getting off the ground and exploration for new oil and gas fields has dwindled. Recently, Colombia and Ecuador have driven tough bargains with foreign companies for the exploitation of the rich Putumayo oil fields.[25]

The question may be raised whether it makes sense for capital-poor countries to use a share of their savings to purchase foreign-owned assets and technologically stagnant activities already within their borders, or to use national funds in industries for which

[24] *Business Week* (October 1, 1966). On more recent developments, discussed below, see *The New York Times* (May 22, 1969) ("Chile to Take Share in Anaconda Control"). Kennecott's Chilean operation accounts for less than a third of its world-wide copper production, while Anaconda obtains more than two-thirds of its copper from its three Chilean mines.

[25] For a description of Ecuadorian negotiations with Texaco and Gulf see *The Economist para América Latina* (April 16, 1969), and *The New York Times* (April 28, 1969). The last sticking point in the negotiations has been Ecuador's insistence on owning the vital trans-Andean pipeline. As indicated by *The Times*: "Tariffs on use of the pipeline would be a way of exacting additional revenues from the consortium. It would also be a strong bargaining point if the Government later wishes to negotiate a new contract, since the oil field is useless without transportation to the sea."

335

plentiful foreign funds are available. If foreign interests being bought out reinvest those funds in other activities within the same country, one may question the net macroeconomic impact of the whole exercise. The answer to these queries depends very much on the details of each agreement; answering them *a priori,* perhaps using a competitive model, would miss much of their point. The Perón purchases appear in retrospect as an unwise use of funds; purchase prices were excessive and the desired control over railroads and public utilities could have been achieved at lower cost by a more intelligent use of Argentine bargaining power and public policy instruments. No attempt was made to persuade foreign investors to reinvest their cash in Argentina. The Mexican and Chilean actions, however, have resulted in advantages beyond the reduction of future profit remittances abroad which must be balanced against the cost of those operations:

1. The political "clearing of the air" resulting from greater national control over an activity that public opinion considers of key importance can have beneficial economic side effects. "Chileanization" of copper mines has led to large expansion plans, after many years of stagnant output.[26] In Mexico, the "Mexicanized" electricity companies early in 1962 placidly raised rates to levels that would have created a social storm under foreign sponsorship. Mexicanization of sulfur cleared the way for full-scale development of Mexico's sulfur.

[26] The Chilean agreements of 1966 have not "cleared the air" completely, however. Debate has continued over the price paid for Kennecott assets, and over Anaconda's reluctance to share its interest in Chuquicamata and El Salvador. The enthusiastic reception given in the U.S. press to the 1966 copper agreements made many Chileans wonder whether they were good bargains. Continuing high world copper prices have led to doubts as to whether Chile is getting a fair share of profits, especially vis-à-vis Anaconda. Friction increased early in 1969, when it was discovered that Anaconda had been surveying on its own for new deposits, even though its agreement with the government provided for joint explorations of new lands. See *The New York Times* (May 6, 1969). Chile is now pressing for 51% control of Chuquicamata and El Salvador, and a new copper surtax adjusted to world prices. The 1966 Chilean agreements illustrate Kindleberger's point: "In bilateral monopoly bargaining in public, it may be that no outcome satisfactory to the company will be acceptable to the body politic." Ref. 1, p. 162.

336

2. By buying a place in the board of directors of vertically integrated activities, governments gain access to valuable cost accounting information. By training not only its own cost accountants, but also its own cadres of copper technicians and engineers, Chilean bargaining power is increased vis-à-vis the foreign companies. Threats by foreign investors to leave can be met with less trepidation. Tax disputes can be handled with richer data. The logistics and mysteries of international merchandising may become less overpowering. Note that to reap benefits from better cost accounting information the host country need not "unfairly" get access to technological knowledge that the foreign investor may have developed with costly research investments. But it is true that part of these benefits to host countries will come about from sharing with foreign investors world market power. Chile and Venezuela show as little inclination as Anaconda and Standard Oil to make world markets for copper and oil more competitive.

3. Motivations to save are manyfold. The incentive of owning a "commanding height" of the national economy long in the hands of foreigners could generate savings that otherwise may not come forth. The level of national savings may not, therefore, be independent of investment opportunities perceived by a country's private and public sectors.

4. Prodding foreign investors out of "traditional" sectors and into new activities may squeeze larger DFI contributions of technology and risk-taking, while placing on foreigners the burden of getting new enterprises going.

As indicated earlier, most of fresh U.S. DFI in Latin America during the 1960s has been in "new" activities, such as manufacturing. Fear that such DFI may become an uncontrollable torrent under a Latin American Common Market and that foreign companies will be the main beneficiaries of trade liberalization has hampered regional integration efforts. With the European experience very much in mind, there has been much talk of the need to coordinate Latin American policy toward DFI and to set up the bases for Latin American multinational corporations.[27] Another

[27] As put by Professor P. N. Rosenstein-Rodan: "The EEC countries have

fear is that DFI, within a common market, will produce regional imbalances, favoring some countries while neglecting others, just as before foreign-owned public utilities centered in capital cities and neglected the countryside.

The concern is warranted if, as Kindleberger and Johnson suggest, common markets lift the attention of U.S. business to a wider horizon, focusing interest in fast-growing markets.[28] This apprehension has been reflected in the popularity of slogans such as: "Either *we* integrate ourselves, or *they* will integrate us," and "Integration should be from the inside and from below, not from the outside and from above."[29]

The case for a common Latin American front in negotiations with foreign investors is obvious and strong. Self-defeating competition over incentives could be minimized and Latin American bargaining in such areas as oil, copper, and other minerals could be increased. (Most countries already have public enterprises in these fields.) Joint action could also provide a way around the sticky problem of guarantees and arbitration. On the whole, Latin American governments view U.S.-inspired guarantee and insurance schemes for DFI with skepticism and suspicion, and have flatly rejected the World Bank's convention on the settlement of investment disputes as an infringement on national sovereignty and contrary to national constitutions. Guarantees and arbitration procedures offered multilaterally by Latin American nations, and administered jointly by them, perhaps with the help of regional or subregional

---

been unable to achieve anything approaching a common policy on foreign investment. One measure of wealth is that waste one can afford. Latin America is not as rich as Europe. In the field of multinational corporations it can and it should do better." See his "Multinational Investment in the Framework of Latin American Integration," in *Multinational Investment in the Economic Development and Integration of Latin America* (Bogotá Colombia: Round Table, Inter-American Development Bank, 1968), p. 87.

[28] The expansion of U.S. manufacturing investment in Central America since the creation of its common market lends modest support to this view, although here fresh policies of import substitution may provide a better explanation than the creation of the common market *per se.*

[29] This theme is developed by A. García, in "El Diálogo Latinoamericano en el Seminario de Arica," *Estudios Internacionales,* Vol. 2, No. 1 (April-June 1968), pp. 142–148.

institutions, may prove to be a workable and acceptable arrangement.[30] Regional institutions, including the Inter-American Development Bank, would naturally be better suited than national ones for promoting multinational Latin American corporations, and their joint ventures with foreign investors.[31] As with Nacional Financiera in Mexico, they could assist local firms in seeking foreign partners and technology, and could encourage the flow of technical and managerial information within Latin America.

Alas, progress in this field has been painfully slow and prospects for the quick creation of a Latin American Common Market are dim. Early in 1968 there was hope that subregional agreements, like the proposed Andean common market, would create institutions such as the Andean Development Corporation, serving, *inter alia,* as a coordinator of policies toward DFI and as promoter of all-Andean firms.[32] But even this effort is taking long to mature. Meanwhile, pressures from non-Latin American multinational corporations for a free hand in "integrating" the region grow stronger. It is a fact that within the Latin American Free Trade Zone foreign firms, such as IBM, Olivetti, and Ford, show greater integration zeal than most domestic entrepreneurs.

With or without regional integration, the Latin American search for a Rodanesque "new philosophy" or "code of international investment" continues.[33] An idea gaining in popularity as an alterna-

---

[30] The zeal of the Nixon Administration for new unilateral schemes to promote U.S. DFI is viewed with apprehension in Latin America, again on the ground that politics and economics may get hopelessly tangled. The attitude may change if U.S. guarantees are offered only to U.S. DFI accepting Latin American conditions, such as joint ventures with a minimum of 51% Latin American participation. Mexico, incidentally, is opposed to granting any special guarantees to DFI and has not done so.

[31] Mexican and Colombian investments in Central America indicate the rich possibilities, and healthy effect on Latin entrepreneurship, of multinational activities. To some extent, investments by São Paulo industrialists in the Brazilian northeast point in the same direction.

[32] See C. F. Díaz Alejandro, "El grupo Andino en el Proceso de Integración Latino-Americana," *Estudios Internacionales,* Year 2, No. 2 (July-September 1968) (Santiago), pp. 242–257.

[33] Mexico, of course, steadily marches on its own path, applying continued pressure on foreign investors for a minimum of Mexicanization. During 1968 International Telephone and Telegraph's Mexican subsidiary offered 40%

tive to joint ventures, which are resisted by many international corporations, is to have *fresh* DFI face ("ex ante") a gradual program of nationalization, say over 10 or 15 years, under conditions agreed to at the time of its entry into the country. More flexibility is desirable: the initial contract could include just the *option* of nationalization, and provide for periodic *renegotiations* between host governments and foreign investors.[34] Different DFI arrangements, including coproduction schemes, may fit with greater or smaller ease in different "portfolios."

Widespread use by foreign companies of Latin American credit facilities, including sometimes subsidized public credit, has stimulated interest in joint ventures. The argument is that as long as foreign investors are going to tap local savings, host governments should pressure them to take more equity capital and less bank credit, with a presumed net reduction in future profit remittances abroad and greater local control.

---

of its stock to Mexican investors. General Electric sold 10% of its shares and Scripto de Mexico 50% interest to Mexicans during the same year. Pressure is likely to mount on companies such as Ford, General Motors, and Volkswagen, which remain 100% foreign owned. A typical form of pressure remains a request by government officials for a Mexicanization plan from companies requesting import permits. Yet, as Minister Octaviano Campos Salas recently stated: "No matter what may be said, we continue to have more than enough suitors." Foreign investors are coming around to accepting Mexicanization as a permanent fact of life and few prefer to pick up their marbles and leave. On the other hand, during 1967–1968 the Mexican government allowed the purchase of wholly owned Mexican companies, primarily in the food and drug fields, by foreign corporations. It is also noteworthy that Mexico follows a permissive policy regarding profit and amortization remittances abroad.

[34] As put by R. Vernon: "If many business enterprises find it difficult or impossible to operate in Latin American countries through joint enterprises, it is also true that many such countries find it difficult to accept foreign ownership on a basis which appears perpetual in time and total in extent." Vernon suggests a flexible approach: "The problem may be to permit the certainty of a change, where certainty is thought a virtue; and to permit flexibility in cases where that is attractive." See R. Vernon, "Private Long-Term Foreign Investment in Latin America" (January 1967), pp. 18–22 (mimeo). See also Ref. 27, pp. 75–76. The importance and desirability of renegotiations are stressed by Kindleberger in Ref. 1, p. 151: "Renegotiations of contracts with long life when the underlying conditions change is familiar in the Anglo-Saxon tradition. We have renegotiation of government procure-

Dissatisfaction with past policies of import substitution is also leading to a closer look at expansion plans of foreign investors in manufacturing, especially in automobiles. Not only are tariff barriers being reduced; recently Argentina authorized Fiat expansion plans only after that company had promised to cut prices drastically.[35] Other companies still enjoying substantial protection can expect a similar treatment.

In some cases public enterprises and powerful quasi-public private groups are entering into joint ventures with foreign investors, thus equilibrating bargaining power between nationals and foreigners. For example, during 1967 Commonwealth Oil Refining Company and the Venezuelan government, through its petrochemical corporation, IVP, agreed to jointly develop a giant petrochemical complex expected to involve an eventual investment of $400 million. The two companies will share equally in the ownership and financing of the projects.[36] In 1966 the Banco Nacional de México entered, with 51% interest, into a joint venture with Pan American Sulphur and other foreign investors to build a $59 million fertilizer plant.[37] Both the Venezuelan and the Mexican ventures expect that a large part of their output will be exported, also illustrating the new interest of Latin American countries to promote DFI in exporting activities.[38] Joint ventures are sought not only for capital

---

ment when subsequent information reveals that profits would be exorbitant at the costs the contractor is able to achieve." (A point for Chile to note in its present dispute with Anaconda.)

[35] *Business Week* (May 17, 1969). While welcoming DFI, the regime of General Onganía is taking a selective approach. Last year its military rebuffed U.S. Steel Corporation in its first attempt to enter steelmaking in South America. In negotiations with Dow Chemical over a proposed large petrochemical complex it is insisting that its internal prices should not be too out of line with those ruling internationally.

[36] *The Wall Street Journal* (September 28, 1967).

[37] *The Wall Street Journal* (November 22, 1966). The Banco Nacional de México is privately owned but has close links with the public sector.

[38] The new interest in export promotion does not, of course, involve a return to pre-1930 permissiveness toward DFI in export activities. Furthermore, Latin American opinion would probably reject Harry Johnson's hope of linking trade preferences to LDC's to a growing flow of DFI in export activities of LDC's. Indeed, if trade preferences are sold on the ground that they will attract international corporations to LDC's to take advantage of

and technology, but also for the marketing capabilities of vertically integrated foreign companies. There is also preoccupation with restrictions that parent companies may place on the exporting of their Latin American subsidiaries.

Outlook

It is hard to see how the trend toward "Latin Americanization" of old and new DFI could be reversed, whether governments are from the right, center, or left. More control and greater sectoral selectivity are likely; banks, natural resources, public utilities, etc., will be placed increasingly out of bounds for DFI. Joint ventures,[39] coproduction schemes, or gradual nationalizations will be pressed on new foreign investments in "dynamic" industries, while "vegetative" industries may be increasingly reserved for national entrepreneurs. Borrowing rights of foreign investors in domestic capital markets will be restricted. Rules of thumb, coupled with some administrative flexibility, à la Mexico, will gain popularity; while arbitrary,[40] they may provide the only realistic way to handle the complications of second- and third-best situations. Hopefully, the rules will be clear and steady, and will be framed with an eye to obtaining economic and noneconomic targets at minimum cost.

---

them, the appeal of trade preferences to Latin American opinion will be considerably reduced. See H. G. Johnson, "LDC Investment: The Road is Paved with Preferences," *Colombia Journal of World Business,* Vol. III, No. 1 (January-February 1968), pp. 17–21. If trade preferences are not granted to all LDC's across the board, the skepticism would be greater. The Cuban experience with U.S. sugar trade preferences, coupled with U.S. DFI in sugar is worth bearing in mind.

[39] A small but active group of foreign investors from 16 industrialized countries have created ADELA Investing Company to promote joint ventures with Latin American control, meeting with success and popularity. By March 1969 ADELA had authorized 97 investments for a total commitment of $55 million dollars.

[40] DFI in some "vegetative" activities may well be more profitable for the host country than in many fashionable "dynamic" industries. Foreign investment in food processing, for example, has had a very beneficial "backward linkage" effect on Central American agriculture. DFI in commercial activities has, in several instances, brought dramatic improvements in obsolete domestic merchandising patterns.

Coupled with permissive policies on profit and amortization remittances,[41] they may lead to more, not less, DFI.

Some countries may prefer to exercise greater control over sectors now dominated by DFI by more purposeful manipulation of public policy instruments, rather than by equity participation. That may achieve at least cost economic and other objectives in some cases, especially in the large countries. But historical evidence also shows that easily reversable credit, fiscal, and exchange policies, used by themselves, often yield much friction and unstable relationships between foreign investors and host governments. Without implying that the Mexican model can or should be copied by all Latin American countries, it may be observed that in Mexico those policies are successfully used as complements to, rather than substitutes for, Mexicanization.

Conciliation of conflicting Latin American goals will not be easy, and will frequently lead to inconsistent and hesitant behavior. Desire for joint ventures may decrease the welcomed inflow of foreign technology; fulfillment of export targets could require greater foreign presence in export activities; some of the funds needed for buying foreign firms within the country may have to come from reduced public programs benefiting the masses; a larger share of foreign bond over equity financing will introduce rigidities in the balance of payments, without necessarily reducing total costs of foreign capital *cum* technology. Leaders will be tempted to use rhetoric to hide these tradeoffs.

The Latin American preference for bond over equity financing and for hiring technology independently of equity capital may become more practical if developed countries succeed in creating a liberal and expanding world economy, with a minimum of control over markets for commodities, technology, and capital. In that environment, Latin American countries could reduce the costs of technology and financing by judiciously taking advantage of the variety of U.S., European, and Japanese investors, stimulating com-

---

[41] Some have noted that when a Latin American country imposes restrictions on profit remittances, they rise, and when restrictions are abolished, they fall.

petition among them. The benefits to responsible LDC governments of such a situation is already reflected in favorable conditions on some suppliers' credits.

Rising Latin American nationalism is not likely to be eliminated by pointing to its possible economic costs. Stable and responsible governments can minimize such costs and harness nationalistic feelings to the task of development, perhaps turning costs into gains, while a massive presence of DFI can weaken national solidarity, impairing the government's ability to coax sacrifices from the public. Nationalism will continue to generate frictions between foreign investors[42] and Latin American countries, and between the U.S. and Latin American governments. That much is inevitable; how serious those frictions are allowed to become depends more on United States' than Latin American statesmanship. United States unseemly support to stubborn positions of its foreign investors (such as IPC) have led, and will lead, to distasteful situations, in which the main losers have been leaders, such as ex-President Belaúnde of Peru, who were supposed to be the main stars of the Alliance for Progress. Skepticism is the natural response when the strong lectures the weak on the evils of nationalism. That message is best preached by the example of the strong.

---

[42] Even taking into account massive Cuban confiscations, it appears that on the aggregate the risk-insurance premium that presumably is added to DFI profit rates in Latin America have amply covered the losses arising from actual confiscations.

CHAPTER FOURTEEN

JAPAN AS HOST TO THE INTERNATIONAL CORPORATION

M. Y. Yoshino

Prewar Attitudes

The strategy Japan pursued in achieving rapid industrialization during the past century has many remarkable aspects. Particularly noteworthy was her intense determination to maintain political as well as economic independence in the process of industrialization. In fact, at least in the early Meiji era (1868 to 1912), industrialization was not the end in itself, but only a means to maintain national independence in the face of serious foreign threats. Thus, it is quite understandable that the Meiji leaders deliberately restricted the entry of foreign capital. With a remarkable degree of discipline they avoided foreign direct investment. This policy was, in part, motivated by their desire to protect struggling Japanese industries against foreign competition. What they feared most, however was foreign ownership and management control of Japanese industries through direct investment. Whenever foreign capital was deemed absolutely necessary they showed a most definite preference for loans.

This cautious attitude, even bordering on timidity, with which the Meiji leadership treated foreign direct investment presented a striking contrast to the aggressiveness with which the nation sought advanced foreign technology. The Meiji leaders, much to their credit, realized in the very early phase of industrialization that importation of advanced foreign technology could be achieved without foreign ownership or control. In this, they saw the possibility of achieving rapid industrialization without compromising their over-riding goal. Indeed, a popular slogan of the early Meiji era, *Wakon Yosai* (The Japanese Spirit and Foreign Technology), aptly describes the sentiment of this period. This set the basic tone of the Japanese attitude toward foreign direct investment throughout the prewar decades.[1]

The tight restrictions against foreign investment became gradually relaxed beginning around the turn of the century as the nation achieved rapid industrialization and foreign threats became less imminent. Even then, direct foreign investment remained rather small in absolute sum, and much of it took the form of joint ventures. The Zaibatsu-dominated business community essentially shared the view of the political elite and zealously guarded its independence. Significantly, even during this period the most important reason why Japanese firms sought foreign joint ventures was to obtain advanced foreign technology.

The foregoing brief review of the basic attitude toward foreign investment prior to World War II is intended to give the reader a perspective for examining subsequent developments, since only in this context is it possible to understand fully the Japanese policy toward foreign direct investment in the postwar decades. True, times are different, but there are some interesting and significant parallels between the pre- and postwar years.

After the War

As in the prewar era, foreign investment, particularly direct investment in Japan, has been comparatively small in postwar decades despite a number of attractive features that the country offers. Japan is now a major industrial nation with a large internal market of its own. The nation's GNP is expected to be second only to the

---

[1] For details of the magnitude and role of foreign direct investment in prewar Japan see: S. Okita and T. Miki, "Treatment of Foreign Capital — A Case Study for Japan" in J. Adler and P. W. Kuznets, eds., *Capital Movements and Economic Development* (New York: St. Martin Press, 1967), pp. 139–156; and W. W. Lockwood, *The Economic Development of Japan: Growth and Structural Change 1868–1938* (Princeton: Princeton University Press, 1954), pp. 321–323.

United States in the free world this year. Japan has a well-educated and trained labor force. Moreover, she enjoys a high degree of political stability unknown in the rest of Asia. Thus, in many respects, Japan is a very attractive country for international investment.

The cumulative book value of all types of foreign investment made in Japan in the postwar period stood at $5,735 million at the end of 1967. The breakdowns are even more revealing. As is evident in Table 1, the combined total of portfolio and direct investment accounts for less than one-fifth of the total foreign capital inflow during the postwar years; the rest is in some form of loan. Particularly significant is the fact that the total direct investment is only a third of this combined sum and represents a mere 6% of the cumulative total of foreign capital inflow between 1949 and 1967.[2] The limited foreign direct investment in Japan is, of course, due largely to the very restrictive policy that the Japanese government has adopted in postwar years. While restricting foreign direct investment, Japan, as in the prewar period, aggressively sought out advanced foreign technology. Between 1950 and 1968 Japanese firms signed over 9,800 licensing contracts with foreign firms, for which they paid a staggering sum of $1.46 billion. Indeed, foreign technology has played an important role in Japan's postwar economic growth. Especially has foreign technology been critically important in the development of highly technically oriented modern industries such as chemical, petrochemical, electronics, and synthetic fibers. Let us now examine the evolution of Japanese policy toward foreign direct investment.

Foreign Exchange Control Law

In 1949, Japan enacted a Foreign Exchange Control Law and the following year a Foreign Investment Law, which have served as the chief instruments to control foreign direct investment. The basic policy that was to prevail for some time was clearly stated in

[2] In terms of national origin, U.S. firms account for over 65% of the total direct investment. It is also interesting to note that over 75% of the foreign direct investment is concentrated in three key industries, petroleum, chemical, and machinery.

Table 1. Foreign Capital Inflow in Postwar Japan (thousands of dollars).

| Fiscal Year | Total* | Shares | | Beneficiary Certificate | Debenture | Claimable Assets Arising from Loans | External Bonds Issued |
		Acquisition of Stock and Proprietary Interest	Participation† in Management				
1949–1950	3,150	3,150	2,572				
1951	17,352	13,326	11,646			4,026	
1952	44,751	10,123	7,166	146	25	34,457	
1953	54,926	5,002	2,687	562		49,362	
1954	19,307	3,970	2,467	58		15,279	
1955	52,214	5,101	2,309	52	7	47,054	
1956	103,302	9,520	5,360	115	15	93,652	
1957	135,597	11,490	7,282	128		123,979	
1958	272,967	11,350	3,698	116	28	231,473	30,000
1959	154,890	27,031	14,561	214	30	127,615	
1960	211,658	74,151	31,593	555	20	127,132	
1961	577,529	116,142	40,170	1,280	77	387,605	9,800
1962	678,823	164,668	22,619	650	86	358,419	72,425
1963	884,302	185,262	42,656	798	247	503,945	155,000
1964	912,784	84,845	30,645	1,828	851	650,760	194,050
1965	528,506	83,331	44,643	398	2,726	379,551	174,500
1966	457,097	126,735	39,812	390	261	329,711	62,500
1967	847,785	159,834	29,777	284	123	637,544	50,000
1968	1,589,643	488,824	50,564	282	31	921,526	178,980

* Figures include reinvestment.
† The acquisition of shares exceeding 10% (since July 1, 1967 — 15%) of the total share issue of one company in the case of designated industries or 15% (since July 1, 1967 — 20%) in the case of nondesignated industries.
Source: *Economic Statistics Annual 1968* (Tokyo: The Bank of Japan, 1969), p. 242.

Article 1 of the Foreign Investment Law. It stated that direct foreign investment was permitted in Japan only when it contributed (1) to the attainment of self-sufficiency and the sound development of the Japanese economy and (2) to the improvement of Japan's balance of payment. As long as the foreign investment meets these requirements, the law unconditionally guarantees the remittance of the principal as well as profits overseas regardless of the country's foreign exchange position. Significantly, the law explicitly recognizes the eventual desirability of free entry of foreign capital and pledges that restrictions will be removed as circumstances permit. The law also established the Foreign Investment Council (FIC) under the juridiction of the Minister of Finance as the chief advisory body on matters relating to direct foreign investment.

During the first several years after enactment of the law, the Japanese government vigorously adhered to the two requirements indicated earlier. As Japan achieved her economic recovery and began her drive for rapid growth in the latter half of the 1950s, the government began, albeit slowly, to relax the very strict restrictions against foreign investment. The criteria for screening underwent a significant change from admitting only those investments with positive contributions to prohibiting those deemed "harmful" or less desirable. By the early 1960s, foreign investment was permitted in Japan as long as it did not (1) unduly oppress small-sized enterprises, (2) seriously disturb industrial order, and (3) seriously impede the domestic development of industrial techniques.

After 1963, the restrictions were further relaxed. During the earlier years, the maximum foreign ownership allowed was 49%, but by 1963 joint ventures on a 50-50 basis became commonplace. Firms in consumer-related industries were now permitted entry under the Foreign Investment Law. Moreover, the government began to allow joint ventures in vital industries in which, up until then, only licensing had been possible. Still, each investment application had to go through individual screening and was rigorously examined by the Foreign Investment Council.

In 1956 the government had made an important exception to the screening requirement: that is, as long as foreign firms were willing to forego the explicit guarantee of repatriation of principal and profit, they could invest in Japan without specific government approval. The subsidiaries established under this provision came to be known as "yen companies." Notwithstanding some obvious disadvantages, there were some advantages to this provision. International companies in consumer-related industries which had experienced difficulty in obtaining government approval were now able to enter the rapidly growing Japanese market and establish wholly owned subsidiaries in Japan. The provision was abolished in 1963 in anticipation of Japan's acceptance of Article 8 of the International Monetary Fund (IMF), which required all subscribing nations to guarantee repatriation of principal and earnings of international corporations. During the six-year period, 1956 to 1963, 316 yen companies were established (with estimated total capitalization of around $90 million).

Policy to Mid-Sixties Evaluated

Thus Japanese policy toward direct foreign investment before the mid-1960s had several noteworthy features. First of all, it was highly restrictive both as to types of industries and extent of foreign ownership. The government screened each application on an individual basis. The maximum foreign ownership allowed was 50%, reflecting a strong and long-held Japanese aversion for foreign ownership and control of her industries. Second, the criteria for screening foreign investment were stated with characteristic vagueness, giving the government officials and the Foreign Investment Council considerable latitude. Along with complex bureaucratic machinery and administrative procedures, this presented a formidable obstacle and served as an informal, but nevertheless real deterrent to international firms contemplating entry into Japan. At the same time, the administrative latitude given to the bureaucracy in the selection of foreign investment gave it considerable power (albeit informal), vis-à-vis the Japanese business community. Finally, the Japanese government consistently and persistently encouraged, through formal and informal means, technical licensing rather than direct investment.

Japanese strategy toward foreign investment through the mid-1960s was sound in that it gave sufficient protection to domestic

350

industries to enable them to achieve initial recovery and rapid subsequent growth. It also provided necessary protection and encouragement for newly emerging technically oriented industries to let them get well established. By the mid-1960s, however, the changing domestic and international situations began to build up pressure for gradual liberalization of this policy.

Pressure for Change

The primary reason, of course, lies in the phenomenal success with which Japan achieved her rapid economic growth in the postwar years. Within a decade and a half after her defeat, Japan emerged as a leading industrial nation of the world. As a tangible demonstration of this, Japan in 1964 accepted Article 8 of the IMF regulations and also joined the Organization for Economic Cooperation and Development. Japan had indeed become a full-fledged member of the world's advanced nations, a fact that brought considerable pride to the honor-conscious Japanese. With this, of course, came a set of obligations, not the least important of which was the liberalization of restrictions concerning direct foreign investment.

Since Japan maintained the most restrictive policy toward foreign investment among its member nations, the OECD, at the insistence of the United States, began to prod Japan into relaxation of these restrictions. The United States, having an important stake in Japan, also intensified its pressure on Japan independently through formal as well as informal channels. As important as these external thrusts were, there were equally intense, though less obvious, pressures being generated internally for capital policy liberalization. By the mid-1960s the Japanese themselves began to recognize the need for some liberalization from the point of view of their own national interest.

First, as the Japanese market became more attractive, it became increasingly difficult for Japanese firms to obtain advanced foreign technology through licensing. This is readily understandable, since large international corporations were anxious to establish a permanent basis of operations in the growing Japanese market. International corporations began to use their advanced technology as a

351

wedge to demand equity participation and a less restrictive investment climate. Thus, no longer able to rely predominantly on licensing, an increasing number of Japanese corporations were compelled to form joint ventures in order to obtain coveted foreign technology. Having enjoyed a partial success with this strategy, international corporations further pressed for a less restrictive investment climate. Thus, Japan came under increasing pressure for capital policy liberalization in order to ensure continued access to advanced technology. At the same time, a growing number of Japanese firms began to see advantages in establishing continuing ties with major international firms. They, for their own benefit, began to advocate more favorable investment regulations for international firms.

The second powerful reason for change in policy is the desire on the part of Japan to improve the climate for her exports. The fact that the Japanese economy is highly dependent upon exports needs no elaboration here. The Japanese business community is keenly aware that its very success in the export market has resulted in restrictive measures in a number of countries. It is particularly concerned with what it fears is a surge of protectionism against Japanese imports in the United States. Realizing the importance of *quid pro quo* in international negotiations, it became aware of the potential value of using capital policy liberalization as a bargaining instrument to improve the climate for Japanese exports. Progessive Japanese business leaders also believe that eventually Japanese corporations too must become multinational in their operations in order to remain viable in the international market. In fact, while Japanese direct foreign investment is still negligible in absolute volume, it is increasing at a rapid rate. A number of Japan's leading corporations have now begun to examine the prospect of establishing manufacturing operations overseas. These business leaders are aware that Japan must relax her restrictions before they can demand more favorable treatment of their investments overseas.

Third, the business community is also fearful of the real possibility that unless Japan is willing to relax her restrictive climate, foreign investment, at least in part, may be diverted to other Asian nations. This would not only affect Japanese exports to these areas adversely, but these nations would become serious competitors in the world market sooner than the Japanese would like to see. They are quick to point out that in some industries Hong Kong, Taiwan, and South Korea are already posing a serious competitive threat to Japan in the world market.

Fourth, some business leaders as well as economists argue for capital policy liberalization on the ground that it will benefit Japanese industries as well as consumers. They hold a view that Japan's strategic industries have been overprotected to their long-run detriment. They argue that the best way to strengthen Japanese industries is to expose them to the full rigor of international competition. This "shock treatment," painful as it may be, will be for the best long-run interest of the Japanese industries as well as the economy as a whole.

The advocates of this view maintain that liberalization of foreign investment restrictions will help improve managerial practices and productive efficiency of Japanese firms. They recognize certain weaknesses in Japanese managerial practices and are concerned with long-run implications of the "managerial gap." They also argue that free access by international firms to the Japanese market will be in Japan's best interest from the point of view of consumer welfare. The widely held notion that international corporations, if freely admitted to Japan, will eventually drive out Japanese competition is discounted and confidence is expressed that Japanese industries are too strong to be dominated by foreign firms. Some business leaders also see in capital liberalization a possibility of reducing the very pervasive government influence in business activities.

Resistance to Liberalization

Thus, by 1966, a number of forces, both exogenous and internal, were creating pressures for capital liberalization; but at the same time there were several powerful forces that were vigorously opposed. Among various interest groups objecting to liberalization, interestingly, most vehement was the state bureaucracy, namely various ministries that took a strong protective interest in various industries that came under their respective jurisdictions. As might

353

be expected, industry groups that might be adversely affected by capital policy liberalization also strenuously objected to it. Thus, the bureaucrats, trade association officials of various industry groups, and executives of individual firms often formed a powerful alliance to block liberalization of restrictions against foreign investment when it began to affect any given industry.

Among the major objections to such liberalization, the most frequently cited reason is competitive vulnerability of Japanese industries. True, Japanese industries have shown tremendous growth in the postwar era, but they are still on the whole too weak and vulnerable to be exposed to the full rigor of competition from giant international corporations. Three specific areas of concern are cited. One is the wide disparity in the total size of leading Japanese and international corporations as measured by such criteria as the total sales, capacity, capital, and overall productivity. For example, in terms of sales, General Motors is roughly 18 times as large as Toyota, Japan's leading automobile manufacturer, and 6 times as large in terms of total unit output. General Electric's sales are 8 times as large as those of Hitachi, Du Pont's nearly 10 times as large as those of Mitsubishi Kasei.

It is also frequently argued that not only is the domestic market small, but for a number of reasons peculiar to Japan, its industries are unnecessarily fragmented and suffer from strong internal competition. As a result they are unable to achieve an optimum size of operations.[3]

The second area of concern is a high debt-equity ratio common to almost all Japanese firms. In most firms their very rapid postwar growth has been debt financed. As a result, debt-equity ratio typically runs 4 to 1, saddling Japanese firms with high fixed financial charges and a certain degree of inflexibility. In contrast, it is noted that large international corporations have tremendous financial resources at their command, and access to low-cost funds that they could deploy to the serious competitive disadvantage of Japanese firms.

[3] For details see M. Y. Yoshino, *Japan's Managerial System: Tradition and Innovation* (Cambridge, Mass.: M.I.T. Press, 1968), pp. 162–177.

The third area of concern relates to the technological gap. Easy access by Japanese firms to foreign technology throughout the postwar decades has tended to stymie their own research and development efforts. For example, in 1967 Japan spent less than 1.7% of her GNP for research and development. Moreover, the Japanese government, unlike those in a number of other advanced nations, has played only a limited role in this area. Government expenditure accounts for only 30% of the total, while the remainder has been borne by the private sector. Research expenditure has been rather small in most of the critical industries. The average per company R and D expenditure among Japan's 14 chemical firms in 1967 was only about $\frac{1}{30}$ of the sum spent by Du Pont. In the electrical machinery industry seven Japanese firms on the average spent only about 2% of their sales for R and D in 1967 whereas General Electric and Texas Instruments spend 6 and 6.7%, respectively.

Whether or not such gross indicators effectively measure the competitive vulnerability of Japanese industries is seldom questioned. Other factors cited are access by international corporations to low-cost sources of raw materials, and their strong marketing capabilities. The latter are particularly a source of a special concern to Japanese firms in consumer industries where marketing expertise has been traditionally limited. They also fear the well-established brand names of international corporations. The foregoing examples provide powerful arguments for government officials and some industrial leaders to advocate that capital liberalization is premature and that more time should be allowed for Japanese industries to improve their competitive ability.

Another strong argument against foreign investment liberalization is the need to protect small firms. Government officials and small business interests argue that this sector of the Japanese economy is particularly vulnerable to foreign competition. Small business still occupies an important position in the Japanese economy, as indicated by the following statistics. In the manufacturing sector, enterprises with less than 300 employees constitute 99.3% of all business establishments are responsible for some 70% of employees and 50% of the value of output. In distribution, the

355

predominance of small establishments is even more striking. Nearly half of wholesaling and almost 90% of retailing establishments have less than four employees.

Protection of small enterprises is critical for a number of reasons. First, small business firms as a whole are poorly financed and inefficiently operated. Second, owners and managers of small firms and their organized interests have considerable political power, which the ruling Liberal Democratic Party cannot ignore. Third, small firms are important to large firms, in unique and intricate ways. Finally, small firms faced a number of grave problems, the most serious of which is a growing labor shortage. Traditionally, small firms compensated for their inefficiency and inadequate financing by relying chiefly on the abundance of low-cost labor. Confronted with a serious labor shortage, they are now forced to change and to undertake fundamental rationalization. It is argued that protection against foreign competition is essential during this critical moment.

Still another objection is based on the very character of international corporations, namely their overriding commitment to optimize the profit of their world-wide operations rather than those of any single country, and their ability to avoid, to an important degree, any national jurisdiction.[4] This deep-rooted concern over the multinational corporation found elsewhere is indeed widely shared among the Japanese. Some businessmen and government officials subscribe to a not unpopular notion in other parts of the world that international corporations are inherently bad and would behave unscrupulously if given a chance. They argue that if such concerns were freely permitted entry into Japan they would bring to bear their tremendous managerial, technological, and financial resources and drive out indigenous firms, and would not hesitate to seek monopolistic power. They would be insensitive to the government economic policies, accepted managerial practices, and, to borrow a popular Japanese expression, disrupt industrial order.

[4] For example, see R. Vernon, "Multinational Enterprise and National Sovereignty," *Harvard Business Review,* Vol. 45, No. 2 (March-April 1967), pp. 156–172.

356

There is a widespread fear that a nation-state would be relatively powerless to deal with these problems. Those who subscribe to this point of view cite a number of recent cases, particularly those in Western Europe where there have been direct confrontations between multinational corporations and the nation-state.

Another factor contributing to the uneasiness that the Japanese feel toward international corporations stems from the particular pattern of government and business relationship that evolved in Japan during the past century. While its statuatory power is limited, the government exerts a pervasive influence over the private sector, and it does so largely through informal guidance, subtle pressures, and intricate power play. This has not only been consistent with Japanese tradition, but the pattern appears to offer some definite advantages both to bureaucracy and business. Of course, behind the informal pressure lies the government's ability to reward those willing to cooperate and penalize the recalcitrants. The business community, though not always willingly, has been generally responsive to the government's guidance. The government, of course, is far from convinced that it can expect the same degree of loyalty and responsiveness to its guidance from subsidiaries (particularly those wholly owned) of international corporations.

Behind the government's resistance to liberalization also lies the fact that the control over foreign investment, technical licensing, and allocation of foreign exchange has given the relevant ministries enormous leverage in dealing with the business community. In addition to the characteristic reluctance of the bureaucracy to give up power, government officials feel that there has never been a time when they would need this leverage more than they do now. As noted earlier, the government ministries are anxious to strengthen the competitive capacity of Japanese industries in order to prepare for eventual capital liberalization according to their own blueprints. This means, among other things, limiting "excessive" competition, avoiding uneconomic duplication of capital investments, coordinating capital investment plans, and encouraging joint actions and mergers. These cooperative actions among individual firms are by no means easy to bring about and the government feels that it needs every bit of persuasive power that it can muster. In fact, foreign capital liberalization at this time would mean the loss of an important power at the very time when it is most needed.

There is still another key consideration. Intense nationalistic sentiment prevails in Japan. The physical isolation, centuries of self-imposed seclusion from the rest of the world throughout much of the Tokugawa era, and its cultural tradition, have made Japan highly ethnocentric and nationalistic, and encouraged the development of strong group solidarity. Traditionally, therefore, any entity other than its own was looked upon with immediate suspicion. This may sound contradictory in view of the great enthusiasm with which the Japanese have absorbed certain aspects of foreign cultures, particularly technology. Careful examination, however, reveals that cultural borrowings have been selective and, more importantly, highly controlled. Japanese history is replete with evidence that the presence of actual or imagined foreign threats has resulted in a very effective and almost immediate mobilization of national energy. Thus, it is not without reason that impending capital liberalization was popularly dubbed as "the second coming of the blackships." The reference, of course, is to the arrival of Commodore Perry's blackships in Tokyo Bay in 1853, challenging Japan at gunpoint to open diplomatic and commercial relations with the United States.

This ethnocentricism, coupled with the absence of extensive "cosmopolitan" exposure, has led to a rather provincial outlook among some Japanese. Often they are not capable of evaluating Japan objectively in relation to other nations. This has resulted in an exaggerated fear that since Japan is so attractive as a market, international corporations would enter Japan almost at any cost if the present restrictions were removed. Seldom recognized by those holding this view is the fact that international corporations have other attractive investment opportunities, and enter Japan only if they can justify their investment.

The Course of the Debate

Thus, by 1966, the liberalization of foreign direct investment policy touched off intense debates both within the government bureaucracy and the business community. In fact, it had become a major national issue. The Ministries undertook a number of studies to assess the possible impact of liberalization on key industries under their respective jurisdictions. Particularly active in this regard has been the Ministry of International Trade and Industry. The MITI undertook in late 1966 a detailed study of 110 industries and concluded that 90% of them would be adversely affected by capital liberalization.

In early 1967, the Foreign Investment Council was reorganized and turned into a blue ribbon committee consisting exclusively of distinguished persons from the private sector under the able leadership of Tohru Kobayashi. Also, a special advisory committee consisting of outstanding experts was organized to assist the Council.

The reorganized Foreign Investment Council was instructed by the Finance Minister to recommend a policy of capital liberalization. Each relevant Ministry was charged with the responsibility of designating those industries where a less restrictive policy might be feasible. The Ministries, particularly MITI, were far from enthusiastic about this liberalization, and after intense consultation and negotiation with various industry groups each submitted a list to the FIC. All of the leading business associations including the powerful Federation of Economic Organizations, Japan Chamber of Commerce, and a number of influential trade and industry associations, made their views known. Characteristically, they took a rather cautious stand. The Council held a number of public hearings, consulted with various interest groups, and in the best Japanese tradition sought as broad a consensus as possible.

The Council made its recommendations to the Finance Minister on June 2, 1967. The recommendations consisted of two parts. In the first part, the Council articulated the basic policy Japan should follow in capital policy liberalization. In the second part, the Council made specific recommendations regarding the first phase of liberalization for immediate implementation.

Recommendations of the Foreign Investment Council

First, examine the salient features of the general policy recommendations. At the very outset, the Council stated in no uncertain terms that Japan was determined to carry out the policy of capital liberalization at her own initiative, because it was deemed to be consistent with the best long-run national interest. The Council clearly rejected the notion that Japan was undergoing such liberalization in response to external pressures.

Second, the Council recommended that liberalization be carried out in a series of steps to be consummated by the end of fiscal year 1971. Third, the report clearly stated that liberalization did not mean totally unrestricted access to the Japanese market by multinational corporations. While 100% foreign ownership will be allowed in some industries, liberalization will proceed primarily on the basis of joint ventures.

The Council's report also included suggestions as to what steps the government and Japanese firms must take in the face of a more liberal policy toward foreign investment. The report urged the government to take the following steps. (1) To prevent economic and social disorder or imbalances that may result from large-scale entry of foreign capital into Japan. (2) To create and sustain an economic environment in which Japanese enterprises can compete with large multinational firms on equal terms. (3) To strengthen the competitive capacity of individual Japanese enterprises and reorganize the structure of Japan's key industries so as to withstand competition from large-scale international corporations.

The Council cautioned Japanese firms against their past tendency complacently to seek government protection, and emphasized the importance of careful investigation and planning in entering into any collaborative arrangements with multinational firms. The report also exhorted Japanese firms to approach foreign ventures with confidence based on equal partnership.

Also included in this report were a number of guidelines to be followed by international corporations operating in Japan. This is the first time that guidelines that apply to all foreign firms across the board have been formally stated. While suggestions for the Japanese government and enterprises were indicated with characteristic vagueness, the guidelines for foreign firms were expressed with unusual specificity. They consisted of the following ten points:

1. Seek coexistence and prosperity with Japanese enterprises through joint ventures on an equal partnership basis.

2. Avoid concentration of investment in specific industries.

3. Avoid suppressing small enterprises when entering into industries characterized by small firms.

4. Cooperate voluntarily with the Japanese effort to maintain proper industrial order.

5. Avoid entering into unduly restrictive arrangements with parent companies abroad, and do not resort to unreasonable restrictions concerning transactions or to unfair competition.

6. Take positive steps toward developing Japanese technology, and do not hamper the efforts of Japanese industries to develop their own technology.

7. Contribute to the improvement of the nation's balance of payments through exports and other means.

8. Appoint Japanese to the board of directors and top management positions and make shares of company stock available to the public.

9. Avoid closures of plants, or mass dismissal, and unnecessary confusion in employment and wage practices by paying due regard to the prevailing Japanese practices.

10. Conform to the government economic policy.

Indeed, these guidelines are extensive, touching on almost every key aspect of the conduct of multinational corporations in Japan.

Consistent with its policy that liberalization be carried out in a series of stages, the Council in its report made specific recommendations for the first stage. In doing so, it made three important policy decisions, setting the tone for the subsequent stages. These decisions were (1) liberalization will proceed on an industry basis; (2) distinction will be made according to the degree of foreign ownership; and (3) distinction will also be made between establishment of new enterprises and acquisition of Japanese firms.

For the first stage, the Council designated 50 industries, or more accurately, product groups in which at least some measure of liberalization would be carried out. These industries were further grouped into the first and second categories. Included in the first category were industries in which a maximum of 50% foreign ownership would be allowed without individual screening, provided that the venture satisfies certain basic conditions. Thirty-three of the 50 industries were placed into this category, including household appliances, sheet glass, phonograph records, cameras, acetate, pharmaceuticals, restaurants, and so on.

The Council recommended that in the second category, consisting of 17 industries, 100% foreign ownership be allowed. Major industries included in this category were ordinary steel, motorcycles, beer, cement, pianos, cotton and rayon spinning, hotels, and shipbuilding of limited size. The Council also imposed three specific conditions that must be met by the first category of industries to qualify for automatic permission. These provisions were to provide additional safeguards to ensure equality in joint ventures. They are:

1. The Japanese partner (or partners) that own at least 50% of the shares in the joint ventures must be engaged in the same line of business as the contemplated joint venture. Moreover, one Japanese partner must own at least a third of the total shares of the joint venture.
2. The Japanese representation on the board of directors in the contemplated joint venture must be greater than the proportion of Japanese ownership in the venture.
3. The joint venture must operate under Japanese commercial law and there should be no provision that the consent of a particular officer or a stockholder be required to execute corporate affairs.

Joint ventures even in first-category industries must go through individual screening if they do not meet the foregoing three conditions. As noted earlier, the Council made a clear-cut distinction between newly established operations and acquisitions of going indigenous concerns. The foregoing first-stage recommendations apply only to newly established operations. Reflecting the extreme sensitivity of the Japanese toward "takeover" of existing firms by foreign interests, the Council recommended only a very limited liberalization. Specifically, automatic permission is granted if the

362

total foreign ownership of a company is not more than 20% and any single foreign stockholder's share does not exceed 7%.

In addition, the Council recommended that application procedures be streamlined for the liberalized industries. Similarly, the Council urged the simplification of both application and screening procedures for nonliberalized industries and recommended that the time required for individual screening be shortened.

Implementing the Report

The Council's report was approved by the Cabinet in its entirety on June 6, 1967 and on the first stage of capital liberalization went into effect on July 1, 1967. The first stage produced few results. It is difficult to conceive that foreign steel firms or manufacturers of motorcycles would rush to Japan, even if highly prized 100% ownership were now permitted. The great majority of first-category firms did not hold much appeal to foreign firms. This can be seen from the fact that more than a year went by before the first joint venture was established under the liberalized program.

The Foreign Investment Council deliberately took a very cautious approach in the first step. Opinions arguing for more substantial liberalization were not entirely absent; however, the government Ministries as well as industrial groups that might be adversely affected by more extensive liberalization showed strong resistance. The Council, anxious to achieve a broad consensus, settled for a token liberalization.

The first round of liberalization, though of limited effect, was significant in that it was a clear expression of Japan's determination for capital liberalization, and it made clear the basic approach and timetable. It also served notice to nonliberalized industries that liberalization was indeed imminent, and that they should make serious efforts toward preparing themselves for this eventuality. In fact, a number of significant mergers and joint actions among various firms in several key industries have taken place since 1967, most of which have been designed to strengthen their competitive capacity.

By June 1968, Japan had completed liberalization in the area of technical licensing in all but a few key product categories such as atomic energy, defense, computers, and petrochemicals. Beginning around mid-1968 the second round of capital liberalization came under serious consideration. All concerned fully expected that the second round had to produce considerably more results than the first. New pressures began to mount. Particularly noteworthy is the pressure brought about by American automotive industries to break down ironclad restrictions both in regard to imports and to direct investment. In December 1967 a series of intense negotiations began between the two nations which resulted in Japan agreeing, among other things, to remove import restrictions on engines and parts by 1972 and to give favorable consideration to applications by foreign automobile firms to manufacture parts in Japan.

Equally significant was the fact that the leadership of the Japanese business community became more favorably inclined to capital liberalization. A growing positive sentiment toward capital liberalization was particularly notable among the leadership of the powerful Federation of Economic Organizations. Several reasons can be cited for this new attitude.

First, the forward-looking business leaders became increasingly concerned over the negative attitude of the government as well as of some industry groups toward capital liberalization. This, they felt, has given an impression to the rest of the world that Japan was reneging on her international obligations, creating an undesirable image for the country, and causing unnecessary hostility. Second, they sensed the inevitability of capital liberalization, and with their characteristic pragmatism, they concluded that it would be more advantageous for Japan's long-run national interest to seize the initiative rather than to react reluctantly to exogenous pressures. Progressive business leaders realized the importance of exerting their leadership in planning for the second stage of liberalization to prevent the future course from being determined predominantly by the bureaucrats. Third, the Federation leaders also expressed their serious concern over what they considered excessive government protection over certain industries, and these industries' tendency complacently to depend on it. They became increasingly convinced that well-planned and well-managed capital liberalization would stimulate industrial reorganization and increase productive efficiency. Perhaps their most fundamental reason is their growing confidence in the dynamism of Japanese industries and their ability to withstand foreign competition.

Amid these pressures and counterpressures, formal deliberations began in the fall of 1968 on the second phase of capital liberalization. The Foreign Investment Council, whose membership was now increased to 15, was instructed by the Finance Minister to present specific recommendations. As previously, the various Ministries engaged in extensive consultations and discussions with various industry groups under their respective jurisdiction to designate specific industries that could be liberalized.

The Foreign Investment Council, now consisting almost exclusively of prominent business leaders, and reflecting the attitude of the mainstream of business leadership, took a considerably more positive attitude toward capital liberalization than previously. It prodded the Ministries, particularly the MITI, to do likewise. As before, the various business and industry associations had also undertaken intensive studies of their own and made their views public. On February 5, 1969, the Council made the final recommendations to the Finance Minister. In doing so, the Council basically followed the same approach as it had in the first round. The Council designated an additional 135 and 20 industries or product groups as Category I and II, respectively. The second phase went into effect on March 1, 1969.

Industries now designated as Category I, where up to 50% foreign ownership is allowed, include meat processing, instant coffee, farm machinery and implements, precision measuring instruments, toys, wigs, and automobile tires. Also newly added to this category are a number of service industries such as insurance, parking lots, amusement parks, and single-unit specialty retail establishments. Those designated as Category II (in which foreign ownership may be 100%) includes sausage made from fish, animal fats, tin plate, sake brewing, steel sheets and pipes, fluorescent lamps, and a number of service industries such as barber shops and beauty parlors. In addition, nine industries previously designated as Category I have been shifted to Category II. Included

365

in this change were restaurants, electrical machinery and equipment, tape recorders, and large-scale shipbuilding.

Several noteworthy features can be observed regarding the second round of capital liberalization. It was somewhat less extensive than anticipated, particularly in view of the changing sentiment among the leadership of the Japanese business community. The FIC deliberately included a few reasonably attractive industries in the second phase of liberalization (The Japanese aptly describe these as "loss leader" industries), but the great majority of those included on the list held little appeal to foreign firms. In the face of vigorous opposition from the Ministries and specific industry groups, the FIC decided to settle for a less ambitious program. A number of strategic industries came under deliberation, including detergents, cosmetics, aluminum refining, and, of course, the three most critical industries, distribution, petrochemicals, and automobiles. The final list, however, included none of these.

The most controversial issue in the second-stage deliberations was the status of the automobile industry. This pitted the FIC and the Federation of Economic Organizations on the one hand against Japan's rapidly growing automobile industry, vigorously supported by the Ministry of International Trade and Industry, on the other. The Federation leaders became seriously concerned over the highly protective environment in which Japan's automotive industry was operating and the industry's persistent resistance to capital liberalization. They were concerned over the strained relations, even bordering on hostility, that characterized the recent United States–Japan automobile negotiations mentioned earlier.

The Federation leadership felt that Japan's automobile industry has developed to the point where it can withstand foreign competition, and urged the industry to take positive steps toward liberalization. The Federation leaders and the FIC were fully aware that immediate liberalization would be out of the question, but they urged the industry to make a definite commitment as to when it would agree to capital liberalization. The industry group argued that, although Japan's automobile industry is the second largest in the world, its total output is less than half that of General Motors, whose annual sales are larger than Japan's national budget.

It also pointed out that total outstanding shares of Toyota Motors at current market value are only about one-fifth of the annual profit of General Motors. Based on these arguments and others, the automobile industry, though not always able to present a unified front, steadfastly resisted the mounting pressure. While neither the Federation nor the Council was able to extract a definite commitment from the industry, the latter has become fully aware of the pressure and informally agreed to some measure of liberalization prior to 1972.

The Foreign Investment Council initially planned to include in its report to the Finance Minister definite plans and timetables for the subsequent stages; but in the face of strong opposition from the MITI, and because of certain technicalities, it did not make them part of the formal report. Instead, the FIC chose to make its view known in the form of the Council's opinion as attached to the main report. In this opinion, the Council urged some measures of liberalization in two of the critical industries — automobile and distribution — as early as feasible, and also recommended gradual liberalization of Japan's restrictions regarding foreign direct investment by Japanese firms.

The Prospect

We have reviewed recent developments in Japanese efforts to liberalize her rather strict foreign investment regulations. What is the prospect for the future? I fully expect that Japan will complete her capital liberalization by 1972 as planned. The only major contingency that may force the alteration of the plan is the anticipated "crisis" of 1970 when the United States–Japan Security Pact, which caused a considerable stir in 1960, comes up for renewal. It is anticipated that the left wing will use this issue as a rallying point for launching an all-out attack on the conservative establishment. But, barring a rather unlikely turn of events, Japan should by 1972 go a long way toward the policy of capital liberalization.

Japan will grant automatic entry for all but a few industries, providing that they meet a set of predetermined conditions. The so-called "negative list industries" where individual screening continues to be required (and the chances of their approval will be minimal), will include only a handful of very essential industries such as those relating to defense, natural resources, atomic energy, computers, and public utilities. I expect that, by 1972, both automobile and petrochemical industries will be liberalized. It is noteworthy that the Federation of Economic Organizations has gone on record as favoring keeping the negative list industries to a minimum. It should be noted, of course, that liberalization will progress largely in the form of 50-50 joint ventures. Wholly owned foreign subsidiaries will be allowed only in those industries where Japanese firms have undisputed competitive superiority.

As we have seen, some significant changes are currently taking place in Japanese policy toward direct foreign investment. We have attempted to examine the process of change as well as the forces that are responsible for it. Japan has long held rather a restrictive policy toward foreign investment. This was quite consistent with her traditional economic, cultural, and political orientation. Until recently, this strategy had been effective in terms of the goals Japan set out to achieve. However, a series of recent developments, both endogenous and exogenous, began to challenge the restrictive policy, forcing Japan to adopt a more liberal posture toward foreign investment. This set off intense debates among all parties concerned.

In formulating a new policy, various interest groups have brought to bear their different and often conflicting demands and pressures. In the best Japanese tradition extensive consultation and vigorous bargaining ensued in the search for a viable compromise and consensus. Out of these evolved Japan's current policy toward capital liberalization. Only in this very broad context can Japan's response be fully understood.

Before concluding, I must at least mention another important question. This is the possibility that upon completion of capital liberalization, the bureaucracy may resort to the familiar administrative guidance to guide, if not restrict, the behavior of foreign firms, so that they will not pose a serious competitive threat to Japanese industries. By administrative guidance is meant informal government guidelines, suggestions, and admonitions communicated to the business community through frequent discussion and consulations. Such informal guidance is by no means unique to Japan, but nowhere else is it practiced so extensively and regarded so importantly as it is in Japan. True, administrative guidelines carry no legal power, but business firms can ignore them only at their own risk.

The Japanese bureaucracy has found discriminate use of administrative guidance as a highly effective instrument in guiding Japanese industries and it may choose to use this time-tested approach in controlling the behavior of foreign firms. In fact, the potential ability of the government to do so may well be a sufficient deterrent to foreign firms not to fully capitalize on their competitive strength. In fact, it is rumored that in prodding certain reluctant industries to agree to liberalization, the Ministries have given them implicit assurance that the government will stand ready to employ administrative guidance to keep foreign firms in line. How far the bureaucracy will resort to this practice is by no means certain, but it is a consideration that multinational corporations interested in Japan cannot ignore.

PROSPECTS FOR THE FUTURE

CHAPTER FIFTEEN

FUTURE OF THE MULTINATIONAL ENTERPRISE*

Raymond Vernon

In the field of social sciences, there is no such thing as being qualified to predict the future. Predictions of the behavior of social institutions are notoriously unreliable. The process whose outcome is to be predicted generally falls in that nasty category of human activity known as games between adversaries, not in the more manageable category of games against nature. Accordingly, one dare not make simple extrapolations based on historical relationships.

Still, wherever man shapes policy, he needs prediction on which to frame his policy. Let me launch this exercise by identifying the factors that I consider to be most critical in shaping that future.

Models for Projection

In order to deal with a phenomenon as complex and as heterogeneous as the multinational enterprise, one has to begin with some gross simplification; the peculiarities, idiosyncracies, and irrationalities that are so important in explaining the individual actions of individual firms have to be set aside in a search for basic forces and tendencies. In brief, some kind of "model" of multinational enterprise behavior has to be constructed and tested as a basis for projection.

After exposure to the available evidence, I find the relatively straightforward competitive model, with its emphasis on factor

* The preparation of this paper was financed by a grant from the Ford Foundation to the Harvard Business School.

prices and factor endowments, to have only a limited utility as a basis for projection. The strength of multinational enterprise, such as it is, seems based on nonclassical factors such as proprietary knowledge and upon advantages of physical and organizational scale. Its motives for existence include profits, to be sure. But the path to profits is perceived as inseparable from absolute growth, and as involving a process of minimizing risk, offsetting threat, and hedging against uncertainty — all this in a setting in which the actors are few and fairly well identified. The first step in any projection, therefore, is to pin down the critical elements in the oligopolistic process that animate the multinational enterprise.

The role of the market. The evidence is reasonably clear that many enterprises have become "multinational" in order to penetrate or protect a market that they feared could not be served by exports.[1] The history of U.S. direct investment in foreign mar-

---

[1] For the investment process within the investing firm, and the considerations that seem relevant in the process, see Y. Aharoni, *The Foreign Investment Decision Process* (Boston: Harvard Graduate School of Business Administration, 1966), especially Chaps. 3–7. For the results of other surveys on the motivation question in international investment, see R. S. Basi, *Determinants of United States Direct Investments in Foreign Countries* (Kent, Ohio: Kent State University Bureau of Economic and Business Research, 1963); A. N. Hakam, "The Motivation to Invest and the Locational Pattern of Foreign Private Industrial Development in Nigeria," *Economic and Social Studies*, Vol. 8, No. 1 (March 1966), p. 50; G. L. Reuber and F. Roseman, *The Takeover of Canadian Firms, 1945–1961: An Empirical Analysis*, Economic Council of Canada, Special Study No. 10 (Ottawa; Queen's Printer, 1969); National Industrial Conference Board, *U.S. Production Abroad and the Balance of Payments* (New York: NICB, 1966), p. 63; A. Stonehill and L. Nathanson, "Capital Budgeting and the Multinational Corporation," *California Management Review* (Winter 1967); R. F. Mikesell, ed., *Private and Government Investment Abroad* (Eugene, Oregon: University of Oregon, 1962), p. 89; *Overseas Operation of U.S. Industrial Enterprises, 1960–1961* (New York: McGraw-Hill, 1960); National Planning Association, *Case Studies of U.S. Business Performance Abroad*, 11 case studies (Washington, D.C.: NPA, 1955–1961); H. J. Robinson, *The Motivation and Flow of Private Foreign Investment* (Menlo Park, California: Stanford Research Institute, 1961), Investment Series No. 4, p. 24; D. M. Phelps, *Migration of Industry to Latin America* (New York: McGraw-Hill, 1936), pp. 43–87; M. Kidron, *Foreign Investments in India* (London: Oxford University Press, 1965), pp. 253–256; B. L. Johns, "Private Overseas Investment in Australia: Profitability and Motivation," *Eco-*

kets, covering the full century during which such investments have been occurring, is rich with the evidence of the importance of that kind of factor. The process generally began with the acquisition by a U.S. enterprise of some sort of innovational lead — some technical or organizational skill, some production or marketing capability, that was not widely shared by others. United States businessmen have repeatedly developed markets in Canada, Britain, and Western Europe for manufactured goods, exporting products that were based on such a lead; then they have shifted their supply strategy to one based on production from an overseas subsidiary closer to these foreign markets.

The reasons for the shift were usually clear. At some point, the overseas markets of U.S. business grew large — sufficiently large so that much of the scale economies of production could be captured overseas. Where tariffs were imposed and where freight costs had any importance, that situation arose sooner than otherwise.

Besides, as the U.S. innovator's original lead began to be appropriated and imitated by others, the incentive of the innovator to consider whether average production costs in the overseas market might be lower than the marginal costs of output delivered from the United States began to take on a certain urgency. Where the specialized external economies of the U.S. environment did not seem to matter very much, and where the ordinary mix of industrial labor skills available in most industrialized countries seemed sufficient for production purposes, the examination often led to a decision on the part of the U.S. businessman to invest in overseas production facilities.[2]

nomic Record, Vol. XLIII (June 1967), pp. 257–261; W. Winiata, *United States Managerial Investment in Japan,* unpublished Ph.D. thesis, University of Michigan (1966), p. 110.

[2] The sequence is described at much greater length in R. Vernon, "International Investment and International Trade in the Product Cycle," *Quarterly Journal of Economics,* Vol. LXXX (May 1966), p. 190. For a similar rationale, developed some years earlier, see S. H. Hymer, *The International Operations of National Firms,* unpublished Ph.D. thesis, M.I.T.; also C. P. Kindleberger, *American Business Abroad* (New Haven: Yale University Press, 1969), p. 11 *et seq.*; and B. Balassa, "American Direct Investments in the Common Market," *Banca Nazionale del Lavoro, Quarterly Review* No. 77 (June 1966), p. 134. The same kind of motivation for overseas direct

There have been cases, of course, in which the initial competitive edge that the businessman thought himself as possessing was one that could not be tested in the first instance by way of exports. In these cases, his decision to use his apparent competitive advantage as a basis for setting up an enterprise in a foreign country has generally involved more risk. Take, for instance, the foreign investment decisions of the food processing companies whose final product, such as green peas or margarine, seems unrelated to sophisticated skills and innovation. Companies of this sort have seen themselves as having a special capacity for mobilizing, financing, and directing the activities of independent farmers; for standardizing and controlling quality in the mass manufacture of tricky organic materials; and for controlling the distribution of perishable products in a way that reduced the threat of deterioration. Skills of this kind, where they exist, generally have to be exercised close to the market; the available choices for those who thought they possessed the skill was either to license a foreign producer, or to take the investment plunge without previously testing the waters by way of exports.

Cases of this kind are to be found not only in the field of manufactured products but also in the sale of services. When skill in purveying services is involved, it is especially difficult to use the export route in order to test the marketability of what one has to offer. Here again, one usually has to test one's marketing advantage by setting up a subsidiary abroad. This is what lay behind the bold overseas expansion of U.S. life insurance companies in the 1880s, of U.S. banking organizations after World War I, and of U.S. hotels, supermarket companies, and management advisory services after World War II.

Investment decisions are, of course, usually the result of a complex amalgam of factors. Still, there is considerable evidence for the view that many investment decisions of multinational enterprises have been stimulated, not by the desire for bold initiatives aimed at exploiting some perceived advantage in organizational skill or technological information, but by a much more defensive

---

investment by United Kingdom firms is suggested in J. H. Dunning, "Further Thoughts on Foreign Investment," *Moorgate and Wall Street* (Autumn 1966), p. 20.

consideration. The literature is rich in allusions to such defensive behavior in the oligopolistically structured industries where the bulk of such investment occurs.

The simplest case of a defensive investment is that of a U.S. industrial supplier who is invited by a major U.S. customer to follow the customer abroad in order to supply him at some foreign location. The subtle threat in a failure to follow such advice is generally not missed by the supplier.

But there are other variants in the defensive investment pattern. Picture a U.S. businessman in a carefully balanced domestic industry whose business horizon stops at the water's edge. Suddenly, one of his domestic rivals makes a move beyond his ken, setting up a local producing subsidiary in Turkey or Peru. For the U.S. firm that has not yet made a move, the problem is to determine the intent of the innovator. Can it be to preempt a market hitherto unknown to the laggard firm, one that will soon be perceived as highly attractive; or can it be to generate a new supply of the product, on a cost basis that can undercut U.S. sources? It is a complacent businessman who, lacking firsthand knowledge, can push such worries and uncertainties wholly out of his mind. And if our defensive businessman has little faith in any investigatory process for so large and uncertain a decision, if he believes principally in learning by doing where initial information is limited, then an obvious response is to match the investment move of his innovating rival.

Besides, imitation offers the best chance of leaving the oligopoly undisturbed. If both investors are right, an opportunity exists for the follower to share the innovator's benefits. If both prove wrong, there may be a problem of absorbing the cost of the error; but if the oligopoly is collectively strong, the cost of any error can be passed on. But if the innovator proves right and there is no imitation, then the oligopoly balance is imperiled.

In the occasional cases in which European parent enterprises have acquired U.S. subsidiaries, similar motivations sometimes seem to have played a role. Olivetti's well-publicized acquisition of Underwood in the United States was inspired by a desire to share with its U.S. rivals all the stimuli and challenges that the U.S.

market was presumed to afford.[3] If U.S. firms were prodded and aided by their environment to generate new products and processes, so the argument went, then one could best protect one's self from the rivalry of U.S. firms by being exposed to the same set of stimuli.[4]

Responses of this sort on the part of firms outside the United States have not been frequent, however. Perhaps a shortage of finance capital contributed to the infrequency of such responses. More likely, however, the problem for large European firms has been to identify the technological or organizational advantage that might serve as a basis for helping them survive the cold plunge into the large, competitive American environment. It is probably no coincidence that those that took the plunge generally did have some technological lead at the time of entry: Pechiney's American aluminum plant was one of the most advanced in the world; Olivetti had reason to believe that she brought real production strengths to her American subsidiary, not readily matched by her U.S. competitors. But the possession of a clear technological lead on the part of firms outside the United States is not all that common. And as long as this is so, the Olivetti-Pechiney kind of response will be slow in coming.

The search for raw materials. While the pursuit and protection of markets have been one driving force in the generation of multinational enterprises, the pursuit and protection of raw-material sources have been yet another. With their markets well secured, companies that once had relied upon domestic raw materials or

[3] Cases of the Harvard Business School, *Ing. C. Olivetti & Co. S.P.A.,* (*A-1 . . . A-6*) (1967). If Olivetti has been aware of the earlier Unilever example, that example would only have bolstered the company's convictions. As Unilever's historian sees it, Unilever's penetration of the U.S. market in the first half of the century was important principally for the stimulus it gave to the whole system's technical and marketing skills. C. Wilson, *Unilever, 1945–1965* (London: Cassell, 1968), pp. 228–236.

[4] Pechiney's motives in acquiring an interest in Howmet in the United States, on the other hand, seem to have been based partly on the availability of cheap power for the production of aluminum, a motive that does not fit the pattern in the text. See "Pechiney Multinational," *Entreprise,* No. 679 (September 14, 1968).

378

upon foreign materials that others were producing, found them-selves reaching abroad to control offshore raw-material sources. The motives for such overseas investment were various. In re-viewing those motives, one must not overlook such straightforward drives as a search for cheaper raw materials; nothing more com-plex than that seems to have sparked the early operations of the Braden and the Guggenheim interests in Chile and Mexico, for instance. But the motives explicitly articulated by the big overseas raw-material investors have often been more complex. What are these drives?

In a world in which the number of independent sources of raw-material supply is low, industrial processors of the material are uneasy about their likely treatment in times of shortage. If some of their suppliers are also rival processors, then the uneasiness takes a more acute form; for then the supplier is in a position, in times of shortage, to price his raw material at levels that would drive the processor out of business. The obvious response has been for the fabricator to search diligently for his own controlled sources of supply.[5] The consequence has been that international trade flows in highly concentrated industries such as copper, aluminum, lead, zinc, and bauxite, are dominated by the interaffiliate sales of international companies; and, further, that the geographical pattern of trade flows is better explained by the affiliate relationships of the buyer and seller companies than by any other measurable factor, such as distance.[6]

The defensive response has gone further in certain respects. Raw-material exploitation is a chance affair from many different points

[5] For oil, see E. T. Penrose, *The Large International Firm in Developing Countries* (London: George Allen & Unwin, 1968), pp. 40–51, 150–172; and J. C. McLean and P. W. Haigh, *The Growth of Integrated Oil Com-panies* (Boston: Harvard Business School, 1954); for aluminum, Organiza-tion for Economic Cooperation and Development, *Gaps in Technology, Nonferrous Metals* (Paris; OECD, 1968), pp. 38–47 (mimeo). More gen-erally, E. T. Penrose, *The Theory of the Growth of the Firm* (Oxford: Basil Blackwell, 1968), p. 147.

[6] J. E. Tilton, "The Choice of Trading Partners: An Analysis of Inter-national Trade in Aluminum, Bauxite, Copper, Lead, Tin, and Zinc," *Yale Economic Essays*, Vol. VI (Fall 1966), p. 474.

of view. First, there is the risk of failing to find a producing mine or well. Then there is the risk of having the production blocked, whether by strikes, acts of God, or governmental interference. There is a strong incentive, therefore, for a firm to multiply the sources of its supply and to spread them geographically without strict regard for least-cost considerations.

The seeming downgrading of simple cost analysis is produced by still another factor, that of unpredictability. One cannot always say if North Sea gas, or Alaskan and Nigerian offshore oil, or Peruvian copper is cheap or dear, at least not in time for the knowledge to be useful. Moreover, irrespective of the cost of the new source, one always has to guard against the possibility that it may be given privileged access to some major market. If others are plunging ahead, therefore, the risks of inaction may be very high.

Of course, the ultimate reaction in risk avoidance is for prospective rivals to pool their efforts in new high-risk areas. That pattern is to be observed in the many joint ventures among producer firms in the exploration and exploitation of crude oil and minerals.[7] This reaction reduces the possibility that any one of the producing rivals can have a very different experience from any of the others, whether in the vagaries of prospecting or in the subsequent costs of operation.

Integration and scale. In response to stimuli of the sort just described, multinational enterprises have extended their reach, moving in an uninterrupted spread upward to their sources of raw material and downward toward their markets. As a result, there has been a remarkable increase in the number of overseas subsidiaries of U.S. parents over the past few decades. The growth is well docu-

---

[7] A recent manifestation of some of these drives is British Petroleum's venture into Alaskan oil and the U.S. retail market; see, e.g., *The Economist* (March 8, 1969), p. 62. While the motivations of all parties to that venture were exceedingly complex, the force of the oligopoly incentive balancing was apparent throughout the transaction. The Royal Dutch/Shell entry into North America decades ago represented still another variant of oligopoly behavior. Reacting to Standard Oil's penetration of the Netherland Indies, Royal Dutch entered the United States, thus posing a threat to Standard if it misbehaved; see *The Royal Dutch Petroleum Company,* Diamond Jubilee Book (The Hague, 1950), p. 16.

mented in the case of a group of 187 such parents whose overseas activities have been traced back to 1900; this group of 187 probably accounts for over 80% of U.S. foreign direct investments in manufacturing outside of Canada. At the end of World War I, the number of foreign subsidiaries in this group somewhat exceeded 250; by 1929, it had reached 500; by 1945, it was just under 1,000; by 1957, about 2,000; and by 1967, over 5,500.[8]

There is a good deal of persuasive evidence, albeit of an unstructured sort, that the nature of the multinational enterprises has tended to change during the process of spread. Recall how much stress was placed earlier upon the primacy of the U.S. market as the genesis of the dynamic forces that led to investment. In the case of the manufacturing enterprises, a firm-specific technology or firm-specific organizational skill provided the jumping off point for the U.S. parent into foreign markets. In the case of the raw-material producers, overseas investment was originally motivated in part by a concern to prevent prospective rivals from threatening the home market with the help of low-cost foreign supplies.

In the course of time, however, the process of vertical and horizontal spread has tended to place multinational enterprises with U.S. parents in a global arena. It is true that the markets of the United States retain a dominant place inside these multinational structures. But the non-U.S. business of such systems has been growing far faster than their U.S. business. Along with this shift, the antennas that U.S. firms employ to scan their business environment have increased in reach and power. As a result, the major raw-material producers have come to think of themselves as operators of a global logistical system — carrying their product from wellheads or pitheads all over the world to markets equally dispersed, using any channel that makes business sense. The giant automobile companies have gradually taken a similar global approach. Their propensity for producing components in one country for assembly in a second and marketing in a third has grown enormously. The same can be said of firms producing components for

[8] Some of the increase in numbers was probably the result of a conversion of branches to subsidiaries, but the factor was not important enough to account for the growth.

381

standardized electronic products, such as radios and television sets.

One can, of course, overstate the importance of the global view-point among the multinational enterprises. The U.S. oil companies probably look upon their new oil discoveries on the Alaskan north-ern slopes with a special satisfaction, a satisfaction that a Canadian discovery would not quite impart. And the U.S. automobile com-panies' decision to produce the new 1970 compact car lines in the United States was probably induced by a set of calculations that was not entirely confined to comparisons of cost in rival locations; ques-tions of relations with the U.S. government and U.S. labor unions were surely involved. Nevertheless, the relative weight of U.S.-based considerations has declined, even if the rank-order position of such considerations has not yet changed.

To speculate effectively about the future of multinational enter-prises, one is obliged to confront the question whether such enter-prises may be parlaying an initial advantage derived from some firm-specific capability, such as proprietary technology or access to a scarce raw material, into a more enduring advantage based on the sheer size of the enterprise. Need one assume that long after IBM's unique skill in the production of third-generation computers has been disseminated to the world, IBM will retain its business ad-vantage on the basis of the sheer size it has meanwhile managed to attain?

This is an extraordinarily complex question, one to be ap-proached with a certain diffidence. Multinational enterprises have almost certainly increased in relative prominence over the past few decades. There is a certain amount of evidence that U.S. firms engaged in multinational activities have higher rates of growth, as well as a higher return on capital, than do U.S. firms in similar industries which confine their activities to domestic markets.[9] There is also some evidence that the foreign subsidiaries of multinational enterprises have generally been growing faster and producing more efficiently than the local competition they confront in the overseas markets where they are located.[10] According to some back-of-the-

[9] This conclusion is based on an as yet unpublished study by my colleague, Professor Lawrence E. Fouraker.

[10] The data on growth rates are firmer than those on productivity. See

envelope estimates, the business of such enterprises outside their home countries may total as much as $500 billions of goods and services, about one-quarter of the gross product of the non-Communist world.[11] Until one can look at the record of growth and profitability by individual product lines rather than by industries, however, he feels unsure of the meaning of the data he confronts.

At the present stage, one is reduced to armchair speculation concerning the nature of the competitive strengths that seem to be associated with multinational enterprises, speculation supported here and there by data and illustration. This sort of rumination suggests that the strength of multinational enterprises is usually based in the first instance on firm-specific capabilities. Multinational enterprises are identified with the development and application of new products and processes and with prolonging the proprietary advantages of such products and processes through adaptation and geographical spread. That advantage, in turn, seems to rest on a number of different types of scale advantage, including scale economies associated with the insurance principle, economies of the utmost importance in the innovating stage. There may be added economies that go with the establishment of a global information network that can efficiently accumulate knowledge regarding sources and markets. In any case, multinational enterprises are not identified with the manufacture of such standardized products as steel bars and rods, gray cloth, or plywood; but they are identified with products whose specifications are in flux. The dichotomy is not all that clear, of course. A few seemingly standardized products, such as automobiles, appear to enlarge their scale economies of production or distribution with such regularity and persistence that the advantages of the multinational enterprises are maintained. This may be part of the explanation for the international dominance of U.S. cigarette subsidiaries as well.

D. T. Brash, *American Investment in Australian Industry* (Cambridge, Mass.: Harvard University Press, 1966), pp. 27, 171; J. H. Dunning, *American Investment in British Manufacturing Industry* (London: George Allen & Unwin, 1958), passim.

[11] J. Polk, "The Economic Implications of the Multinational Corporation," U.S. Council, International Chamber of Commerce (February 14, 1969), p. 15, (mimeo).

But if production and distribution scale economies cannot be counted on to grow constantly, one can see why the development of the multinational enterprise may be self-arresting. As the technology or organizational skill associated with a given line of manufactures is disseminated and appropriated by the world at large, the multinational enterprise may begin to lose any advantage based on its original proprietary lead in the affected line. If the demand for the product or service grows rapidly and if the optimum level of production or distribution for the individual firm grows more slowly, then the market may be able to accommodate more and more entrants. If multinationality entails overheads and inefficiencies not shared by its national rivals, the advantage may even be reversed.

There have been very few systematic tests of this semantical model, as far as I am aware.[12] Some industries, such as the copper industry and the petroleum industry, seem to be responding simultaneously to both the elements that strengthen the position of multinational enterprise and those that weaken it. In these industries, one can discern both a tendency toward more complete vertical integration on the part of existing firms and a tendency toward the introduction of new producers at the refining and exploiting stages.[13] With both tendencies occurring at the same time, it is unlikely that the usual measures of industry concentration and industry dispersion will help much to illuminate the trend.

One also sees some lines of manufacture, however, that appear to behave consistently with the hypothesis of self-arresting growth. The tendency is apparent, for instance, in nine major petrochemicals, whose industry structure has been traced from their genesis to their present state. In this case, the early dominance of multinational enterprises was rapidly eroded over the decades by the entry of national producers.[14] More impressionistically, one seems

[12] A more detailed version of this model will appear in an article by R. Vernon, "Organization as a Scale Factor in the Growth of Firms," in J. W. Markham, ed., *Industrial Organization and Economic Development* (Boston: Houghton Mifflin, to be published).

[13] See the sources cited earlier in footnote 5.

[14] In these nine petrochemicals, 100% of the "initial" plants were those of multinational enterprises; but in the first following stage — a stage of very rapid growth — 59% of the additional plants established were those of multi-

to see the same tendencies in such relatively "mature" industries as metal industries, paper production, consumer electronics, and other consumer hardgoods. The conclusion to be drawn is trite, but significant: the scope of multinational enterprises depends in part on how rapidly technology is disseminated to national companies and assimilated by them.

The elements projected. If oligopoly responses play as dominant a role in the behavior of multinational enterprises as this analysis suggests, then any projection of the future of such enterprises depends on how such enterprises define the geographical scope of their markets in the future. In industries where a basis for oligopoly exists, what is the scope of the geographical area that the principal participants will scan for opportunity and for threat?

Three or four decades ago, it was already clear that the main participants in some industries were beginning to think of their arena as global in scope. This was certainly true of the oil industry, of some of the nonferrous metal industries, and of certain branches of the chemical and machinery industries. But there was a wistful hope among the leading participants of these industries that uninhibited competition could be held in check. Large firms that had the competitive power to extend their reach to global markets were often prepared to forego that possibility if their prospective competitors in other countries would agree to limit their reach as well.

Until World War II, therefore, cartels were endemic in the industries characterized by high concentration and large firms; and one guiding principle of many of these cartels was to allocate markets on geographical lines to each of the participants in the cartel.[15] Partly as a result, the process of interpenetration by large firms in the markets of their rivals in the period between the two world wars seems to have slowed down. The activities of the overseas manu-

---

national enterprises; in the second following stage, a period of slower growth, the comparable figure was 47%; and in the third following stage, one of still slower growth, the figure was 35%. Adapted from R. B. Stobaugh, Jr., *The Product Life Cycle, U.S. Exports, and International Investment,* unpublished D.B.A. thesis, Harvard Business School (1968).

[15] For a summary of these developments, see my "Antitrust and International Business," *Harvard Business Review,* Vol. 46 (September-October 1968), p. 78.

facturing subsidiaries of U.S. firms grew only slowly up to World War II;[16] and the spread of the Western Hemisphere subsidiaries of European firms, with the exception of a few ebullient drug and machinery companies, also seems to have been arrested.

In the years immediately following World War II, however, U.S. businessmen no longer seemed interested in maintaining a geographical division of world markets. European businesses, though slower on the whole to respond to the change, also show signs of breaking out their geographical shells. If the above arguments have any validity, then one of the lines of response of the large European firms acting to reduce the threat of their U.S. competitors and to reestablish oligopoly equilibrium will be to accelerate their investments in the Western Hemisphere. One might then picture the reestablishment of some sort of uneasy stability in the highly concentrated industries, approximating the kind of unspoken half-truce that is characteristic of such industries in national markets.

But how important are we to assume that oligopolistically structured industries will be in the future, especially those industries in which multinational enterprises have exhibited their greatest strength?

The rate at which businessmen attempt to develop new products and processes is a key variable. If multinational enterprises do possess some advantage over others in developing and exploiting opportunities of this sort in their early proprietary stages, then the proportion of world business in the hands of such institutions should grow in periods of rapid change. The assumption that is fashionable at the moment is that such change is exponential in nature; but, like any such asumption, this is a projection based on not much more than casual extrapolation. Still, we can probably take it for granted that the rate will continue to be high for another decade or two if not longer.

The second kind of question is whether the advances of the

---

[16] For our 187 multinational enterprises, for instance, the number of such subsidiaries outside the Western Hemisphere at the outbreak of World War II was under 600; by 1967, the comparable figure would rise to over 3,000. The characteristic pattern of cartel agreements was to assign Western Hemisphere markets to U.S. participants.

386

future are likely to involve high developmental costs and prolonged developmental time schedules of the sort that offer very large firms a competitive advantage. Will the direction be such as to emphasize jumbo innovations like fourth-generation computers, new power plant technology, and new airframe advances; or is the stress to be on the development of products that are smaller and more manageable in risk terms, as in the field of optics, photography, and metallurgy? Insofar as one can discern a trend over the past few decades, the movement toward huge discrete innovational steps involving relatively large commitments on the part of the developing agent seems to have grown.[17] But it is not apparent how one can determine what should be expected in the future.

As one turns from the rate and form of innovation to future trends in transportation and communication, the basis for projection seems somewhat more solid. Here, it is reasonably sure that the spectacular decline in costs and increase in efficiency which have been evidenced in the past century will continue. Air freight promises to grow at rates that will equal its past record of 20% or so in real terms, as larger and more economical equipment replaces the existing stock. Sea freight facilities will also increase in efficiency, even if at a less spectacular rate, as containerized sea shipments expand and specialized carriers continue to be developed. Improvement in the international transmission of sounds and images also can be expected to continue.

The implications of these changes for the growth of multinational enterprises are extraordinarily complex and subtle. Take the issue of communication improvement. We may be in for a period in which information is not only generated more quickly but also appropriated more quickly. Multinational enterprises may be in a

---

[17] Evidence on the magnitude of the effort associated with successful industrial innovation and development is beginning to accumulate; on the whole, the materials suggest that the time and money commitments involved in industrial innovations of any significance are depressingly large. See, for instance, R. R. Nelson, ed., *The Rate and Direction of Inventive Activity* (Princeton: Princeton University Press, 1962), pp. 279–358; IIT Research Institute, *Traces: Technology in Retrospect and Critical Events in Science*, Vol. 1 (IIT, 1968); E. Mansfield, *The Economics of Technological Change* (New York: W. W. Norton, 1968), pp. 99–133.

position to quickly build new caches of firm-specific information, creating a basis for a competitive lead; but they may confront an environment in which that information will be appropriated and applied more rapidly by national companies. It is hard to say, on the basis of this factor alone, whether the multinational enterprises will strengthen their relative position or weaken it.

To the extent that enterprises manage to keep a proprietary hold on their technological and organizational resources, the basis for a tight oligopolistic structure may yet exist in some industries. In the foregoing it was observed that easier communication will widen the scanning frontier of enterprises in such industries so that the market with which they identify themselves and the competitors to which they respond will be more broadly dispersed than ever. The scanning of broader horizons, however, need not lead to more overseas direct investment; it may simply lead to more exports and imports on the part of enterprises, while they confine their actual investment to national markets. What can one say about the relative use of investment, rather than trade, as a means of penetrating overseas markets?

In the usual multiplant locational model, location is a function of the shape of the production cost curve plus transport costs. If production scale economies increase, the propensity to export from some central producing point will grow; and if transport costs decline, the tendency for centralizing production will grow stronger still. On the other hand, if aggregate demand increases, the optimum-sized plant may be found to serve a smaller area, so that more plants may be needed.

The usual model, however, carries us only a little way in the international context. In international investment, locational decisions are colored, even dominated, by other considerations: by a need to learn by doing, by a fear of the imposition of national trade barriers, and so on. The simple locational model is swamped by factors of this sort, and the basis for any solid projection evaporates.

Any predictive exercise concerning the future of the multinational enterprise entails either an extraordinarily complex model or a bold intuitive leap; and it is not evident on its face which is the superior course. My intuitive estimate is that multinational enterprises will maintain their prominence in the output of world goods and services, and may even enlarge their position somewhat in the next decade or so. Their prominence will be more evident in the advanced technological sectors and in the industries that are reliant on raw materials that are subject to oligopoly control. Multinational enterprises will be less evident with respect to the more mature and standardized products. Indeed, mature industries that are now dominated by multinational enterprises, such as consumer electronics and cigarettes, could very well become more nationally oriented in their ownership and structure.

If guesses of this sort prove valid, they still suggest difficulties for multinational enterprise. According to my projection, such enterprises will seem to be controlling and preempting certain especially sensitive areas of economic activity: industries whose raw materials are sold in a well-controlled, oligopolistic market, and industries whose technology is under tight control. In short, multinational enterprises are likely to maintain their strength in those areas of economic activity to whose control national governments are most sensitive. That is why I anticipate the continuation, perhaps the heightening, of tension between the multinational enterprise and the nation-state.

Role of the State

Whether or not the multinational enterprise grows in importance relative to national industry, the propensity of such enterprise to establish itself in the more sensitive areas of national life is bound to evoke a defensive response on the part of sovereign states. The form and intensity of that response no doubt will vary from one country to the next, as it has in the past. Factors of a cultural, historical, and social sort will certainly affect the level of tolerance, as the cases of Canada and Belgium attest. That tolerance will also depend on the economic costs and benefits of the foreign investment as perceived by the people and the government in the host country. Despite those national differences, however, there are a number of general lines of response that one can envisage.

Limiting the right to do business. Many countries profess in

389

principle to grant national treatment to foreign-owned business; but few apply the principle without substantial qualifications.[18]

In the less-developed countries, qualifications on the national treatment principle have always been of major importance. For various reasons, governments in most of these countries have developed the practice of negotiating with foreigners over the terms of their entry and of applying conditions they would not impose on domestic investors. This practice grew up originally partly because of the nature of foreigners' investments, rather than because of their foreignness. Many of these early investments involved raw materials, the title to which was vested in the state, so negotiation could hardly be avoided. Besides, the early foreign investors encountered no settled structure of domestic law relevant to the operation of their enterprises. Corporate tax law, labor law, and other statutory enactments necessary to define the relations between business and the state were lacking; the rights and obligations of such investors, therefore, had to be determined by contract. Finally, raw-material producers generally required physical control over extensive stretches of remote, underdeveloped territory. In those cases, there were added issues to be elucidated: questions of developing and controlling roads, ports, and power; questions of administering justice; and so on.[19]

Although the underdeveloped condition of many countries led them initially to apply a case-by-case approach to foreign investors' proposals, most of these countries retained that approach after the original reasons for it had disappeared. The practice of judging

[18] The principle, as V. Folsom observes, is founded on the biblical admonition, "One law shall be to him that is homeborn, and unto the stranger that sojourneth among you." (Exodus 12:4); see his "Rights and Duties of Foreign Investors Abroad," *The Rights and Duties of Foreign Private Investors* (New York: Matthew Bender, 1965). The practice is mired in complex qualifications; see H. Walker, Jr., "Provisions on Companies in the United States Commercial Treaties," *American Journal of International Law,* Vol. 50, No. 2 (April 1965), pp. 373–393.

[19] For a brief summary of problems and practices associated with such arrangements, see R. Vernon, "Long Run Trends in Concession Contracts," *Proceedings of the American Society of International Law,* Sixty-First Annual Meeting, Washington, D.C. (April 27–29, 1967).

each case on its individual merits by that time was well fixed in administrative procedures. Besides, there were chronic balance of payment difficulties to deal with, providing a new reason for close control over any activity that might give rise to foreign transactions. In the administration of balance of payment regulations, distinctions in the treatment of foreign-owned enterprises inevitably developed.

If governments in the less-developed countries had not applied a case-by-case approach to foreign investment, however, the foreigners would probably have insisted upon it. The Damoclesian character of balance of payment controls often led foreign investors to negotiate for some assurances on entry. Besides, the widespread tax-exempting powers in many countries for "new and necessary industries" or "pioneer industries" or industries located in backward regions tempted foreign investors into negotiation for such exemptions.

By the 1960s, however, the tendency to apply special conditions of entry for foreign-owned enterprises could be found not only in the less-developed countries but in many countries that were well along in development.[20] Even in the United States, limitations of this sort — some of them of rather long standing — existed in a number of business activities. Foreign-owned corporations were limited in their right to do business in banking, and were excluded from doing business in public broadcasting, coastwise shipping, minerals exploitation on public lands, and a number of other activities.[21]

Other advanced countries were imposing similar limitations, varying in scope and effect. In France, for instance, foreign-owned

[20] For general surveys, see United Nations, *The Status of Permanent Sovereignty over Natural Wealth and Resources* (New York: United Nations, 1962), pp. 7–62; National Industrial Conference Board, *Obstacles and Incentives to Private Foreign Investment, 1962–1964* (New York: NICB, 1966); S. Hymer, *National Policies Toward Multinational Corporations* (1969, mimeo); U.S. Bureau of International Commerce, Department of Commerce, *Overseas Business Reports,* various dates and countries.

[21] D. F. Vagts, "United States of America's Treatment of Foreign Investment," *Rutgers Law Review,* Vol. 17, No. 2 (Winter 1963), p. 74.

oil companies had been limited in their refining and distribution activities since the late 1920s[22]; a systematic screening of all proposed foreign investments had been in effect since the early 1960s.[23] In the well-publicized case of Japan, all foreign direct investments have been under tight control for two decades; in the late 1960s, the only industries for which foreigners had unrestricted establishment rights were 15 or so sectors that foreigners could be counted on to avoid, such as brewing, ice manufacturing, cotton spinning, and steel.[24] Even Britain, despite its long tradition of maintaining a liberal regime on capital movements for nonresidents, was quietly negotiating with major foreign investors over the terms of entry.

The results of the negotiations between investors and host governments are sometimes recorded in formal agreements, under which the foreign enterprise assumes various explicit commitments in the fields of finance, production, marketing, control, labor practices, or equity-sharing. In other cases, where the style of a nation's administration is such as to boggle at explicit agreements of this sort, "assurances" are required of the foreign investor — "assurances," for instance, that the enterprise will expand exports or production, will train local managers, and so on.[25]

In recent years, as the screening and conditioning of foreign investment have grown more widespread, the range of practices discriminating against foreign-owned enterprise seems to have widened as well. The use of "buy at home" preferences, a long-established policy of government procurement agencies, has now been extended to "buy at home except from foreigners." The procurement officers of some governments are no longer content to screen their suppliers simply by determining whether they are producing locally; local ownership of the producing facilities also is a basis for preference. British government agencies give preference to the product of

[22] J. McArthur and B. R. Scott, *Industrial Planning in France* (Boston: Harvard Business School, 1969).

[23] A. W. Johnstone, *United States Direct Investment in France: An Investigation of the French Charges* (Cambridge, Mass.: M.I.T. Press, 1965).

[24] Organization for Economic Cooperation and Development, *Liberalization of International Capital Movements — Japan* (Paris: OECD, 1968).

[25] J. H. Dunning, *The Role of American Investment in the British Economy*, PEP Broadsheet 507 (February 1969).

British-owned computer companies, French agencies to French-owned companies, and so on. Now that European governments are subsidizing research on a fairly broad scale, officials administering the subsidy programs are beginning to raise questions over the ownership of national corporations that apply for subsidy; otherwise, they fear that they may be financing IBM's research in fourth-generation computers. In countries where access to local capital markets is a licensed privilege, the same sort of ownership consideration is being taken into account.

My expectation is that, in the years just ahead, the criterion of ownership will figure even more in the treatment of enterprise than has been the case in the past, and that the tendency will exist both in the advanced and in the less-developed countries. But it is important to make a distinction at this point between discriminatory forms and discriminatory effects. It is not at all clear that nations will actually be able effectively to increase their discrimination against such companies. Indeed, it is here that the nub of the problem can be said to lie. With different degrees of intensity, practically all countries feel that something has been lost if their national industries are not nationally owned; but most countries are also aware that at times more is lost by excluding the foreigner than by admitting him. As the years go on, if multinational enterprises increase somewhat in scope and power, it seems likely that nations will feel that both kinds of losses are growing — that the loss associated with a diminution of national ownership is growing, and that the loss that would be associated with terminating the trend is growing too. That, at least, seems a reasonable inference if the size of efficient units of technology, money, and markets continues to grow. As a result, the issue will be elevated from one of moderate importance in the affairs of nations to one that is rather more significant.

Of course, an uneasy equilibrium might conceivably emerge, an equilibrium sustained on the one hand by the need of national governments for the money, magic, or markets of the multinational enterprises, and, on the other hand, by the urge of multinational enterprises to expand their reach. But I am inclined to doubt that such an equilibrium can be long sustained. If transportation and communication are improving as rapidly as I have suggested, the

393

urge of the more dynamic industries to integrate production and distribution facilities across national boundaries is likely to become more intense. To be sure, if new trade barriers appeared, such barriers could reduce international cross-hauling. But if trade barriers were to reappear widely among advanced countries — an unlikely phenomenon — this would affect only the placement and function of subsidiaries, not their establishment. The other rewards and advantages of a multinational strategy, including the advantages that go with the interaffiliate transmission of technology and money, still would be present. The conflict between a global strategy on the part of multinational enterprises and a desire to retain national control on the part of the governments will be heightened. From time to time, in a spasm of frustration, there will be repressive acts on the part of individual states. How then will the multinational enterprises respond to this heightened state of tension?

Reaction to tension. The first instinct of multinational enterprises, we can be sure, will be to deal with the intrusions of governmental bodies on their own, without trying to elevate their problems to an intergovernmental issue.

The reaction is understandable enough. So far, multinational enterprises have displayed a remarkable capability for surviving in an environment of uncertainty and risk. Their confidence in their ability to deal with governmental hostility in the future is high. They are aware that trying to pit government against government may have a price, in terms of ill will and retaliation; and even when pressure is exercised by so powerful an advocate as the U.S. government, one cannot be sure it will work.

Of course, there is always the possibility that multinational enterprises might urge governments to develop some kind of agreed international order that would ease their lot. But even that kind of initiative has its dangers. Although a more elaborated international order conceivably could increase the predictability of the environment in which such enterprises operate, it would be hard to picture such a regime that did not at the same time reduce their flexibility of response. Accordingly, when multinational enterprises begin to feel the breath of governments at their backs, the disposition is to find some formula that relieves the pressure locally without widening the role of government. "Codes of fair conduct," "sharing ownership with local interests," and similar formulas are generally advanced. Actions that involve intergovernmental threat or intergovernmental collaboration take a very low place in the list of possible responses.

Not all intergovernmental measures are ruled out, however. Enterprises concerned with international business have been known to support limited and selective intergovernmental agreements where they feel such agreements would be helpful. After all, the International Convention for the Protection of Industrial Property — a convention safeguarding the rights of inventors and their assignees to secure patent protection in foreign countries — has been operating for 85 years or so; similarly with protective clauses in the field of trademarks. Bilateral treaties of establishment — sometimes dubbed "treaties of friendship, commerce, and navigation" in their more archaic form — have been negotiated between pairs of nations for many years; and bilateral treaties for the avoidance of double taxation have been sponsored by business interests where needed. But if U.S. enterprises looked charily on the uninhibited extension of such intergovernmental regimes, they would not be exhibiting an obvious kind of irrationality.

One is led to assume that if some more elaborate international regime should eventually emerge, it will not be because foreign investors were clamoring for it. More likely, it would arise out of a recognition on the part of governments that for one reason or another their interests demanded such a regime. That development could come about eventually if governments — particularly the U.S. government — began to distinguish their national interests from the interests of their multinational enterprises rather more explicitly than they have in the past. The possibility that this divergence of interest may occur is somewhat increased by the trend toward the multinationalizing of business; that is, by the increase in the relative importance of the "foreign" element in the total business of multinational enterprises. The growth in that element of the business increases the frequency of incidents in which the sovereign's capacity to enforce some national policy — such as a national monetary policy, a national antitrust policy, a national trading-with-the-enemy policy, or a national employment policy —

seems to have been weakened. The realization that there are problems in this regard is nothing new; the question is whether the problems will grow.

That there will be some increase in such problems seems plausible in its face. For numerous reasons, multinational enterprises are not easily subjected to national policy. The problem appears not only in a form that is familiar to host countries, that is, in the context of applying national policies to foreign-owned enterprises; it appears also in a form that applies especially to the capital-exporting country. The home government, when deliberating whether to apply its jurisdictional power to the full, is obliged to consider the reactions of other governments. For fear of offending other governments, for instance, the United States finds itself obliged to move judiciously and with circumspection when it applies national regulations that might bear on the behavior of overseas subsidiaries. Problems have arisen in the application of its trading-with-the-enemy regulations, the institution of its antitrust suits, the imposition of controls on its direct investment flows, and so on.

Besides, there is a possibility that the issue could become more symmetrical. Until recently, the United States has not seriously had to confront the implications of the fact that France may be in a position to influence the business policies of Pechiney's U.S. subsidiary in the U.S. market. Heretofore, the shoe has been on the other foot; accordingly, the United States had tended to belittle the problem, as indeed it deserves to be belittled when gauged in pragmatic terms. But if some of the highly concentrated manufacturing industries should become more international in their structure, then the United States may begin to develop some of the reactions heretofore associated with host countries.

If the United States should develop those reactions, the possibility of concerted response by nations will be somewhat greater than it appears at present. But what kind of response is likely to be generated? Here, one strays beyond the limits of projection into that of almost pure speculation. But perhaps a little speculation is justified.

What nations shortly will discover when they turn to a concerted approach is that the heart of the problem is its least tractable part:

396

how to ensure that the fruits of such enterprises' operations are distributed among such nations in some "equitable" way. No one is likely to need much persuading that a tight case-by-case regulatory approach would be impossible in practice and very likely destructive in outcome. The principles of any negotiation, if not their implementation, will probably have to be comparatively simple; and, being simple, they may well have to allow some of the more vital problems posed by the multinational enterprise to go by the board.

One area in which some relatively arbitrary and simple principles could probably be negotiated is in the field of taxation. The progress that has been already achieved in the negotiation of bilateral agreements paves the way for the extension and multilateralization of tax arrangements. Besides, this is a field in which multinational enterprises themselves may see some advantages in pressing for the negotiation of agreements; this would be especially true if national taxing authorities, through increasing sophistication, managed progressively to reduce the value to these enterprises of their present flexibility. That flexibility depends partly on the inefficiency and limited competence of these authorities. As the company's discretion in areas like international transfer pricing, overhead allocation, debt in lieu of equity, and other familiar areas of accounting choice are reduced by more aggressive action on the part of national tax authorities, the firms themselves may perceive advantages in greater international tax collaboration. The approach to collaboration would presumably require the nations concerned to look upon intimately related affiliates as if they were a single enterprise. The problem would then be to define and allocate the profit of the enterprise irrespective of where that profit might nominally appear.

Another area that lends itself to international collaborative effort is the avoidance of clashes between sovereign states arising out of their joint jurisdiction over subsidiaries.[26] In this area, one could picture a set of agreements based on several interrelated principles. The first principle would be that, with regard to certain areas

---

[26] The word "subsidiaries" is used loosely here. The same points may well apply to other types of entity located abroad that have a jurisdictional personality in the host country, even if technically they were branches.

of national policy, no government would try to influence the overseas subsidiaries of its national companies by coercion of the parent.
An agreement of this sort, if multilateral in scope, would be confined to nations that saw something to be gained in a reciprocal
commitment; and it would be confined to subjects in which the self-
imposed restraint did not raise the specter of significant injury to
the participating countries. One could picture, for instance, agreements of this sort among the advanced countries, covering activities
in the fields of antitrust, trading with the enemy, corporate disclosure, corporate financing, and so on. Since such agreements
might ease the lot of the multinational enterprises themselves, it is
even possible to envisage eventual support from that quarter.

A second principle emerges as a natural corollary of the possibility just mentioned. This is the revitalization through international
treaty of the principle of national treatment for foreign nations —
but a revitalization accompanied by the rehabilitation of the Calvo
clause; that clause, it will be recalled, would deny all domestic
rights and remedies to any foreign-owned subsidiary if it invokes
the diplomatic support of a foreign government (for which read
"the United States") in a dispute with its host government.

Each of the two principles so far suggested requires some kind
of international adjudicating mechanism in order to be operative.
Countries are bound to be accused of violations from time to time.
Besides, no responsible country could withdraw its protective shield
from the overseas subsidiaries of its nationals unless it left behind
some set of credible safeguards which might take the place of that
shield.

An approach of this sort would have a somewhat greater chance
of being launched among the advanced countries alone than on a
global basis. For one thing, most U.S. parent firms, being understandably disposed to the avoidance of the untried, would probably
prefer to limit any innovation of this sort to the comparative safety
and security of the advanced countries' jurisdictions. Moreover,
many of the less-developed countries would probably resist any
proposal that assigned an important role to international adjudica-
tion, fearing the internal domination of the advanced countries in
any intergovernmental tribunal.

398

The probability that this approach would be confined to the advanced world is enhanced by another major factor. Nations involved in any agreements that relinquished their hold on overseas subsidiaries would probably wish to protect themselves from the risks that the subsidiaries' new-found freedom would imperil some important national objective. Accordingly, there might well be a need for a joint commitment on the part of the countries concerned to launch on a continuous, nonstop process of policy harmonization in the fields in which they were accepting restraints upon their exercise of sovereign power. One would not expect that the harmonization process would lead to identical national policies in these fields. In the business of trade with the Communist bloc, for instance, the present differences in national levels of control are probably quite tolerable. In the field of antitrust, on the other hand, other governments might have to be persuaded to exert some kind of control over agreements likely to be harmful to the other governments concerned; this might mean, for instance, persuading various countries to extend their anticartel legislation to export cartels, which usually are exempted from national antitrust laws. In short, where large differences existed and where these were perceived as generating major risks for any of the countries concerned, one could surely hope to find eventually the means of reducing these risks.

If all these things were done, however, some of the most difficult aspects of the operations of multinational enterprises — difficult in the sense that they challenge the control of member states in their own economies — would still lie outside the reach of these agreements. For instance, national employment policy and national monetary policy would still be subject to the actions of the multinational enterprises to a degree that might prove intolerable for the nations concerned.

One way to "solve" a difficult problem is to submerge it into an even larger one. In this case, the larger problem is already waiting in the wings. The threat to national policies will be mounting from many different directions: not alone from the existence of the multinational enterprise, but also from the shrinkage of trade barriers, the improvement in transport and communication, and so on. These are likely to raise issues of sovereignty that may, in the end, dwarf the multinational enterprise problem. Perhaps when that occurs, the resulting institutional adjustments will deal with the multinational enterprise as well.

INDEX